D1711404

HISTORY OF JOURNALISM IN THE UNITED STATES

HISTORY OF JOURNALISM IN THE UNITED STATES

BY

GEORGE HENRY PAYNE

GREENWOOD PRESS, PUBLISHERS
WESTPORT, CONNECTICUT

Originally published in 1920
by D. Appleton and Company

First Greenwood Reprinting 1970

SBN 8371-2817-X

PRINTED IN UNITED STATES OF AMERICA

TO

THE MEMORY OF

THEODORE ROOSEVELT

WHO UNDERSTOOD THE NEWSPAPER—

AND NEWSPAPERMEN

PREFACE

Man frequently knows little about the phases of existence with which he comes into daily contact. As frequently he is not even curious regarding them. He telephones for a taxicab, is whisked to a labyrinthine terminal in time to catch an express, which clanks across viaducts conjured up by engineering's sheerest magic — usually without query save that prompted by solicitude for his comfort of the moment. Man goes, comes, and eternally accepts, en route. His, for the most part, is a *post facto* viewpoint. Effect is what really concerns him. He is likely to be bored by those who expound cause.

Among the commonest and least comprehended ingredients of living is the daily newspaper. More powerful than public school or college, more vitally affecting destiny than all the churches of all the sects, it thrusts its well or ill conceived messages into the homes and minds of the millions. Coral like, it has reared itself into an all encircling reef, upon which beats the tidal wave of world politics or laps the insignificant ripple of village chatter. The roar of the tidal wave and the lap of the ripple are what men think they hear. Actually they do not. What one hears is the note of the reef — the newspaper. Wherefore let us consider its beginnings.

Never have citizens needed more urgently an understanding of the genesis and development of journals which — although they may deny it — shape their trend of thought, their ethics and tastes, and their interest in the matter of national honor. To review compactly the pedigree of American journalism, detachedly and simply, has been the intent of Mr. Payne. He has done it.

This book may well prove to be profitable reading for earnest and careless alike — both perforce are members of the great army of newspaper consumers. It will repay, amply, snatched perusal in the city room of any Park Row between assignments — how many reporters can pass a genuine test in the fundamentals of a profession into which they are putting even more of themselves than their fellows of the law and medicine? Finally, it will be worth a great deal to students in the schools of journalism, so rapidly increasing throughout the country. For seven years I have watched mature minded young men and women leave Morningside to help get and write the news you and I read. They and their sort must know the background of their craft. A decade ago one embarked upon a newspaper career in an almost jocund spirit of adventure. The jocund spirit and the flavor of adventure will persist, but let us carry with us the records and the maps — old fashioned though they be — of the pioneers, strong and weak alike, who made the newspaper of to-day possible.

Robert Emmet MacAlarney

Columbia University

INTRODUCTION

"Democracy," says John Morley, "has come to mean government by public opinion." Like democracy itself, public opinion is a new power which has come into the world since the Middle Ages. "In fact," declared E. L. Godkin, "it is safe to say, that before the French Revolution nothing of the kind was known or dreamt of in Europe. There was a certain truth in Louis XIV's statement, which now seems so droll, that he was himself the state. Public opinion was HIS opinion. In England, it may be said with equal safety, there was nothing that could be called public opinion, in the modern sense, before the passage of the Reform Bill." [1]

Mr. Godkin, however, ignored the fact that, as early as 1738, Joseph Danvers rose in the House of Parliament and declared that Great Britain was then being governed by a power "that never was heard of as a supreme authority in any age or country before . . . it is the government of the press." [2]

Before England knew of this power, this new authority, it was established in America. De Tocqueville thought he saw, in the first Puritan who landed on these shores, the embodiment of democracy, but it was in the acquittal of the printer John Peter Zenger in 1734 that the first evidence of government by public opinion triumphant was given. The law was against him and

[1] *Unforeseen Tendencies of Democracy.*

[2] *Parliamentary History,* x, 448.

legal precedents pointed to his conviction, but his lawyer appealed from the law to public opinion and the result was his acquittal —" the dawn of the Revolution."

The ideal of government by public opinion has been more nearly achieved in this country than elsewhere. With all the faults that foreign critics see in our government, it is admitted that, from the beginning, we have moved steadily toward that ideal. From De Tocqueville to Bryce, the critics have found only those faults that are in themselves the result of inactive public opinion. De Tocqueville's fear that the rights of minorities would be ignored has been proved groundless. In democracy or in a government by public opinion, minorities are as powerful as they are right. Our greatest reforms are the work of minorities, our greatest advances the triumph of the far-seeing few. The American Revolution itself was a minority movement, and it was successful only when public opinion was aroused. Mill's doubts before the Civil War about the evil effect of slavery, as well as Bryce's just criticism of our municipal government, have all been answered as public opinion has been aroused.

To assume that government by public opinion would be perfect would be to assume that man is perfect. At times the student may be disheartened or the philosopher dismayed, but, as long as the sovereign power rests with the people and the people are civilized, there is bound to be progress, for democracy itself is as positive a sign of evolution as is religion.

Those who regard democracy with misgiving are generally those who are more interested in man's written record than in man's place in nature. The entire recorded progress constitutes but the most superficial part of man's entire development. Assuming the human race to be 240,000 years old, and accepting the most generous figures on Egyptian and Mesopotamian civilization, civilized man has existed only ten thousand years, or one-two hundred and fortieth part of the life of the human species. It is only in the last two hundred years that there has been a definite concept as to progress, unless one wishes to accept the gropings of Heraclitus and Lucretius as part of man's evolution toward an understanding of himself. How feeble then seem those doubts as to the future, when one contemplates the inevitable forces that are working toward man's progress!

That men will not easily be led from the lines of their accustomed thought, born of the instincts for immediate comfort and domination, is inevitable. For years we were in the habit of regarding the Middle Ages as great periods of darkness, when the human race went to sleep. We know now that scholarship was kept alive by the very monks who were formerly accused of strangling thought, and that the races that were then being slowly civilized were destined to give to humanity some of its greatest blessings. So when democracies seem to turn over, and the will of the people seems to be thwarted; or when, as frequently happens, some particular community refuses to respond to the call of those who assume that they have the greater vision, it is well to remember that the march of humanity's progress is as imperceptible as is the motion of the earth to those distant cousins of ours who still go on all-fours.

Since Turgot wrote his memorable essay on progress, we have learned to look on man's state as progressive so long as there is a development in man's intelligence. The moral sentiments, whether of utilitarian origin or not, are great factors in developing man's intelligence, and in turn intelligence develops the moral sentiments. So, where there is an intelligent people there will be a will to be free, and where there is a will to be free there will be a desire to be right.

The development of democracy in America is one of the greatest examples in recorded history of this law of progress — the triumph of democracy has always been the triumph of the moral sentiments.

How far democracy developed journalism and how far journalism developed democracy is an interesting question. That the democracy of ancient Greece, limited monarchy that it was, existed without journalism is true. But government was local and dealt purely with the affairs of those residing within the dema; the community being small, and the Greeks being a garrulous and politically developed people, they were able by word of mouth to keep track of their affairs. As soon as the government stretched out it became, not a democracy but a tyranny.

What is plainly evident is that the printing press was invented at a time when people were becoming restive. They had progressed to a point where they were no longer satisfied with the old servitude. Once given an invention by which man's thoughts might be communicated to others with a minimum of labor and expense, journalism was inevitable. The humblest effort to make it effective, such as that of Benjamin Harris, thus becomes an important page in our history.

Indifference to the history of journalism has been ascribed to the fact that research into those departments of knowledge that do not lead to an academic career is usually neglected. That comparatively few writers have been attracted to the subject is all the more remarkable in view of the fact that it is over a hundred and fifty years since the press in this country began to assume political functions. While the early historians entirely neglected this phase of our development, later writers have touched on it, but always most inadequately.

"Newspaper government," says the historian Rhodes, "we have with us, and it must be reckoned with"; yet little attempt has been made to investigate the origin of the political power of the new estate.

At a time when journalism has risen to the dignity of an academic career,— a time when it is conceded that it represents, if it does not furnish, the public opinion that makes and unmakes governments,— an inquiry as to its origin and development as a political power would seem to be, at least, labor not wasted. It is proposed in this book to trace the development of that power as it lies in the story of journalistic development.

It is recognized that this is only one of the many aspects from which journalism may be studied. A German economist, calling attention to the fact that the history of journalism has been a neglected study, declared that it is a study of the most direct concern to the political economist, for the reason that the newspaper was "primarily a commercial economic contrivance forming one of the most important pillars of contemporary economic activities." [3] Such a view is not justified by a research into American journalism, for we find that it is in affecting political results that its representatives have been most successful.

The history of journalism in America cannot be separated from the development of the democratic idea. The very first editor in this country, the forgotten and neglected Benjamin Harris, in all his interesting struggles represented that idea, for his fight was for freedom of expression, the very essence of democracy. With us democracy has come to mean sovereignty of the whole

[3] Buecher, *Industrial Evolution*, p. 216.

body of the people; the achievement of that sovereignty was of the slowest development, and frequently the battle was made nowhere else than in the meagre and forgotten journals.

To journalism, then, democracy owes, not only its strength but, in whole or in part, all of its important victories. No political advance has been made in this country without the aid of the press; all of our democratic achievements have been accomplished with the help of men who were, in the beginning, regarded as mere mechanics, poor printers, or who were, in later periods, grudgingly given credit and political recognition as the representatives of a not entirely welcome social and political phenomenon.

Journalism, in turn, owes to democracy its enjoyment of enormous privileges, its practical admission into the government. In the preliminary skirmishes for liberty in this country, the people found that the free press was a powerful weapon by which they were able to wrest from tyranny the power of government. They found that through the press they could keep their own phalanxes compact, a difficult task in a country spread over the great area of the thirteen colonies.

"A free press" became their shibboleth. When a nation was born and the political thought of the philosophers of the eighteenth century had taken root, it was the press that made the battle for the extension of the suffrage and that wrested from the minority the power which, in a democracy, must be with the people. The abolition movement, variously explained, was a development of the democratic idea. What the statesmen of that time failed to realize was that there could not exist in a democracy a class, such as the slaveholders, claiming to have property rights in human beings. The press that took up the cause of the negroes did not represent the black men; it was impelled to action by the moral sense of those who had recently achieved sovereignty and who, subconsciously perhaps, acted as much for their own protection as for the betterment of the blacks. The low condition to which the poor whites were sinking at the South shows that a condition worse than slavery was possible, if the right to own human beings were not abolished.

Thus the development of democracy meant increase of the power of journalism. Strange and crude were the instruments of this journalism, it is true, but elegance and refinement are characteristic of neither biologic nor social evolution. The manners of men are rude, and, as journalism developed,— as a more or less illegitimate or "poor white" brother of literature,— it was subjected, helpfully in most cases, it is true, to criticism either by those who had little interest in the political significance or by those who were politically and socially opposed to the purposes to be achieved.

Strange instruments, as I have said, appeared in the course of this development. The elder Bennett and the *Herald,* as it was edited for years, would hardly seem the agents of either a moral or political development. Yet, distasteful as were many of his early exploits, and immoral as was his espousal of the slavery cause for purely commercial reasons, the elder Bennett did the country and democracy a great service, for he caused people to read newspapers in large numbers. He gave them news of events that lay about them daily, and of which they had little consciousness; he interested them in themselves and their fellow beings, he quickened their sense of life, thereby increasing their political power.

History is often read in terms superimposed by men

with no sympathy for the story they are unfolding. The story of the evolution of such an institution as journalism should have very little to do with questions of taste or literature, except as they hindered or assisted the objects for which the journalist strove. Of all the editors in America, Bryant was pre-eminently literary, yet his influence was never so great as that of Bennett; even among the literary class he never achieved such influence and power as did Godkin, who wrote not a single poem.

We have spoken of journalism as the poor white brother of literature, a despised relative. In these later days it has become, with the impetus of being accepted as offering an academic career, something more; it might now be described as literature in action,— action first and action last. The artist may achieve success in journalism, as Dana did, but he must first be a man of action. The journalist must first see the truth, he must be one who is not deceived by the lie.

To tell such a story and to outline properly the relations of the press to government and to the people has necessitated a somewhat compact marshaling of a world of facts, the importance of which has been, not that they have been unrelated before, but that they show how resistless has been the law of advancement. The career of Benjamin Harris has been set forth in as careful detail as research would permit; this seems necessary if we are to understand journalism's very beginning, a beginning that makes luminous the struggle of Zenger and those patriots who made the Revolution possible.

The mere fact that Harris' name seemingly passed into oblivion does not mean that his influence was naught. Although directly, that influence was little, it was great in an indirect way, for the James Franklin who came back to Boston in 1719, to be the spokesman of the "Hell-Fire Club," that first organization of liberals, brought back with him from London a spirit that was as directly traceable to Harris and the other pioneers of journalism as the independent spirit of the pre-Revolutionary editors was traceable to Zenger. And as Zenger leads to Sam Adams, Adams leads to Jefferson and Hamilton and Duane and Coleman; Bennett to Greeley and Pulitzer to Hearst, a certain inevitableness marking the progress of the story.

CONTENTS

APPENDICES

HISTORY OF JOURNALISM IN THE UNITED STATES

HISTORY OF JOURNALISM

CHAPTER I

HISTORIC PREPARATION FOR JOURNALISM

Mayflower leader a printer — Democracy and the press — Interest in the "newes"— Public opinion vs. English government — Persecution of authors and printers in England — L'Estrange, first licensor of the press — First newspaper in English — English politics reflected in New England — Printing in Boston — Political development affecting publication.

Among the one hundred and two passengers on the *Mayflower,* which brought to this country in 1620 the first body of men who were to give to the American nation its character and tendency, was William Brewster. In addition to being the spiritual guide of the little group, Brewster had the experience, unusual in those days, of having been a practical printer. A man of education, he had been sent to jail for his religious beliefs, and with others of his faith had sought refuge in Holland. He had procured a printing press and in Leyden, where the press was untrammeled, had published a number of books attacking the English authorities.

The day before the Pilgrims landed, they drew up, in the cabin of the *Mayflower,* their celebrated agreement, based on the idea of equal rights for the general good — "The birth of popular constitutional liberty," Bancroft calls it. In any case, it was the first expression of the democratic idea toward which humanity had been painfully toiling for centuries.

These two facts are important in the history of journalism.

The greatest of all liberties, it is said, is the liberty of opinion. Within a comparatively few years of the *Mayflower's* sailing, there had come, following the revival of learning and the development of the art of printing, an impetus toward freedom of expression such as the previous centuries had never known. How much the democratic idea — the democratic tendency that came with Christianity — owes to printing and how much the invention of printing owes to the growth of this idea is one of those nicely balanced questions that is not to be entered into here.

In "De Natura Deorum," Cicero put forth the idea of printing books, but there the idea rested for centuries. It was the fact that the world was stirring in the fifteenth century and that the revival of learning had brought about a demand for books, on the part of those who were not able to afford the great vellum manuscripts, that brought the printing press. It has been observed that the processes used in the printing press "are as old as the first medal which was ever struck."

We know that the Romans could have invented the printing press, and probably would have, were it not that slave labor satisfied their wants.[1] There was among them the demand for publication; Dionysius of Halicarnassus tells of "thousands" of writers on the subject of Roman History alone, and Martial reports that copies of his "Epigrams" sold for six sestertii, less than the cost of a book to-day. But slave labor took the place of the printing press, and the ingrained belief that reading as well as thinking belonged to the ruling class rendered

[1] H. M. Alden, "Why the Ancients had no Printing Press," in *Harper's Monthly*, Vol. XXXVII, p. 397.

the great organ of modern civilization unnecessary.

But the printing press came to awaken man to his possibilities — the philosophies of the ages sweeping down into the great under mass to awaken them to manhood — and one of the first evidences that the apparently inert majority, lying under the governmental impact, were shaking off the lethargy of brutedom, was the interest in "Newes," itself a new word.

As early as 1561 we find references to doggerel reports of recent events that were being printed under the title of "Newes out of Kent" and "Newes out of Heaven and Hell," and during the reign of Elizabeth, papers were printed giving news of the time in order to keep the people interested in the defense of the realm.[2] This was a development of the written news-letter, which had its origin in the idea of keeping the wealthy informed, just as the wealthy Romans were kept informed by letters from Rome.[3] But we must look to the end of the reign of James the First, says the Harleian manuscribe, for the time when "news began to be in fashion."[4] The first attempt to treat of the general "newes," in a regular series of newspapers, issued weekly, was when Nathaniel Butters, acknowledged father of the newspaper, brought out in London, on May 23, 1622, the first issue of the *Weekly Newes.* This was followed by the establishment, here and there throughout Europe, of the Gazettes, intended in the beginning for the merchants and courts, but soon to pass into the hands of those far removed from Kings and Courts.

[2] For account of the interesting forgery of a newspaper in Elizabeth's time, see Disraeli's *Curiosities of Literature;* Andrews, *History of British Journalism,* Vol. I, p. 22; Chalmers, *Life of Ruddiman,* p. 114. See Appendix, Note A.

[3] See Cicero and Horace.

[4] See Appendix, Note A.

The men who came to this country on the *Mayflower* were men who, with their forbears, had been furnishing England with much news long before they set sail. They were, in the main, of the mass of people. They were men who had been persecuted, who had suffered, who had been jailed in England for their principles and for striving for their liberty, though they had little in common with the Barons who through Magna Charta had wrested from the Crown the power of absolute rule.

These Puritan insurrectionists had been nurtured by the printing press. Beginning with the struggle to hold religious views that were interdicted by the government, they had broadened gradually into unconscious exponents of free government; and the government, seeing that it was from the press that they had gained courage and boldness, subjected the press to a rigorous censorship, printing being forbidden, save in London, Oxford and Cambridge, as far back as Queen Elizabeth's time.

When Brewster and his flock first left England, they went to Leyden, where, as in no other place in Europe, there were free schools, and where, as Motley says,[5] "every child went to school, where almost every individual inhabitant could read and write, where even the middle classes were proficient in mathematics and the classics and could speak two or more modern languages." Campbell says, that during the sixteenth century "this little country published more books than the rest of Europe put together, and while England was suppressing and censoring the press, the author here was free to express his thoughts so long as he committed no libel and wrote nothing to offend the public morals." [6]

[5] *History of the United Netherlands*, Vol. IV, p. 137.

[6] Campbell, *The Puritan in Holland, England and America*, Vol. II, p. 343; Rogers, *Story of Holland*, p. 220.

When these Pilgrims landed in America, the great wilderness that was to take centuries to subdue, they had, in the fact of Brewster's apprenticeship and the compact referred to, the germ of the free press and the journalism that was to become a world factor in humanity's development.

It was not until 1639 that the first printing press was imported into this country; even then the settlers were living under such conditions of savagery as England had not known for nearly a thousand years.

Wilderness that it was, these Pilgrims had brought with them very definite ideas, many of them gained during the sojourn in Holland; while in many respects they were still only keeping pace with those of their class in England in intellectual growth, they were far advanced in political thought. A small community of not more than a few thousand was more easily influenced than the population of the thickly settled country whence they came. Such an event, therefore, as the founding of Harvard University and the legacy of Brewster's library, in which there were eight books that he himself had published in Leyden, was bound to have its influence on the intelligent section of the public mind. Not only were those in the colony affected by these and similar evidences of liberal thought, but the character of immigration was affected, as we see from the fact that between 1630 and 1647, one hundred university men came to New England from the continent. Such immigration could not do otherwise than broaden the current.

New England, however, was still a colony under the rule of the mother country, and was still greatly influenced by the thoughts of those Englishmen who had remained on the other side. A second printing press was brought over in 1660. Two years later, with only two presses in the colony, the Government of Massachusetts, following the example of the mother country, appointed a licensor of the press, and in 1664 a law was passed permitting printing only in Cambridge, and then only by those licensed.

In the time elapsing between the sailing of the *Mayflower* and the establishment of the censorship, a little more than forty years, the folks in the colonies had been hearing of strange happenings at home. Journalism in England had been born. The first newspaper, *The Weekly Newes,* had appeared, but at a time when authors, printers and importers of prohibited books were being subjected to the most barbarous persecutions, treatment that recalled to the Pilgrims the conditions that had driven them to Holland.

Despite all persecutions, the fight in England was on in bitter earnest. More than thirty thousand political pamphlets and "newspapers" were issued between 1640 and the Restoration, two thousand bound volumes of which are now to be found in the British Museum.[7]

While Charles the Second was a less vindictive persecutor of the press than either his grandfather or his father had been, he had to deal with a refractory Parliament, without which the beginning of journalism would never have been written in the seventeenth century. It was a period, too, which saw the rise of political parties in England, the Whigs and the Tories. Both upheld the monarchy, but the Whigs stood for the limitation of authority within the law, while the Tories were for absolutism in both Church and State.[8]

It was in his desire to cope with the growing evil of

[7] See Knight's *Old Printer and Modern Press,* also Disraeli's *Curiosities.*

[8] May, *Constitutional History of England,* Vol. II, p. 21.

publication and the free press that King Charles fanned the flames that he would fain have quenched. He appointed, in 1663, Sir Roger L'Estrange as licensor of the press and surveyor of the printing offices.

Americans are not accustomed to think of this remarkable cavalier and journalist as connected with the newspaper history of this country; yet connected he is in the most interesting way — directly through Benjamin Harris, as we shall see in another chapter, and indirectly through his persecutions and general whacking of heads, both of editors and publishers, toughening the fiber of those who were founding the Fourth Estate, and providing examples of heroism for those editors in this country who in their turn went to jail as part of the routine of a not over-respected profession.

It was L'Estrange who was selected to answer Milton's "Areopagitica," which he did under the brutal title, "No Blind Guides Needed," a fair sample of his wit. From pamphleteer he became, on his appointment as licensor of the press, a full-fledged journalist, issuing in 1663 the *Public Intelligencer.* For this posterity is indebted to him, for an able journalist he was; considering that his business was to suppress printing and prosecute printers, he set about it in the very best way calculated to encourage the one and stiffen the other.

The *Public Intelligencer* gave way in 1665 to the *London Gazette,* the first official newspaper in English, a purely governmental publication, containing in the most meager and formal fashion such news as the government wished to publish. But the damage was done, for what the government could do others could do, and despite the licensor, pillories and prisons, the printers became busy with their defense of a free press and popular rights. When it is realized that thirty thousand of these pamphlets were printed in a comparatively few years, it is seen that they were no mean workers.

The Licensing Act, which had been passed shortly after the accession of Charles II, expired in 1679, and for a short while several newspapers — the *Protestant Intelligence,* the *True News,* etc.— were published by the Whigs, but the twelve justices, under Chief Justice Scroggs, declared that it was a criminal act at common law to publish any political news without the King's license.[9]

As this allowance was given only to the London *Gazette* and to L'Estrange's new paper, *The Observator,* life for the journalists was just as unbearable as when the license act was in force. James II, however, was not satisfied with this common-law protection, which was ample enough, as the printers and writers, who had served in jail under it, could testify, and in 1685, immediately after his accession, censorship of the press was revived.

Those were sad years for our Protestant Pilgrims on the edge of the wilderness in New England, but not dull ones. There was no need of any license law to keep them from printing seditious pamphlets or newspapers, for Indian wars, smallpox and the severe New England winters kept them engrossed without the aid of political discussion, while their material troubles divided their attention with the struggle against heresy and sin. Though they were all of the same sect and religious belief, it was no easy matter to maintain harmony in matters spiritual.

Persecutions in the mother country had helped largely to increase emigration to the colonies, although the newcomers soon found that on this side of the ocean government was far from humane,— Radcliffe's ears had been

[9] May, *Constitutional History of England,* ii, 105; State Trials, vii, 929.

cut off, and he had been banished from the colony because he criticized the government and the church. It was a cruel age, and perhaps it would be too much to expect that these men, cast off into a new world, would develop refining processes over and above those of their mother country.

Another new-comer, Roger Williams, soon clashed with the intolerant authorities, and the over-bold innovator was driven out of the colony to found a more liberal one of his own.

A woman was another conspicuous disturber of the colony's smug self-content. Mrs. Hutchinson arrived in 1634 with an apparently harmless message, but one calculated to disturb the colonists. "She brought with her," said Governor Winthrop, "two dangerous errors; that the person of the Holy Ghost dwells in a justified person, and that no sanctification can help to evidence to us our justification." Of course, no self-respecting Puritan government could stand such heresy, but the plain people, with an aptitude for theological hair-splitting that later generations can scarcely appreciate, took Mrs. Hutchinson and her two heresies to their bosoms; in order that there might be peace and unanimity in the community — according to the Puritan idea of a good community — it was necessary to banish Mrs. Hutchinson and several important men of the colony who had become converts.

The importance of Mrs. Hutchinson is due to the fact that about the time of her appearance there began to be great nervousness over the problem of witchcraft. Winthrop, in his journal, suggested that her devilish doctrines might have been inspired by a real witch.

Despite these troubles, the colony prospered, spiritually as well as materially. Harvard College was founded in 1636. By 1645 the colonists were producing more than they needed, exporting was begun, and vessels were built, the latter industry thriving so well that by 1665 they had built about eighty ships of from twenty to forty tons and twelve of over one hundred tons.[10]

England began to take notice of this colony, whose prosperity was being noised about. In 1673 the colony had five iron-works, the products of which were used exclusively by the colonists, and along with this opulence, the people began to get beyond the control of the church so that we hear more and more about sin and its allure. In 1675 King Philip's War broke out, and for two years there was a sanguinary conflict. In the same year the first fire of importance swept away forty-five dwellings and several large warehouses, but the greatest catastrophe was when King James, on his accession to the throne, took away the charter of the colony and appointed Governor Andros to rule over these sturdy believers in their right — and their ability — to rule themselves. All the annoyances possible from a tyrannical representative of a tyrannical king, Andros inflicted. Though the colonists murmured and met in secret, it was not until they had learned of the Revolution in England and of the invasion by the Prince of Orange, that they seized Andros and his associates, restoring the old form of government.

Despite these activities and interests, the colonists were far from indifferent toward the spirit of the times, and the happenings across the seas. Many ships brought news of the home-land, and the news-letters, direct precursors of the newspapers, not only brought news from the other side but developed the habit of wanting news about themselves. Religious news was the most important item, as might be expected in a community of eight thousand inhabitants where the intense religious fervor,

[10] Skelton, *Story of New England,* 96.

of the type that this generation knows as the spasmodic revival, was not a matter of a week or a month, but had been the business of the colony from the time when their grandparents had come into the wilderness and, with the aid of God, had built up a thriving city.

There were book-stores and culture of a kind, but just as we see cities, communities and nations influenced and swayed by dominant intellects, so here the dominating intellects were men whose culture was narrow; men who, representing generations of persecution for their beliefs, had grown to hate all not closely allied with their own sect; men who, like Cotton Mather — though he was a leader, with none quite like him — saw God only in the thunder and the storm, and never dreamed that humanity could be led to reverence the Deity through the simple processes of Eternal Law, unfolding and unraveling man's liberty, equality and happiness.

CHAPTER II

THE FIRST NEWSPAPER IN AMERICA

Contemporary indifference to Harris — His important part in struggle for free press — Prosecuted by Jeffreys — Jailed and pilloried for seditious publication — Imprisoned for second time — His arrival in America — Opens coffee-shop — Publishes first newspaper in America — Reasons for suppression — Author of *New England Primer* — Returns to England — Date of death unknown.

Into this settlement came Benjamin Harris, arriving, according to one authority, in 1687; according to the Boston Town Records, in 1686. If ever a community needed a particular type of man, Boston of this period needed Benjamin Harris — London bookseller, printer, "brisk asserter of English liberties," and later on the author of the *New England Primer.* That he was suppressed and driven back to the London from which he had come, was the misfortune of a colony not liberal enough to welcome him, for he was of the type of the earlier Pilgrims and of those later New Englanders who directed the fight for independence.

Contemporary records afford us little information about Harris, though he left his impression on the journalism of two countries and was an exceptional figure in the fight for a free press in both England and America. That he has been neglected by those who have come after him, has been due, not so much to indifference to him personally as to the general indifference to the journalist who fails, no matter what the cause.

A robust, interesting character was Harris, whose contribution to the history of two continents is deserving of a better fate, for nowhere is there even a biography of him, though in his day both American and English authorities knew him well and had to take official cognizance of his endeavor to enlarge the scope of the press and to unshackle the budding journalistic idea.

Although the part he played in England as one of the most assertive of Whig journalists was not inconsiderable, apparently it brought him no attention when he came to this country, where the authorities, vigorous believers in their own liberties though they were, did not propose to undergo any unnecessary risks in behalf of so combative and unpopular a person as Harris.

The first venture of which we have any knowledge is his publication in London, begun on July 7, 1679, of the *Domestic Intelligence,* more a political periodical than a newspaper, for newspapers were not permitted. With other publications of a similar type, it served the purpose of keeping alive the Whig fight against Tory principles and religious persecution. Harris had his following in London even then, for we learn that the Green Ribbon Club sent its political paragraphs to him regularly. On the other hand, he had vigorous opponents, and one of his rivals, Nathaniel Thompson, accusing him of "lifting" the "stories" of his competitor, thus characterized his new venture:

"There hath lately dropped into the world an abortive birth by a factious, infamous, perjured antichristian, a senseless lying pamphlet, by the name of the *City and Country News.* This is the first of his offspring that ever bore name, the rest being spurious and illegitimate, like his natural issue, which he either durst not own, or would not bring to the font to receive the marks of

Christianity no more than himself. This pamphlet-napper and press-pirate hath cruised abroad since he put up for himself, to make a prize of other men's copies, to stuff his own cargo with ill-gotten profit, making his business cheating and usurpation, to defraud all men, and by factious libels to sow sedition amongst the people, and frighten allegiance from the subjects' bosoms. Now I have yourselves and all honest men to be judges, whether of the two be the best intelligence; he having not only stolen from other intelligences, but likewise from mine, to make up his senseless scrawl, as particularly the relation of Mr. Carte the Jesuit, taken in St. James, which he inserted in his for want of matter, three days after the same was published by me, in a single half-sheet; and this is the whole proceeding of this infallible news-monger." [1]

In the spring of 1680 Harris was arrested for publishing a then famous *Appeal from the Country to the City,* in which the King was openly criticized. He was tried before Chief Justice Scroggs by the infamous Jeffreys, and what has been preserved of the record shows that the pioneer journalist of America was, even in those times of bullying judges, an independent and courageous soul.

At the trial, his neighbors testified that he was a quiet, peaceable, "fair-conditioned" man, but the Chief Justice over-rode all the testimony, declaring him to be the "worst man in the world"— surely a great distinction in times that knew many evil men — and sent the jury out with an open intimation as to the kind of verdict that was expected from them.

The courtroom was crowded with Harris' sympathizers; that he was not without friends among the jury is

[1] Cooke, *History of Party,* i, 363.

shown by the fact that one of the jurors asked if they might not take the seditious pamphlets with them to look over. This was refused. Harris himself had asked if he might not address the jury. This also was denied.

The opening speech of Recorder Jeffreys indicates that Harris' well-wishers gave free vent to their emotions, for the prosecutor hoped that the large numbers present had come to "blush rather than to give encouragement" to Harris' great crime.

That the hope was not well founded is shown by the recorded fact that when the jury brought in a verdict of "Guilty of selling the book," — a plain evasion, and a direct slap at the irascible Chief Justice, — "there was a great and clamorous shout." But the court was not going to allow the jury to interfere with the business in hand, and the foreman was informed that it was his duty to say "Guilty," which was done, and then came words from Harris that are just as fine as some of the expressions that have made famous other champions of liberty. Before he was sentenced, he earnestly besought his lord ship that he might be sent to any other prison than Newgate, the horrors of which live with the pits of ancient Syracuse, but the request was denied, whereupon he said: "I hope God will give me patience to go through with it."

There is something of the best of American journalism in that simple declaration — it was the attitude of Zenger, whose willingness to combat authorities meant so much in pre-Revolutionary times; it was the spirit of Garrison, and it has been shown in a hundred and one ways, when the freedom of the press and the idea of democracy have been challenged by authority.

He was sentenced to pay a fine of £500, to stand in the pillory one hour, and to find sureties for his good behavior for three years. Indeed, had it not been for Justice Pemberton, the Lord Chief Justice would have added that he should be "publicly whipt."

On the 17th of February he was stood in the pillory "over against the Old Exchange" in London, and his friends were again to the fore, for they interfered with one of the main sports of the day, inasmuch as "his party hollowed and whooped and would permit nothing to be thrown at him." [2]

The next we hear of him is on April 27, 1680, when he announces that he has "for several weighty reasons," [3] laid down his paper, *The Domestic Intelligence*. Both action and reasons seem most logical, in view of the fact that the communication is dated from "King's Bench Prison in Southwark."

For a while, neither the indecency of his trial nor the severe punishment meted out to him broke Harris' spirit, and he addressed to Scroggs "Twenty-four Queries" which furnish interesting comment on the trial of libel cases at that time. But his suffering must have been severe, and it was even suggested that his death was planned.[4]

It is not surprising, therefore, that we find Scroggs, at the trial of Harry Care, another writer of seditious pamphlets, declaring that Harris, deserted by his friends, had sent him word that he was ready to "cry quits." Thereupon the learned judge read the noisy crowd in front of him a lecture, pointing out that behavior like that of the "unfortunate man Harris" leads to no good,[5] and that Harris' friends had neglected to pay his fine of £500, which he said would have been about five shillings apiece,

[2] Luttrell, i, 34.

[3] Andrews, *History of British Journalism*, i, 70.

[4] *Sir Roger L'Estrange*, 271.

[5] *State Trials*, vii, 931.

"if they had been as free of their purses as they were of their noise and acclamations." [6]

On September 18th [7] he was examined and is said to have given some information, unfortunately too soon, for in December, Scroggs and Jeffreys suffered impeachment and humiliation at the bar of Commons, Harris' own trial and conviction being cited in the impeachment of the former.[8] The dread hand for a short time was removed from the press and Harris merrily proceeded with his *Intelligence,* but was soon in hot water with his contemporaries as to who was telling the truth. In the spring he was arrested again on a political charge. The following year he heard that another warrant was out for him, and insisted upon being arrested while a friend of his — one Bethel, a Whig — was sheriff, showing that Mr. Harris had political wisdom as well as editorial pugnacity.

But the foresight proved unavailing and again he went to gaol. This time he broke down before the punishment, and is said to have disclosed the names of those who had written the offending articles that he had published. At least, it cannot be said that he feared to go to jail, nor can it be denied that he went with courage and with fortitude.

After this, until he appears in America, we find no record of his activities, although his friend, John Dunton — the "crazy book-seller," Macaulay calls him — speaks of his keeping a coffee-house, and refers to his wife, "like a kind rib," defending him when he was placed in the pillory, referring doubtless to the punishment that was meted out to him by Scroggs.

Dunton, when he came to New England with a cargo

[6] *State Trials,* vii, 1126; also *Sir Roger L'Estrange.*

[7] Luttrell, i, 127.

[8] Cobbett, *Parliamentary History of England,* iv, 1274.

of books, wrote to a friend in 1686 that Ben Harris — tired, like so many of those who were emigrating, of trying to make a living and battling for liberty in England — was contemplating coming to America. Dunton viewed the project dubiously, for while he admitted that Harris " had many good thoughts," he had " wanted the art of improving 'em and could he fix his Mercury a little, and not be so volatile, he would do well enough." He gives us our only idea of Harris' age by declaring that he is advanced in years and at best can only hope to " scuffle through this world."

Harris had little intention of " scuffling through," for that very year he appeared in Boston and opened up a " Coffee, Tea and Chucaletto " shop.

A year later he was printing books and employing printers at what he called the London Printing House.[9] In the diary of Samuel Sewall, the return of Harris from London is noted on January 25, 1688, and in the fall of the same year, when Sewall himself sailed for England, Harris was again on board.

Sewall states that the day after they sailed " the wind came out at North East to our great discomfort," and Harris read the twenty-first chapter of Proverbs, " which is the first chapter I heard read on ship-board. . . . I must heed that voice — he that wandereth out of the way of understanding shall remain in the congregation of the dead."

The picture of Harris in America compares well with the Harris we have seen in England; he arrives in the country and is speedily in touch with its most distinguished judge; he has hardly been here two years when, with an energy unusual in those days, he embarks on a fourth winter ocean voyage in company with the judge, who

[9] Ford, *New England Primer*, 31.

marks him as a man of unusual piety, as well as of stout heart.

The trip abroad must necessarily have been for business purposes, whether for books or in relation to his "Coffee-house." The coffee-clubs took the place of the "saloons" of another epoch when the politician or propagandist discovered there a receptivity for his ideas that he would not have found in less social and convivial places.

It is more likely that his trip had to do with the paper which he was to issue. Without further intimation, so far as any of the contemporary records show, without fanfare or preliminary advertising, *Publick Occurances* appeared on September 25, 1690 — the first newspaper to be printed on this continent — published from Harris' "London Coffee House," the printing being done for him by Richard Pierce.

The first issue was printed on three pages of a folded sheet, leaving the last page blank, there being two columns to a page, each page being about eleven by seven inches.

Harris begins by declaring that his purpose is to furnish the country once a month with an account of "such considerable things as have arrived unto our notice," a promise calculated to arouse the interest of the dwellers in the wilderness, who must have been hungry for news of their fellow-men. He promises that he will take pains to collect his news and will "particularly make himself beholden to such persons in Boston whom he knows to have been for their own use the diligent observers of such matters."

Thirdly he states, "that something may be done toward curing, or at least the charming, of that spirit of lying which prevails among us; wherefore, nothing shall be entered but what we have reason to believe is true, repairing to the best fountains for our information. And when there appears any material mistakes in anything that is collected, it shall be corrected in the next.

"Moreover, the Publisher of these Occurances is willing to engage, that whereas there are many false reports, maliciously made and spread among us, if any well-minded person will be at the pains to trace any such false report, so far as I find out and convict the first raiser of it, he will in this paper (unless just advice be given to the contrary) expose the name of such person as a malicious raiser of false report. It is supposed that none will dislike this proposal, but such as intend to be guilty of so villainous a crime."

Then followed the news or "Occurances," which — considering that this was seventy years after the landing of the Pilgrims on Plymouth Rock, and two hundred years after the invention of printing — shows that our pioneer journalist was not lacking in what is now called news-sense. We are informed that the Christianized Indians in Plymouth had appointed a day of Thanksgiving, and their example is commended to other non-Indian neighbors in a line that seems sarcastic.

There is a brief mention of the fact that two children had been stolen by Indians from the settlement of Chelmsford, the correspondent and not the editor being responsible for the fact that names are not given.

From Watertown there is communicated the news that an old man (again the correspondent neglects to give the name) "having lost his wife, fell into a fit of melancholy during which the devil took possession of him with the result that one morning early in the month he was found hanging in the cow-house." It is noted that the small-pox is abating in Boston, but that another disease — seeming to be more or less of a malignant fever, not unlike the influenza with which this generation is acquainted — is growing into a common thing, and the report states that three hundred and twenty people had died by the last visitation of smallpox.

Two fires are reported, and with much feeling it is noted that in one of them a PRINTING PRESS (the capitals are Harris') had been destroyed.

It was in his account of the battle with the French and Indians that Harris printed news which was to be his undoing. Read even to-day his report of the expedition against the French and the use of the friendly Maquas by Governor Winthrop is not bad reporting when one considers that reporting had yet to be developed or even inaugurated. It was a report, however, that contained matters that the authorities were not desirous of having printed, for it told how the Indian allies of the colonists had treated the French prisoners with great barbarity. Harris protested against trying to subdue Canada with the assistance of "these miserable savages."

Stout old Benjamin Harris, fine old Whig — even in the wilderness he was on the side of humanity and progress, to the very great displeasure of the authorities. Two days after publication, Judge Sewall noted in his diary that the paper had appeared and that it had given "much distaste" because it was not licensed and because of the "passages referring to the French King and the Maquas." Four days later the legislative authorities took the matter up officially, sagely ruling that it contained "reflections of a very high nature," and strictly forbade "anything in print without license first obtained from those appointed by the government to grant the same." [10]

We learn from Sewall, under date of the following

[10] *Sewall,* i, 332 and ii, 345; Felt, *Annals of Salem,* 14.

May, that even though suppressed as a publisher, Harris was still a private purveyor of news, for he brought the information that Captain Leisler and Mr. Millburn had been executed in New York. The same year a partnership was formed with John Allen and a printing shop of their own was set up. Evidently he was working back into the graces of the authorities, for, a short time after, he was made the official printer and ordered to print the laws " that we the people may be informed thereof."

But the spirit of Harris could not be contented in the colonies so long as the mother country afforded greater prospects for safe political activity to one of his ardent temperament. Though the *London Gazette* was the only paper published while the licensing act was in force, the keen interest in the news was satisfied at the coffee-houses in London and by the news-letters throughout the country. The official paper was edited by a clerk in the office of the Secretary of State, who published nothing but the dullest doings of the government. The censorship law expired on May 25, 1695, and within a fortnight thereafter, Harris, back in London, was once more on the ground with the announcement that the *Intelligence Domestic and Foreign* that had been suppressed by tyranny, fourteen years before, would again appear.

CHAPTER III

THE FIRST JOURNALS AND THEIR EDITORS

The news-letter of England — In America — Postmaster as editor — America's first newspaper — *The Boston News-Letter* — Origin — Character of paper — Its lack of enterprise — Brooker and the second paper — Appearance of James Franklin — Conflict with the authorities — Benjamin Franklin's journalistic beginning.

The news-letter, of ancient origin, filled the place of newspapers in England as well as in America, long before the first newspaper appeared. In the mother country the news-letter had become an important political engine.[1] One writer in particular, a high-churchman named Dyer, whose letters were much circulated in manuscript, was twice sent to prison for his anti-government writings.

Eagerness for news, so persistently thwarted by the government, caused the people of London to flock to the coffee-houses, while censorship was being exercised, as the Athenians of ancient times flocked to the market-place. To some extent this satisfied the Londoners, but people in the provinces were obliged to depend on news-letters. These were prepared by writers who wandered from one coffee-house to another, gathering material for weekly epistles with which to enlighten the country folk. It was an evidence of the material well-being of a country gentleman that his news-letter arrived weekly to supply him with the gossip of the great city.[2]

The demand for news-letters brought about, in 1695,

[1] Macaulay, *History of England,* v, 2459.

[2] Macaulay, *History of England,* i, 381.

a half-printed and half-written news-letter called the *Flying Post,* which declared that any gentleman who had "mind to oblige his country friend or correspondent with this account of publick affairs" might purchase it for twopence and on the blank half of the sheet "write his own private business or the material news of the day."[3]

While the American mind, as developed in the colonies, was in advance of the contemporary culture of Europe in the science of politics,[4] the homogeneous character of the colonists, or rather their practical unanimity in matters of religion, led to an absence of the acrimonious political debate that marked England at that time, although the example of the mother country was to bear bitter fruit.

Little demand for political discussion existed in America, but there was a great demand for news, and since there were but few coffee-houses, such as London contained, it was natural that the postmaster should be the central figure for the trade in gossip.

The first postmaster of Boston was Richard Fairbanks, who in 1639 was officially declared to be the person at whose house all letters were to be delivered.[5] The smallness of the compensation, however, led the postmasters to devise various means by which their slight income might be augmented, so that in 1703 we find John Campbell — an active citizen of Boston, interested in the first charitable society of the country,—[6] adding to his meager income by supplying the colonists outside of Boston with the news and gossip that came to him as postmaster. Nine of these letters, addressed to Governor Winthrop of

[3] Andrews, *History of British Journalism,* 87.

[4] North, *The Newspaper and the Periodical Press,* 10.

[5] Drake, *History of Boston,* 247.

[6] Drake, *History of Boston,* 455.

Connecticut, show Campbell as a faithful, if not an inspired, reporter of the events of the day.[7]

That the memory of Harris' attempt with the first newspaper still lingered is shown by Campbell's reference to his own letters as journals of *Publick Occurances,* although it is evident that the summary treatment accorded Harris' publication had chilled any printer or writer who might have thought of a second attempt along similar lines. But the newspaper was bound to come, especially when the newspapers in the mother country were attracting so much attention and exercising so great an influence on the public mind.

With the expiration of the censorship in England in 1695,— for which relief so much was owing to John Locke's argument before Parliament [8] — journals sprang up by the dozen, and, though America remained dependent on the news-letter and belated copies of London papers for its information, England was flooded with newspapers and newspaper discussion. The first daily newspaper in London made its appearance in 1702; and the same year that Campbell started what was really the first newspaper in America, Daniel Defoe started his *Review* in London.

So it might be said that the appearance of the *Boston News-Letter* on April 24, 1704, was not so much a sign of progressiveness as an evidence of the backwardness of the colonies. Samuel Sewall, the faithful diarist, records under this date, the fact that the *News-Letter* had come out and that he had taken the first copy ever carried "over the river" to President Willard of Harvard University. We do not hear now of the lamentations that accompanied the virile publication of Benjamin Har-

[7] *Massachusetts Historical Society,* ix, 485.

[8] H. R. Fox Bourne, *Life of John Locke,* ii, 312–315.

ris, for Campbell was careful to publish his paper "by authority" and to print nothing that would offend the authorities or religious leaders such as Mather, who had waxed so indignant over the Harris publication.

Most of the paper is taken up with extracts from the London *Flying Post* and the *London Gazette* of the previous December. This was doubtless a very safe introduction. When it came to printing the local news, the harmless Campbell restricted himself to recording several particularly eminent deaths and the announcement of a sermon by the Reverend Mr. Pemberton, of extensive influence. There was a short, snappy account of a sea fight between the English and the French and the story of a scare about French ships appearing off Rhode Island,—several "marine items," as they would be called to-day, and then his announcement that he would be ready to take advertisements and subscriptions, prices to be furnished by calling on Mr. Campbell himself at the post office.

There is none of the spirit of Harris here, no burning indignation against conditions, such as marked the great journalists and later made journalism the voice of the people, nor during his career as editor do we find Campbell showing any desire to bring about a better condition of affairs or any other evidence of the progressive spirit. It is, therefore, not to be wondered that Campbell's colorless publication had a hard struggle.

Truly a timid spirit was poor Campbell, whose paper persisted for fifteen years without character or progress, but with frequent pitiful requests for contributions and assistance. We find him pleading, the year after he had established the paper, that the post office was paying him very little money, and that, despite the fact that a number of merchants had promised to contribute to the support of his weekly *News-Letter,* he had not made anything by it. He begged the Governor to grant him some allowance "to encourage him in said duty for the future," a petition that resulted in his being allowed six shillings or six pounds, the exact amount not being decipherable.[9]

Fifteen years after he had started the paper he appealed to the public for assistance, stating that he had "supplied them conscientiously with publick occurances of Europe and with those of these, our neighboring provinces, and the West Indies,"[10] although he admitted that at one time he had been a little matter of thirteen months behindhand with the news. The time had come, he said, when he must have assistance, frankly admitting that his circulation was not over 300 copies, although some ignorant persons had spread about a report that he was selling upward of a thousand. He therefore pleaded, the good postmaster, that those who had not paid for the half year's subscription would please come forward to his house in Cornhill and lay down the cash.

Campbell's lack of success aroused little sympathy, for while some of the fault may have been with the authorities, we cannot help contrasting his puny and generally uninteresting gazette, which had held the field for sixteen years without a rival, with the great development of journalism, in the mother country. It was during these sixteen years that Addison, Swift and Steele were, as Henry Morley says, "teaching the English people to read" in journals which, if they did not come up to modern ideas and high standards of journalism, were bridging the chasm between journalism and literature and establishing for the former an authority, a political and social standing that

9 *Historical Magazine,* viii, 31.
10 August 10, 1719.

was to count for much in the battle for a free press and political liberty.

New forces, affecting those interested both in literature and politics, were at work in England; chief among these forces was "the tendency to exalt the common good of society at the expense of special privileges."[11] Within a few years after the *News-Letter* was established, the circulation of the papers in London was about 44,000, the papers named being the *Daily Courant, General Remark, Female Tatler, General Postscript, Supplement, British Apollo, London Gazette, Postman, Postboy, Flying Post, Review, Tatler, Rehearsal Revived, Evening Post, Whisperer, Postboy Junior, City Intelligence* and *Observator.*

What was more surprising was that when the Whigs came into power in 1715, with George the First, there was no sympathetic reaction in a journalistic way in the colonies as might have been expected. Campbell's journalistic career suffered a severe blow when in 1719 he was removed as postmaster and a William Brooker was appointed in his place. Campbell, on being summarily dismissed, declined to send his newspaper through the mail, with the result that on December 21, 1720, Brooker brought out the first number of the second newspaper published in America, called the *Boston Gazette,* which was also a newspaper "published by authority" and was printed by James Franklin, who with his celebrated brother was to play an important part in shaping the early journalistic history of colonial America.

Brooker was a more able man than Campbell, as he showed in the controversy that followed between the two pioneer journalists, both of whom incidentally established that connection between journalism and political office

[11] Stevens, *Notes on English Politics,* 1702–1750.

which has persisted to our day and doubtless has had something to do with the journalist regarding himself, in this country more than in any other, as entitled to direct governmental support and reward. We shall see curious and sometimes rather tragic instances, as we progress, of the endeavor on the part of editors to unite the functions of journalist and politician.

Brooker's paper was the same size as Campbell's and was issued from the post office as the latter's had been. This fact was gall and wormwood to old Campbell, who showed the first spirit evidenced in his journalistic career, by attacking his rival in really modern fashion, declaring that he pitied the readers of the new newspaper — "its sheets smell stronger of beer than of midnight oil — it is not reading fit for people!" Certainly this was the thrust direct, and a fine evidence that after the long sleep that might be said to have characterized Campbell's editorship up to this period, he was at last awake and was appearing as the original sponsor of the personal note that was afterward to be so seldom missing from American journalism.

Right modern, too, was Brooker's rejoinder, intimating that editor Campbell was discussing many things in order to confuse the public mind as to the fact that he had been "removed, turned out, displaced or superseded" from the post office, although it seemed to his successor that "removed" was the "softest epithet."

Before leaving Campbell, it may be said for him in extenuation that some of the dullness of his journal was but a reflection of the life he depicted, and it can also be said that much of the dreariness of New England life was due to the reign of the Mathers. Brooks Adams has well observed that the one weak point in the otherwise strong position of the Massachusetts clergy was that they were not permitted to make their order hereditary.[12] But the Mathers came near establishing a dynasty. It was a Mather who cried out against the Benjamin Harris publication; it was a Mather who made it necessary to have printing done in New York when occasion arose for criticizing those stern New England divines, and it was unquestionably the spirit of the Mathers dominating in New England that led the community to stand, for sixteen long years, the dull and phlegmatic journalism of John Campbell.

James Franklin, who now appeared as printer of the new postmaster's newspaper, had studied his trade in London, whither he had been sent by his father, Josiah Franklin, whose paternity of thirteen children made it necessary for him to devote some thought to the occupations which they were to follow.

Benjamin Franklin, in his autobiography, is far from kindly toward his brother, and of his father he gives us not as much to indicate his importance as does the chronicler Sewall in several short lines. The Puritan Pepys, as Senator Lodge has called Sewall, shows what our modern yellow journalist would call a keen news sense when he records on February 6, 1703, that "Ebenezer Franklin of the South Church, a male infant of sixteen months old was drown'd in a tub of suds, February 5, 1703."[13] In 1708 Sewall preached at the house of Josiah Franklin "the eleventh sermon of the Barren Figtree."[14] He records going to a meeting at Franklin's house in 1713, when Benjamin was in his eighth year and probably had the privilege of sitting very still and listening to the wonderful elders. In 1718 Sewall, having

[12] M. C. Crawford, *Old Boston in Colonial Days,* 165.
[13] *Sewall's Diary,* ii, 73.
[14] *Ibid.* ii, 236.

"set the tune" for twenty-four years, found that he was wandering off the key and suggested that Josiah Franklin take his place in church.

James Franklin's trip to London had done much for him and much for journalism, for he came back from a London that was full of politics and journalistic combat. The influence of these early journalistic masters was broad and deep, as we learn from Benjamin Franklin's biography, wherein he states that he taught himself to write excellent English prose by modeling his style upon that of Addison and Steele; an evidence indeed that the colonies were ripe for better journalism, when the son of a soap-maker, at the age of thirteen or fourteen, was imitating the pioneer newspaper stylists.

The *Boston Gazette* made little impression on the life of the colony, except as it stirred up a controversy with the old postmaster, Campbell, who continued to abuse Brooker — possibly to the merriment of the community but with no advantage to either gentleman, for in a few months Brooker lost both the postmastership and the *Gazette,* the latter passing from postmaster to postmaster, apparently as the property of the office, or rather as a perquisite of the position.

Between 1719 and 1739, the *Boston Gazette* was owned and conducted by no less than five postmasters. Each of these, of course, was entitled to give the printing of the paper to whomsoever he would. When the paper passed into the hands of Brooker's successor, the printing was taken away from James Franklin. The young printer, with his London ideas and London training, and with the intelligence that was evidently a family possession, determined to start a paper of his own and, on August 7, 1721, there appeared the first number of the *New England Courant.*

The new editor had no intention of abiding by the policies that had characterized his predecessors, for in the first number he attacked the *News-Letter* as a " dull vehicle of intelligence," which brought down upon him the wrath of old Campbell. What was of more importance was that Franklin, his paper appearing when the town was being ravaged by smallpox, attacked the practice of inoculation, which caused Cotton Mather to condemn his paper as " a vile production," and to regret that it could not be suppressed as a libelous sheet.

Franklin, we learn from his brother Benjamin, had some ingenious and intelligent men among his friends, who backed him in his venture and anonymously contributed articles to it. This group was described by the clergy as a " Hell-Fire Club."

The attack of Cotton Mather on the *Courant* helped as much to make it popular as did its own courage and freedom of expression. The town was divided over the novelty of this kind of journalism and some even stopped James Franklin on the street to remonstrate with him, while others attacked him in the *News-Letter* and in the *Gazette*. The audacity of the publishers turned out to be a good business venture, for they picked up forty new subscribers, which was then a great increase, no newspaper having more than three hundred circulation at that time.

It was at this time that Benjamin Franklin began, under the name of " Silence Dogood," his contributions to the paper, which are so closely modeled on the essays of Addison in the *Spectator* that it has been suggested that he had the original book open before him when he wrote them.

The paper continued in its course, criticizing and occasionally referring with sarcasm to the government, until the General Court took the matter in hand. A committee was appointed to consider the charges, and it finally decided, on the issue of January 14, 1722, that the tendency of the paper was to mock religion and government and that, therefore, James Franklin should be forbidden to print and publish his paper or any other paper or pamphlet like it unless what was to be printed was first submitted to the secretary of the province.

Franklin, however, refused to submit his manuscript as ordered, with the result that the General Court ordered "that James Franklin no longer print the newspaper." The publisher's friends held a meeting, and as young Benjamin Franklin, then only sixteen years of age, had developed talent, first as a printer's devil and then as a contributor to the paper, it was decided to print the paper in his name and on February 11, 1722, Benjamin Franklin made his début as editor.

The policy of the paper, however, continued to be dictated by James Franklin, and the following summer trouble again arose between the paper and the government when the *Courant* criticized the Massachusetts authorities for their failure to give chase to a pirate that had appeared off Block Island. The authorities decided "that the said paragraphs are a high affront to this government" and ordered Franklin to be imprisoned in Boston. After a week's confinement, the records of the General Court show a petition from him "that he may have the liberty of the yard, he being indisposed and suffering in health by the said confinement," and upon his promising not to endeavor to escape, this privilege was granted to him.

Several weeks afterward the council again called attention to the free-thinking character of the writings in the *Courant* and its habit of reflecting on his majesty's government, and the publisher had to put up one hundred pounds as security for his good behavior.

Meanwhile Benjamin Franklin and his brother had quarreled, as he relates in his biography, and in the fall of 1723 the enterprising young man, who was to take such a part in the development of this country, sailed for New York without a formal farewell.

For several years after his departure the paper was printed in his name, but it weakened in spirit and, in the beginning of the year 1727, it ceased publication, and James Franklin accepted the invitation of his brother John in Newport and moved his printing press to that colony.[15]

[15] McMaster, *Benjamin Franklin,* 23.

CHAPTER IV

PHILADELPHIA AND THE BRADFORDS

William Penn, the patron of the press — William Bradford's arrival and first trouble with the government — His defense of right to print — Leaves colony for New York — Return of Andrew Bradford — His troubles with the government — First newspaper in Philadelphia — Benjamin Franklin and his enterprise.

In Boston, Philadelphia and New York, American journalism had its beginnings; strong, characteristic, combative beginnings, with many clashes against the authority that sought to stifle it — authority that was in a very short time to learn its power. In the development of the press and the growth of the power of public opinion, it was in these three cities that the struggle for democratic ideas was keenest, and here, too, the brains employed were the ablest. We also see that journalism can function at its best only where it is an active participant, if not the leader, in the fight for democratic ideas and popular rights. In later years the papers throughout the country came to be the great organs of public indignation and reform, achieving success for the causes espoused, and distinction and influence for the journalists who dominated them, but only as they were combative, democratic and representative of the people.

"It would be perfectly reasonable to expect that it (journalism) would reach its highest development in the cities," says J. Allen Smith; "here modern democracy was born; here we find the physical and social conditions which facilitate interchange of thought and concerted action on the part of the people."[1] In these cities, too, we find public opinion immediately affecting the daily life of the people, with the result that the cities were more democratic than the country, where there were no newspapers.

It was in Philadelphia that the first printing press outside the New England colonies was established by William Bradford, a Quaker, who came to America with Penn's colonists in 1682. Through his father-in-law, also a Quaker, Bradford, when very young, met William Penn, and the Great Proprietary, when he was about to sail for Pennsylvania, arranged to take young Bradford with him, that the new colony might have the benefit of a printing press. This was a most fortunate situation for the young man; not only did he have the patronage of a great and wealthy proprietor, but Penn's own taste in literature and his attitude toward the press were those of a man of extreme intelligence and liberality.[2] While it was in Boston that the first newspaper was started, and while New York was the scene of the first notable battle for the freedom of the press, it is to the Philadelphia of William Penn that one would naturally look for leadership in the struggle for a free press, and subsequent history shows how small and apparently unimportant incidents frequently contained within themselves the germ of great influence. It is true that on the *Mayflower*, with the Pilgrims, came Brewster, with the liberality toward the press that one might assume from his having been a publisher himself, but Pennsylvania's history can more than offset this by pointing to the care that was taken — when the *Welcome* brought hither William Penn and the

[1] *Spirit of American Government*, 251.

[2] Edward Armstrong, *Address before the Historical Society of Pennsylvania*, November 8, 1851.

men who were to settle the new colony — that a printer should be included among them, with the understanding that his was to be a free press and, above all, that he was to have the power to print the laws for the people.

Himself an author of a notable little book, *The Fruits of Solitude,*— interesting even at this day,— Penn showed, in times that were dark indeed, a foresight that makes both democracy and journalism in America his everlasting debtors. The great glory of Philadelphia in the history of journalism is the name of Franklin, but it is hard to conceive Franklin attracted to the place, had it not been for the spirit of liberality with which Penn had endowed his colony.

Bradford went back to London, after his visit with Penn, and in 1685 prepared to return here. He brought with him letters of introduction which stated that he was coming over to be a printer of Quakers' books and asked the Quakers of the colonies to patronize him, as they would thus be sure to get genuine Quaker books and not those containing heresy. The first book known to have been issued from his press is an almanac for the year 1686, printed in the latter part of 1685. Bradford, with the genius of his craft, clashed with the government in this publication, by referring to Penn as "Lord Penn." The Provincial Council summoned the man who had edited the almanac for Bradford, ordered the printer to blot out the words "Lord Penn" and warned him that he "was not to print anything but what shall have lycence from ye Council." [3]

In the early part of 1688, at the instance of some of the women of Philadelphia who were opposed to the holding of a fair too far from the fashionable section of the city, Bradford printed a paper of protest which resulted in

[3] *Minutes of Provincial Council,* I, 115.

bringing his efforts once more to the notice of the Council; this time, however, it was the subscribers who were called before them.

Two years later the Governor and the people became involved in a dispute as to the extent of their respective rights, and one of the leaders of the colony, Joseph Growden, had Bradford print the charter. Party spirit ran high, and Bradford, scenting trouble, was careful enough to send out the work without his imprint. Once more he was in clash with the government, this time called by the Governor, as he says, to accuse himself. In the course of an ingenious evasion, he declared that one of the things for which William Penn had asked him to come to the colony was to print the laws, and the only reason why he had not printed them was that he had no particular orders to do so. Bradford held out for the right to print the laws, declaring that the charter had been printed in England, and showed a fine sense of his rights by refusing to answer questions until he was faced by his accuser.[4]

In his next clash with the authorities Bradford, on trial for printing a seditious pamphlet for one of the warring factions, showed that he had a fundamental understanding of the rights of publishers. He conducted his own examination, and objected to two of the jurors on the ground that they had already formed an opinion. In the conduct of his case, he laid the ground-cloth for the many libel dramas that were to follow — notably in the case of Zenger — the successful issue of which meant so much to the colonies in their struggle for freedom.

Bradford was permitted to go free, but as he had been interfered with from the first publication he had attempted, he was heartily sick of the colony, especially as the

[4] An account of this interview in Bradford's own handwriting now hangs in the Hall of the New York Historical Society.

Quakers themselves, in their church council, had decided that he ought to submit to them in addition to the censorship already established by the government. The council of the City of New York in 1693, acquainted with the conditions in Philadelphia, passed a resolution at the instigation of Governor Fletcher, declaring that "if a printer will come and settle in the City of New York for the printing of our Acts of Assembly and Publick Papers" they will give him forty pounds for his salary and he could "have the benefit of his printing besides what serves the Publick." Bradford promptly accepted.

This was the beginning in New York, a beginning most auspicious and interesting; reflecting great credit on Fletcher, who, though not the most liberal or understanding of governors, was nevertheless a good friend to Bradford, and saw to it, as long as he was in office, that the printer received those increases in salary and those little extra allowances which were so welcome, even to a pioneer in the cause of journalism and the free press.

From this time to the establishment, in 1725, of the *New York Gazette,* the first newspaper in New York City, Bradford's life was uneventful, although fairly successful. He became a well-known vestryman of Trinity Church and was a conspicuous person in the community, of decidedly different mold from the complaining and complacent Campbell of Boston. In 1709, with an eye to the future, he sought to establish his son Andrew, who had now come to man's estate, in Rhode Island, where the prospects of liberal treatment were good. The negotiations evidently came to naught, and in 1712 Andrew was established in Philadelphia, as his father's partner.

Here, temporarily, we must leave old Bradford, but not without commenting on the ability and foresight of the man. If the pioneers of journalism were in Boston, it was Philadelphia and New York, but especially Philadelphia, that first produced the men who gave it vigor, force, reason and character.

Andrew Bradford was seven years of age when his father moved to New York, where, under his tutelage, the boy was versed in the trade that he was destined to follow. In 1712 he moved back to Philadelphia, and in 1714, by arrangement with the assembly, he issued "Bradford's Law of 1714."

From 1712 until Samuel Keimer, Benjamin Franklin's first employer, appeared on the scene in 1723, Bradford was the only printer in Pennsylvania. In addition to his printing, he ran what would to-day be called a general store, where he sold, as he advertised, a variety of goods from "beaver hats" to "pickled sturgeon."

Although his father, from the time of his removal to New York and his occupation of the position of official printer to the end of his life, showed Tory leanings, Andrew Bradford was decidedly of the Whig faith. There is, however, consistency in the fact that it was the son, representing the spirit of free discussion, who started a newspaper in Philadelphia several years before the father started one in New York.

The *American Weekly Mercury,* the third paper in the colonies, made its first appearance on December 22, 1719. It resembled the New England journals, was 15 inches by 12½ inches in size, and appeared weekly, generally on Tuesday. Like the New England papers, it printed little of the local news, with which everybody was supposed to be conversant, but was made up principally of extracts from foreign journals.

Like his father in his younger days, Andrew Bradford was soon in a clash with the government, for in the issue of January 2, 1721, a paragraph appeared expressing the hope that the General Assembly "will find some effectual remedy to revive the dying credit of the Province and restore to us our former happy circumstances." For this implied criticism he was haled before the Provincial Council, where his defense was that the paragraph had been written and inserted without his knowledge by a journeyman.

In 1721 Andrew Bradford eliminated the name of his former partner, John Cobson, and from that time on the imprint read "Philadelphia: printed and sold by Andrew Bradford at the Bible in Second Street and also by William Bradford in New York where advertisements are taken in," the fact of the same paper being sold in New York and Philadelphia tending to broaden the views and the outlook of the citizens of both cities.

It is interesting to note Bradford's "editorials," as showing that the editors, even in those early days when there were but three or four of them and they were far apart, were watching each other; and that while James Franklin was having his trouble with the Colonial Government in New England, Andrew Bradford, whom Benjamin Franklin calls illiterate, was defending the *New England Courant* and its publishers.

"My Lord Coke observes," commented Bradford, in the first newspaper defense of a free press, "that to punish first, and then inquire, the law abhors; but here Mr. Franklin has a severe sentence passed upon him, even to the taking away of his livelihood, without being called to make an answer. An indifferent person would judge by this vote against courts, that the Assembly of Massachusetts Bay is made up of oppressors and bigots, who make religion the only engine of destruction to the people, and the rather because the first letter in the *Courant,* of the 14th of January, which the assembly censures, so naturally represents and expresses the hypocritical pretenders to religion. This much we could not forbear saying, out of compassion to the distressed people of the province, who must resign all pretences to sense and reason, and submit to the tyranny of priestcraft and hypocrisy." [5]

Naturally, therefore, when young Benjamin Franklin ran away from Boston and arrived in New York, it was to William Bradford, a printer famous even to young Franklin, that he applied for work. Franklin tells us that Bradford advised him to go to Philadelphia, informing him that his son Andrew had lost his only workman. When he called at Andrew's house in Philadelphia, father Bradford had arrived in Philadelphia before him, having traveled on horseback. He introduced Franklin to his son, who received him civilly and gave him a breakfast. Bradford had at the time no need for a new employee, but told Franklin of another printer in town, one Keimer, who perhaps would employ him. If not, Franklin was told, he would be welcome to lodge at Bradford's house, and a little work would be found for him to do now and then until the situation bettered. This is Franklin's own statement; yet he does not hesitate to refer slightingly to both the son and the older man, who even went to the trouble of taking him to see the new printer, Keimer.

It was while he was in this same Keimer's office that Franklin came under the notice of the Governor of Pennsylvania, Sir William Keith, who took a fancy to him and proposed one day "over the Madeira" that the young man should set up a printing shop of his own. On the strength of Keith's promises Franklin went abroad to purchase supplies, but when he arrived in London found that Keith had no credit there. For eighteen months he worked in various printing-houses and, the

[5] *Mercury*, February 26, 1723.

venture into commercial life having failed, went back to Philadelphia and worked for Keimer until 1728, when he and one of his associates, Hugh Meredith, set up a printing plant for themselves. He was hardly established in this when the idea of a newspaper of his own came to him. He was preparing to issue it when his former employer, Keimer, hearing of the project, anticipated them, and issued, in 1728, the first number of the *Universal Instructor in All Arts and Sciences,* or the *Pennsylvania Gazette.*

This publication, as might be expected from its origin and the ignorance with which Franklin endows Keimer, made little impression on the community. Keimer struggled along up to the twenty-seventh number of the paper, when there was a week's delay, which he later explained as being due to the fact that he had been " awak'd when fast asleep in Bed, about Eleven at Night, over-tir'd with the Labour of the Day, and taken away from my Dwelling, by a Writ and Summons, it being based and confidently given out, that I was that very Night about to run away, tho' there was not the least Colour or Ground for such a vile Report."

He was released, through the forbearance of his creditors, and struggled on until number 39, when, the circulation being reduced to ninety subscribers, the paper was sold for a small price to Franklin and his partner Meredith, and continued as the *Pennsylvania Gazette,* the second paper established in Pennsylvania.

Of Franklin, as editor and publisher of his own paper, it is to be said that, in this year, 1728, he came to his task — one might even say his mission — unusually well equipped. From the age of twelve, when he was apprentice to his brother James, to the time when he took hold of the *Pennsylvania Gazette,* he had been steadily gaining experience such as had fallen to the lot of no other man in the colonies. He tells us himself that he studied style by copying Addison and Steele when a mere child. With his brother, he had suffered because of the autocratic spirit of the times when James Franklin and his associates were making, in their small way, an interesting beginning in the battle for a free press.

He knew the Bradfords, William and Andrew, personally. He knew the personnel of the printers in the colonies as probably no other man did. He had had an interesting and intensive training in England for eighteen months, and the philosophical bent that he showed in the first essay written for his brother's paper, the *New England Courant*, was now to be given full sway, with a development that was to hold two continents in rapt admiration and a result that was to make his native country his everlasting debtor, for Franklin, the great editorial-political genius used the success that came to him to swell the current of influence that was making for liberty and democracy.

In the meantime the advent of Bradford the elder marked the beginning of truly historical developments in the colony of New York.

CHAPTER V

PRINTING IN NEW YORK—THE ZENGER TRIAL

Early political divisions — Oppression by the Conquerors — Foundation for the Whig party — William Bradford invited to the colony — *New York Gazette,* the first paper — Maladministration of Governor Cosby — Zenger brings out the *Journal* — Attacks government — His arrest and trial — Andrew Hamilton's great speech — Its importance in the history of the country.

While the printing press did not appear in New York Colony until some years after there had been presses in Massachusetts — and even in Pennsylvania, a colony settled after New York — there was, in the Dutch settlement, greater encouragement for a free press than in either of the other two, at least in the beginning. This was partly due to the fact that, when the Dutch colony had been taken over by the English, there had grown up two parties more equally divided than was the case in any of the other colonies — parties divided somewhat as the Whigs and the Tories later were. The governing class was arrogant, inasmuch as the government represented the conquerors; on the other hand, the governed class in the colony of New York, representing some of the rich burghers and old Dutch families, was not as docile as the laboring and governed class of other colonies. Having been, in former days, the rulers of the colony, and therefore accustomed to public discussion, its members were quick to use the printing press to air their grievances.

An early evidence of liberality in the new colony is shown by Benjamin Fletcher, who, when he became Governor of New York in 1692, realized that both Massachusetts and Pennsylvania had advanced more rapidly in this direction than had New York, and therefore caused to be passed by the assembly a law which was practically an invitation to William Bradford of Philadelphia to set up his printing press in New York. In 1696 Fletcher reprinted an issue of the *London Gazette* which contained an account of the engagement with the French preceding the peace of Ryswick.[1]

As early as 1668, Governor Lovelace, the second English Governor, had expressed a desire to have a printer in the colony, and he tried to get one from Boston.[2] Following the accession of James the Second, one of the first instructions given to Governor Dongan in 1686 was to see that no one did any printing without first obtaining a license. With the brighter prospects which followed the Revolution of 1688, Governor Fletcher had the Council pass, on March 23, 1693, the resolution above referred to, by which " the sum of £40 current money of New York per annum for his salary " was offered to any printer who would settle in the colony and print the Acts of Assembly.[3]

Bradford, tired out with continual wrangling with the authorities in Pennsylvania, accepted this offer, as we have seen, and the following October the first warrant for his press was issued.

Although the printer had been invited by a representative of the government, it was not long before those opposed to the interests of the Crown attempted to use the

[1] Hudson, *Journalism in the United States*, 50.

[2] Wallace, *Address on William Bradford*, 60.

[3] *Council Minutes*, vi. 182.

press. Two years after Bradford was established, the Assembly asked permission of the Governor "to print their journal," a request that resulted in the House being dissolved. But while Fletcher was in power, Bradford's course was prosperous and smooth, and continued so until Fletcher was succeeded by the Earl of Bellomont, who, being a reformer, believed in low salaries and much work.

A clash came after the Earl had had a long conference with the Indians — "the greatest fatigue I ever underwent in my whole life," he wrote. "I was shut up in a closed chamber with sixty Sachems who, besides a stench of bear's grease with which they plentifully daubed themselves, were continually either smoking or drinking drams of rum — for eight days." He decided that this heroic performance justified a printed report. Bradford, however, refused to print it, as he considered it a private diary and not a public paper coming within his contract. Bellomont retaliated by charging Bradford with neglecting his duty, and appointed one Abraham Gouverneur in his place. Bradford won, however, by anticipating the advice of Comte de Buffy: "Take good care of yourself; be persuaded that if you will only let your adversary die before you, it is he, not you, who has lost the case." Bellomont died before he was able to do any serious damage to Bradford, or to diminish his influence and lessen his power in the colony.

We have told in the previous chapter how the printer increased his business and how he sought, when his son Andrew became of age, to start the young man's career in Rhode Island, finally establishing him in Philadelphia in 1712. Following the new movement of the day, and imitating Andrew in Philadelphia, at the age of sixty-two Bradford established the first newspaper in New York; in 1728, having a paper in Philadelphia owned by his son and one in New York owned by himself, he purchased a large paper factory in Elizabethtown and thus rendered both establishments independent of the British manufacturers. Bradford edited his own paper until he was eighty years of age, when he retired, transferring it to James Parker, by whom it was conducted after 1743.

Bradford's very partisanship had its usefulness to the opponents of the Colonial Government, and when the crisis came,— as it did over a mere matter of salary — it was from his office and by his apprentice, John Peter Zenger, that the most effective blow was struck at the despotism of the government.

Between the death of Governor Montgomery, on June 30, 1731, and the arrival of Governor Cosby on September 18, 1732, Rip Van Dam, the senior member of the Council, occupied the executive chair. Over a dispute as to who should receive the fees of the office, which amounted to about £6000, the Governor *pro tem.* and Cosby went to court. In order to carry his case, the Governor removed Chief Justice Morris and appointed James DeLancey in his place, an act of arrogance that caused a great deal of acrimony among the colonists. Cosby showed his contempt for them in other ways, calling them, in an official report, "A lazy, good-for-nothing crowd, filled with the spirit of insubordination,"[4] who were drawing their inspiration, he declared, from trouble makers in Boston. The opposition decided to have their own paper, and on the 15th of November, 1733, they brought out the first number of the *New York Weekly Journal* under the auspices of John Peter Zenger, an apprentice of Bradford, who had come to him as a poor young immigrant.

The records of Zenger's life are very meager. He

[4] *New York Documents*, v, 937.

was one of a large number of Palatines who were sent to America in 1710 by Queen Anne. His mother, his sister, and his younger brother arrived with him, the father of the family having died on shipboard. After serving an apprenticeship of eight years with Bradford, Zenger went to Maryland to try his fortunes there, but met with little success. For a few years he struggled at his trade; he joined in partnership with Bradford in 1725, but the partnership must have been of short duration, as there is only one book extant showing the imprint of their joint names. In 1726 Zenger, a poor, struggling German printer, started in business for himself. His shop was of small size and he printed a few political tracts and a number of unimportant books, principally theological in character and written in Dutch. In 1730 he printed the first arithmetic published in the colony.

In the very first issue of the *New York Weekly Journal* there appeared an article on the liberty of the press which was used as the text for many others, all filled with direct allusions to Cosby and his conduct. Several numbers were condemned by Cosby to be burned as containing "Scurrilous, Scandalous and Virulent Reflections," — these were numbers 7, 47, 48 and 49.[5] The first of these was largely taken up with a bold and vigorous criticism of the Governor for permitting a French man-o'-war to enter New York Harbor — ostensibly for the purpose of provisioning, but more likely in order, the Journal asserted, to spy upon the works and fortifications of New York. These numbers also contain critical mention of the fact that the Governor invited but a few members of

[5] Number 7, December 17, 1733.
Number 47, September 23, 1734.
Number 48, September 30, 1734.
Number 49, October 7, 1734.

the Council to sit in session with him on matters of State, and that these invariably were his appointees and favorites. Numbers 47, 48 and 49 were primarily taken up with the publication of an anonymous letter, purporting to be from a New Jersey settler who undertook to criticize and hold up to ridicule "the Nullity of Law" in New York Province and the maladministration of Governor Cosby.

As a result of these attacks, Cosby issued a proclamation offering a reward of £50 for the discovery of the author of said "Scandalous, Virulent and Seditious Reflections," and on Sunday, November 17, 1734, Zenger was arrested on a charge of libel.

When brought before the Chief Justice on November 20th, his bail was fixed at £800, which he was unable to raise, but he was finally allowed to have pen, ink, and paper, which he had been previously denied. For the next nine months, Zenger edited his paper in jail.

It has been said that Zenger deserved little credit for his fight for a free press, as he was a poor printer without much education and the articles that did all the damage were written by wealthy and cultivated gentlemen of the period.[6] It is to be sincerely hoped that this was not so, in view of the fact that the important and wealthy men who took part in Zenger's fight allowed him, for nine months, to languish in jail because of their failure to raise the amount of his bail. Zenger was really a strong, courageous citizen, who, while he may not have written some of the learned articles in his paper, was the one who stood for them, showing a great deal more character and vigor than the anonymous, if educated, contributors. It is a sad comment on their gentle descent that they allowed another man to go to jail for what they had written.

[6] Rutherford, *John Peter Zenger.*

In the first issue after his arrest Zenger apologized for missing an issue, on the ground that, not only had he been without pen, ink, and paper, but he had been held *incomunicado.* He promised them " by the liberty of speaking to my servants through the hole of the door of the prison to entertain you with my weekly journal as formerly," and this he did until the trial took place, on August 4, 1735.

When the trial came up Zenger's counsel, William Smith and James Alexander, denied the competency of Chief Justice DeLancey and of Judge Phillips who sat with him, which objections were treated by DeLancey as contempt of court, and both lawyers were excluded, by another order, from further practice.

To the amazement of the court and of Cosby's party, when the case finally came to trial Andrew Hamilton, the celebrated lawyer of Philadelphia — the ablest attorney in the colonies, and a warm personal friend of Benjamin Franklin — walked into court to defend Zenger.

Hamilton is said to have been eighty years of age at this time, and he was known throughout the colonies as a man of great ability. There was a romantic mystery about him. It was known that Hamilton was not his real name. It was said that he had fled from Europe after having killed some one of importance in a duel. He was unquestionably of gentle blood, but whatever the cause of the mystery, he carried his secret to the grave. He had acquired a handsome practice and much wealth in the colonies, and in 1712 had gone to England, where he was admitted to the bar. On one of his trips to Europe he sailed with Benjamin Franklin.

The appearance of Hamilton dumfounded the Cosby adherents. He opened the case by offering to prove the truth of the statements in the alleged libel. This was overruled by DeLancey, who, as an appointee of Cosby, was naturally on the side of the Governor. As a matter of fact, though, the law as it then stood was on the side of the Chief Justice.[7]

From the time of the Star Chamber there had been little addition to, or development of the law with regard to seditious offenses. It was under the law as laid down by Lord Chief Justice Holt that Zenger was being tried: "If people should not be called to account for possessing the people with an ill opinion of the government, no government can subsist. For it is necessary for all governments that the people should have a good opinion of it." [8]

This was still the law of England, and necessarily of the colonies. It is said that a great deal of the vivacity and energy used at that time in cases where the liberty of the press was concerned, was due to the fact that the lawyers realized the insecurity of the legal foundation of that liberty.[9] We have seen how William Bradford was tried under this law, but in his case the jury was instructed to find whether the papers printed by Bradford tended to weaken the hands of the magistrates as well as to find whether Bradford printed it. "*Comme la vèritè, l'erreur a ses héros.*" [10]

The law had already been tested and accepted in the colonies. In 1702 Colonel Nicholas Bayard was charged with alleged libels which were not put in evidence but which were declared to contain charges that "the hottest and ignorantest of the people were put in places of trust," and on this verbal statement Colonel Bayard was sen-

[7] Lewis, *Great American Lawyers,* i, 32.
[8] *Howell's State Trials,* xiv, 1128.
[9] Stephen, *History of the Criminal Law of England,* ii, 349.
[10] Lewis, *Great American Lawyers,* i, 35.

tenced to be hanged, drawn and quartered. The sentence, however, was not carried out.

Hamilton, therefore, approached his trial knowing well that he must acquit Zenger, not by the law, but by the feeling in the community — the growing feeling among human beings that the law was wrong.

It was to this feeling that he appealed — in a larger sense it was to the yet unborn feeling of Nationalism that he addressed himself, and in this connection alone his speech is one of the important documents in the history of the rise of the American republic. But it was a novel doctrine that he enunciated; even to those whose interest he espoused it must have come with a shock when he declared, "What strange doctrine is it to press everything for law here which is so in England!"

That Hamilton appreciated, as did those who were back of Zenger in his fight, that it was not a local matter, or a personal vindication that was sought, is shown by one of the concluding paragraphs:

"The question before the Court, and you, gentlemen of the Jury, is not of small or private concern; it is not the cause of a poor printer, nor of New York alone, which you are trying. No! it may, in its consequences, affect every freeman that lives under a British government, on the main of America."

He ridiculed the assumption that power must always be protected. It was a beautiful river while it was kept within bounds, but when it overflowed its banks, it bore down all before it and brought destruction and desolation wherever it went. Liberty was the only bulwark against lawless power, which in all ages had sacrificed the blood of the best men that had ever lived to its wild and boundless ambition.

"I hope to be pardoned, Sir, for my zeal upon this

occasion: it is an old and wise caution that 'when our neighbor's house is on fire, we ought to take care of our own.' For though, blessed be God, I live in a government where liberty is well understood, and freely enjoyed; yet experience has shown us all (I'm sure it has me) that a bad precedent in one government is soon set up for an authority in another; and therefore I cannot but think it mine, and every honest man's duty that (while we pay all due obedience to men in authority) we ought at the same time to be on our guard against power, wherever we apprehend that it may affect ourselves or our fellow-subjects."

Hamilton pleaded that he was unequal to such an undertaking, that he labored under the weight of many years, and that he was borne down with great infirmities of body. But old and weak as he was, he declared it to be his duty, if required, to go to the utmost part of the land, if his service would be of any use to stop persecutions set on foot by the government, to deprive people of the right of remonstrating and complaining against the arbitrary actions of men in power.

It was usual, he continued, for men who injured and oppressed the people, men who provoked them to cry out and complain, to use those very complaints as the foundation for new oppressions and persecutions:

"It is the best cause; it is the cause of Liberty; and I make no doubt but your upright conduct, this day, will not only entitle you to the love and esteem of your fellow-citizens, but every man, who prefers freedom to a life of slavery, will bless and honor you, as men who have baffled the attempt of tyranny; and, by an impartial and uncorrupt verdict, have laid a noble foundation for securing to ourselves, our posterity, and our neighbors, that to which nature and the laws of our country have given us a right — the liberty — both of exposing and opposing arbitrary power in these parts of the world at least, by speaking and writing truth."

In a short time the jury came in with a verdict of "Not guilty," and "there were three huzzas in the hall," writes the triumphant Zenger in his own account of the trial, "which was crowded with people; and the next day I was discharged from my imprisonment."

The freedom of the city was conferred upon Hamilton by the corporation of the City of New York, and he was escorted to his sloop with drums and trumpets, when he was about to return to Philadelphia.[11]

Not only on this side of the ocean, but in London, the case attracted wide attention. It was printed in New York, Boston and London. The *Pennsylvania Gazette* of May 11, 1738, published the following letter from its London correspondent:

"We have been lately amused with Zenger's trial which has become the common topic of conversation in all the Coffee Houses, both at the Court End of the Town and in the City. The greatest men at the Bar have openly declared that the subject of Libels was never so well treated in Westminster Hall, as at New York. Our political writers of different factions, who never agree in anything else, have mentioned this trial in their public writings with an air of Rapture and Triumph. A Goliath in learning and politics gave his opinion of Mr. Hamilton's argument in these terms: 'If it is not law it is better than law, it ought to be law and will always be law wherever justice prevails.' The trial has been reprinted four times in three months, and there has been a greater demand for it, by all ranks and degrees of people, than there has been known for any of the most celebrated

[11] Fiske, *Dutch and Quaker Colonies in America,* ii, 25.

performances of our greatest Geniuses. We look upon Zenger's advocate as a glorious asserter of public liberty and of the rights and privileges of Britons."

"It is, however, worth remembering, and to his honor," said Horace Binney, "that he was half a century before Mr. Erskine, and the Declaratory Act of Mr. Fox, in asserting the right of a jury to give a general verdict in libel as much as in murder, and in spite of the Court, the jury believed him and acquitted his client." [12]

The view of Judge Cadwalader [13] is more appreciative:

"Reform, through legislation, may be effected with little difficulty as compared with administrative reformation of jurisprudence without legislative aid. The Advocate who can effect the latter, especially where political considerations are involved, must be a mental giant. One great excellence of the system of trial by jury is that it affords the means of gradually producing such reformations without revolutionary peril. Propositions in this argument, which were, strictly speaking, untenable as points of Anglo-American Colonial law, prevailed, nevertheless, at that day, with the jury. These propositions have been since engrafted permanently upon the political jurisprudence of this continent. If that speech to the jurors who acquitted Zenger had never been uttered, or had not been reported, the framers of the Constitutions of the several states might not have been prepared for the adoption of provisions like that of the Seventh Section of the Declaration of Rights in Pennsylvania."

The immediate effect of the trial was to increase Zenger's popularity and the prestige of his paper, although

[12] *Pennsylvania Magazine* — Leaders of the Old Bar of Philadelphia, xiv, 7.

[13] *Pennsylvania Magazine,* xvi, 18.

there was no visible evidence of this in such things as increased advertising. But the effect of his stand may be seen in the plea by William Bradford in his journal,[14] that it was not true, as Zenger had said in his paper, that Bradford published only such news as the government permitted him to print, nor was it true that he submitted his news to the Governor before printing. He declared that he was a free and independent citizen, printing the news wherever he found it, making mistakes occasionally, he admitted, but that was the fault of his informants. He protested that the object of the Zenger attacks, as far as he was able to understand them, was "to deprive me of my bread; for who will buy my papers if they can be induced to believe that I have a constant respect to (or am constant publisher of) Falsehood and Dislike to Truth," showing the shrewd old printer in an amusing light, for he was then well along in life, with printing establishments in Philadelphia and New York, a paper mill in New Jersey, and no real need to worry about his living or who would buy his papers.[15]

On the other hand, sixteen years later, Zenger having died in 1746 and the paper having passed into the hands of his son, a real need had fallen on a family that a grateful community should have rewarded; at least to the point of preventing such a pitiful plea as that made by John Zenger, the son — "I have worn my clothes threadbare" waiting for delinquent subscribers, some of whom, he laments, are as much as seven years behind.

The trial of Zenger was the forerunner of the great struggle of the Revolution, no less an authority than Gouverneur Morris admitted. It was the greatest battle fought on this side of the water for a free press and

14 March 28, 1736.
15 See Appendix, Note B.

a greater journalism. It was, however, no more than a continuation of the fight of lone Benjamin Harris; and, like Harris, like James Franklin, who had fought a similar but less conspicuous battle, we find Zenger, his work done, passed, forgotten.

CHAPTER VI

RISE OF THE FOURTH ESTATE

Development of journalism in connection with democracy — Growth of spirit of nationality — First call for congress of colonies — Conditions under which press grew — Benjamin Franklin — His aid to other printers — Progress slow in South — Gradual withdrawal of government interference — Meeting of colonial congress — Franklin's plan for union of colonies.

In the short period of forty-four years we have seen a new institution born and developed into an actual power — the veritable creation of a new Estate. Like so many other institutions of civilization and progress, it apparently prospered in adversity; it fed on the oppression that would have annihilated it.

Little wonder that there was small understanding by contemporaries, or even by those who were able to take a view from afar, of the importance of this event. The power of the Commons itself, the Third Estate, was almost of recent origin; yet it had taken centuries, with the people in continual warfare for their rights, to build it up and to establish it.

But that there should spring up, overnight, as it were, another Estate, a power hitherto unknown,— a power which, in the language of Burke, should be more powerful than the Lords Spiritual, the Lords Temporal and the Commons combined,— was something that only the mind of a Burke could understand. We have seen that power born amid vicissitudes in the wilderness of newly settled colonies. Henceforth the history of the country is not of kings nor battles, but largely of that power and of those wielding it.

From now on the history of journalism is not of its own struggles, but of the struggles of the ideas for which it stands. The thing itself is established. Henceforth it is a story of development; development in close connection with the idea of democracy, from which it sprang, to whose influence it owed its quick growth, and to which in turn it contributed as no other single factor in civilization, except Christianity, has contributed.

Politically and economically the colonies were preparing for a change. They were no longer the separate settlements in which the advent of the first printer was an historic advance, nor yet were they groping imitators of conditions at home, where the publication of a newspaper was a revolutionary breaking away from the foundations of government. In the time that a bare half-dozen papers had been established, the colonists had accomplished a complete *volte face.* Instead of looking to England for complete guidance, there was, as Andrew Hamilton expressed, a resentment at the continuous citation of English authority. In Hamilton's speech we find the idea put forth — for the first time, I believe — that, if the law of the mother country is wrong, the duty of the colonists is to correct it.

With such a start in so brief a time, it was but a step to a declaration of complete independence. But as a stepping-stone to such a declaration, there was necessary a feeling of nationality. While the printing press and the new institution did much to develop that feeling, the main cause was the necessity for protecting the lives of the colonists — first from the common foe on the outside, and in the final development, from the encroachments of the mother country that had failed to appreciate or understand the spirit and ideas that had grown up on this side of the water.

Chronologically, the beginning of the national spirit is almost coincident with that of journalism. In 1689, one year before the appearance of Harris as a newspaper publisher, Jacob Leisler, as the self-constituted representative of the new monarchs, William and Mary, had seized the government of New York and, desiring to strengthen himself as well as his cause against the adherents of the old government, had appealed to the other colonies to unite against the opponents of the Prince of Orange. While the answers to the invitation were all cautious, there was enough response to this first inter-colonial correspondence of a political nature to show, despite the differences among the colonies, that underlying all was the "powerful element of political affinity."[1]

The sacking of Schenectady by the Indians and the murder of nearly all the inhabitants the following year[2] brought about the first call for a general congress in America. The congress met and decided on measures for the protection of the colonists, but no suggestion was made as to a permanent organization. In fact, the timidity with which the whole subject was approached was shown by the apologetic explanation of the Governor of Massachusetts that "the congress had been called to meet a conjuncture, until more express commands should be received from the king." There was not at this time the slightest desire to set up either an independent nation or independent colonies; on the contrary, there was evident the most loyal devotion to the monarchical principle.[3]

1 Frothingham, *Rise of the Republic*, 85.

2 February 8, 1690.

3 *Rise of the Republic*, 98.

It was, indeed, for the purpose of serving the monarchy that the first suggestion for a union of the colonies came about. The declared object of William Penn's plan of 1698, for two persons from each colony to meet once a year for a better understanding among the colonies, was frankly that "the English colonies may be more useful to the crown." [4] Charles Davenant commended this plan of Penn's, comparing it to the Grecian Court of the Amphictyons.[5] Others took up this idea from time to time,[6] many reasons being given as to the necessity for such a union, but none with the idea of independence or of any lessening of the royal control. Under the authority of the crown a number of meetings were held in the meantime, generally with the purpose of arranging for the common defense or to make treaties with the Indians.

Though there was unquestioned loyalty to the crown, the principle of local self-government was, nevertheless, strongly implanted in the colonists; in fact, the inducement was put forth in the newspaper advertisements and

[4] *Rise of the Republic,* 98.

[5] *Ibid,* 112.

[6] The plan proposed by William Penn, in 1697, for an annual congress had left in the minds of the colonists a deep impression. The result was that, when Franklin revived the idea, the people themselves rose to welcome it; and as he descended the Hudson he was greeted by cheering throngs as soon as he entered the City of New York. The boy who had first entered New York City as a runaway apprentice was revered as the mover of American Union.

In the same year, 1754, that Franklin was proposing his Union of American Colonies, David Hume, who had felt the hollowness of the political philosophy that then dominated Europe, turned to America and, expressing a belief that must have been in the minds of other men, said, "The seeds of many a noble state have been sown in climates kept desolate by the wild manners of the ancient inhabitants, and an asylum is secure in that solitary world for liberty and science."

Bancroft's *History of the United States of America,* iii, 81-83.

tracts that Europeans who settled in America would have a share in the making of the laws under which they lived. The "moral discoveries," as they were called later, of *Habeas Corpus* and trial by jury, of popular representation and a free press, were their inherent rights, though the last named was but now to come into their light. Against these ideas and this spirit the various governors, constituting themselves defenders of the royal prerogative, were almost continuously in clash. The reports sent by these governors tended to irritate the British ministry, resulting in instructions which further stiffened the resistance of the colonists.[7]

It is well to remember that, despite all the love for the mother country, from the passage of the Navigation Act up to the final break there was never a time when there was not in every colony more or less feeling on the part of the colonists against some act of the royal government, feeling that led to developing the controversy between the colonists and the crown — "the natural rights of man on the one hand and the authority of artificial institutions on the other;"— and it was this exercise of absolute power on the part of the once beloved mother country that eventually brought the colonies together in a spirit of opposition.

This in very brief was the political condition in the colonies when the press of North America — six papers — began to play a part in the politics and development of the nation that was to be. To these six — the *Boston News-Letter*, the *Boston Gazette*, the *American Weekly Mercury* of Philadelphia, the *Pennsylvania Gazette* of Philadelphia, the *New York Gazette*, and the *Maryland Gazette* of Annapolis — were added the following:

South Carolina Gazette, Charleston, Jan. 8, 1732;

[7] Chalmers, *Revolt of the Colonies*, i, 307.

New York Weekly Journal, New York, November 5, 1733;

Boston Evening Post, Boston, August 11, 1735;

Virginia Gazette, Williamsburg, 1736.

As the historian Rhodes said later of Horace Greeley, no single man in his time influenced so many people as did Benjamin Franklin, the editor and publisher of the *Pennsylvania Gazette.* Franklin started off briskly to make his paper a notable one, announcing that the paper would be issued twice a week, a practice he shortly afterward discontinued as not entirely profitable. To increase his circulation he originated the practice, still popular to-day, of writing letters to the editor, creating a number of imaginary characters and engaging in disputes with himself in order to draw the public into the editorial circulation-building net, wherein they write letters and buy many copies of the paper in which their names are printed.

To all this was added the humor that he had tried in Boston; and he originated the editorial paragraph. In commenting on the rumor that a flash of lightning had melted the pewter buttons off the waistband of a farmer's breeches, he observed, "'Tis well nothing else thereabouts was made of pewter." [8]

His progress from that time on was rapid. The list of achievements which added to his fame and fortune included the writing and publication of "Poor Richard's Almanac," which he began in October, 1732. Refraining from no step that would lead to his success, we find him in 1736 elected Clerk of the Assembly and afterwards becoming a Member of it, combining thereby his journalistic strength with a political position, a combination that journalists of America were thereafter to emulate in great numbers.

[8] McMaster, *Benjamin Franklin as a Man of Letters,* 68.

Such was the early development of the great Benjamin Franklin, and such the beginning of his great influence.

But it was not only by his example — the towering example of success — and by his influence that Franklin aided the beginning of journalism in America. He was the thrifty financial partner and abettor of other pioneers. The importance of this aid can hardly be estimated, for at a time when the new profession — though it was a "trade," the trade of printing that editing still came under — needed friends, it meant more than one can realize now to have a man of Franklin's ability, eminence and success express his belief in the material possibilities of his vocation in so unanswerable a fashion as by the risking of his own money. There is no doubt that he, being the very living example of the "poor boy" legend, has been the inspiration of the venturesome spirit of Typothetæ, not only in this country but the world over; with the result of many Horace Greeleys, it is true, but also with many disappointments and failures in the unwritten records of journeymen printers who wandered beyond the appointed time, until wandering became a habit.

In modern terms, he, more than any one else, put printing and journalism on a business basis. He was not content with the success that he was achieving in his own city, but he penetrated into other colonies. He set up Lewis Timothy, the publisher of the *South Carolina Gazette,* at Charleston in 1733, on a basis of partnership.[9] Timothy was one of three printers who went to Charleston as a result of the offer, on the part of the Colonial Government, of a £1000 premium to encourage a printer to settle there.[10] Franklin tells us that he visited New-

[9] *Franklin's Works,* i, 195. (Bigelow Edition.)
[10] Thomas, ii, 153.

port and, when his brother James died, Benjamin, to make amends to him for having run away from Boston, set up his son in the printing business, the son being the James Franklin, Jr., who afterward became the editor of the *Newport Mercury*.[11] He was also the partner of James Parker, the publisher of the *Gazette* in New York City.

Meanwhile, the demand for the printing press and for news journals spread throughout the colonies. Journalism developed in the South more slowly than in the North, a larger proportion of the Southerners living on their own land, especially in Maryland and Virginia; as a result, there was a sense of individual freedom which did not produce that political spirit that knits men together for a common purpose.[12]

Politics develops with the town, but on the other hand the landed proprietor developed a sociability and hospitality not found in the towns — a sociability and hospitality, however, that went to make a ruling class and not to make a democracy or to encourage democratic institutions. Virginia particularly lagged behind the other colonies in this regard. In the early days of the printing press the one attempt in Virginia to keep abreast of the new movement had been promptly quashed. In 1682 John Buckner published the Virginia laws of 1680; he was immediately summoned before the council and forbidden to do any more printing until the consent of the king had been given him, with the result that "for forty-seven years not another type was set in the Old Dominion." [13]

The backwardness of Virginia in this respect was partly due to the attitude that is shown in the statement of

[11] *Franklin's Works*, i, 199. (Bigelow Edition.)
[12] W. H. Browne, *Maryland*, 16.
[13] McMaster, *Franklin*, 37.

Governor Berkeley, when reporting in 1671 on the condition of the colony: "Thank God, we have no free schools nor printing; God keep us from both." [14]

Express orders were given to Lord Effingham, on his appointment as Governor in 1683, not to allow the use of a printing press in the colony. It was not until 1766 that the colony had more than one printing press. This belonged to William Parks, who had established a paper in Maryland, but finding Virginia a more profitable field, had left Annapolis and moved to Williamsburg, where he established in 1736, under the patronage of the Governor, the colony's first newspaper, the *Virginia Gazette.*

If the South lagged behind, Pennsylvania forged ahead. In 1742 William Bradford, grandson of the publisher of the *New York Gazette,* brought out the *Pennsylvania Journal and Weekly Advertiser.* The publication came out as a strong Whig paper, devoted to the interests of the colonists. On the 31st of October, the day before the Stamp Act was to go into effect, it appeared in mourning, with a skull and cross-bones over the title. On the border of the first page was an engraving of a coffin, under which was this epitaph:

The last Remains of
THE PENNSYLVANIA JOURNAL
Which departed this life, the 31st of October, 1765,
of a stamp in her Vitals
Age 23 years.

Thomas Bradford, son of the publisher, was taken into partnership in 1766. The Bradford family distinguished themselves not only in printing and in journalism, but on the field as well. Bradford was a major of Militia at Trenton, was at Fort Mifflin, and came out of the Princeton fight a Colonel.

[14] Gordon, *History,* i, 53.

In Maryland, the *Gazette,* which had died under Parks in 1736, was revived in 1745 under the direction of Jonas Green, and this paper in 1765 announced its suspension because of the Stamp Act, but the suspension was brief. It was soon re-continued and was published weekly by Green and his descendants until 1839, when another Jonas Green, great-grandson of the original proprietor, discontinued it and a paper called the *St. Mary's Gazette* took its place.

In New York the New York *Evening Post* was issued for about a year by Henry De Forrest, appearing first in 1746. The spread of the journalistic spirit was shown by the fact that two attempts were made about this time to print papers in German, one being published by Sower in Germantown, in 1739, and the other by Armbruster in Philadelphia in 1743.

About this time Boston, too, added to its list of newspapers. Ellis Huske, whose son is supposed to have recommended the obnoxious Stamp Act to the government in 1765, was made postmaster in 1734. Following the example of Campbell and the others, he got out a paper called the *Boston Weekly Post Boy.* This paper lived for nearly a quarter of a century without any particular distinction.

The *New England Courant* case, in which James Franklin was involved, was the last instance of an attempt to revive and enforce censorship in Massachusetts. The failure of the General Court to restrict the freedom of the press by insisting that a license be granted by the Secretary of the Province, marked the end of the old order of things; from that time on there was at least a partial freedom for the press.[15]

That the government itself recognized this condition is

[15] Duniway, *Freedom of the Press in Massachusetts,* 102.

shown in two indirect ways. On May 13, 1725, the Council had ordered that the newspapers must not print "anything of the Publick Affairs of this Province relating to the war without the order of the government," which order by implication meant that the printers might print anything else that they chose.[16]

On September 2nd of the same year the council, on the complaint of a minister who declared that he had been wrongfully treated in the Boston *News-Letter,* ordered that "His Honor the Lieut. Governour give his orders to the publishers of the several newspapers not to insert in their papers these words — published by authority — or words to the like import for ye future." [17] This indicated that the government did not intend to assume the responsibility of supervision, nor did it desire such control; but the old habit of leaning on the government was still so strong that, in December, 1729, it was necessary for the Council again to order the printers of the newspapers not to state that they were published by authority.[18]

With the departure of James Franklin, there was a short period of colorless newspapers, and although there were sharp political disputes, such as those over the Governor's salary and the issue of Bills of Credit, the editors themselves took no sides, acting merely as printers or publishers of the papers.

Not until Thomas Fleet appeared as the printer and publisher of the *Evening Post* did the press of Boston again become interesting. He conducted this paper from 1735 to 1758, with sarcasm and vivacity — so much so that he was declared by the preachers to be "a dangerous

[16] *Council Records,* viii, 198.
[17] *Council Records,* viii, 272, 273.
[18] *Council Records,* ix, 189, 190.

engine, a sink of sedition, error and heresy." That he understood the value — and the dangers — of the fight in which he was engaged is shown, however, by his reprinting an account of the Zenger trial in the *Evening Post* of May 29, 1738, under the head of "The Liberty of the Press."

Although there was a great deal of liberty as compared with the previous century, political items might still render the publisher liable to prosecution. In March, 1742, Fleet, having picked up, in conversation with a naval officer, an item to the effect that Sir Robert Walpole was to be taken in custody, was haled before the Council, and the attorney general was ordered to prosecute him. The prosecution, however, was never pushed.

It was at the suggestion of the Lords of Trade, sent to several of the governors in a letter dated September 18, 1753, that an American Congress, based on the principle of representation, was convened for the purpose of making a treaty with the Six Nations, to prevent them from aiding the French or uniting with the Indians under French influence. The suggestion, which was to mean so much to the colonists, awoke enthusiasm only among the royal governors, the newspapers as a rule making no reference to it. This Congress was called to meet at Albany June 14, 1754, and Benjamin Franklin urged it in the Philadelphia *Gazette,* using the device, "Join or Die." [19]

On June 19, 1754, the Congress met at Albany, then a compact Dutch city of three hundred houses and 2600 inhabitants. The men present from the various colonies, while mainly champions of the royal prerogative, were also, in some instances, distinguished upholders of the

[19] *Pennsylvania Gazette,* May 9, 1754 — Copied by the *Boston Gazette,* May 21, 1754.

people's rights; among them were Benjamin Franklin of Pennsylvania and William Smith, who had been one of the counsel for Zenger in his great fight for the liberty of the press.

It was here that Franklin put forth his plan for uniting the colonies, which, it was finally voted, the commissioners should lay before their constituents for consideration. But the people were not yet ready for such an advance. The *Boston Gazette,* July 23, 1754, simply noted that "the Commissioners from the several governments were unanimously of the opinion that such a union of the colonies was absolutely necessary."

Here and there the idea of uniting gained converts. Later, a fervid writer in the same paper wrote: "I hope and pray the Almighty, that the British colonies on this continent may cease impolitically and ungenerously to consider themselves as distinct states, with narrow, separate and independent views; . . . and thereby secure to themselves and their posterity to the end of time the inestimable blessings of civil and religious liberty, and the uninterrupted possession and settlement of a great country, rich in all the fountains of human felicity. To obtain this happy establishment, without which, I fear, it will never be obtained, may the God of heaven grant success to the plan for a union of the British colonies on the continent of America." [20]

The colonists needed more than perfunctory urging, and the plan was denounced in public meeting, from the fear that it would tend to increase the power of the crown rather than to strengthen the people. The Commissioners themselves were not enthusiastic. The real reason for the rejection of the plan of union was the attitude of the ministry of George III toward the colonists.

[20] *Boston Gazette,* October 1, 1754.

The new king believed that America was growing wild, and that the institutions with which America was identifying itself were opposed to the British Government. Immediately after the peace of Paris, orders were issued directing the execution of the Sugar Act, the Navigation Act, and those arbitrary laws which had long been urged by the Lords of Trade, laws which contemplated bringing the colonists under the absolute control of the mother country. "The Sugar Act," said the Boston *Evening Post,* "has from its first publication (1733) been adjudged so unnatural, that hardly any attempts have been made to carry it into execution."

A general meeting was urged and it was suggested that a committee write to every maritime town in the province. The *Boston Gazette* of January 16, 1764, says that the merchants were communicating their actions to every town. The Boston *Evening Post,* for February 13, 1764, has an account of the meeting of the merchants of New York, held at Mr. Burn's Long Room.

The acts of the Lords of Trade were oppressive to the point of arousing those who were at heart neither Tory nor Whig, and thereby strengthened the Whig party in America, a party believing in the principles of, and claiming an ancestry in, Buchanan and Languet, Milton, Locke and Sidney . . . "of the political school whose utterances are inspired and imbued with the Christian idea of man." [21] We shall see how the seed of democracy, warmed by the battle for a free press and greater personal freedom, grew overnight into a sturdy plant, under the influence of hot resentment against these moral wrongs.

The first organized action took place in Boston on the motion of Samuel Adams, on the 24th of May, 1764.

[21] *Rise of the Republic,* 165.

This was the caucus which was to play such an important part in history, and which advertised in the Boston *Evening Post* of May 14, 1764, requesting, of the freeholders, power to act against the obnoxious trade regulations.

Even to this time, there was no hostility to the monarchical principle, nor any desire to set up an independent nation;[22] still, while the newspapers that were being printed did not directly encourage anti-monarchical feeling, the mere fact of their being printed more or less against the wishes of the Governor encouraged the idea of a nation, which was slowly germinating.

The national feeling received encouragement — not from colonists alone, who were in frequent clashes with their governors, or from the journalists who were obliged to suffer from the oppression and narrowness of the latter — but from outside sources.

Daniel Coxe had proposed, in 1722, that there should be a "legal, regular and firm establishment," uniting all the colonies, but still loyal to Great Britain, for even up to 1749 the belief of the majority of the colonists was that "our constitution is English, which is another name for free and happy, and is without doubt the perfectest model of civil government that has ever been in the whole world."[23]

Journalism began to give the colonists a sense of their own individuality, "not merely by passionate appeals, but by virtue of its prime office of collection and circulating intelligence by disseminating the facts that enabled the public opinion of one community or political center to act on other communities."[24] To a great extent, the importance of this new agency in giving strength and force

[22] *Rise of the Republic*, 98.
[23] *Boston Independent Advertiser,* May 29, 1749.
[24] *Rise of the Republic,* 130.

to the elements of progress in the colonies has been overlooked. That these efforts were increasing the democratic tendency and awakening the communities to self-consciousness, may be seen by the rejection of the Albany plan of confederation on the ground that it was not "democratic" enough,—to use the words of Franklin, who was one of the commoners for Pennsylvania. He tells us in his autobiography that it was on his way to the conference that he drew up his plan [25] which after debate was unanimously adopted. "Its fate was singular," writes Franklin, "the assemblies (of the colonies) did not adopt it, as they all thought there was too much prerogative in it, and in England it was judged to have too much of the democratic." But at least the concrete idea of a Union was before the people.

The difficulties with the colonial government, oppressive as they were, were not as important as the difficulties attendant on the finding of adequate protection against the French and the Indians, and the idea of a nation was to come originally out of the latter condition rather than the former. In the Albany conference, Franklin, the printer and editor, was the one man of vision; he, a man of the people, was the leader; he who had come up from nothing, the prototype of the Greeley journalist-statesman, was the one man that made the conference a memorable gathering. Men who had hitherto looked down upon the press, who had regarded papers as "miserable sheets," began to see their usefulness. In the next chapter we see that these men did not disdain to use these sheets for the cause that they held sacred, leading the way for their later use by even the scholarly Jefferson and Hamilton.

[25] Franklin's *Autobiography*, i, 243.

The journalistic efforts of this time may not seem inspiring but the spirit of James Franklin in Boston, of Zenger in New York, and of the Bradfords in Philadelphia, was spreading throughout the colonies even though the tendencies were not observed by the colonists themselves. These were preliminary battles, the results of which were to be seen in the fight against British autocracy.

CHAPTER VII

THE ASSUMPTION OF POLITICAL POWER

Boldness of the press — Boston the "Hub" of the fight — Samuel Adams — Daniel Fowle — The Boston *Chronicle* — Thomas and the *Spy* — Tribute to democracy and journalism — The Whig Club — Alexander McDougall — "45" — Hugh Gaine and John Holt — Holt's activities for the patriots' cause — William Goddard — Washington's letter to Goddard — The Green family — Press in other colonies.

At practically the same time that there began to spread throughout the colonies the idea of a nation — before there was yet a well developed idea of independence — the Fourth Estate began to show conscious power. The new institution was no longer a thing of threads and patches. Although there were at the date of the Albany conference hardly more than a dozen journals in the colonies, and none at all in at least six of them, the liberty of the press was already one of the most firmly rooted ideas in the colonies. The boldness of the men who, but a few decades before had been almost outlaws, established for themselves and their calling a respect and a following that made them a primary factor in the struggle into which the colonies were about to enter. The new institution took its place among the active factors in the organization of human society, adapting itself progressively to the "wants which it itself created and fostered." The tasks to which this institution — scarcely out of infancy — addressed itself were no less tasks than the freeing of a people and the foundation of a nation.

The people were beginning to be sovereign. The press,

as the leaders in the revolutionary movement said over and over again, was the expression of that sovereignty. It was also the instrument by which the people were aroused to oppose oppression. Having taken unto themselves the right to question authority, they could not even understand the attitude of those who still looked to the king as the sole source of authority. It was not conceivable to them that only a few years before Louis XIV, entering the French Parliament in his hunting-dress and great boots, with whip in hand, had been in a position to declare: " The mischievous consequences of your assemblies are well known. I therefore order this, which is met to discuss my edict, to be at an end," [1] or that their own king, Henry VII, when Parliament refused to pass his appropriation bill, had sent for the members and, glowering at them, declared that if the bill failed to pass he would chop off their heads.

There were many, not only in England but in the colonies who still believed that the king represented this same kind of power and authority; but the men who were leading public opinion, who were insistent on the rights of the people, were men who had developed a point of view that could little comprehend such authority.

The Provinces in this short pre-Revolutionary period presented a spectacle unusual in political history, and particularly unheard-of at that time. The law-making body in England did not have the right of publicity. Public meetings and the press were still controlled. In France, the people were a negligible element, and in Germany there was little free discussion of political affairs. This revolution by public opinion was therefore, to those who were out of sympathy with it, like some strange apparition.

[1] Voltaire, *Age of Louis XIV*, ii, 2.

The idea of a nation was slowly passing into the minds of the people, but many still believed that a recognition of the rights of the colonies could be achieved without a severance of political relations with the mother country. The great idea of a free and independent nation, as it rose in the minds of the people, left its traces in the journals of the day, and it was to those journals that the idea owed much.

Even before the independence of the country was thought of, prophecies as to the future greatness of America were being made in Europe, and these were bound, in time, to have their effect on the colonists. The spectacle of a nation in the process of formation was an attraction to the clear-visioned philosophers, such as Berkley in England and Turgot in France. A few far-seeing patriots dreamed of a nation; Franklin, with continued vision, prophesied that the Mississippi Valley would become, in a comparatively few years, a populous and powerful country.[2] Internal conditions, too, were adding to the leaven. About the middle of the eighteenth century a wave of democracy swept over the province of New York and spread to other provinces, in consequence of which suffrage was considerably extended.[3]

Ignorant of occurrences on this side of the water, and unable to understand the temper and the new beliefs of the people who had once been loyal and unquestioning subjects, the British Government, by a series of acts calculated to check their democratic tendencies, irritated the colonists and finally roused them to the point of revolution. To awaken in the Americans a sense of indignation over their wrongs; to keep alive their resentment that they might, by cohesive action, break down the defense

[2] Sparks, *Works of Franklin,* iii, 70.

[3] Edwards, *New York as an Eighteenth Century Municipality,* 243.

and repel the attack of the Tories when they finally saw the necessity for attack and defense — this was the work of a comparatively few men, who, when they were not journalists themselves, either became journalists, or else, like Thomas Jefferson in Virginia, induced others to take up the cause through the press.

Papers were now being published regularly in Boston, Newport, New York, Philadelphia, Annapolis, Williamsburg (Virginia,) and Charleston. But it was in Boston that this fight took place — Boston, the cradle of American liberty and the birthplace of American journalism. It was from Boston that the campaign of publicity and propaganda was directed, for it was vitally necessary that Boston should arouse the other colonies, in order that she might not find herself single-handed in the very unequal struggle in which she had engaged.

There was in Boston one man who recognized the power of journalism, the first man in America to use it for political purposes — Samuel Adams. It was to Adams and a group of his young friends that the first political newspaper in the colonies owed its existence. On January 4, 1748, the *Independent Advertiser* was issued in Boston by Gamaliel Rogers and John Fowle, the leading printers of the colony, who had already published the *American Magazine,* from 1743 to 1746. They were the first in America to successfully manufacture ink, and the first American impression of the New Testament in English had been printed by them.

The *Advertiser* was started as the result of the activity of a political club, formed by the man who was to be the "Father of the Revolution." The paper, it is said, was begun on the strength of the communications promised by the members. [4] That the group of young

[4] Wells, *Life of Samuel Adams*, i, 15.

men associated with Adams took themselves and their task with becoming seriousness, is evidenced by the pertinent and well-written address with which the opening number saluted the public, stating their purpose to be, inasmuch "As our present political state affords matter for a variety of thoughts," to insert whatever of general interest might appear proper to publish. They declared that they were of no party, nor would they promote any narrow private designs. "We are ourselves free, and our paper shall be free — free as the Constitution we enjoy — free to Truth, Good Manners and good Sense, and at the same time free from all licentious Reflections, Insolence and Abuse." [5]

The *Independent Advertiser* reflected the sentiments of most of the colonists at that time, their point of view being friendly and even affectionate toward the mother-country. "Our Constitution is English, which is another name for free and happy, and is without doubt the perfectest model civil government that has ever been in the world."

A free press, the right of habeas corpus, trial by jury and popular representation were all regarded as English institutions — the gift of the mother-land. Even Washington himself, in 1756, spoke of showing his obedience to "the best of Kings." [6]

In April, 1750, Rogers and Fowle dissolved partnership and the paper was discontinued, but the work of Samuel Adams went on. The part played by the great patriot and the *Boston Gazette,* with which his name is so closely associated, is so important a part of the history of journalism that it has been reserved for another chapter. A paper of the same name had been published

[5] *Independent Advertiser,* January 4, 1748.
[6] *Pennsylvania Gazette,* September 16, 1756.

from 1753 to 1755, by Samuel Kneeland, but the journal of Edes and Gill, the journal which was to make American history, did not appear until April 7, 1755, after Kneeland's paper had passed away.

The name of Daniel Fowle, however, is entitled to further mention, for in a persistent fight with the authorities he proved that the printer was no longer a poor fellow at whom any representative of the government might bark. In October, 1754, he was arrested for printing an anonymous pamphlet, supposed to be an attack on the House of Representatives. He was accused of printing the libel and was sent to jail, but as the prosecution failed to establish his guilt, the case was dropped. The following year he brought suit for £1000 damages for illegal imprisonment, and finally in 1766, after continued litigation, he was awarded £20 — establishing, if not the right of the printer to a fair trial, at least a monument to his combativeness and his insistency.

"Living in the family of Daniel Fowle's brother," says Isaiah Thomas, himself a notable printer and the first historian of printing in America, "I early became intimately acquainted with the whole transaction, and deep impressions were then made upon my mind in favor of the liberty of the press." [7]

It is easy to understand how a long, bitter fight by an apparently humble printer against the powerful government had its effect on the imagination of other printers and writers.

With so aggressive an adversary as Samuel Adams in the field, and one proving himself to be so capable a journalistic combatant, the defenders of the crown were driven to the use of his own weapons. One of the most loyal of these defenders was the old *News-Letter,* which

[7] *History of Printing in America,* i, 337.

became for a while, under new hands, a vigorous figure in the arena.

John Draper, an industrious and scrupulous journalist, had conducted the *News-Letter* for thirty years. When he died, in 1762, it passed to his son, Richard Draper, who earned the reputation of being the best reporter — "the best compiler of news in his day." [8]

The *News-Letter,* under the Drapers, had achieved a certain distinction and much authority, although it did not have a large circulation. Richard Draper was a strong supporter of the royal cause and, as a sign of his devotion, he added the King's arms to the title of his paper. He died in 1774, and his widow attempted to carry it on with the assistance of a young printer and bookseller, named Boyle. Boyle was a patriot, however, and as the paper was developing more and more into an out-and-out Tory sheet, he retired. While the British occupied Boston the paper flourished, but when they left it ceased to exist. The widow Draper left Boston with the British troops and received a life pension from the British Government. She has been immortalized in Trumbull's poem, "M'Fingal." Thus ended ingloriously the first newspaper printed in America, its end as little inspiring as was its beginning. It was cordially hated by the patriots. It was the only paper printed in Boston during the siege, and was ardent in its defense of the British troops and their various acts.[9]

The *Boston Chronicle* appeared on December 21, 1767, to back up the Tory cause, though at first it seemed inclined to be impartial, even going so far as to print the celebrated letters of the *Pennsylvania Farmer*, by John Dickinson. The *Chronicle* was one of the first evidences

[8] *Memorial History of Boston,* ii, 392.

[9] *Memorial History of Boston,* ii, 392.

that the Tory forces realized the necessity for using methods that they had once despised. Its very publication was a frank admission that the first battle in the great fight for popular sovereignty had been won; it was an admission that, after all, public opinion had to be considered.

The men who were entrusted with the undertaking of keeping the populace "from being misinformed" were John Mein, a bookseller of some literary ability, and John Fleming, a printer.

John Mein was the founder of the circulating library in Boston. He had come to the colony from Scotland but three years before, bringing with him an assortment of books, Irish linens and other merchandise. The necessity of some organ to defend the Crown was apparent to the shrewd Scotchman, who formed a partnership with John Fleming, another Scotchman then resident in the colony. Fleming was sent abroad to procure the best materials and workmen possible. They opened a printing shop in 1766, and the following year the *Chronicle* was brought out.

As might be expected, this representative of authority was mechanically superior to those journals which were dependent on popular support. It was the most ambitious endeavor in newspaper printing that the continent had yet seen. It was printed on a whole sheet quarto, after the fashion of the *London Chronicle,* containing only reading matter in the way of news and extracts from the European papers. Despite the fact that its superiority was commented on, it sold at the same price as the other Boston papers. It was unquestionably subsidized by the British Government.

The neutrality which was at first assumed, soon began to give way to the necessity for espousing the weakening

Loyalist cause, and Mein undertook the abuse of the Whig leaders in Boston. The result was that public indignation was so thoroughly aroused against him that he was obliged to leave the colony, sailing for England in 1769. Very shortly after the *Chronicle* began to fall away, even with the bolstering-up that the Colonial Governor gave it, and it was discontinued in 1770. [10]

The endeavor to reach those who were not as yet interested in the newspapers led Zechariah Fowle and Isaiah Thomas to bring out the *Massachusetts Spy,* August 7, 1770. "It was calculated," says Thomas, "to obtain subscriptions from mechanics and other classes of people who had not much time to spare from business." Three issues a week were planned and the first number was scattered free throughout the town. The venture, however, was premature, and at the end of a month the noble design succumbed.

The following year Thomas brought out a paper of the same name, with the announcement that it was "open to all parties, but influenced by none." In two years, he says, his paper had the largest circulation in New England. [11] At first the Tories contributed a few essays, but its Whig leanings were evident, and it soon became an outspoken supporter of the Liberty cause.

The Loyalists gave warning in 1774 that, in the event of an outbreak, not only the leaders of the patriots but "those trumpeters of sedition, the printers, Edes and Gill and Thomas" would be properly punished.

Thomas, who was the sole controlling factor in his own paper, was much more vehement than Edes and Gill, who allowed the more scholarly writers to control their policy; Thomas was trying to arouse the laboring

[10] Sabine, *The American Loyalists,* 463.

[11] *History of Printing in America* ii, 249.

class, the plain people, whereas the *Gazette* appealed to the more cultivated.

In his narrative of newspapers,[12] Dr. Eliot said of these writers for the *Spy* that they were " most of them young men of genius, without experience in business or knowledge of the world." But it is of such men that enthusiasm for the right is born. They furnish the passion without which there cannot be war, when many of those who, while seeing the righteousness of war, are dominated by intellect, weaken and hesitate.

It is to Thomas that we are indebted for the first history of journalism, which is included in his comprehensive History of Printing, published in 1810. In his own resumé of this period, commenting on the part that the journals played in preparing the public mind, and his own endeavors to arouse the laboring classes, he says: " Common sense in common language is necessary to influence one class of citizens as much as learning and elegance of composition are to produce an effect upon another. The cause of America was just; and it was only necessary to state this cause in a clear and impressive manner to unite the American people in its support."[13]

This is the statement of Thomas, one of the men who fought for the cause, not only as a publicist but as a soldier — as one of the journalists of Liberty, as well as of America. He knew better than any modern historian what it was that aroused the colonists, what it was that made them fight. It is an eloquent tribute to democracy as well as to journalism.

When the young printer began the publication of the *Massachusetts Spy*, he was in his twenty-seventh year.

[12] *Massachusetts Historical Collections,* i, 64-79.
[13] *History of Printing in America,* ii, 251.

He tried to be fair to the Government, but his convictions were all with the colonists. At first the Government tried to buy him. Failing in this, more strenuous methods were attempted, but he was undaunted and continued to increase his circulation and his influence. He was prosecuted for libel but no indictment could be obtained. His vehemence attracted attention throughout the country and his paper was burned by the hangman. Several attempts, he says, were made to prosecute him; the Loyalists in North Carolina burned him in effigy, and a regiment of British soldiers paraded before his house, threatening to tar and feather him.

The part of the papers grew more important as the contest grew warmer. John Adams was disturbed, as one might expect, by the vehemence of Thomas,[14] but that vehemence was necessary, in order to arouse and stir the people. With the issue of July 7, 1774, Thomas threw all caution to the winds and his paper appeared with "a new device," a snake and a dragon. This device was spread across the paper; the dragon representing Great Britain and the snake, which was divided into nine parts, representing the colonies. Under it, in large letters, were the words, "Join or Die!" "This device," Thomas proudly stated in his history, "appeared in every succeeding paper whilst it was printed in Boston."

Like Franklin and some of the earlier printers in the colonies, Thomas was not satisfied with the paper in Boston alone, but reached out and established a paper in Newburyport, called the *Essex Journal.* As the situation grew more critical in Boston, however, he sold this, and his efforts were restricted to the *Massachusetts Spy,* which assumed such an important part in the conflict that it was openly said that, the day the British actually began hos-

[14] *Familiar Letters of John Adams to His Wife,* 11.

tilities, Thomas would be among the first to suffer. Anticipating their action, he brought out his last number in Boston on April 6, 1775, and quietly started moving his types and press to Worcester. On the 19th of April, hostilities began, but Thomas was safely away and, on the 3rd of May, he reissued the *Spy* from the town of Worcester.

It is from a contemporary Loyalist writer, Thomas Jones, that one gets the best view of the journalistic activities of the New York patriots of that time. The history of Judge Jones is a far from non-partisan performance, but it abounds in spicy information. In 1752 the Whig Club was formed, by William Livingston, William Smith and John Morin Scott — all graduates of Yale, " A college remarkable for its persecuting spirit, its republican principles, its intolerance in religion and its utter aversion to Bishops and all Earthly Kings." [15]

The club proceeded at once to attack the established church and to deride monarchy, by bringing out a weekly paper called the *Independent Reflector,* and later one called the *Watch Tower.* The latter was really the front page of Gaine's *Mercury,* written by William Livingston; the former was distinguished through the fact that the Reverend Aaron Burr, Smith, Livingston and Scott were the principal contributors. It was printed by one James Parker.

Jones further informs us that in the *American Whig,* published in 1769, the villainous statement was printed that " this country will shortly become a great and flourishing empire, independent of Great Britain; enjoying its civil and religious liberty, uncontaminated and deserted of all control from Bishops, the curse of curses, and from the subjection of all earthly kings." The General As-

[15] Jones, *History of New York,* i, 5.

sembly having been won over to the side of the crown, numerous attacks were made upon it, among them a printed handbill accusing its members of treachery. A reward was offered for information as to the author, with the result that James Parker, who had printed it, and who was threatened with the loss of the small political position he held, gave information that Alexander McDougall was the author.

"The method lately used in New York to post up inflammatory handbills," states a contemporary of this particularly famous one, "was the same as used in England at the time of the Pretender. It was done by a man who carried a little boy in a box like a magic lantern, and while he leaned against the wall, as if to rest himself, the boy drew back the slide, pasted on the paper, and shutting himself up again, the man took the proper occasion to walk off to another resting-place."

Concerning McDougall's activities during the war, his short biographies are explicit, but of his career up to that time, it is to the unfriendly Jones that we must turn. He was the son of a poor milkman, we are told, who had taken up seafaring as a vocation, finally becoming the captain of a privateer.

The Tory historian pays him an unusual tribute: "He was a principal promoter and encourager of the unhappy disputes which raged with such violence in the colony for many years, terminated in a rebellion, in a dismemberment of the empire, in almost a total destruction of thirteen valuable provinces and in the loss of not less than 100,000 brave men." [16]

Surely such a man is worthy of our attention, especially in view of the fact that he was, if not one of the editors, at least one of the principal contributors to Holt's

[16] Jones, *History of New York,* i, 26.

paper, the *New York Journal,* which now became the leading organ of the patriots.

McDougall was arrested on the information of Parker; he refused to give bail and was committed to prison. Because of the connection of the number forty-five with his commitment — the proceedings of the Assembly voting the handbill libelous were printed on the forty-fifth page of the journal of that body — "45" became a magic number for the patriots. It was also the number of John Wilkes's *North Briton,* which had been declared by the House of Commons to be a scandalous and seditious libel.

The *Journal* continued to make a hero of him, regaling the public with the exhilarating information that on the 45th day of the year, 45 gentlemen went down to jail and dined with Captain McDougall on 45 pounds of beef, cut from a bullock 45 months old, drank 45 bottles of wine in 45 toasts, etc. The use of numbers as rallying cries was then in vogue, not only in New York but in Massachusetts, where, when Governor Bernard asked the colony to rescind its circular letter to the other colonies, the request was rejected by a vote of 92 to 17. The "Illustrious 92" then became a favorite toast of all gatherings of the patriots.

McDougall was not liberated until March 4, 1771.[17] After his first short term in jail, he gave bail, but the suit was never prosecuted. In the following December, he was arraigned before the Assembly; because of his answers he was held in "high contempt" and was again sent to jail when the Assembly was prorogued.[18]

McDougall's own account of his arrest was printed in Holt's *Journal,* February 9, 1770, dated from the "New

17 *Documents Relative to Colonial History,* New York, viii, 213.
18 *Documentary History of New York,* i, 323.

Gaol" and addressed "To the Freeholders, Freemen and Inhabitants of the Colony of New York and to all the friends of Liberty in North America."

He was brought into the presence of the Chief Justice:

"His Honor said to me:

"'So, you have brought yourself into a pretty scrap.'

"To which I replied:

"'May it please your Honor, that must be judged by my peers.'

"He then told me that it was fully proven that I was the author or publisher of the above mentioned paper, which he called 'a false, vile, and scandalous libel.'

"I replied again:

"'This also must be decided by my peers.'"[19]

When McDougall, almost a year later, was called before the Assembly to answer to the indictment for libel, he refused to answer questions on the ground that they would tend to incriminate him.

"The House has power to extort an answer, and will punish you for contumacy if you refuse to reply," stated De Noyellis, who was responsible for the charge.

"The House has power to throw the prisoner over the bar or out of the window, but the public will doubt the justice of the proceedings," exclaimed George Clinton — later to be the first Governor of New York State — who was the only lawyer who dared appear for McDougall.[20]

While there were many distinguished contributors, the important editors of this period were Hugh Gaine and John Holt. The *New York Mercury* came out in 1752, under the auspices of Gaine; but it was the *New York Journal* or *General Advertiser*, issued by Holt in 1770,

[19] *New York Journal*, February 15, 1770, 2, 3.

[20] Booth, *History of the City of New York*, ii, 461.

which remained the organ of the Liberty Party until the capture of the city in 1776.

Gaine was made famous by Philip Freneau, who attacked him in verse. He was an industrious journalist, for he not only collected his news and set it up, but printed his papers, folded them and delivered them. His career indicates that he was of a volatile disposition, and he was accused of taking whichever side of a question was the most profitable.

John Holt had begun his career in New York as an associate of James Parker, the informant on McDougall. Parker, one of Bradford's apprentices, had established in 1743, with the backing of Franklin, a new weekly, called the *New York Gazette* or *Weekly Post Boy*, which was a continuation of William Bradford's periodical. The same year he began the publication of a monthly called the *American Magazine and Historical Chronicle*.[21] Parker, with William Weyman, whom he had taken in as a partner, was arrested in 1756 for printing an article offensive to the Assembly, but both were discharged almost immediately on apologizing to the Legislature, paying a fine, and giving the name of the writer of the article, a missionary named Hezekiah Watkins.

Holt was the editor of the *Gazette* up to 1766, when he brought out or revived the *New York Journal*. He early established a reputation for courage and patriotism. The attitude of the public toward him is shown in a letter which he printed in 1765, and which he declared had been thrown into his printing house:

"*Dulce et decorum est, pro Patria mori.*

" Mr. Holt, as you have hitherto proved yourself a Friend to Liberty, by publishing some Compositions as had a Tendency to promote the Cause, we are encouraged to hope you will not be

[21] Booth, *History of the City of New York*, i, 382.

deterred from continuing your useful Paper by groundless Fear of the detestable Stamp-Act. However, should you at this critical time, shut up the Press, and basely desert us, depend upon it, your House, Person and Effects, will be in imminent Danger: We shall, therefore, expect your paper on Thursday as usual; if not, on Thursday Evening — take care. Signed in the Names and by the Order of a great Number of the Free-born Sons of New York.

"JOHN HAMPDEN."[22]

"On the Turf, the 2nd of November, 1765."

It is interesting also to read his statement that offense had been given to many of the inhabitants of the city by the advertisement of a play at a time of public distress "when great numbers of poor people can scarce find means to subsist."[23] The play was produced, and the indignation of the public over the fact that people should go to a place of entertainment at a time when others were starving caused a mob to break in and gut the theater — "many lost their hats and other parts of dress."

Although not as virulent nor as able as the *Boston Gazette*, or the *Massachusetts Spy*, from this time on Holt gave the patriots a service that was second only to that of the New England papers. In 1774 he dropped the King's arms from the first page, substituting for it Franklin's serpent cut in pieces, with the motto "Unite or Die." When the British took possession of New York he moved to Esopus, now Kingston, and when that village was burned in 1777, he went to Poughkeepsie, and there stayed until the peace of 1783, when he came back to New York and continued his publication, the title of which was the *Independent Gazette* or the *New York Journal Revived*.

The heartiest response to the newspaper and patriotic activities of Boston naturally came from the New Eng-

[22] *New York Gazette*, November 7, 1765.
[23] *New York Gazette*, May 13, 1766.

land colonies. The desire to have a paper in Rhode Island that would more fairly represent the point of view of the Whigs than did the *Newport Mercury,* the one paper published there, led the Governor to encourage William Goddard, one of the famous printers of the time, to establish the first printing press in Providence, and in 1762 to publish a newspaper there, the *Providence Gazette.*

What Samuel Adams and his group were doing in Boston, Stephen Hopkins, the Governor of Rhode Island — "a far-seeing and accomplished statesman," comparable in intellectual traits with Benjamin Franklin, according to one authority — did almost as well in that little colony.[24] He was not only the author of a strong pamphlet that drew out the "Halifax Gentleman," the first Loyalist writer in the field, but his contributions to the *Providence Gazette*[25] helped to build the paper up as a patriotic organ, to counteract the efforts of the Loyalists, and to arouse the men of the colony to a full sympathy with the patriots of Boston.

William Goddard, the publisher of this paper, was as important in his field as Hopkins was in his. Not meeting with sufficient encouragement in Providence, which was a small place, he moved to New York and worked with John Holt on the *New York Gazette and Post Boy.*[26] In 1766 he went to Philadelphia and became the partner of Galloway and Wharton, both Loyalists, in the *Pennsylvania Chronicle.* In 1773, having found the venture unprofitable, Goddard went to Baltimore, where he started another newspaper. Here he devoted himself to working out a plan for a line of post-riders

[24] Tyler, *Literary History of the American Revolution,* 64.
[25] W. G. Foster, *Stephen Hopkins,* ii. 48.
[26] Sabine, *The American Loyalists,* 326.

from New Hampshire to Georgia, in opposition to the Post Office establishment of the crown. He traveled through the colonies, leaving the care of his printing affairs to his sister. The scheme was successful, and he was made surveyor of the roads, expecting to succeed Franklin as Postmaster General.

Bache, Franklin's son-in-law, was appointed to succeed him, and Goddard, in disgust, threw up his position and resumed the publication of the *Maryland Journal.* Two articles which he printed in 1777 caused the Baltimore Whig Club to notify him to get out of town. He appealed to the Assembly for protection and remained in town, but was mobbed on several occasions. In 1792 he sold his press and moved to Rhode Island.

Goddard was an intimate friend of General Charles Lee, who had endeavored to supplant Washington as Commander-in-Chief, and, failing, had retired in disgrace after the battle of Monmouth in 1778. Lee was the writer of "Queries," which brought Goddard into trouble with the Whig Club in 1779.[27] At his death in 1782, Lee bequeathed valuable real estate in Virginia to Goddard, and also his private papers. While preparing these for publication, Goddard informed Washington of their contents, assuring him of his wish to avoid injuring his feelings. The answer of Washington is worthy of reproduction:

"Mount Vernon, 11th June, 1785.

"SIR:

"On the 8th inst. I received the favour of your letter of the 30th of May. In answer to it I can only say, that your own good judgment must direct you in the publication of the manuscript papers of General Lee. I can have no request to make concerning the work.

"I never had a difference with that gentleman, but on public ground; and my conduct toward him upon this occasion, was

[27] Sabine, *The American Loyalist,* 328.

only such as I conceived myself indispensably bound to adopt in discharge of the public trust reposed in me. If this produced in him unfavorable sentiments of me, I yet can never consider the conduct I pursued with respect to him either wrong or improper, however I may regret that it may have been differently viewed by him, and that it excited his censure and animadversions.

"Should there appear in General Lee's writings anything injurious or unfriendly to me, the impartial and dispassionate world must decide how far I deserved it from the general tenor of my conduct. I am gliding down the stream of life, and wish, as is natural, that my remaining days may be undisturbed and tranquil; and, conscious of my integrity, I would willingly hope that nothing will occur to give me anxiety; but should anything present itself in this or in any other publication, I shall never undertake the painful task of recrimination, nor do I know that I shall even enter upon my justification.

"I consider the communication you have made, as a mark of great attention, and the whole of your letter as a proof of your esteem. I am, Sir, your most obedient humble servant,

"GEORGE WASHINGTON."[28]

Mr. Goddard.

Connecticut showed a steady development. The first paper in that colony appeared in the same year with the *Boston Gazette*, 1755. The *Connecticut Gazette*, as it was called, was the enterprise of James Parker and John Holt.

The *New London Summary*, which appeared on August 8, 1758, the title afterward being changed to the *New London Gazette*, brought to the fore the indefatigable Green family, whose contributions to printing and journalism grew like the family tree, for wherever a member of this family was to be found, there was a pioneer with the printing press.

A most important addition to the patriotic papers was the *Connecticut Courant*, brought out by Thomas Green at Hartford in December, 1764, the same *Hartford*

[28] Thomas, ii, 357, 358.

Bartholomew Green, the Emigrant, arrived 1632.

Samuel,
came with father; printed the Indian Bible; d. 1702
aged 88; Cambridge.

Samuel, b. 1648, d. 1690 Boston	Bartholomew, d. 1732 Boston
Timothy, b. 1679, Boston; removed to New London, 1714; d. 1757	Bartholomew, Jr. Boston 1751 removed to Nova Scotia
Timothy, Boston; removed in 1752 to New London.	John Boston; d. 1787

Samuel, d. 1752; with his father; his three sons were printers in Connecticut	Nathaniel, New London	Jonas, Philadelphia and Annapolis [29]

Courant that ranks as one of the leading papers of the country to-day. In conjunction with Samuel Green, the proprietor of the Hartford paper brought out the *Connecticut Journal and New Haven Post Boy* in October, 1767. In this paper appeared the earlier essays of John Trumbull, one of the first of America's poets. Not the least interesting point in Trumbull's many-sided career appears in a news item in the *Connecticut Gazette* for September 24, 1757. This states that, at the age of seven, he passed the entrance examination to Yale, a feat which necessitated his being able to write Latin prose and to read Cicero and Virgil, as well as the four Gospels in Greek. While taking the examination, he was held in the

[29] *Memorial History of Boston,* ii. 406.

lap of another student, the grown-up student being twelve years old. It was Trumbull's ambition, as expressed in the series of essays that he contributed to the *Journal,* to reform the controversial manners of a time when, as he said later, "the press groaned with controversy," and when the writing was marked with "absurd pedantry, unrelenting partisanship and the extravagance of misrepresentation." [30] To be remembered, in connection with the future developments of journalism in America, is the fact that in one of these essays he attacked those Americans and Christians who were building up fortunes through their participation in the African slave trade. [31]

It was in the *New London Gazette,* beginning September 6, 1765, that Stephen Johnson published his five essays addressed to the Freemen of the colony of Connecticut. In them he not only protested against the right of the British Government to tax the colonies against their will, but, with a boldness unusual at that time, against conditions that, if continued, would result in a "bloody revolution." Like others of the men who used the pen to arouse the colonists, Johnson was a Congregational pastor. He afterwards showed on the battle field that he had the courage of his convictions.

In Virginia, "unaided by an active press they learned from nature what others learned from philosophy." [32] While it was not through journalism or the printing-press that Virginia was to make its principal contribution to the pre-Revolutionary contest, the importance of a paper that would set forth the Whig cause was seen by no less a person than Thomas Jefferson.

[30] Tyler, *Literary History,* 200.
[31] *Connecticut Gazette,* July 6, 1770.
[32] Bancroft, *History of the United States,* iii, 87.

In the other colonies the newspapers, as they appeared, echoed more or less vigorously the defiance proclaimed by the larger cities. No paper was published in New Hampshire until August, 1756, when Daniel Fowle started the *New Hampshire Gazette* at Portsmouth. It came out vigorously against the Stamp Act, and continued to be published as usual without stamps. Fowle regarded his own experience with the Boston authorities as a good example of a tyrannical government suppressing a free press, and as late as 1770 he reprinted parts of Andrew Hamilton's speech in behalf of Zenger, as matter that his countrymen should have ever in mind.

In January, 1765, the *Portsmouth Mercury and Weekly Advertiser* appeared. In its opening address to the public it announced that it would print all the news, even if opposed by an "arbitrary power," since the news was necessary to the people if they were to have those liberties which were "dearer to them than their lives." The paper, however, was not as well handled or printed as the *Gazette,* and succumbed at the end of three years.

To summarize, there were in 1775, five newspapers published in Boston, one at Salem, and one at Newburyport, making seven in Massachusetts. There was at that time one published at Portsmouth and no other in New Hampshire. One was printed at Newport, and one at Providence, making two in Rhode Island. At New London there was one, at New Haven one, and one at Hartford; in all, three in Connecticut; and thirteen in New England. In the province of New York, three papers were then published, all in the City of New York. In Pennsylvania there were on the first of January, 1775, six; three in English and one in German, in Philadelphia; one in German at Germantown; and one in English and German at Lancaster. Before the end of January, 1775, two newspapers in English were added to the number from the presses in Philadelphia, making eight in Pennsylvania. In Maryland two; one at Annapolis, and one at Baltimore. In Virginia, there were but two, both of these at Williamsburg. One was printed at Wilmington, and one at Newbern, in North Carolina; and one at Savannah in Georgia, making thirty-four newspapers in all the British colonies which are now comprised in the United States.[33]

[33] *History of Printing*, ii, 187, 188.

CHAPTER VIII

THE *BOSTON GAZETTE* AND SAMUEL ADAMS

Adams a great journalist — His remarkable industry — Associated with Jonathan Mayhew — New group takes up patriotic struggle — *Gazette* office headquarters of patriots — Boston Tea Party planned there — James Otis and Joseph Warren among editorial contributors — Important contributions of John Adams — Notable writings of Samuel Adams — Attacks on *Gazette* — Edes and Gill threatened — The days before the Revolution — Edes dies in obscure poverty.

If Massachusetts was the leader in the events before the Revolution, and she unquestionably was, Samuel Adams was the leader in Massachusetts, and the organ through which he swayed the people was the *Boston Gazette*. There is not an American schoolboy who is not familiar with the names of Samuel Adams, "Father of the Revolution" and of John Adams, "Statesman of the Revolution," but probably very few people are fully aware of the great extent to which these two used, and how much they relied on, that very important pre-Revolutionary newspaper.

The history of the *Boston Gazette* is the history of its influence, which came not only from its notable contributors, but from its courageous and able editors and printers, Benjamin Edes and John Gill. It takes not a tithe from the statesmanlike reputation of Sam Adams that he was, after Franklin, America's greatest journalist, though indifference to this aspect of his career has been the attitude of most of the historians of this period.

In order to write adequately the history of journalism,

it is necessary to re-read the documents and publications of this period; even the writers of later date have written under the prejudice against journalism that marked its beginning. It is not until we have such modern and broad-minded historians as Rhodes, McMaster and Roosevelt that we begin to get a proper appreciation of the part played by journalism, even in the primitive sections.

Samuel Adams was born in Boston in 1722, and graduated from Harvard in 1740. An undergraduate essay was on "Liberty," showing the drift of his mind; and, from the time when it became evident to him that there could not be happiness in the colonies until England had receded from her position, he never neglected an opportunity to stir the colonists in every way possible.

His biographer tells us that the Boston people, going home late at night, would pause as they passed his window, where the lights shone far into the morning hours, and observe that it was "old Sam Adams" writing the pieces for the paper that roused his countrymen to a sense of their wrongs. It was not alone what he wrote himself, but what he succeeded in getting others to write, that stirred the people. He was an industrious editor, engaged in a great campaign, continually suggesting to able men that they take up this or that question in the public press. So anxious was he to get matter into the papers that one of Governor Bernard's spies was able to tell of a quarrel between Otis and Adams over the latter's desire to rush into print.

It has been said that he had the instinct "of a great journalist willing to screen his individuality behind his journal." We have heard little of Samuel Adams, journalist, because it was not in journalism itself, any more than it was in literature or in oratory, that he was interested. Journalism, literature, oratory, for him were but means by which the people were aroused. His very anonymity made him a power, and from 1755 to the breaking out of the war, though he was the most industrious, the most effective and the most able of the men writing for the papers, he was the least identified. He seldom, if ever, published anything under his own name, but carried on, sometimes over periods of several years, controversies under different *noms de plume*. His biographer gives a list of twenty-five of these disguises that he assumed, among them: "An American," "A Tory," "A Son of Liberty," "An Elector in 1771," "Candidus," "Determinatus," "Populus," "Cedant Arma Togae," "Principiis Obsta," "A Religious Politician," and "Shippen."[1]

We have seen in the previous chapter how Adams began his fight for liberty by the formation of a club and, after its formation, by the publication of the *Independent Advertiser*. He was then a young man of twenty-six. When the paper failed, because of business difficulties, he was still very young — only twenty-eight. Between that time and the start of the *Boston Gazette* in 1755, he became a man of maturity, a statesman, a ripened combatant. During those five years he gathered about him the men who were to be famous as the group that defied England, brought about the Revolutionary War and inaugurated the movement that led to American independence.

In the columns of the *Independent Advertiser* was printed the sermon of Jonathan Mayhew, in which the distinguished Unitarian set forth the idea that these colonies should be not only free and independent, but should become a republic. This sermon has been called

[1] Wells, *Life of Adams.*

"The Morning Gun of the Revolution."[2] Mayhew died, but in the two years that the *Independent Advertiser* was being published, Adams had opportunity to study and gauge the men in the community who might be drawn together in the fight which he had undertaken. John Adams soon became closely associated with him in the group, which numbered, among others, such men as James Otis, Oxenbridge Thatcher and Joseph Warren.

The office of the *Boston Gazette*, on Court Street, was recognized as the headquarters of the Revolutionary leaders, and here Warren, Otis, Quincy, John Adams, Church and others less known, held frequent meetings. Here they watched the public sentiment of the country respond to their publications, read the exchanges, went over the proofs of their contributions, in fact went through what to-day would be considered an editorial council. It was in the back room of the *Gazette* office that the "Boston Tea-Party" was planned.

It was said that the ablest and most interesting of all the protégés of Samuel Adams was Joseph Warren. Warren was then about twenty-seven years of age and for some years had been a contributor to the newspapers, thereby attracting to himself the attention and respect of Adams. In February, 1768, he vigorously attacked Governor Bernard in the *Gazette*. His attack "drew blood," for Bernard endeavored to have the legislature act in the matter, and, upon its refusal, prorogued that body.

James Otis was the counterpoise for the impetuous Samuel Adams. He was the scholar and the cultivated writer. In 1762 he published a pamphlet, "A Vindication of the Conduct of the House of Representatives of the Province of the Massachusetts Bay." John Adams

[2] *Memorial History of Boston*, iii, 119.

later said that it contained most of the solid thought of the philosophic writings of the Revolution. It was Otis who aroused John Adams with his speech against the Writs of Assistance and brought him into the newspaper circle, and he was the one patriot whom Governor Hutchinson challenged to a newspaper duel, grimly informing Otis that he had "been cutting out work for him in the papers." [3]

Another brilliant contributor was Josiah Quincy, Jr., who was admitted to the Bar in 1768. When the British soldiers made their appearance in Boston, he published in the *Gazette* of that year, under the signature of "Hyperion," a series of essays. Joseph Warren's oration on the anniversary of the Boston Massacre in 1772, though he defended the soldiers against the popular feeling, stirred the imagination of the patriots; printed in the *Boston Gazette* on March 17, 1775, it was copied throughout the colonies.

The part played by his kinsman, John Adams of Braintree, is second only to that of Samuel Adams himself, though the "Statesman of the Revolution" had not the direct hand in either the journalistic or the political divisions that the Boston Adams had. The fire that burned in the mind of John Adams was very often rekindled by the ardor of Sam Adams. It was the literary art that fascinated the man who was to be the second President of the United States; it was the idea, the cause, that inspired the "Father of the Revolution." John Adams' more conservative soul rebelled at the excesses of the newspapers, and yet there is a great tribute to Messrs. Edes and Gill in his dissertation on the Canon and Feudal Law, which was printed in the *Boston Gazette* in four numbers, and which, like so many other

[3] Tudor, *Life of James Otis,* 102.

writings of the day, both in newspapers and pamphlets, was an endeavor to find a legal basis for getting rid of the tyranny of the British Government.

In 1774 and 1775 John Adams wrote the "Novanglus" letters, which were among the most important contributions to the *Boston Gazette.* They were answers to letters that had been written by Daniel Leonard and printed in the *Massachusetts Gazette,*— one of the names of the *Weekly Advertiser.* Leonard's letters defended the course of the English Government and tried to make it appear that the colonists had no substantial grievance. Adams was then opening the congress in Philadelphia and when he returned and found that these letters, which were signed "Massachusettsensis," were making a deep impression, he began his series of letters in the *Gazette,* defending the course of the colonies in declaring that America would defend her rights and that submission was not to be thought of.

The last of these letters appeared with the date of April 17, 1775. Two days later, April 19th, the battle of Lexington took place, and the newspaper war gave way to the fight of arms. These letters were reprinted during the war and were widely read, both then and afterward. In the words of Charles Francis Adams, "they formed a masterly commentary on the whole history of American taxation and the rise of the Revolution."

When we come to discuss Sam Adams' own part, it must be said first, that never before in the history of a people had there been such a successful endeavor to conduct a public issue within peaceful lines, while, at the same time, nothing was omitted that would arouse the public to a full sense of the importance of the events that were taking place. English historians, even in this century, comment with amazement on the fact that the same public that called for the punishment of those British soldiers who were responsible for the Boston Massacre viewed with calmness the spectacle of the defense of these same "murderers" by John Adams and Josiah Quincy; and immediately after the verdict — in which all but two were acquitted — chose John Adams for their representative in the Assembly. For this condition credit belongs more to Sam Adams than to any other individual.

He showed his leadership in many ways; not the least was in making himself very popular among the mechanics and laborers. When he could not pour forth his convictions at a town meeting, he would harangue the ship carpenters working on a block of wood above the tide, or debate with a small shopkeeper, caught in a leisure moment. Nor was this enough; the day done, in a study adjoining his bedroom, he wrote night after night. His right to the title of "Father of the Revolution" rests on many instances of his initiative, but principally on the fact that he drafted the first public denial of the right of the British Parliament to put in operation Grenville's scheme of the Stamp Act, and that in this document he made the first suggestion of the union of the colonies for the purpose of redressing their grievances. He was appointed, in May, 1769, a member of the Committee to instruct the Representatives just elected and the Committee left the drafting of the instructions to Adams alone.

It was in the following September, when Adams was again appointed to prepare instructions — these instructions taking the place of the political platform of to-day, that he collaborated with his kinsman, John Adams, who had been delegated to undertake a similar task for the representatives of Braintree. This was a historic collaboration, an important event in the history of the American Revolution.

The *Boston Gazette* printed these documents and they went through all the towns in Massachusetts, becoming the platform of the Province. In 1772, Sam Adams organized the Committee of Correspondence in more than eighty towns, and no town was without its copy of the *Gazette*.

Never was there more artful journalism than that in which the Boston Massacre was used to inflame the public mind. It might be said that Adams showed himself a consummate reporter. He was always in the court, and followed the trial carefully, consistently taking notes and then printing over the signature of "Vindex," his own review of the case. He was a believer in "shirt sleeve diplomacy." When he sent Franklin a long letter, retailing the grievances of the colonies against the government, he printed the letter in the *Boston Gazette*.

In a communication to the *Gazette* in December, 1768, written under the nom de plume of "Vindex," he showed his political sagacity when he pressed home on an English opponent of America the argument that if the colonists admitted they had no right to be represented when taxed, they were admitting that they were slaves, and that their property was not actually their own. However faulty the logic, the point roused the colonists and was the beginning of limitless discussion

The illegality and uselessness of billeting troops was a theme with which it was easy to stir his readers; and it can be easily imagined what the effect was on those hardy New Englanders, resentful to the core, when they read his appeal:

"I know very well that some of the late contenders for a right in the British Parliament to tax Americans who are not, and cannot be, represented there, have denied this. When pressed with that fundamental principle of nature and the constitution, that what is a man's own is absolutely his own, and that no man can have a right to take it from him without his consent, they have alleged, and would fain have us believe, that by far the greater part of the people in Britain are excluded the right of choosing their representatives, and yet are taxed; and that therefore they are taxed without their consent. Had not this doctrine been repeatedly urged, I should have thought the bare mentioning it would have opened the eyes of the people there to have seen where their pretended advocates were leading them: that in order to establish a right in the people of England to enslave the colonists under the plausible show of great zeal for the honor of the nation, they are driven to a bold assertion, at all adventures, that truly the greater part of the nation are themselves subject to the same yoke of bondage. What else is it but saying that the greater part of the people of Britain are slaves? For if the fruit of all their toil and industry depends upon so precarious a tenure as the will of a few, what security have they for the utmost farthing? What are they but slaves, delving with the sweat of their brows, not for the benefit of themselves, but their masters? After all the fine things that have been said of the British Constitution and the boasted freedom and happiness of the subjects who live under it, will they thank these modern writers, these zealous asserters of the honor of the nation, for reducing them to a state inferior to that of indented servants, who generally contract for a maintenance, at least, for their labor?" [4]

As the tragic hour approached, his appeal became more

[4] *Boston Gazette,* December 19, 1768.

ardent: "Is it not enough," he cried, "to have a Governor an avowed advocate for ministerial measures, and a most assiduous instrument in carrying them on, model'd, shaped, controul'd and directed, totally independent of the people over whom he is commissioned to govern, and yet absolutely dependent upon the Crown, pension'd by those on whom his existence depends, and paid out of a revenue establish'd by those who have no authority to establish it, and extorted from the people in a manner most odious, insulting and oppressive? Is not this indignity enough to be felt by those who have any feeling? Are we still threatened with more?"[5]

At length, as "Observations" in the *Boston Gazette,* September 27, 1773, Samuel Adams wrote:

"This very important dispute between Britain and America has, for a long time, employed the pens of statesmen in both countries, but no plan of union is yet agreed on between them; the dispute still continues and everything floats in uncertainty. As I have long conplated the subject with fixed attention, I beg leave to offer a proposal to my countrymen, namely, that a CONGRESS OF AMERICAN STATES shall be assembled as soon as possible, draw up a Bill of Rights, and publish it to the world; choose an ambassador to reside at the British Court to act for the United colonists; appoint where the congress shall annually meet, and how it may be summoned upon any extraordinary occasion, what further steps are necessary to be taken, etc."[6]

Three weeks later, October 11th, in the *Gazette,* appeared the following:

"But the question will be asked — How shall the

[5] *Ibid,* October 2, 1772.

[6] Hosmer, *Samuel Adams,* 238.

colonies force their Oppressors to proper Terms? This question has been often answered already by our Politicians, viz: 'Form an Independent State,' 'An American COMMONWEALTH.' This plan has been proposed, and I can't find that any other is likely to answer the great Purpose of preserving our Liberties. I hope, therefore, it will be well digested and forwarded to be in due Time put into Execution, unless our Political Fathers can secure American Liberties in some other Way. As the Population, Wealth and Power of this Continent are swiftly increasing, we certainly have no Cause to doubt of our Success in maintaining Liberty by forming a Commonwealth, or whatever Measure Wisdom may point out for the preservation of the Rights of America."

John Adams, Thomas Cushing, Thomas Paine and Samuel Adams departed for Philadelphia, and Congress was established; when it adjourned, October 26th, a special convention was appointed for May 20, 1775. The battle that Adams had made had been won, to a very large extent, for it was not Adams against the British Government; it was not Boston against the British Government; it was not even New England against the British Government; it was the united colonies of America that had taken up the war begun in Boston, practically by a single individual.

It must not be assumed that the *Boston Gazette* was allowed to have the field unattacked. Governor Hutchinson was keenly sensitive to the fact that seven-eighths of the people of Boston — the calculation is his own — read no paper but the *Boston Gazette,* and for that reason the *Massachusetts Gazette* (the old *News-Letter*) was furnished with articles and built up in every way possible that it might hold its own against the *Boston Gazette* and Adams. The *Massachusetts Gazette,* which was also known as Draper's *Gazette,* was paid liberally, but no matter how well paid the contributors were, the Tory papers were unable to obtain a large circulation. The two most important writers were Thomas Hutchinson himself and Jonathan Sewall, the Attorney-General of Massachusetts, the latter being the most forceful contributor to the Royalist papers. Hutchinson, a man who undoubtedly loved his country, a man of unquestioned ability, was almost a match for Adams. He drew to him also Daniel Leonard, one of the ablest writers of the time.

When we come to the *Boston Gazette* itself, it is well to remember that, though the newspapers were small in size and poorly printed, they exerted a powerful influence; their appeals reached practically every threshold, and through them "the sense of national life was becoming intense and vivid." The mind of America at this time was very keen. Montesquieu, Priestley, Bacon, Bolingbroke, Milton, Locke and Harrington were quoted and known almost in the wilderness, and Edmund Burke was able to say "I hear that they have sold nearly as many of Blackstone's Commentaries in America as in England."[7]

History must ever be grateful that Benjamin Edes and John Gill were bold and fearless publishers. The Stamp Act and the Boston Massacre, the Tea Tax and the closing of the port of Boston, the conduct of the British soldiers and many oppressive measures against the colonies were handled in this paper in a way to arouse the indignation of the colonists and to make patriots of them. The *Gazette* was "a great power in the community. Rarely in our history has a single newspaper met a difficult crisis, maintained its principles with more

[7] *House of Commons,* March 22, 1775.

splendid ability, or exercised so powerful an influence over the minds of men."[8] Governor Bernard himself declared it the most "factious newspaper" in America, while the copies sent abroad gave to the thoughtful men of Europe the first insight into the profound character and understanding of the men who were leading the Revolutionary movement. But no greater tribute could be paid than that of John Adams, printed in the paper and addressed to Edes and Gill:

"But none of the means of information are more sacred, or have been cherished with more tenderness and care by the settlers of America than the press," he said. "Care should be taken that the art of printing should be encouraged, and that it should be easy and cheap and safe for any person to communicate his thoughts to the public. And you, Messieurs printers, whatever the tyrants of the earth may say of your paper, have done important service to your country by your readiness and freedom in publishing the speculations of the curious. The stale, impudent insinuations of slander and sedition, with which the gormandizers of power have endeavored to discredit your paper, are so much the more to your honor. . . . And if the public interest, liberty, and happiness have been in danger from the ambition or avarice of any great man, whatever might be his politeness, address, learning, ingenuity, and, in other respects, integrity and humanity, you have done yourselves honor and your country service by publishing and pointing out that avarice and ambition. . . . Be not intimidated, therefore, by any terrors, from publishing with the utmost freedom, whatever can be warranted by the laws of your country; nor suffer yourselves to be wheedled out of your liberty by any pretences of politeness, delicacy,

[8] *Memorial History of Boston,* iii, 134.

or decency. These, as they are often used, are but three different names for hypocrisy, chicanery and cowardice. Much less, I presume, will you be discouraged by any pretenses that malignants on this side the water will represent your paper as factious and seditious, or that the great on the other side the water will take offense at them. . . . I must and will repeat it, your paper deserves the patronage of every friend to his country. And whether the defamers of it are arrayed in robes of scarlet or sable, whether they lurk and skulk in an insurance office, whether they assume the venerable character of a priest, the sly one of a scrivener, or the dirty, infamous, abandoned one of an informer, they are all the creatures and tools of the lust of domination." [9]

These are noble words indeed, and as we go on with our story, they will be worth recalling, when we come to realize that they were used by the same man who later on, when President of the United States, was the supporter of the Alien and Sedition Acts, the failure of which was necessary in order to put an end to the endeavor in this country to shackle the press.

Of all the patriots, it was Sam Adams whose head the British Government most desired. Edes and Gill, too, were openly threatened, as was Isaiah Thomas, the publisher of the *Massachusetts Spy,* referred to in a previous chapter. The decision to move on the stores at Lexington and to put an end to the military training was, to every patriot, the call to arms. At the same time that the *Massachusetts Spy* suspended and started moving its types and press to Worcester, Edes quietly moved an old press and one or two improved fonts of type to Watertown, and there the paper was printed until the evacuation of Boston by the British, when he returned

[9] *Life and Works of John Adams,* iii, 457, 458.

in November, 1776. The partnership seems to have been dissolved when Edes decided to move the paper to Watertown and Gill remained in Boston. [10]

When Edes returned and resumed publication, he took into partnership his two sons, Benjamin and Peter, until 1784, when Peter retired from the scene and in 1795 started the Kennebec, Maine, *Intelligencer*. The *Gazette* was continued until 1798 by the old man himself, his sons having left him. The year before it was discontinued, in the issue of January 1, 1797, he began his salutation with the statement that "The aged editor of the *Gazette* presents the compliments of the season to his generous benefactors, and invites all those who have any demands on him to call and receive their dues;" this gentle introduction leads into the main purpose of the salutation, which is to ask the many who owe him money, especially those who are two, three or more years in debt, to discharge their arrears, "as the editor has found it impossible to live upon the wind and promises equally uncertain."

He recalls the time when the *Gazette* was a power; when its circulation was "upward of 2,000." He now states that he has only a circulation of 400 and hardly any advertisements.

The following September, the paper, at the close of its forty-third year, went out of existence. In his valedictory, the old editor states sorrowfully: "The cause of liberty is not always the channel of preferment for pecuniary reward." He recalls the fact that Adams, Hancock and Otis were his chosen intimates in the days when the country was in danger; and advises his countrymen to cherish their liberties and maintain their virtues. He bids them farewell.

[10] *Nelson,* i, 267.

"It is beneath a patriot to mourn his own misfortunes."[11]

A visitor found him in 1801, in a house on Temple Street, Boston, "with spectacles on nose, a venerable old man, bent over the case, setting type for shop bills, while an elderly female, his daughter, beat and pulled at the press," the last picture of the pioneers of American Liberty. Two years later, neglected, forgotten, weighed down with poverty, he died.

[11] *Buckingham*, i, 205.

CHAPTER IX

JOURNALISM AND THE REVOLUTION

False impression of strength of Continental Army — Tories outnumber Patriots — Number of papers in colonies — Lieutenant-Governor Colden and Hugh Gaine — Attitude of British toward journalism — Samuel Loudon — His publication closely watched — Rivington's *Gazette* boycotted — Sears and McDougall wreck office — Encounter with Ethan Allen — Double-dealing of Gaine's *New York Gazette* — *New Jersey Gazette* assists Patriot cause — Tory papers picture misfortune of Americans — Change in attitude of people toward press — Encouragement of writers.

In the minds of most Americans, this country was, during the Revolution, a great battlefield on which for seven years there was continuous clash of arms. As a matter of fact, of the three million people in the country, at no time were more than a small part engaged in the war. During the campaign of 1777, Washington's army never exceeded 11,000 men. [1]

In the spring of 1777, when the Continental Congress was enjoying its greatest authority and when, through the generosity of France, the financial condition of the temporary government was at its best, so that it was able to make liberal offers of bounties, only 34,820 were obtained, despite an earnest appeal for 80,000, less than one-fifth of the male population. [2] The total number of men in the field for the year, including militia, was 68,720. In 1781 the total number of men in the field was only 29,340, despite the great military action.

[1] Fiske, *American Revolution,* ii, 27.

[2] Fiske, *Critical Period,* 102.

Although what has been called the war of argument ended with the battle of Lexington on April 19, 1775, and that date, as Professor Tyler says, becomes the divisional point in any history of America or American development, it is, nevertheless, not true that the journalism of the colonies stopped in its development or its importance. The picture of an entire country engaged in battle for seven years is a companion piece to another equally false; that of an entire country fighting the British troops and their paid support. The truth is that the difficulty of holding the patriots themselves in line was the principal cause of the prolongation of the war.

The Tories asserted that they were numerically superior to the patriots. Lecky declares that the American Revolution was "the work of an energetic minority, who succeeded in committing an undecided and fluctuating majority to courses for which they had little love, and led them step by step to a position from which it was impossible to recede."[3]

The greatest number of Tories was found in New York, while in South Carolina and Georgia they outnumbered the patriots. John Adams, in a letter written in 1813, declared that New York and Pennsylvania were evenly divided, and that only Virginia and New England kept them in line. He also stated that fully one-third of the people were averse to the Revolution[4] and, in general, to the idea of rebellion and separation. Until the opening of hostilities, it was a war of argument, but it became necessary to keep up the argument by propaganda and printing after hostilities had begun. Such action was necessary in order to hold those who were already in sympathy with the American cause, to increase the

[3] Lecky, *History of England,* iii, 443.

[4] *Works of John Adams,* x, 63.

number of patriots where it was possible, and to attack those who were circulating falsehoods intended to weaken the patriotic ranks.

In addition to the Tories, who openly supported the enemy, there were many worthy people who believed that the patriots were "going too far," as well as a number who, as Fiske says, magnified the losses and depreciated the gains.[5] In New York and Pennsylvania there was a large non-English population, both men and women, who had come from the continent of Europe, and in them "the pulse of Liberty did not beat so quickly" as in the English commonwealths of Virginia and Massachusetts. The Quakers of Pennsylvania and New Jersey were opposed to war, and in New York City, which had been the headquarters of the British army and the seat of the principal royal government in America, there was a strong royalist feeling.

If, as Lecky says, the revolution was the work of a minority, and the army itself was so small a part of the population, it is quite evident that the propagandist part played by the forces that converted that minority into a majority, a part greatly undervalued by most of our historians, was not inconsiderable.

At the close of the year 1774, there were thirty-one newspapers printed in English in the colonies, of which twenty-one were Whig. To these thirty-one, between that time and April, 1775, were added three more, one of which was devoted to the patriotic cause, but no less than five went over to the Tory side during the course of the war.

Until the beginning of actual hostilities newspapers were maintained in the principal cities; the activities of the enemy, however, necessitated the removal of several

[5] Fiske, *American Revolution,* i, 56.

of them to more remote places and interrupted or entirely stopped the publication of others.

The papers at that time were not by any means evenly distributed; for instance, Maryland, Virginia, the two Carolinas and Georgia, together could boast of but one more journal than Pennsylvania, and only three more than little Massachusetts. New Hampshire had only the *Gazette*, while in Rhode Island there were both a *Gazette* and a *Mercury*.[6]

Early in the war the British General, Gage, recognized the necessity of putting before the public the encouraging aspect of the British cause. Immediately after the battles of Lexington and Concord, he sent to Cadwallader Colden, Lieutenant-Governor of New York, his own account of these engagements, requesting him to have them printed in some New York paper. Colden's experience is best told in his own language:

"Immediately upon the receipt of your first account of the facts of the 19th of April, I sent it to Gaine to be published in his paper. He desired leave, if asked, to say from whom he got it. I sent my son to tell him he might, and if he chose, might add that I received it from headquarters, which entirely satisfied him, and he promised to publish it on Monday. This was on Saturday evening. On Sunday he returned the copy and let me know that he could not insert it in his paper."

When the British took possession of New York the Whig printers, including Gaine, had to leave and there was no newspaper published. General Howe saw the necessity of keeping the citizens informed and of putting the best face on the British cause, and authorized Ambrose Serle to issue a newspaper and to use Gaine's establishment for that purpose. The issue of September 30th of

[6] Lorenzo Sabine, *The American Loyalists*, 53.

the *New York Gazette* came out bearing Gaine's name, but in the issue of October 7th and those following his name was dropped. Serle, in his report to Lord Dartmouth, tells of acting as superintendent to the *New York Gazette* and gives an interesting view of the governmental attitude toward journalism:

" Among other Engines which have raised the present commotion, next to the indecent harangues of the preachers, none has had a more extensive or stronger influence than the newspapers of the respective colonies. One is astonished to see with what avidity they are sought after, and how implicitly they are believed, by the great bulk of the people.

" The Congress saw the necessity of securing this advantage entirely to themselves and of preventing all publications which might either expose or refute the policy of their measures. A free press, however, teeming with heterogeneous matters, would have at least retarded their great design.

"Government may find it expedient in the sum of things to employ this popular engine; and, if it be impossible to restrain the publication of falsehood, it will be its interest to give power and facility to the circulation of truth. The expense of allowing salary (if needful) to some able superintendents of the press in different colonies, who should in policy be natives of this country, would be too trifling to mention, considering the almost incredible influence those fugitive publications have upon the people. Ever since the press here has been under my direction (from the 30th of September) I have seen sufficient reason to confirm this opinion and have had the pleasure to hear that the papers, which have been circulated as extensively as possible, have been attended with the most promising effects. The advantage to the printer, upon a moderate computation in the present state, will amount to seven or eight hundred pounds a year, Sterling, clear of all deductions. I mention this to show how great the demand is and consequently how prudent it may be for the government to take care with what matter it is supplied.

"I beg leave to refer Your Lordship to the inclosed newspapers for an account of general occurrances. Nothing, to the best of my knowledge, is inserted in them, as New York intelligence, but matters of fact as they have arisen. This little business affords me some amusement, where I have no books and few friends, and engages a part of my time with the satisfaction I am otherwise deprived of, of doing some service to the cause of my King and country."[7]

Thomas Jones, the Loyalist historian, affords us further enlightenment concerning the frame of mind of the opposition as to the attacks made on them by the patriots. It was in the office of Samuel Loudon — who afterward (January 17, 1776) established the *New York Packet,* later being obliged to move it to Fishkill while the British occupied New York — that a reply was to be printed to Thomas Paine's "Common Sense." Loudon unquestionably was a Whig, but according to the account of Jones, Alexander McDougall, Isaac Sears and other "inveterate republicans" having one night imbibed plentifully of "rumbo" (the strong man's drink of the day) went to the house of Loudon and pulled him out of bed. Disregarding the fact that he was both "a Presbyterian and a Republican," they took the manuscript away from him and destroyed all the copies that he had printed. It is doubtful if this "Presbyterian and Republican" printer was much alarmed over the visit, as

[7] Stevens, *Facsimiles,* Nos. 2044–2046.

his actions indicated that he was much in sympathy with the " Sons of Liberty."

This occurred in the summer of 1775. The day following the visit to London, printers of the city were notified that they must cease to print articles in favor of our "inveterate foes, the King, Ministry and Parliament of Great Britain."

Loudon appealed to the Committee of Safety to recompense him for the loss sustained, and was appointed official printer with a salary of £200 a year, to print a weekly newspaper, in which there was to be such information as a future legislature should direct. This was the *New York Packet* above referred to. Doubtless it was a matter of some satisfaction to both Loudon and the patriots that they had, in destroying Tory literature, forced the royalists to assist in establishing a patriot paper.

How closely the provisional government watched over publication is shown in the action of the Committee of Safety, which on December 21, 1777, ordered Loudon to appear before them and explain why he had reprinted in his paper extracts from Gaine's *New York Gazette,* which contained news discouraging to the patriot cause. The following day Loudon did appear and explained that he only printed the extract to show his readers the kind of stuff that was being published in New York.

The Chairman of the Committee, on Loudon's apology, pardoned the offense, declaring that while the House of Representatives of New York had no intention of restricting the liberty of the press, they were determined "not to employ any person who shall do things inimical to the cause of American freedom." [8]

But it is when Jones comes to tell of the attack by

[8] *Journal of the New York Provisional Congress,* i, 781.

Sears on James Rivington's *New York Gazetteer* that he is unable to contain himself over the wickedness, unjustness and villainy of the patriots.

Rivington was a favorite with the Loyalists. He had come to the colonies after a stormy career in London, where he had been a bookseller — fond of horse-racing and good living — with all the proclivities of a Royalist. His *Gazetteer* first appeared April 22, 1773, and was patronized by the royal supporters in all the principal towns. He boasted on one occasion that its circulation was 3,600 — a circulation quite as large as that of any paper, not only in the colonies, but even in Great Britain.[9]

Rivington's success, as well as his virulent pen, had made him a thorn in the side of the Whigs. His paper became known during the war as the "Lying Gazette," and even the royalists commented on his disregard for the truth. In fact he himself warned contributors to be more truthful.[10]

So bitterly were the Whigs opposed to Rivington that members of the party passed resolutions March 1, 1775, recommending "to every person who takes his paper, to immediately drop the same." A similar resolution was passed in Freehold, New Jersey, on the sixth day of March. On the 8th a committee, consisting of Philip Livingston and John Jay, called on him to ascertain the authority for all his false statements; and on the 14th, at a meeting of the Freeholders of Ulster County, New York, a resolution was passed to have "no connection or intercourse with him." His case was examined by the Provincial Congress and referred by them to the Continental Congress, then in Philadelphia, to whom he ad-

[9] Rivington's *New York Gazetteer,* October 13, 1774, No. 78.
[10] July 10, 1782.

dressed his defense, declaring that "his press had always been open and free to all parties."

He stated that, while an Englishman by birth, he was an American by choice, and that it was his wish and ambition to be a useful member of society. He also stated that he employed sixteen people, costing him nearly £1,000 annually. This reply was dated May 20, 1775. On the 7th of June the Provincial Congress granted him permission to return to his house, and recommended to the inhabitants of the colony that he be unmolested, as he had apologized for his previous remarks and attitude.

Washington, on June 5th, 1775, passed through New York on his way from Mount Vernon to Cambridge; following this visit, New York was ordered by the Continental Congress to raise her quota of 3,000 men. The city presented the curious spectacle of being the seat of two governments, each denouncing the other as illegal. On August 23rd Captain Lamb and a party of "Liberty Boys" removed the twenty-one guns at the Battery, during which operation shots were exchanged. The royal Governor, Tryon, fled aboard the frigate "Asia," but continued to direct violent attacks on the Sons of Liberty through Rivington's *Gazetteer,* which now became the representative of the royalists.

Among the men whom Rivington had sharply attacked was Isaac Sears,— conspicuous for his zeal in the earlier patriotic movements,— who had recently moved to New Haven and there raised a company of cavalry. Rivington having become bolder and bolder, Sears took it upon himself to put an end to his activities. Arranging with McDougall and other patriots the details of the raid, he rode into the city with his men and, armed to the teeth, entered Rivington's house, demolishing his plant and carrying off the types, which were converted into bullets. The loyalists indignantly condemned the act as evidence that the patriots were trying "to restrain the freedom of the press." [11]

Rivington used this ill-treatment as a means of courting British favor. He went to England to procure a new press, and succeeded in securing appointment as King's printer for New York. When the British recaptured the city he returned and, beginning with October 4, 1777, issued his paper anew. He was received as a martyr, welcomed with congratulatory verses and with a public dinner, and from that time on the *Royal Gazette,* as he now called his paper, told not only the bitter truth about the Revolutionists but as much more as imagination could conceive and Rivington and his "lying staff" could invent.

That he was determined to recoup his fortunes is shown by the advertisement that he carried for several weeks after he had once more established his paper.

"James Rivington," he announces, "has brought back from London an extra fine assortment of London snuffs, shoes, gentleman's silk stockings, fishing tackle, magnifiers, buckles, small-swords, toothpick cases, pen knives, nail scissors, sleeve buttons, etc." [12]

Rivington was a man of unquestioned ability. As one who espoused and defended the Royalist cause, he adopted the royalist costume and dressed in the extreme of fashion — curled and powdered hair, claret-colored coat, scarlet waistcoat trimmed with gold lace, buckskin breeches and top-boots — and he was very fastidious as to the society he kept and the wine he drank. His contempt for the revolutionists is shown in his own story of his treatment

[11] Lamb and Harrison, *History of New York City,* ii, 49.

[12] *New York Royal Gazette,* November 1, 1777.

of Ethan Allen, the truth of which is not established in any of the biographies of Allen:

"I was sitting," said Rivington, "after a good dinner, alone, with my bottle of Madeira before me, when I heard an unusual noise in the street, and a huzza from the boys. I was in the second story, and, stepping to the window, saw a tall figure in tarnished regimentals, with a large cocked hat and an enormous long sword, followed by a crowd of boys, who occasionally cheered him with huzzas, of which he seemed insensible. He came up to my door and stopped. I could see no more. My heart told me it was Ethan Allen. I shut down my window and retired behind my table and bottle. I was certain the hour of reckoning had come. There was no retreat. Mr. Staples, my clerk, came in paler than ever, and clasping his hands, said:

"'Master, he is come.'

"'I know it.'

"'He entered the store and asked if James Rivington lived there.'

"'I answered, "Yes, sir." "Is he at home?" "I will go and see, sir," I said; and now, master, what is to be done? There he is in the store and the boys peeping in at him from the street.'

"I had made up my mind. I looked at the bottle of Madeira — possibly took a glass.

"'Show him up,' said I, 'and if such Madeira cannot mollify him, he must be harder than adamant.'

"There was a fearful moment of suspense. I heard him on the stairs, his long sword clanking at every step. In he walked.

"'Is your name James Rivington?'

"'It is, sir, and no man could be more happy than I am to see Colonel Ethan Allen.'

" 'Sir, I have come —'

" 'Not another word, my dear colonel, until you have taken a seat and a glass of old Madeira.'

" 'But, sir, I don't think it proper —'

" 'Not another word, colonel. Taste this wine; I have had it in glass for ten years. Old wine, you know, unless it is originally sound, never improves by age.'

"He took a glass, swallowed the wine, smacked his lips and shook his head approvingly.

" 'Sir, I come —'

" 'Not another word until you have taken another glass, and then, my dear colonel, we will talk of old affairs and I have some droll events to detail.'

"In short, we finished two bottles of Madeira, and parted as good friends as if we never had cause to be otherwise." [13]

During the time that Rivington was in Europe arranging for a new outfit, the British side of the controversy was set forth by Hugh Gaine, once a patriotic editor, but later — for business reasons — an enthusiastic Royalist. Gaine's double-dealing had been noted for some time, but it remained for the war to develop his talents to their full. When the British took possession of the city he fled to Newark, New Jersey, and apparently edited his patriotic paper there. His paper in New York was continued by the British. The only known file of the Newark issue shows Mr. Gaine running along very smoothly until his issue of November 2, 1776, when he apparently suffered what the modern alienists would describe as "brainstorm" for he takes both sides in the same issue, an article in one column referring to the ease with which "our troops" beat the "Britishers," while in an adjoining column, he recounted the skill with which "our" troops

[13] Lossing, *Field-book of the Revolution,* i, 508.

had trounced the "rebels." Apparently this was too much for the patriots and there ended Mr. Gaine's double venture, and from that time he devoted his talents entirely to the British cause and his New York paper.[14]

When the war ended Gaines, unabashed, petitioned the Legislature to be allowed to remain in the city, which he was permitted to do. Philip Freneau gave Gaine national fame by ridiculing him in verse, a sample of which, explaining why he deserted the Americans, follows:

> "As matters have gone, it was plainly a blunder,
> But *then* I expected the Whigs must knock under,
> But I always adhere to the sword that is longest,
> And stick to the party that's like to be strongest:
> That you have succeeded is merely a chance,
> I never once dreamed of the conduct of France!
> If alliance with her you were promised — at least
> You ought to have showed me your *star of the East,*
> Not let me go off uninformed as a beast.
> When your army I saw without stockings or shoes,
> Or victuals or *money* — to pay them their dues,
> Excepting your wretched congressional paper,
> That stunk in my nose like the snuff of a taper," etc.

But Gaine was not daunted. He stayed along and, on July 23, 1788, when New York celebrated the adoption of the Constitution, he was one of the marshals of the great parade!

After the desertion of Gaine during the campaign in New Jersey, the necessity for answering the attacks and the ridicule of James Rivington's *Royal Gazette,* led Governor William Livingston of New Jersey to aid Isaac Collins in establishing the *New Jersey Gazette* at Burlington. This paper, like some of the other patriotic journals, was obliged to move from town to town when

[14] *New York Gazette and Weekly Mercury,* September 21st to November 2nd, 1776, Nos. 1301 to 1307. This file of the Newark issue is in the New York Public Library.

the situation dictated prudence, but kept up its issuance with reasonable regularity. [15]

Livingston had had considerable training in newspaper work; in 1752 he had edited the *Independent Reflector*, and it was he who, in February, 1765, commenced a series of papers entitled the *Sentinal* which were published in Holt's *New Jersey Weekly Post Boy*. He was a steady contributor to the *New Jersey Gazette*, under the *noms de plume* of "Hortentius" and "Scipio," and on those occasions when he was presiding over the Council of Safety, somewhere in the mountains or woods of New Jersey, his gifted daughters are said to have written the caustic articles for him. [16]

The Tory editors found solace in recounting the misfortunes of their foes. The fall of Continental money, or the impoverishment of the rebel provinces, provided a subject for much jesting. "At Boston," said Gaine, "the people are starving and rebellious; food was brought them from the South by a land carriage of 1,700 miles; damaged Bohea tea, transported in this way from Charleston, was selling at $15 a pound; West India Rum was $12 a gallon; a plain surtout brought $60 and not a single hat could be bought in all Boston. The Yankee privateers had been chased from the seas by the King's ships; and the chief supplies of the Eastern states were wholly cut off. Trade was sunk; gold and silver had disappeared. Of the vile Continental currency a cart-load was not worth a dollar; and a piece of coin was not to be seen in all the New England states."

In the South the provinces were described as being even more unhappy, half the soldiers being depicted as laid low by fever while the other half were longing to enjoy

[15] Lamb and Harrison, ii, 175.
[16] Theodore Sedgwick, Jr., *Life of William Livingston*, 248.

once more the protection of King George. The people of Maryland were preparing to rise and reconquer the province. Connecticut was in a state of riot and disorder from one end to the other, and everywhere the people were sick of the unnatural war and were anxious to bring it to an end.

Such was the pabulum that was distributed, not only to the Loyalists but to the many weak-kneed patriots who came within the sphere of influence of the New York and Philadelphia papers. To counteract such statements was in itself a difficult task; in addition the patriotic press not only had to deny what was untruthful in the Loyalist press, but had to write, in the face of undeniable misfortune, what would be encouraging and would keep the weaker element from getting still weaker.

A feature of importance in a review of journalism during the Revolution was the changed attitude of the public toward the new institution. From indifferent onlookers in the contest between the first printers and the government; from slowly awakened people, conscious of their rights, but not particularly interested in the press that had awakened them, they had now passed to the point where the freedom of the press was asserted by them as boldly and as proudly as it was asserted by the press itself; it was now regarded as their instrument, to which they had every right and in which the setting forth of their views was not to be stopped. They now proclaimed it the great engine of civilization and, as one of them declared, "The test of truth, the bulwark of public safety and the guardian of freedom." [17]

This changed attitude made it necessary that the press be allowed such encouragement as was possible; it was

[17] *Connecticut Commercial Gazette,* November 1, 1765, quoted in Barry's *History of Massachusetts,* second period, 275.

the beginning of the desire for news, the supplying of which in the middle of the next century was to be found so profitable by many editors, but especially by the Greeleys and the Bennetts. This changed attitude on the part of the people was what led Washington — the first general in history to do so — to carry with him a literary assistant. This assistant was Thomas Paine, a born journalist if there ever was one, and his series of essays, called "The Crisis," was read to every corporal's guard.

Thomas Paine arrived in America November 20, 1774, with a letter of introduction from Benjamin Franklin to his son-in-law, Richard Bache. For eighteen months Paine edited the *Pennsylvania Magazine* or *American Museum,* and during that time the magazine was "A seed bag from which this sower scattered the seeds of great reforms, ripening with the progress of civilization." [18]

He was for republican equality and against privilege. He was the first to urge an extension of independence to the enslaved negro; the first to arraign monarchy, to denounce dueling, to suggest more radical ideas of marriage and divorce, to call for justice for women and kindliness toward animals, and to advocate national and international copyright.

It was while he was working on the *Pennsylvania Magazine* that he composed "Common Sense," with an effect "which has rarely been produced by types or paper in any age or country." [19] Leaving the *Pennsylvania Magazine,* he joined the army "as a sort of itinerant writer, of which his pen was an appendage, almost as necessary and formidable as its cannon." When the spirit of the colonists drooped he revived them with his

[18] Moncure D. Conway, *Life of Thomas Paine,* 47.
[19] Cheetham, *Life of Thomas Paine,* 55.

writings, the first number of "The Crisis" appearing in December, 1776, beginning with the famous lines: "These are the times that try men's souls." In January, 1777, the second number was published, and the remaining six appeared at irregular intervals. When the first number reached England, it was ordered to be burned by the common hangman near Westminster Hall, but a mob assembled and put out the fire by throwing on it dead dogs and cats.

The lot of the patriot editors was not always the happiest, but it had its later compensations. When the British took New York, Holt was obliged to flee with his presses to Esopus (Kingston), which then became the seat of the New York government. When this place was taken and burned by the British, October 16, 1777,[20] he fled with the government. Indeed, George Clinton, the Governor, and Holt with his printing press (he had now been made Provincial printer), practically constituted the government. As long as there was a printing press and a rowboat to take it away in, the government of New York was non-capturable.

Poughkeepsie was the next official resting place. Here Holt issued his paper regularly until January 6, 1782, when he announced that "as the people have been greatly inconvenienced because they have not known what laws have been passed in the past few years" he had acceded to the request of those in authority and would discontinue the publication of his paper for the time being, in order that he might devote his time to the printing of the laws.

He promised that when the paper was resumed it should be better than it had ever been and parenthetically observed that the period of non-publication would give

[20] *Public Papers of George Clinton*, ii, 457.

those who were behind in their subscriptions an opportunity to catch up. [21]

The evacuation of Boston by the British, early in the war, allowed the patriot journals to hold sway there unmolested. For three years, during which Newport was in the hands of the enemy, the *Newport Mercury* was published at Rehoboth, but upon their withdrawal the paper was brought back to Newport, and there resumed its original influence under the editorship of Henry Barber.[22]

The only paper in Baltimore, Goddard's *Maryland Journal and Baltimore Advertiser*, gave the patriots no little concern. Associated with Goddard was Colonel Eleazer Oswald, one of the finest artillery officers in the American army — a man who, despite his services in the patriot cause, suffered because of his association with Goddard, when the latter's friendship for Charles Lee led him to take up Lee's fight against Washington. Goddard was mobbed for his attacks on General Washington and Oswald left Baltimore and went to Philadelphia.

As might be expected from the leading position of the city in both politics and journalism, the service rendered by the Philadelphia papers was second to none during the war. When the British entered the city, however, both the *Pennsylvania Gazette* and Bradford's *Journal* suspended publication. The *Pennsylvania Packet* or *General Advertiser* followed the example of Holt and moved with the government up to Lancaster, where it remained until the British withdrawal. The *Packet* was owned by Dunlap and Claypoole and afterward became the first daily paper in America.

21 For Holt's official record, see *Public Papers of George Clinton*, iv, 548, 659, 791, 821, 831; v, 116-623-626, 633; vi, 252, 869; vii, 193; viii, 24, 33.

22 Greene, *Short History of Rhode Island*, 248.

Imitating the *Mercury* of Hugh Gaine, the *Evening Post* of Philadelphia did not move out with the American troops, but remained behind to welcome the Britishers. When Washington regained his position the editor unsuccessfully endeavored to reëstablish old friendship; unlike Gaine, he was not successful.

The *Pennsylvania Ledger,* a Tory sheet which had been suspended for a year before the occupation by the British, blossomed anew when Philadelphia changed hands, and when the British moved out of the city the paper moved with them. The *Royal Pennsylvania Gazette* was started by the British themselves, which would indicate that the advice of Serle to use the newspapers as much as possible had been transmitted to the commanding generals.

The reward of the patriotic editors at the end of the war came in the form of great influence and, in some cases, — that of Isaiah Thomas, for instance — wealth and prosperity as the country developed. A number of Tory editors sought refuge in Nova Scotia and New Brunswick and established papers there.

One or two of them remained in this country, however, and finally succeeded in living down their reputations. A "literary fair" was held in New York in 1802 and Hugh Gaine, then acclaimed the oldest living bookseller, was chosen President of the bookselling fraternity, showing how soon the people forget,— and forgive.

CHAPTER X

AFTER THE REVOLUTION

Critical period in American history — Greater interest in the news — Prominence of journals and writers — Press held in contempt as the representative of the people — Characteristics of papers — Bareness of life of laboring class — Russell and the *Massachusetts Sentinel* — Loyalty of Russell shown — First daily in America — Thomas Greenleaf — His office wrecked.

The war is ended, and there has come into existence a nation in which the liberty of the press is one of the canonical principles. During the brief period from the time of achieving independence to the adoption of the Constitution, there are to be severe tests of the metal of the people — it is to prove indeed the critical period in American history. It is unique in history as a period in which there was little other government than that by public opinion. The glory of that period was the adoption of a constitution that has made the American Republic a leader among nations.

With the protection and encouragement of the press as one of the fundamental principles of the new nation, its history is now one of development, and of participation in the development of the government.

With the end of the war there came an end, of course, to the Loyalist press. To a great extent, it might be said that the patriotic press also passed away — not physically, but as a political power — for new conditions brought new problems and with these problems new men arose; men who, in their cleverer use and more up-to-date handling of the new institution, made the pioneers of the pre-Revolutionary days seem small and insignificant.

To add to these generally favorable political conditions, there was a development of physical conditions, so important in the modern newspaper. In the first place, the war had furnished a great incentive to American manufacturing; types, presses, paper and ink were now manufactured in this country. The citizens of the cities in which various papers were printed had been aroused by the struggle before the war and by their suffering during the war, and had lost their self-interest which had made them indifferent to the doings of the outside world. Their conception of life had been broadened sufficiently to make them take a greater interest in the "news." The residents of the different states had come to know that they were, after all, Americans, citizens of one country. They had become familiar with the fact that important newspapers were published in different parts of the country.

The interest in public matters diversified on the first reaction. This is true after all wars. But in a very short time a few absorbing themes were arousing the people. The depreciated currency and the large debt — as well as a lack of power in Congress, resulting in that body being treated with the utmost contempt in the press — led to chaotic conditions, bordering almost on anarchy, as we see in the movement against lawyers and judges. But even in this time, when there was no rule but the rule of public opinion, and when, unfortunately, there was no leadership such as that to which the people had become accustomed, there was still such a great respect for public opinion, that, out of all the disorder and chaos, there came a strong and remarkable government.

It was in the fight over the adoption of the Constitution that those journals and writers that were to become conspicuous leaders of public opinion came to the fore. It was here that the lead was assumed by New York, its geographical position having given it an advantage which was freely used by its not always scrupulous politicians.

For the next twenty years the press of the country was practically under the dominance of two men; and though both would have indignantly resented the suggestion that their activities brought them within the classification of active journalists, of one of them at least, Alexander Hamilton, it is true that his public career after the war was as closely identified with the journalism of the country as were the men who actually earned their living by writing for and printing the newspapers.

With the prejudices against the trade — prejudices inherited from England, the social ideas of which still dominated the nation — it was understandable that men who prided themselves on being "gentlemen" should disown too close an association with a calling such as "Printing," which had yet to live down its early stigma.

What is to-day regarded as the very strength of the press was then a great cause of its being held in some contempt — it actually represented the people, the "rabble"; it came from the people, its mechanical artificers were of the people, and therefore, except when it was properly "led," it was not considered a power for good. This distrust of the masses was not shown in the attitude of the statesmen of the period toward the press alone — it was, as one writer has said, a characteristic of the eighteenth century. It was a widespread belief that the commonwealth must depend on the "powers, estates and vested interests" rather than on the masses of the people, who were a danger unless "led or repressed." [1]

The prejudice was active, not only with the men who made use of journalism in developing the policies of their respective parties, but among the men of later generations who undertook to write the history of their country; and, as we shall see, a century was to pass before journalism came to be considered as having a professional status sufficient to entitle it to a place in the curriculum of a reputable university.

When the end of the revolutionary struggle came, there were forty-three papers in the colonies. The three best of these were the *Connecticut Courant,* the *Boston Gazette* and the *Pennsylvania Packet.* Their news was either very general or very local; the advertisements were matters of particular importance to the people locally. The essays and contributed editorials were of interest to those of culture and to those who had ideas and theories as to the government. For the academic and literary, there was poetry and sometimes ponderous literary work. The *Boston Weekly Advertiser* printed as a serial, "Robertson's History of America," which ran through one hundred and fifty numbers.

The lack of news concerning the country in general was due almost entirely to the difficulties of transmission. The Post-Office would not carry the papers and the post-riders had to be bribed to take them along with the letters. It took six days for a letter to go from Boston to New York, or nine days in bad weather; still, when a paper arrived in a small village, nearly all the adult population gathered around the minister while he read it from start

[1] Walker, *Making of the Nation,* 150.

to finish. The dignity and prosperity of a town were established by the fact that it supported a weekly journal.[2]

The absence of political parties gave emphasis to the two great divisions of society, i. e., the rich and the poor. Unskilled labor was paid but two shillings a day, and it was only by the strictest economy that the laborer kept his children from starvation and himself from jail. He was not considered one of the real people, had no right to vote, lived in low dingy rooms, rarely tasted meat and looked up respectfully to those who were able to vote — those, that is, who were able to pay the tax that gave them the franchise — as his "betters." He dressed in a way that marked him wherever he went: "A pair of yellow buckskin or leathern breeches, a checked shirt, a red flannel jacket, a rusty felt hat cocked up at the corners, shoes of neat's-skin set off with huge buckles of brass, and a leathern apron, comprised his scanty wardrobe."[3]

Spring elections for 1785 found the papers filled with exhortations to the people to oppose all those who were aristocrats. "Beware the lawyers! Beware the lawyers!" was the title of a pamphlet, typical of the times, exhorting them to vote against those who were interested in property and not in human rights.[4] The people were led to believe that the lawyers prospered only as the people suffered, this prejudice going so far that even the judges were notified that the people did not want them to sit.

Another problem that the people had to face was the lack of sound coinage, for counterfeiters and clippers were so busy that it was said that a good halfpenny or a

[2] McMaster, *History*, i, 58.

[3] McMaster, *History*, i, 97.

[4] *New York Packet*, April 7, 1785.

full weight pistareen was not to be found in the States. The papers of the colonies warned their readers to beware of counterfeiters and to take no French guineas "till they had examined carefully the hair on the King's head." [5]

In times past, especially in New England, it had been the ministers who had dominated the community, mentally as well as religiously. The great career of Franklin, already passed into history and associated with newspapers, and the honored names of Samuel Adams, Otis and others, led the people to give stricter attention to the journalists who began to be more numerous and more conspicuous. In turn, young men,—who, in the early days of the colonies, would have chosen the profession of minister, lawyer, doctor, or even school-master — now began to see the possibilities of training for a vocation that had the attraction of wielding great influence in the community.

Not in war so much as in the after-war periods are democracies threatened. This is shown by the critical periods in American history. The reasons are that men will rush to the defense of their homes, but on their return they are restless of their old responsibilities and, with the lack of discipline of a democracy, are apt to listen to the dreamer or the theorist.

When the war broke out, journalism had established itself as an institution and the freedom of the press was no longer a matter that concerned solely the unfortunate printer like Harris, who dared the prejudices, the ignorance and autocracy of the times; the martyrs of the past could have wished for no greater results than those which had come about in but a little over a century — a country

[5] *New York Packet,* April 21, 1785; *Pennsylvania Packet,* May 13, 1784

free from all the old autocratic ideas of the past, liberated from the old tyrannies, not by compromise, but by blood, and carrying aloft, as one of its most important standards, the Liberty of the Press. While the people gave much credit to educated men such as Samuel Adams and John Adams, they gave greater credit to themselves as the class from which had sprung the Franklins, the Zengers and such men as Edes. The success of a cause is dependent on the quality of the fighters that are attracted to it, but we are all a little inclined to concentrate our attention on the socially distinguished rather than on those whose surtouts show wear. The judgments of history are continually being reversed, while such men as Harris and Zenger have had difficulty in getting into history at all. Class consciousness arose in this period through the sense of affiliation with men who were good fighters, even if they were not of the best families or the ruling class.

There was another reason why journalism was to come into its own. Up to the time of the Revolution it was, even when uncensored and free from persecution, at best a tolerated usurper of authority, a disturber of the peace and of conditions as they were. Under the new conditions it was the voice of the people — recognized as such even by those who lamented the democratic tendencies of the times and the growing influence of journalism. Even they were driven to journalism to controvert the "pernicious" theories that were sweeping away the old order of things.

But the new figures in the field were fully alive to their responsibilities as well as to their opportunities. Not only were they unawed by the difference between the humble beginnings of journalism and the mightiness of those who had been dethroned, but they were determined on a still further participation in government, and a further elimination of class distinction.

No better example of the new type of journalist was there than Major Benjamin Russell, who, in addition to learning his business with Thomas, had served six months as Thomas' substitute in the Continental Army. With a partner named Warden, he began, on March 24, 1784, the publication of a semi-weekly, the *Massachusetts Centinel and the Republican Journal.* For forty-two years the paper under his leadership was an actual power, not in the sense that the old *Gazette* had been, as the representative of a group, but because it represented Russell's own personality and responded to his will as he interpreted the public sentiment. In many ways it was the prototype of the great American dailies as we are to see them later in the times of Greeley, Bennett, and others. Gradually, it marked the continuation of Boston's leadership of the Press.

Russell had had a good training in the printing office of Thomas and had earned a majority in the Continental Army. When Major André was executed Russell was one of the guard. As a journalist he showed at once that he had no inclination to play a minor part, and led an attack on those British factors and agents who, now that the war was over, were endeavoring to build up British trade. He put his opposition to business relations with the British on many grounds, but the most effective was that it tended to drain the country of currency, which, in those days of financial confusion, was an alarming prospect.

Although a Federalist, Russell, as might be expected of one bred in New England and sensitive to all its prejudices, did not follow the lead of Hamilton in the matter of advocating liberal treatment of the Loyalists. The antipathies bred by the war, he argued, had taken too deep root.[6]

News, in the sense of personalities, could not be carried further than he carried it in depicting the scene when his sanctum was invaded by an irate citizen, who threatened to kill him. This was a news development that was afterward to be emulated by James Gordon Bennett and other editors attacked under similar circumstances.

When it came to the fight for the adoption of the Constitution, Russell was a tower of strength in the only issue that ever gave the Federalist party any great popularity. But he went further. He organized meetings of the plain people of Boston to urge ratification; and as other states ratified, each ratification was set forth prominently. There is modern enterprise shown in his account of the part he played when the Massachusetts convention, held in a church, came to pass on the Constitution:

> I never had studied stenography, nor was there any person then in Boston that understood reporting. The presiding officer of the convention sat in the Deacon's seat, under the pulpit. I took the pulpit for my reporting desk, and a very good one it was. I succeeded well enough in this my first effort to give a tolerable fair report in my next paper; but the puritanical notions had not entirely faded away, and I was voted out of the pulpit. A stand was fitted up for me in another place, and I proceeded with my reports, generally to the acceptance of the Convention. The doubts that still existed as to whether enough of the states would come into the compact to make the Constitution binding, made the proceedings of the Convention intensely interesting. When the news arrived of the acceptance of it by the state of Virginia, there was a most extraordinary outbreak of rejoicing. It seemed as if the meeting-house would burst with the acclamation.[7]

His loyalty is instanced by the fact that he printed the public laws gratuitously and, when the bill was asked for,

[6] *Centinel,* August, 1784. [7] Hudson, 150.

sent a receipt. Washington himself directed that he be paid:

"This must not be," said Washington, on learning the fact. "When Mr. Russell offered to publish the laws without pay, we were poor. It was a generous offer. We are now able to pay our debts. This is a debt of honor, and must be discharged."

Shortly afterward a check for seven thousand dollars was sent to Major Russell.[8]

It was such ardent advocacy of the Federal constitution, ably backed up by Hamilton in the "Federalist," that brought to the Federal party its main support. While the Federalists were the party in favor of the Constitution the opposition could not stand against them. Once, however, that issue was dead, and the issue became popular control, with the Federalists opposed to popular rights, they lost influence. Party consistency, however, led men like Russell to remain Federalists, and this he did even up to the administration of Madison, when he bitterly opposed the war with England — the last stand of the Federalist party, which practically passed away with the Hartford convention. The election of Monroe marked its complete eclipse, and then followed the "era of good feeling," an expression said to have been originally uttered by Russell.

Although Philadelphia had no such distinctive character as Russell to take up the fight for journalism after the war, it was in this period that Philadelphia offered the country its first daily paper. On September 21, 1784, the *Pennsylvania Packet or General Advertiser* of Dunlap and Claypoole appeared as a daily, evidently in response to a large increase in the advertisements, for in the first issue of this new daily there were plenty of advertise-

[8] Hudson, 152.

ments but not a single line of comment to indicate that the founders of the first daily newspaper on the American continent were aware that they were embarking on a most interesting and historic undertaking.[9]

For some time after the Revolution there was no vigorous newspaper in New York. The *New York Journal,* which we have seen, during the Revolution, fighting on amid difficulties, came back to the city with the English withdrawal; but old John Holt had run his course, dying a year after. The widow and Eleazer Oswald, a relative, continued it until 1787, when it was bought by Thomas Greenleaf, an enterprising printer, son of the Joseph Greenleaf whose writings in the *Massachusetts Spy* had so incensed the royal authorities. Greenleaf had learned his trade under Isaiah Thomas and had worked as a sub-editor of the *Independent Chronicle* of Boston. Beginning November 19, 1787, he issued a daily, the *New York Journal and Daily Patriotic Register,* the first in New York and the second in America. Greenleaf's training, as one might expect, was such as to make him suspicious of the "big wigs" who had gathered in Philadelphia, and, when the controversy started over the adoption of the Constitution, his paper printed the "Brutus" series in answer to the "Federalist." He was not content with mere argument, however. When the Constitution was adopted by the state, and the jubilant citizens expressed their exultation by a parade and a pageant, Greenleaf devoted a column to ridiculing the festivity and those who had taken part in it.

In the following issue he announced that the daily had been given up, pathetically adding that those who intended to withdraw subscriptions "at this juncture of the Print-

[9] The first daily newspaper in England, the *Daily Courant,* had appeared March 11, 1702.

er's sufferings and distress will please to indulge themselves one more reflection on the subject." In the succeeding issue he tells the whole story, admitting the folly of trying to conceal what had happened. The jubilant paraders, roused more by his ridicule of themselves than by his attack on the Constitution, had broken into his place and, though he fired twice at the mob, he was obliged to retreat, while most of his plant was destroyed.[10] It is a good graphic story that he writes, the kind that editors do write as a rule when their places have been attacked or they have been horse-whipped; the mode of punishment for editors, as we shall see, varying with the generations.

After this Greenleaf naturally turned more earnestly to the anti-Federalist party; his was the first Democratic organ in the country, and the first to attack Washington's administration. His alignment with the Democratic party became so complete that in 1789 he was elected a sachem of Tammany Hall. On his death, the *Independent Chronicle* of Boston said, " he was a steady, uniform, zealous supporter of the Rights of Humanity." [11]

The crowning glory of the party was the " Federalist," Alexander Hamilton's great contribution to journalism and political literature. To the publication of the " Federalist" in the newspapers of the country has been ascribed the fact that the doubting country accepted the Federal Constitution.

In the Federal convention that met in Philadelphia in 1787, there was no real appreciation of the democratic character of the nation. In that convention, democratic sentiment was in a weak minority; the Federal union was

[10] *New York Journal and Patriotic Register,* July 24, July 31, August 7, 1786.

[11] September 24, 1789.

the work of the commercial people of the seaport towns, the planters of the slave states, the officers of the Revolutionary army and the property-holders.[12]

This lack of realization was reflected, first, in the fear that the executive might assume the powers of a king; secondly, in the long serious discussions which led to the complicated machinery by which the choice of the president was left to an electoral college. This, it was intended, should consist of estimable and well-informed gentlemen who would meet and select, after calm and lofty debate, the best possible candidate, according to "their own unfettered judgment."

So little did the Fathers realize that there was, aside from the legislative, executive and judicial branches of government, a fourth factor, the power of public opinion, that it was a matter of astonishment to them that in the very first instance public opinion reduced the electoral college and its estimable gentlemen to mere automatons.

The fear of the conservative element was that the voters of the country were so widely scattered that they would not be informed on the questions or the character of the men at issue. There was not the slightest indication throughout the entire convention that the makers of the constitution appreciated the great power of public opinion and the changes it was going to make in their Constitution.

True it is that Benjamin Franklin sat in this convention and was one of its most conspicuous figures; from him, the once poor printer who had risen to great power and authority, visions as to the power of the press in the future might have been expected.

But Franklin was old, the last fifty years of his life had been spent in courts, in diplomatic usage, in polite

[12] *Life of John Adams,* i, 441.

and scientific circles — a far cry from the simple democratic beginnings in Boston and Philadelphia, when he had been so keen an analyst of the average man's heart and aspirations.

Samuel Adams, another great democrat whose vision might have helped the convention, was at home, a disappointed and disapproving man. John Adams and Thomas Jefferson were both abroad.

No other clause of the Constitution has so little reflected the ability of the Fathers as the one relating to the election of the president. The greatness of the men who wrote this constitution looms always larger and larger — an assembly of demi-gods, Jefferson called them,— for they possessed in an unusual degree the faculty of statesmanship, and of seeing clearly what would be the results of a political act. That they failed to see the power of public opinion was one reason why the Constitution was so bitterly opposed that they were unable to have it adopted until, following the suggestion, or rather the demands, of Samuel Adams and Thomas Jefferson, the pledge was given that, as soon as it was adopted, amendments would be passed containing the essential provisions of the Bill of Rights, guaranteeing freedom of speech and of the press.

On Alexander Hamilton fell the burden of defending the Constitution, and under his leadership was founded the first of American parties — the Federalist party. The methods of party warfare that he inaugurated were to be, in outline, the methods of the next century; the use to which he put the newspapers emphasized more than ever their importance in American government.

With every other aspect of Alexander Hamilton's many-sided career, except that of a journalist, every American schoolboy is familiar. It was, his biographer states, a brilliant newspaper description of a hurricane that decided his career at the age of fifteen. He was then an orphan, of romantic parentage, living in one of the West Indian islands; this bit of writing led the principal people of the island to decide that he ought to have a larger career than Santa Cruz afforded and, in accordance with his wishes, he was sent to New York to be educated. He early distinguished himself on the side of the patriotic cause as an orator and conversationalist; almost from the time he arrived in America he was a contributor, especially on political subjects, to the *New York Gazette,* and later to the other journals.

It is for the essays that Hamilton wrote with Madison and Jay under the title of the "Federalist" that the journalism of the period is noteworthy. They have, from the influence that they gave to the press of the time, been likened to the letters of Junius, which, appearing in the *Public Advertiser* of London during the year 1765, went far to counteract the feeling in England that everything connected with journalism was superficial and ephemeral.

The first of these essays, afterward to be famous as the most profound treatises on government, was written by Hamilton in the cabin of a sloop as he came down the Hudson. It was first published in the *Independent Journal* of New York, on October 27, 1787, and not in the *Independent Gazetteer,* which was edited by Colonel Eleazer Oswald, a friend of Greenleaf; a man unlikely to be made a confidant by Hamilton — their differences, in fact, leading Oswald to challenge Hamilton to a duel in 1798.[13]

[13] This error is made by Professor McMaster in his *History of the People of the United States,* i, 583, and repeated by John Fiske, *Critical Period of American History,* 341.

Not only did Oswald and his paper oppose Hamilton and his political theories, but toward the English, with whom Hamilton sympathized, Oswald carried his opposition so far that he had been called

From October, 1787, until the following April several numbers of the "Federalist" appeared every week and were copied by the friendly papers, or by those with whom the Federalists had influence, throughout the country. William Duer wrote several, and both Jay and Madison were contributors, but the main burden fell on Hamilton. In one of the very last numbers he answered the criticism that there was not, in the Constitution, a specific declaration in favor of a free press:

"In the first place," he stated, "I observe that there is not a syllable concerning it in the Constitution of this state; in the next I contend that whatever has been said about it in that of any other state, amounts to nothing. What signifies a declaration, that 'the liberty of the press shall be inviolably preserved'? What is the liberty of the press? Who can give it any definition which would not leave the utmost latitude for evasion? I hold it to be impracticable; and from this I infer that its security, whatever fine declarations may be inserted in any constitution respecting it, must altogether depend on public opinion, and on the general spirit of the people and the government. And here, after all, as is intimated upon another occasion, we must seek for the only solid basis of all our rights."

With such words, especially when the wonderful unselfishness that was back of them and the lofty conception of duty that inspired them were known, the doubters were put to flight, but the distrust due to the feeling that omissions had been made in the preparation of the Constitution was the beginning of party strife. The nobility

the first American Fenian. He died of yellow fever in New York on September 30, 1795, and his body is buried in St. Paul's Churchyard; in spring and summer it affords a shady noon resting-place for the girl employees of the same *Evening Post* that was once William Coleman's.

of Hamilton's character and the great ability and worth of his contributions shine nowhere more clearly than in these writings, but the very political division that he created as he labored was one that was to bear, for him, bitter fruits. Hamilton, in his fight for the adoption of the Constitution, stirred many others, but none more notable than John Dickinson. Signing himself "Fabius," Dickinson came to the defense of the new Constitution, his writings displaying marked literary ability, as well as a knowledge of government second only to that shown in the "Federalist."

The founder of Dickinson College had to suffer many bitter aspersions on his loyalty, despite his great contribution to the political cause in the "Farmers' Letters," previously referred to.

In 1798, in a new series under the signature "Fabius," printed in the "New World," Dickinson took the high ground that it was the duty of Americans to forget the insults of Genet and to work out a policy toward France that would show "the proper sense of gratitude to that country."[14]

Although a frequent contributor to the newspapers, Dickinson was not oblivious to their faults, as is shown by the letter which he wrote to the publisher of every newspaper in Philadelphia when he was about to be married, in July, 1770; a letter with a very modern appeal.

Gentlemen:

I earnestly entreat as a favor of great weight with me that you will not insert in your newspaper any other account of my marriage than this: "Last Thursday, John Dickinson, Esquire, was married to Miss Mary Morris." An account of the expressions of joy on the occasion will give me inexpressible pain, and very great uneasiness to a number of very worthy relations.

[14] Stille, *Life of Dickinson,* 296.

The new Constitution was to bring new journals and new editors. In the *Gazette of the United States*, of April 25, 1789, it is stated that on the Saturday previous "the most illustrious President of the United States arrived in this city. At Elizabethtown he was received by a deputation of three senators and five representatives of the United States, and the officers of the state and corporation, with whom he embarked on the barge for the purpose of wafting him across the bay. It is impossible to do justice to an attempt to describe the scene exhibited in his Excellency's approach to the city."

The same paper also noted the arrival of the schooner *Columbia*, Captain P. Freneau, eight days out of Charleston. On board was "Dr. King, from South Africa, with a collection of natural curiosities, particularly a male and female ourang outang." As the escort for Washington proceeded up the bay, Captain Freneau, poet, seaman and scholar, brought his ship — with its cargo of monkeys — into line and sailed along with the gorgeous procession that was escorting the President-elect to the capital city.

As the editor of the *National Gazette*, Freneau was, more than any one else, to be responsible for the political acrimony that marked the beginning of government in this country. To him John Adams traced his downfall. It was this man, Freneau, of whom Jefferson said, when Washington had practically urged him to get rid of his services, that he (Freneau) and his paper, the *National Gazette*, had done more than any other single agency to combat the Hamiltonian political theories and to keep the country from all monarchical ideas.

CHAPTER XI

GROWTH OF PARTY PRESS

Reticence of Hamilton — The *Gazette of the United States* — John Fenno — His difficulties — Jefferson's estimate of importance of newspapers — His attitude toward Hamilton — Philip Freneau selected to reply to Fenno's writings — Government position offered Freneau — Hamilton attacks Jefferson.

One may search in vain through the correspondence of Hamilton for light on the important part in journalism that he was to play during the remaining years of his life. One looks especially for some inkling of Hamilton's own thoughts as to the significance of the moves that led to the launching of what was to be a gigantic political press. But there is not a word, and, considering the greatness of the tasks that confronted him — establishing the credit of the nation not the least among them — it is not surprising that his purely political activities are not set forth at length. There is no hint as to what he thought of his own newspaper activities; it is all behind the scenes, and for light we must go elsewhere than to his correspondence or his biographies; the charges of his adversaries forming, in fact, the chief source of information.

When we consider that Hamilton owed his education to a cleverly written newspaper article, and that he had seen, in the articles comprising the "Federalist" how he might sway a nation through his writings, it is but natural that when he was no longer a contestant for power, but in power; no longer a secretary or a mere aide, but an important official of the government of the United

States — his mind should turn as it did. On April 15, 1789, there appeared in New York, the seat of the new government, a NATIONAL newspaper, the *Gazette of the United States,* superior in plan and make-up to any paper then in existence. Its prospectus proclaimed its ambition to be the organ of the government; it would print the debates and the important papers; it would contain from time to time serious and thoughtful articles on government; it wished for the patronage of people of wealth and culture because they would find there such reading as would please them, and it did not neglect to add that it also wanted the good-will of the " mechanics " — Lincoln's " plain people " were then addressed as mechanics.

The editor and publisher of this paper was John Fenno of Boston, a school teacher — a man without a biographer, although it was his paper and the articles appearing therein that brought about the famous quarrel between Jefferson and Hamilton. All that is known about him is that he was a native of Boston, born August 12, 1751, and that he was a teacher for several years in the Old South Writing School, Boston. Why it was that this man — unknown in New York, undistinguished either as printer or writer, and apparently without means — came to New York to establish a national organ for the party of which Hamilton was the most conspicuous leader, is not revealed in any of the documents of the correspondence of the time, with one single exception.

The exception is a letter from Christopher Gore of Boston, introducing Fenno to Rufus King, a leading Federalist — later to be one of the first United States Senators from New York. Gore stated that Fenno had conceived a plan for a newspaper " for the purpose of demonstrating favorable sentiments of the federal constitution and its administration," and went on to say: "His literary achievements are very handsome, and from long acquaintance I am confident his honor and integrity are unquestionable." [1] It is also stated that he had had newspaper experience in Boston, but does not state with whom.

A letter from Fenno to Hamilton in November, 1793, shows that, despite the patronage of the Federalists and the national administration, Fenno was not successful, for he appealed to Hamilton for a loan of two thousand dollars. The reference to previous conferences over his financial condition shows how closely Hamilton followed the project and with what interest he watched its development and troubles. Fenno also delicately hints of one or two positions — "berths," as he calls them — in the Bank of the United States, either of which, apparently, would be acceptable and would help him out of his financial embarrassments.[2]

Hamilton sent this letter to Rufus King with a note suggesting that, if the latter would raise one thousand dollars in New York, he, Hamilton, would raise a thousand in Philadelphia. Apparently this was done, for Fenno continued to defend the Federal party up to the time of his death. That Hamilton's father-in-law, General Schuyler, who had already had experience in newspaper financing in the pre-Revolutionary days, might have been induced to assist in these practical financial details, it is easy enough to conceive. There is no doubt that Hamilton was responsible for the paper. His method of working with editors, as we shall see later in his direction of the New York Evening Post, was such that he could easily have controlled the paper without revealing his direct interest.

[1] *Life and Correspondence of Rufus King,* i, 357.
[2] *Ibid,* i, 502.

The *Gazette of the United States* was, distinctly, what those back of it might have called a high-class paper, perhaps a "gentlemen's paper." It was sixpence a copy and at the very beginning was filled with lofty political thoughts on government, a tone that could have little appeal to those "mechanics" to whom it professed to cater. It was soon in full blast as an organ of those principles of government which Hamilton represented, and which were described by the adversaries of Hamilton as monarchical, because of his expressed belief that government was best conducted when it was not too much subject to the direct control of the people.

The usual impression is that party strife in this country began when Jefferson and Hamilton clashed, but even at this period, 1788 to 1790, while Jefferson was abroad, Hamilton was already in a bitter political battle with those who represented more liberal ideas of government. In this struggle, George Clinton was the leader of the anti-Hamiltonian party in New York State, the *Daily Advertiser* being its chief organ.

It has been customary to ascribe to Jefferson's sojourn in France his democratic ideas and the democratic turn that was given to the anti-Hamiltonian party. The truth is, however, that there was as bitter anti-monarchical party feeling in America before Jefferson went to France or before the French Revolution, as there was afterward. One of the strongest exponents of this feeling was no less a person than Samuel Adams, and as he and others came to see the weakness in Hamilton's position, it was on his lack of faith in the people that they made their attack.

Jefferson arrived in New York on March 21, 1790, and the conditions he found there were, to him, little less than amazing. He was received cordially by the President and offered the courtesy of many dinner parties. "But I cannot describe the wonder and mortification with which the table conversation filled me. Politics were the chief topic and a preference for kingly over republican government was evidently the favorite sentiment. An apostate I could not be, nor yet a hypocrite, and I found myself for the most part the only advocate on the republican side of the question, unless among the guests there chanced to be some member of that party from the legislative house." [3]

During the struggle against England before the Revolution, Jefferson had always shown a strong democratic inclination. When in France he heard of the constitution, and commented on its weakness in the lack of a Bill of Rights. After it was adopted he insisted that there must be amendments protecting freedom of speech and the freedom of the press.

Jefferson's correspondence while abroad reveals the fact that he had been a careful student of the newspapers and regarded them as a potent factor in the new kind of government that was being set up in the United States. Writing to Hogendorp from Paris, on October 13, 1785, he declared that "the most effectual engines for this purpose are the newspapers," referring to the reconciliation between the British Government and America. He accused the British Government of filling the newspapers of England with paragraphs against America, the purpose of which was two-fold; first, "to reconcile their own people to the defeat they had suffered and, second, to keep the English people from emigrating to America." [4]

The importance attached by Jefferson to the home newspapers is shown in a letter sent to Francis Hopkinson

[3] Randall, *Life of Jefferson,* i, 560.
[4] *Writings of Jefferson,* Monticello Edition, v, 182.

from Paris, September 25, 1785, when he states that he had asked for the newspapers to be sent to him "notwithstanding the expense." He discovered, however, that the plan by which they were sent was costing him guineas, and he evolved the plan of having them sent in a box to the Foreign Affairs Office.[5]

Jefferson's belief in journalism as a means of establishing the rule of public opinion is clearly expressed in a letter to Colonel Carrington, January 16, 1787, when he said:

"I am persuaded myself that the good sense of the people will always be found to be the best army. They may be led astray for a moment, but will soon correct themselves. The people are the only censors of their governors; and even their errors will tend to keep these to the true principles of their institution. To punish these errors too severely would be to suppress the only safeguard of the public liberty. The way to prevent these irregular interpositions of the people is to give them full information of their affairs through the channel of the public papers, and to contrive that those papers should penetrate the whole mass of the people. The basis of our government being the opinion of the people, the very first object should be to keep that right; and were it left to me to decide whether we should have a government without newspapers, or newspapers without a government, I should not hesitate a moment to prefer the latter. But I should mean that every man should receive those papers, and be capable of reading them." [6]

In a letter written to Madison from Paris, July 31, 1788, Jefferson said that he thought the new constitution needed only a few more retouches to make it right — and

[5] *Writings of Jefferson,* Monticello Edition, v, 150.
[6] Monticello Edition, vi, 57, 58.

one of the changes necessary was to guard the freedom of the press.[7]

In another letter to Madison, November 18, 1788, he declared that the "Federalist" was the best commentary ever written on the principles of government.[8] His generosity to Hamilton is again shown in his letter to Thomas Mann Randolph, from New York, May 30, 1790, in which he said, "there is no better book than the *Federalist*."[9] Coming from a man who differed from Hamilton so radically, this was a strong statement, doing Jefferson as much credit as it did Hamilton.

To come back to his own country and find such conditions prevailing was to him a great shock. When, in addition to this, Fenno's paper began throwing reserve to the winds, it was only natural that Jefferson's acute mind should see the necessity for concentrated effort.

Despite the denials that were maintained in after years as to the plans of the Hamilton party at this particular time, there is no doubt that Hamilton distrusted the masses, and, in his great admiration for the British government, he allowed his advocates and admirers to go to an extreme that proved his undoing.

We may imagine the indignation of Jefferson when he read in Fenno's paper, a paper that was admittedly under the control of Hamilton, such expressions as the following:

"Take away thrones and crowns from among men and there will soon be an end of all dominion and justice. There must be some adventitious properties infused into the government to give it energy and spirit, or the selfish, turbulent passions of men can never be controlled. This has occasioned that artificial splendor and dignity that are

[7] *Ibid,* vii, 97.
[8] *Ibid,* vii, 183.
[9] *Ibid,* viii, 32.

to be found in the courts of many nations. The people of the United States may probably be induced to regard and obey the laws without requiring the experiment of courts and titled monarchs. In proportion as we become populous and wealthy must the tone of the government be strengthened." [10]

Against these theories the *Boston Gazette* and the other anti-Federalist papers were contenders, but nowhere was there a more able writer than the poet Freneau, who had, after his arrival in New York from Charleston, established himself as a writer on the *Daily Advertiser*. Here he found, among other old friends, James Madison, Henry B. Livingston and the brilliant Aaron Burr, with whom he had associated at Princeton. The new and invigorating associations of New York life appealed to him. He was soon friendly with the leading Democrats, and a conspicuous champion of Democracy. On Jefferson's arrival in New York he found these men congenial spirits, and as resentful as he of the political theories of Hamilton and his friends. On the *Daily Advertiser* with Freneau was John Pintard, who was also a translating clerk in the Department of State.

Early in 1791 the seat of government was moved to Philadelphia, and Fenno's *Gazette of the United States*, in accordance with its plans as announced in the first issue, went on with it to that city. Pintard resigned his position as translator, declining to leave New York for a yearly salary of two hundred and fifty dollars, which was the appropriation for the place, and Madison and Henry Lee urged Jefferson to appoint Freneau in Pintard's place. The necessity of having some organ that would reply to Fenno's, as well as a writer capable of answering John Adams and Hamilton, who were both contributors

[10] *Gazette of the United States*, March, 1790.

to Fenno's paper, had been considered by Jefferson, Madison and Lee. These men had come more and more to the conclusion that, in the words of Gouverneur Morris, "Hamilton hated Republican government," [11] and that they must have an active combatant in the newspaper field.

Jefferson accordingly wrote Freneau on February 28, 1791, offering him the place,[12] but Freneau had ideas of his own and was not inclined to go to Philadelphia. In the meantime Madison had urged the matter on him, while Lee [13] had offered to finance the paper; apparently their arguments were conclusive, for on August 16, 1791, he was appointed clerk for foreign languages in the office of the Secretary of State.

When he went to Philadelphia, Freneau took his printers with him. The plans and prospectus of the new paper were announced, and it appeared ahead of time, on October 31, 1791, under the name of the *National Gazette.* In its first issue there was nothing of the violent partisanship that was later to distinguish it, but its columns were filled with praise for Thomas Paine and Rousseau, and with essays on equality and fraternity. This at once gave offense to the Federalists, who saw that its purpose was unquestionably "to energize the spirit of democracy." To assist in its success Freneau had collaborators — Hugh Brackenridge, a classmate at college and afterward a distinguished jurist, was a frequent contributor, as was also James Madison. Jefferson himself had it continually in mind. He wrote to a friend about it, solicited subscriptions, saw that Freneau had the foreign newspapers, and did everything in his power to make it a success, with the result that, in May, 1792, Freneau

[11] Sparks, *Gouverneur Morris, Life and Works,* iii, 260.
[12] *See* Appendix.
[13] Parton, *Life of Jefferson,* 433.

was able to publish a card stating that the subscriptions had passed beyond his most sanguine expectations.

Jefferson relied on Madison to give Hamilton fitting replies. "Hamilton," he wrote, "is really a colossus. For God's sake, take up your pen and give him a fundamental reply."

It was not, however, the "fundamental" replies of Madison, but the ridicule and savage attacks of Freneau that finally goaded Hamilton to desperation. Proud and sensitive as he was, when he did enter the arena it was not to break a lance with Freneau — a common clerk in the government employ, whom he probably met every day,— but to attack a man who had, he felt, vitalized the opposition to him and given form and momentum to the democratic movement now called the Republican party.

It was in July, 1792, that Hamilton unadvisedly rushed into print under the signature of T. L. attacking Jefferson in this fashion:

> Mr. Fenno:
>
> The editor of the *National Gazette* receives a salary from the government. Quære: Whether this salary is paid for translations or for publications the design of which is to villify those to whom the voice of the people has committed the administration of our public affairs,— to oppose the measures of government and by false insinuation to disturb the public peace?
>
> In common life it is thought ungrateful for a man to bite the hand that puts bread in his mouth, but if the man is hired to do it, the case is altered.
>
> T. L.

Freneau, not realizing who his adversary was, boldly reprinted this attack and pointed out that Fenno was obtaining from various sources far more money than his (Freneau's) two hundred and fifty dollars a year salary. In return for this, he (Fenno) was trying to poison the minds of the people against democracy and Freneau declared that the reader must judge who was the culpable man — himself or Fenno.

The answer to this defense by Freneau came from Hamilton, in a letter signed "An American," in which Jefferson was directly attacked. To this Freneau replied by publishing an affidavit, asserting that Jefferson was not responsible for his paper nor had he ever written a line for it. The fight was now on in bitter earnest. It was at this time that Fenno wrote to Hamilton stating that he was in financial straits.

The bitterness of the fight between the Secretary of State and the Secretary of the Treasury grew to be so uncomfortable for the President, that Washington endeavored to end the bickering between the two members of his cabinet, and asked them, in the name of their country, to cease.

Jefferson's reply to the President very frankly stated his own relations with Freneau, and with equal frankness expressed his belief that it was a patriotic service to give a small position to a man of Freneau's talent, especially when he was so bitterly opposed to the dangerous ideas for which Fenno stood.

What made Jefferson more determined not to withdraw his protection from Freneau was the fact that the country was responding to the appeals of the *National Gazette*. Freneau's paper had now become the leading paper of America, and the humbler Democratic sheets throughout the country, especially in the south, looked to him as to an oracle.

CHAPTER XII

THE EDITOR AND THE GOVERNMENT

Citizen Genet — Freneau's espousal of his cause — Hamilton and the "No Jacobin" papers — Noah Webster and the *Minerva* — William Cobbett — His attack on Callender — Lawsuit cause of his return to England — Benjamin Franklin Bache — Criticism of Washington — Encounter between Fenno and Bache — President's farewell address — Bache's abusiveness leads to wrecking of his office — William Duane and the *Aurora*.

Such was the condition in January, 1793, when, as a contemporary irreverently put it, "Louis Capet lost his caput" and France became a republic. Citizen Genet, ambassador of the new government, arrived in this country and brought with him a new issue — Genet expected America to declare war on England. The people were, to a large extent, in sympathy with France, and Freneau, to whose republican heart the French cause was dear — moreover, he was a Frenchman by descent — espoused the cause of Genet most fervently. Genet's actions, however, brought down on him the disapproval of the administration and aroused against him the Hamilton party. President Washington decided that this was no time for gratitude, and by proclamation called for a neutral course. The friends of Genet and of republican France bitterly protested and Freneau openly addressed the President.

"Sir," said the editor to the President, "Sir, let not, I beseech you, the opiate of sycophancy, administered by interested and designing men, lull you into fatal lethargy at this awful moment. Consider that a first magistrate in every country is no other than a public servant whose conduct is to be governed by the will of the people." [1]

Nor did Freneau stop there; he defended Genet against the President: "Why all this outcry," he asked, "against Mr. Genet, for saying he would appeal to the people? Is the President a consecrated character that an appeal from him must be considered criminal? What is the legislature of the union but the people in congress assembled? And is it an affront to appeal to them? The minister of France, I hope, will act with firmness and with spirit. The people are his friends, or rather the friends of France, and he will have nothing to apprehend, for as yet the people are sovereign in the United States. Too much complacency is an injury done his cause, for as every advantage is already taken of France (not by the people) further condescension may lead to further abuse. If one of the leading features of our government is pusillanimity, when the British lion shows his teeth, let France and her minister act as becomes the dignity and justice of their cause and the honor and faith of nations." [2]

This effrontery led Washington to send for Jefferson and practically to demand that Freneau be dismissed from the State Department. It was then that Washington declared that "that rascal Freneau" had been trying to use him as a distributing agent for his newspaper by sending him three copies every day, and that he (Washington) "would rather be on his farm than be made emperor of the world."

After his interview with the President, Jefferson recorded in his Anas his own impressions. Written for

[1] *National Gazette,* June, 1793.
[2] *National Gazette,* July, 1793.

posterity, it is an interesting picture of the Father of the Country, affords a pleasant view of the writer and is no mean tribute to Freneau.

The President, he tells us, brought up the subject of Freneau's attack on him, declaring that there had never been an act of the government that the editor had not abused.

" He was evidently sore and warm," he goes on, " and I took his intention to be that I should interpose in some way with Freneau, perhaps withdraw his appointment of translating clerk to my office. But I will not do it. His paper has saved our Constitution, which was galloping fast into monarchy, and has been checked by no one means so powerfully as by that paper. It is well and universally known, that it has been that paper which has checked the career of the monocrats; and the President, not sensible to the designs of the party, has not with his usual good sense and *sangfroid,* looked on the efforts and effects of this free press, and seen that, though some bad things have passed through it to the public, yet the good have preponderated immensely." [3]

To answer Genet's appeal to the people against the government, and the Republican editors who were supporting him, Hamilton took up his pen and addressed the public in the papers, signed " No Jacobin," which appeared first in the *Daily Advertiser* and were reprinted by Fenno. No matter how strong the sympathy of the people for France, or how great their gratitude, they realized the justice of Hamilton's statement in his initial paper that the minister of a foreign country has no right to appeal over the head of the President. The government tolerated Genet's impudence as long as possible and then demanded his recall, the attitude of Washington and

[3] *Jefferson's Works,* i, 353.

the arguments of Hamilton having finally brought public opinion around to the administration.

Not content with the *Gazette of the United States* and Fenno's efforts — which from Fenno's own description and his appeal to Hamilton for financial assistance, had evidently not been as successful as the party leaders wished — Hamilton and his friends established another paper, this time in New York, under the editorship of Noah Webster, afterward distinguished as the lexicographer. Webster was already prominent in his home state, Connecticut, having contributed letters, the forerunners of editorials, to the *Connecticut Courant* as early as 1780. During the vigorous debate over the adoption of the constitution he had been one of the conspicuous journalistic proponents of Federalism. He was a man of learning and of great industry, but narrow-minded and exceedingly vain. He believed that he was responsible for the adoption of the Constitution. On the other hand, his work as a teacher and his campaign on behalf of the copyright law had made him a conspicuous person, and when he visited New York in August, 1793, an offer was made to him to establish a paper, the capital for which was provided by Hamilton and King, among others.[4]

As he was, with the members of the Federal party, ardently attached to Washington, Webster accepted the invitation, and the result was the appearance, in 1793, of the American *Minerva,* afterward to be the *New York Commercial Advertiser,* now the *Globe* — the oldest paper in New York City. To Webster was due the introduction of the economical device of setting up a subsidiary paper, which he called the *Herald,* issued semiweekly. It was made up entirely from the columns of the *Minerva* without recomposition.

[4] Scudder, *Noah Webster.*

The next political division in the country came over the treaty with England, negotiated by John Jay. The Republicans were quick to see the unpopularity of this document, which Washington had ratified in August, 1795. Practically every paper in the country teemed with letters or long series of essays denouncing or defending the instrument; chief of these was Hamilton's series of thirty-eight newspaper articles, signed "Camillus," which were printed in Noah Webster's *Minerva*. Some of these were written, it is said, by Rufus King and John Jay.

But the strongest journalistic protagonist of Federalism was William Cobbett, afterward to be famous in England as writer and reformer,— a man of little education but undoubted genius. In 1794 he landed in New York, without friends; from there he went to Philadelphia, where — apropos of the arrival in this country of Dr. Joseph Priestley, who, on account of his criticism of church and state, had found England an uncomfortable place, and had emigrated to America,— the democratic newspapers were making vicious attacks on England. Cobbett, who had had some slight experience in pamphleteering, attacked Priestley and the haters of England in such vicious form as to warm the hearts of the Federalists.

It has been pointed out by a biographer of Cobbett [5] that it was the repressive measures of Pitt in 1794, with frequent trials for sedition, that drove many Englishmen to America. Regarding Philadelphia as the most liberal and philosophic city in the United States, these men made their homes there, and at the same time helped to make that city and the entire commonwealth of Pennsylvania a hotbed of democracy.

[5] Smith, *William Cobbett*, i, 130.

James T. Callender, later to become a storm-center in American politics, was one of these emigrants. He had attacked the Pitt administration for its political injustices, in a pamphlet entitled, "The Political Progress of Britain." Cobbett, having had some success with his attack on Priestley, turned his attention to Callender with equal success. This endeavor resulted in his being likened to a porcupine, and from that time on Cobbett signed himself "Peter Porcupine." For a while his writings were printed as a series in *The Political Censor,* eight numbers of which had appeared up to January, 1797. On March 4, 1797, he brought out the first number of *Porcupine's Gazette and Daily Advertiser,* and for the next two years he was actively engaged in defending himself and his paper and attacking those who were against the English cause and the Federal party.

The virulence with which Cobbett attacked his opponents, and his vituperation of the French people and French admirers, occasioned so much scandal that it was said that John Adams had resolved to order him to leave the United States, under the provisions of the Alien Act — strong Federalist though Adams himself was. The remonstrance of the Attorney-General prevented this action, but Cobbett decided to return without such a mandate, and secretly sold his property.[6] In the end, however, it was a private lawsuit that resulted in his leaving Philadelphia,— Dr. Benjamin Rush, a famous physician and politician of Pennsylvania, having received a verdict of $5,000 damages for a libelous statement against him. *Porcupine's Gazette* was suspended in consequence of this verdict, and the following year Cobbett sailed for England, leaving behind him as a legacy all his virulence and

[6] E. I. Carlyle, *William Cobbett,* 69.

vituperative style, which for years was imitated by the American press.

Considering the briefness of his sojourn in this country and the short time that he was identified with American politics and journalism, Cobbett made, as Henry Cabot Lodge has pointed out, a great and lasting impression.[7] Not only was he one of the founders of our party press, but he was, as Senator Lodge says, "the ablest" of them — certainly the most vituperative. He had a vigorous and impulsive, but a half-educated, mind. This was to be to a large extent characteristic of many of the forceful figures who, in the development of journalism in the new country during the next fifty years, were destined to be the pioneers in America not only of journalism but of the country itself.

The Genet incident brought to the front another vigorous anti-Federalist editor, Benjamin Franklin Bache, the grandson of Benjamin Franklin. As a boy Bache had traveled with his grandfather to Paris, and had been educated in France and at Geneva. He gained some knowledge of printing in the house of Didot in Paris, came back with his grandfather to America in 1785, finished his college studies in Philadelphia, and, on the first of October, 1790, appeared as a full-fledged publisher and editor on the *General Advertiser*. It was not so much under this title as under the title of *Aurora* — which was assumed in November, 1794 — that the paper became a bitter and vigorous opponent of Hamilton and the Federalists.

With the breaking out of the French Revolution, Bache's pro-French sympathies were given full play, and the French ambassador, Genet, had no more vigorous defender than Bache. Whatever of restraint there had

[7] *Studies in History*, 110.

been up to this time, with regard to attacking Washington himself, was disappearing, but it remained for Bache to assail the Father of his Country in most vitriolic fashion. He even went so far in the *Aurora* that when the song, "Hail, Columbia," which had just been written to the tune of "The President's March," was sung at a theater in Philadelphia, he declared it to be "the most ridiculous bombast and the vilest adulation of the Anglo-Monarchical party." [8]

Bache's denunciation of the song "Hail, Columbia" may possibly be traced to the fact that the air had been composed as a tribute to Washington by Pfyles, the leader of the few violins and drums that passed for an orchestra at the one theater in New York, and had been played for the first time when Washington rode over Trenton Bridge on his way to New York to be inaugurated.[9] On the frequent occasions when Washington attended the theater in New York, during the time that the seat of government was in that city, it was always played on his entrance. To the irate democrats it was too reminiscent of monarchical ceremony, and the respect, shown by the spectators' rising from their seats, irritated them.

Bache's feeling against the Federalists was not lessened by an incident which occurred in the spring of 1797. He had gone down to witness the completion of the frigate *United States,* the first naval vessel constructed by the government under the Constitution, and had been set upon and beaten by the son of the builder; the chastisement being, he was given to understand, a punishment for his newspaper abuse of Washington and the government in general. The assault on Bache was, to the Federalists, a source of almost equal jubilation with that caused by the

[8] Scharf and Westcott, *History of Philadelphia,* i, 493.

[9] McMaster, *History of the People of the United States,* i, 565.

successful launching, and it was especially pleasing to "Peter Porcupine."[10]

So bitter did the controversy now become that personal affrays resulted both in and out of Congress. Fenno having charged Bache with being in the pay of France, Bache retorted that Fenno had sold out to the British. The son of Fenno called on Bache and demanded the name of the author of the attack on his father. Bache told the young man to send his father to ask his own questions. The next day the two editors met on Fourth Street and, when Fenno attacked Bache, Bache hit him over the head with his cane. Bache states that, after they had been separated, as he "stooped to pick up his comb," Fenno retreated.[11]

In the midst of this bitter controversy came the announcement of George Washington's intention to give up public life at the close of his presidential term. On September 19, 1796, his Farewell Address was printed in Dunlap and Claypoole's *Daily Advertiser*.

It was not until years later that the facts were made public as to how this particular journal came to be the one selected by the President for his historic announcement. Several days before it was printed he sent for Claypoole, the editor of the *Daily Advertiser,* and informed him that he had for some time past contemplated retiring from public life, but had "some thoughts and reflections upon the occasion, which he deemed proper to communicate to the people of the United States, in the form of an address, and which he wished to appear in the *Daily Advertiser.*" Claypoole's account of the matter is given in his own words:

"He paused, and I took the opportunity of thanking

[10] McMaster, ii, 323, and *Aurora,* April, 1797.

[11] Scharf and Westcott, i, 495.

him for having preferred that paper as the channel of his communication with the people — especially as I viewed this selection as indicating his approbation of the principles and manner in which the work was conducted. He silently assented, and asked when the publication could be made. I answered that the time should be made perfectly convenient to himself, and the following Monday was fixed upon. He then told me that his secretary would call on me with a copy of the address on the next Friday morning and I withdrew.

"After the proof sheet had been compared with the copy, and corrected by myself, I carried another proof, and then a revise, to be examined by the President, who made but a few alterations from the original, except in the punctuation, in which he was very minute.

"The publication of the address — dated 'United States, September 17, 1796' — being completed on the 19th, I waited on the President with the original, and in presenting it to him expressed my regret at parting with it, and how much I should be gratified by being permitted to retain it. Upon which in an obliging manner, he handed it back to me, saying that, if I wished for it I might keep it; and I then took my leave of him." [12]

The stepping down of Washington from the seat of power let loose the political furies. Freneau having retired, Bache had become the chief Republican editor. In the *Aurora* he went as far as a critic could possibly go:

"If ever a nation was debauched by a man, the American nation has been debauched by Washington. If ever a nation was deceived by a man, the American nation has been deceived by Washington. Let his conduct, then,

[12] *Memoirs Pennsylvania Historical Society,* 1864, reprint of edition of 1826, 265. The original "copy" is now in the New York Public Library.

be an example to future ages; let it serve to be a warning that no man may be an idol; let the history of the Federal Government instruct mankind that the mask of patriotism may be worn to conceal the foulest designs against the liberties of the people." [13]

There was scarcely a limit to the abuse that was heaped on him, the *Boston Gazette* — of December 26, 1796, January 16, 1797, and February 13, 1797 — continuing to pile obloquy on the great Father of his Country.

"If ever there was a period of rejoicing," the *Aurora* declared on March 6, 1797, "this is the moment. Every heart, in unison with the freedom and happiness of the people, ought to beat high with exultation that the name of Washington ceases from this day to give currency to political iniquity and to legalize corruption."

The indignation of the people at this attack led some of the veterans of Washington's army to march to the office of the *Aurora* and break into the place, very nearly demolishing it.[14]

After such a tirade it was more or less to be expected that Adams would at least have a reasonably respectful reception when he assumed office. The Republican papers hailed with delight his declaration in favor of popular government, pretending to believe that it came to them as a surprise. Within a few months, however, a speech on French affairs was so distasteful to them that they began abusing him with the same degree of enthusiasm with which they had attacked Washington.

The bitterness between the two factions was checked for a short time by a power before which both had to bow. In the early summer and fall of 1798 there was a recurrence of yellow fever in which the newspaper offices

[13] December 23, 1796.

[14] *Aurora*. March, 1797.

of the city suffered severely, losing in all sixty-two persons, among them being both Fenno and Bache. The death of the latter brought to the front William Duane, one of the most powerful of the early political editors.

Duane was born in the northern part of New York, in 1760. His father died shortly after. His mother, after trying to live in Philadelphia and Baltimore, had gone to Ireland. A dispute with his mother over his marriage — she was a woman in comfortable circumstances — led to his determining to learn some business as a means of livelihood, and he turned to printing. After working for a while in London he went to Calcutta, and there published a newspaper which for a while was very successful. A bold criticism of the East India Company, however, led to his being forcibly put aboard ship and sent to England, while his property in India was confiscated. For some time he was a parliamentary reporter for the *General Advertiser* of London, now known as the *London Times,* but the refusal on the part of the authorities to take any interest in his ill-treatment in India so disgusted him that he finally determined to return to the United States; he arrived here in 1796. He obtained employment as one of the editors of the *Aurora,* and after Bache's death conducted the paper for the widow, whom he later married.

It was against Duane as much as any single individual that the Alien and Sedition laws were directed by the Adams Administration, a fact that makes Duane a singularly interesting person, as the passage and enforcement of those laws led to John Adams' retirement to private life and contributed more than any other event to the passing of the Federalist party.

CHAPTER XIII

ADAMS AND THE ALIEN AND SEDITION LAWS

Attitude of the new President — The control of the press — Oppressive laws — Severity of penalties provided for violation — The President's responsibility — Trial of Duane — Dr. Thomas Cooper — His Defense — Duane's later history — The *Boston Chronicle* indicted — Laws defended by Oliver Wolcott.

Having followed the career of John Adams in the pre-Revolutionary days, when, with Sam Adams, he made the *Boston Gazette* the official organ of the patriots, the student of journalism might well expect that his administration of the office of President of the United States would be marked with a distinctive course in the matter of the Fourth Estate. And so it was, for in the second year of his term there were passed laws, intended to shackle the press and oppress the editors, that aroused a spirit of indignation that contributed not only to his own downfall but to the extinction of his party.

To understand the character of Adams, we must recall that, even at the time when the Massachusetts *Spy* and the *Boston Gazette* were vigorously fighting in the cause of the Revolutionists, he was not the exponent of an entirely unshackled press. In one of his interesting and most illuminating letters, written at that time to his wife, he declared that it was a pity that the papers were not more guided and controlled. Even then he overlooked the fact that the fight for independence was a fight against that very guidance and control, the absence of which he lamented. In this casual expression one sees the germ of the Alien and Sedition Laws which brought about his downfall.

It has been said in his defense — in fact, it was said by Adams himself — that these notorious laws originated not with him but with Hamilton and his friends. However true this may be, they could never have been the laws of the land, had it not been for Adams. The fact is that this famous legislation grew out of the failure of Adams and other Federalists to properly understand public sentiment.

The exposure of the famous X. Y. Z. dispatches, showing an attempt on the part of Talleyrand and his friends in Paris to hold up the ambassador of this government for money, brought to Adams and the Federalists strong popular support in 1798, and turned national sympathy away from the French party. Republicanism was at its ebb; New England was carried in phalanx by the Federal Americans, as they called themselves, and John Jay was re-elected governor of New York by more than 2,000 votes over Livingston. Newspapers that had been neutral began to support the administration, while the *Aurora* and other strong Republican papers suffered heavily in circulation.[1]

For a brief time Adams was the hero of the hour. It was then, in what now seems a moment of madness, that the Federalist leaders conceived the Alien and Sedition acts — aimed, because of the unpopularity of France, against French ideas, and particularly at "Popular Liberty and free speech."[2]

Jefferson, from the vantage ground of the Vice-presidency, was closely watching his opponents in their hour of

[1] Schouler, *History of the United States,* i, 400.
[2] *Ibid,* 404.

triumph. To Madison he sent word that this onslaught on the principles he held dear was about to occur.

"One of the war party," he wrote, "in a fit of unguarded passion, declared some time ago that they would pass the Citizens' Bill, the Alien Bill and a Sedition Bill. Accordingly, some days ago Cort laid a motion on the table of the House of Representatives for modifying the Citizen Law. Other threats pointed at Gallatin, and it is believed they will endeavor to reach him by this bill. Yesterday, Hillhouse laid on the table of the Senate a motion for giving power to send away suspected aliens. . . . There is now only wanting to accomplish the whole declaration before mentioned, the Sedition bill, which we shall certainly soon see proposed. The object of that is the suppression of the Whig press. Bache has been particularly named."

The Alien act, which has been characterized as "without parallel in American legislation," permitted the President to order out of the country all such aliens as he should deem "dangerous to the peace and safety of the United States." Any alien who was found in the country after receiving such an order was liable to imprisonment for three years.

The Sedition act of July 14, 1798, made it a high misdemeanor, punishable by a fine of $5,000 and five years' imprisonment, for persons to unlawfully combine or conspire against the government, or to write, print, publish or quote any false scandal or scurrilous writings against the government of the United States, the President or either House of Congress. Through the efforts of Bayard, a Federalist at that, an amendment was added, amending the common law of libel by permitting the truth of the matter contained in the publication to be given in evidence as a good defense. It will be recalled that this contention, revolutionary in law, was first made in this country by Andrew Hamilton at the trial of John Peter Zenger. But at the time that this amendment was put on the books of the United States Government, it was accepted in only two states, and it was not until after Alexander Hamilton's own great defense of Harry Croswell, as we shall see later, that, by enactment of the Legislature, such a defense was made possible in the State of New York.

The historian Schouler calls attention to the fact that the Alien and Sedition acts, "born in a single session," were not passed in the midst of fierce revolution nor while the country was in any great danger. The law-makers were animated, unquestionably, by a spirit of revenge and a desire to suppress and intimidate those newspapers and writers who had in the past subjected them to forceful, vigorous criticism.[3]

It is true that the press tended toward coarseness and sometimes indecency, but the Jeffersonian press had no monopoly of either. In fact, no one then writing could compare with Cobbett in either bitterness or vulgarity. There is no doubt that many of the leading editors had been exiled from foreign countries, and the scurrility with which they handled one another was such that at the seat of government "hardly a week passed without a scuffle in which one at least of the leading editors was concerned."[4]

What particularly enraged the Republicans when the laws were passed, was the fact that the juries summoned by the marshal were all Federalists, and only Federalists were selected to try those who were indicted. Ten Republican editors and printers were tried and convicted

[3] *History of the United States,* i, 411.

[4] Wharton, *State Trials,* 23.

under the Sedition act, and many others were tried but not convicted.[5]

It is stated, and doubtless the statement is true, that "Mr. Adams' participation respective to the Alien and Sedition laws was confined to his official act of signature."[6] But this in no way excuses him, for by his very signature he made the acts his own. Had his previous utterances been of a more democratic nature, it would not have been possible to have fastened on him the odium for this political mistake. Moreover, his active interest in prosecutions under the Alien and Sedition acts shows that he welcomed this unpopular legislation. It was to him that Pickering, the Secretary of State, gave a thoroughly Federalist description of Duane.

"The editor of the *Aurora,* William Duane," he wrote to the President, "pretends that he is an AMERICAN CITIZEN, saying that he was born in Vermont, but was, when a child, taken back with his parents to Ireland, where he was educated. But I understand the facts to be, that he went from America prior to our revolution, remaining in the British dominions till after the peace, went to the British East Indies, where he committed or was charged with some crime, and returned to Great Britain, from whence, within three or four years past, he came to this country to stir up sedition and work other mischief. I presume, therefore, that he is really a British subject, and, as an alien, liable to be banished from the United States. He has lately set himself up to be the captain of a company of volunteers, whose distinguishing badges are a plume of cock-neck feathers and a small black cockade with a large eagle. He is doubtless a United Irishman, and the company is probably formed to oppose the au-

[5] Bassett, *Federalist System,* 264.
[6] *Works of John Adams,* i, 562.

thority of the government; and in case of war and invasion by the French, to join them." [7]

"The matchless effrontery of this Duane," wrote back Adams in August, 1799, "merits the execution of the Alien Law. I am very willing to try its strength on him." [8] This is hardly the temper of a guileless President being imposed on by the wicked Hamilton, as some of his biographers picture him.

Duane absorbed much of the attention of the distinguished President and his Secretary of State, all of which would go to show that they were as eager to prosecute under the Alien and Sedition Acts as any of the Federalist Congressmen had been to put them upon the books. In Duane's case Adams felt a particular interest, for he afterwards said that Bache and Duane had directed their criticism against him, not because of the principles he was identified with, but because he had, in his negotiations with France, antagonized Dr. Franklin, who had come to hate him.[9]

Not even the presence of yellow fever, which was again severe in 1799, prevented the furious political war. To add to this, the passage of the Alien and Sedition Laws led to disorder, not only in Philadelphia but in other sections of the country. Duane, who had taken an active part in the endeavor to have petitions signed for the repeal of the laws, was indicted for seditious writings. Several months later he was set upon and beaten. Democrats gathered around the office of the *Aurora*, ready to fight those who had attacked Duane, if they returned. One Democrat visited the office of the younger Fenno, editor of the *Gazette*, and assaulted him.[10]

[7] *Works of John Adams*, ix, 4.
[8] *Ibid*, ix, 5.
[9] *Ibid*, ix, 619.
[10] Scharf and Westcott, *History of Philadelphia*, i, 497.

Shortly after the trial of Duane, Dr. Thomas Cooper was arrested for criticism of the government under the provisions of the Sedition Law. It was alleged that he had libeled President Adams in an article published in the *Sunbury and Northumberland Gazette,* of which he was the editor.

One reads so much of the scurrility, vileness and indecency of the press in those days that it is but fair that one of these editors should be allowed to testify in his own defense. Cooper was found guilty. The famous, or rather infamous, Judge Chase, before sentencing him, questioned him as to his financial condition, declaring that he would be influenced by Cooper's ability to pay the fine himself, if the members of the political party with which the editor was associated were not pledged or willing to take up the burden.

"Sir," responded Cooper, "I solemnly aver, that throughout my life, here and elsewhere, among all the political questions in which I have been concerned, I have never so far demeaned myself as to be a party writer. I never was in the pay or under the support of any party; there is no party in this, or any other country, that can offer me a temptation to prostitute my pen. If there are any persons here who are acquainted with what I have published, they must feel and be satisfied that I have had higher and better motives than a party could suggest. I have written, to the best of my ability, what I seriously thought would conduce to the general good of mankind. The exertions of my talents, such as they are, have been unbought, and so they shall continue; they have indeed been paid for, but they have been paid for by myself, and by myself only, and sometimes dearly. The public is my debtor, and what I have paid or suffered for them, if my duty should again call upon me to write or act, I shall again most readily submit to. I do not pretend to have no party opinions, to have no predilection for particular descriptions of men or of measures; but I do not act upon minor considerations; I belong here, as in my former country, to the great party of mankind."

Duane, for whom Cooper was sponsor, has been very roundly abused, and unjustly so. This is understandable when it comes from contemporaries, or from a man like John Quincy Adams, whose father had suffered so much at Duane's hands; it is not quite so understandable when it comes from historians of this generation. Duane occupied a conspicuous and important place in American life, and it is not true, as one historian has said, that "his friendship (almost intimacy) and his loyalty to Jefferson, constituted his claim for recognition." [11]

His later history, like that of most of the early political editors, was unhappy. With the advent into power of Jefferson, Duane opened a store in Washington, in the hope of obtaining the government printing. Gallatin endorsed his application,[12] and Jefferson himself promised to help him in the matter of purchasing supplies.[13]

The various prosecutions under the Alien and Sedition Acts, together with the time he had spent in prison, had reduced his business considerably. In a letter to President Madison he recounted that, in addition to his own family, he had taken care of the progeny of the descendants of Benjamin Franklin. But through all his applications for assistance, he showed himself to be independent, and more deeply interested in the cause of the party

[11] Massachusetts Historical Society, *Proceedings,* xx; second series, 257.

[12] Massachusetts Historical Society, *Proceedings,* xx, second series, 258.

[13] *Historical Magazine,* iv, 63.

with which he was associated than in his own personal affairs.

Later in his life his son, William J. Duane, began to take interest in politics, and became a member of Jackson's cabinet. But the correspondence of the elder Duane reveals him, in November, 1824, broken down, and complaining that he had been unable to borrow any money.

One of the papers that fought the Alien and Sedition acts openly and with vigor was the sturdy old *Independent Chronicle* of Boston. When the laws were enacted, the Legislature of Virginia passed resolutions denying their constitutionality, and sent copies of their resolutions to all the Legislatures. Massachusetts, however, took the side of the President, and passed a resolution upholding the laws and condemning the Virginia resolutions. The *Chronicle* protested against the point of view, held by the Massachusetts Legislature, that denied to any of the states the right "to decide" on the constitutionality of the acts of Congress.

"As it is difficult for common capacities to conceive of a sovereignty," the paper declared, [14] "so situated that the sovereign shall have no right to decide on any invasion of his constitutional powers, it is hoped for the convenience of those tender consciences who may hereafter be called upon to swear allegiance to the State, that some gentlemen skilled in Federal logic will show how the oath of allegiance is to be understood, that every man may be so guarded and informed as not to invite the Deity to witness a falsehood."

This, and a paragraph in praise of the legislators who had favored the Virginia resolution, led to the indictment of Abijah Adams, the bookkeeper of the paper, as Thomas Adams, the editor, was sick in bed, and the authorities had

[14] February 18, 1799.

instructions to indict some one. Abijah was sentenced to thirty days in jail, whereupon the paper scoffingly announced that, although the bookkeeper was in jail and the editor on his back, the cause of liberty would still be upheld.

Another victim of the displeasure of the administration was Matthew Lyon, by some described as the "Wild Irishman," by others regarded as one of the sturdiest of American patriots. He was in the army that captured Burgoyne, and when peace was restored set up a saw-mill, a paper-mill and a printing press near the foot of Lake Champlain, and in 1793, published a small newspaper which he at first called *The Farmers' Library* and later changed to the *Fairhaven Gazette*. He was elected to Congress, and distinguished himself in the House of Representatives by declining to march to the President's house to make the usual formal call of respect.

Lyon was one of the first of those brought to trial under the Sedition law. He had addressed a letter to the editor of the *Vermont Journal* in reply to an attack on his own course in Congress, and it was this letter that led to his indictment. The principal count was founded on the following passage, which reads very mildly to a later generation:

"As to the Executive, when I shall see the efforts of that power bent on the promotion of the comfort, the happiness, and the accommodation of the people, that Executive shall have my zealous and uniform support. But whenever I shall, on the part of the Executive, see every consideration of public welfare swallowed up in a continual grasp for power, in an unbounded thirst for ridiculous pomp, foolish adulation, or selfish avarice; when I shall behold men of real merit daily turned out of office, for no other cause but independency of spirit; when

I shall see men of firmness, merit, years, abilities and experience, discarded, in their application for office, for fear they possess that independence, and men of meanness preferred, for the ease with which they can take up and advocate opinions, the consequences of which they know but little of; when I shall see the sacred name of religion employed as a state engine to make mankind hate and persecute each other, I shall not be their humble servant."

He was tried by a judge distinguished for his vigorous Federal temper, and conducted his own defense, alleging that the articles complained of had been printed before the law was passed. He was convicted, however, and sentenced to four months imprisonment, "and to pay a fine of $1,000 with costs of persecution (*sic*) taxed at $60.96." [15]

As the Federal marshal might lodge him in any jail in the state, Lyon was taken to Vergennes. The use of writing materials was denied him and he was informed that, despite the severe cold of October and November, he would have to buy his own stove if he wished to heat his cell. His friends offered to give bail to the amount of one hundred thousand dollars, but this was refused. While he was in jail he was reëlected to Congress.

His revenge was sweet, for it is said that it was by his vote that Jefferson was made President of the United States in 1801. He went to Kentucky in the same year and represented that state in Congress from 1803 to 1811. During the war of 1812 he ruined himself, financially, in building gunboats for the government.

It will be seen that they were rather sturdy characters that the misguided Federalists sought to punish.

Hamilton himself appears but once as prosecutor un-

[15] White. *Life and Service of Matthew Lyon,* 19.

der the laws that he was charged with having inspired. Greenleaf's *Daily Advertiser* had been changed to the *Argus* and was then edited by David Frothingham; it was, as it had been during the administration of Washington, bitterly anti-Federalist. A paragraph appeared in this paper to the effect that Mrs. Bache had been offered "six thousand dollars down" to suppress the *Aurora,* but that the indignant widow had refused, declaring that she would never dishonor thus the memory of her husband, "nor her children's future fame by such baseness; when she parted with the paper it should be to Republicans only." Hamilton was named as the person back of the offer.

The day after this was printed Hamilton had Frothingham indicted and, despite the fact that it was shown that he had copied the paragraph from another paper, he was found guilty, fined $100, and sentenced to four months imprisonment.

By the Jefferson party the direct charge was made that the laws were an attempt to punish those who either sympathized with France or were in communication with French patriots, or, to be still more general, those who had attacked the Federalist administration.

The defense of the Federalists showed their failure to understand the seriousness of their transgression against modern political theory; the lack of understanding is nowhere better shown than in the defense of the Sedition Laws by Oliver Wolcott, Secretary of the Treasury under Washington and Adams. The fact that censorship of the press had, in the past, been tolerated and encouraged, gave them, as they believed, a historic justification for the violation of popular rights.

"Those to whom the management of public affairs is now confided," concluded Wolcott, "cannot be justified in yielding any established principles of law or government to the suggestion of modern theory." [16]

Even Washington, in a letter to Alexander Spotswood, said that it was time that the country had laws against those aliens who wrote and spoke "for the express purpose of poisoning the minds of our people." [17]

Unfortunately for Wolcott and Adams and the other Federalists, the "modern theory" was ensconced more firmly by the attempt to check it than by any other measure since the similar endeavor on the part of George the Third.

But the political insanity of the Federalists did not end with these attacks on the press and on aliens, which added large forces to those who already believed that a tenet of the Federalist faith was the belief that "there ought to be in America only two sorts of people: one very rich, the other very poor." [18] Fisher Ames expressed the bitterness of the Federalists when he wrote in 1803: "Democracy cannot last." Dennie, the editor of the *Portfolio,* declared: "A Democracy is scarcely tolerable at any period of national history," [19] and this paragraph was reprinted by the Federalist papers.

As if this were not sufficient handicap for a party about to go to the people for a verdict, the leaders quarreled openly among themselves. Hamilton administered the final *coup de grâce* to Adams. A few weeks before the election in 1800 he devoted himself to penning a severe attack on the President, though whether he intended that it should be public property before the election is a question. In any case, Aaron Burr, of all persons, succeeded

[16] Gibbs, *Memoirs of Administrations of Washington and John Adams,* ii, 85.

[17] *Writings of George Washington,* ii, 345.

[18] Pellew, *Life of John Jay,* 275.

[19] Adams, *History of the United States,* i, 85.

in getting copies of the sheets of Hamilton's composition as they were set up by the printer, and scattered them through the anti-Federalist press. In the last week of October the pamphlet itself was released and made certain the defeat of Adams and the election of Thomas Jefferson. William Duane, writing to his friend, General Collot, who had been driven to the other side of the Atlantic by the Alien Law, said: "This pamphlet has done more mischief to the parties concerned than all the labors of the *Aurora*."

The anomaly of Hamilton's using Burr, the man by whom he was afterward killed, to bring about the elevation to the presidency of his bitterest enemy, Jefferson, is not more strange than the manner in which John Adams passed out of political life. One would have expected from the glorious associate of Sam Adams, the man who urged Edes and Gill to hold fast and not be swayed from the true path of patriotic printers, that he would have sensed the folly of the course on which he had embarked. That it was Hamilton, the brilliant editorial writer and manager, who administered to him the final stroke, shows how uncertain and temperamental were the ties. But one leaves the second president with the feeling that he was a lovable old blunderer, and a fine, God-given American, the very best of that great New England stock.

CHAPTER XIV

HAMILTON AND THE *EVENING POST*

Beginning of dissolution of Federalist party — Establishment of *Post* — Cheetham, Duane and Coleman — Duel between Coleman and Thompson — James Thompson Callender — His arrest and trial — Sudden turning against Jefferson — Jefferson's opinion of the press — The Croswell case — Letters of General Philip Schuyler — Hamilton's great speech — His remark concerning Burr — His death.

With this chapter we close the eighteenth century, remarkable for many contributions to human progress, not the least of which was the distinct assumption of political functions by the newspaper press.[1]

Theoretically the Revolutionary War marked the assumption of political functions by the great mass of the people, but actually a majority remained non-active; in fact, until the time of President Monroe, many, even of the white people of the United States,—democracy though it professed to be,— had no actual voting power. In the meantime the will of the people was expressed through the newspaper press.

The Alien and Sedition Laws were the last attempts by the government in power to check the development of the Fourth Estate and the exercise of its acquired political power. Those who believed in government by a select minority felt that such power in the hands of irresponsible persons, such as editors and printers, was a danger to the community; especially dangerous to those who were the political representatives of the old order of things.

[1] Henry Jones Ford, *American Politics*, 108.

But the Federalist attack failed; the Federalist party was defeated and, with the advent of Jefferson into power, there began the dissolution of the first political party in the country, the only one to misinterpret so wilfully the character of the government that this was to be.

It is unfortunate that those who write of this period, even after so many years, do so with some of the acrimony of the times. To admire Hamilton is to disparage Jefferson, and *vice versa.* In this regard the student of journalism is more happily placed than the student of politics, for to both men journalism is largely, and very nearly equally, indebted. The most influential conservative paper to-day, the New York *Evening Post,* was Hamilton's own undertaking, while to Jefferson's belief in the masses, and in a government resting on a broad popular appeal, we owe much of the development of the great popular journals that came later with what was called the cheap press, the press for "even" the workingmen.

The very success of this conservative press has proved the justification of Hamilton's industry, though it is never the conservative press that rules the country. Nevertheless we shall see it, under the leadership of Godkin and others, one of the most effective forces in the country for certain specific governmental reforms.

The political triumph of Jefferson in 1800 "was an event of importance in the history of the world." [2] It marked, moreover, the retirement of Hamilton from national life, although he could not and did not give up his interest in the affairs of his state. It was this, more than a desire to found a national organ, that led him, shortly after the inauguration of Jefferson, to establish with John Jay and a group of Federalists, the New York

[2] Gordy, *Political Parties in the United States,* i, 382.

Evening Post, November 16, 1801. William Coleman, a Massachusetts lawyer, who at one time had been associated with Aaron Burr, was made the editor. His opponents gave Coleman the title of "Field Marshal of Federal Editors" and he was unquestionably the ablest man in the country in his line.

It is to him that we owe what knowledge we have of Hamilton's editorial methods. Hamilton, it seems, was in the habit of seeing Coleman late in the evening, whenever the latter felt the necessity of the statesman's assistance. "He always kept himself minutely informed on all political matters," was Coleman's confidential statement to a contemporary; "as soon as I see him, he begins in a deliberate manner to dictate and I to note down in shorthand; when he stops, my article is completed."[3] A very humble note for an editor, but Hamilton was then a powerful political figure, with a position in his state not very dissimilar to that which Theodore Roosevelt occupied in our own time, after his retirement from office.

In New York State there was a particularly bitter struggle, because here were located Aaron Burr,— now Vice-president under Jefferson, although secretly opposed to him — and Hamilton, the acknowledged leader of what remained of the Federalist party. Burr's endeavor to make himself a leader of the anti-Jeffersonian party led to vicious attacks on him by the *American Citizen,* edited by James Cheetham, one of the vigorous editors of the day. Duane, editor of the *Aurora,* and Coleman, editor of the *Evening Post,* constituted, with Cheetham, a triumvirate of editorial pugnacity and vivacity.

As Burr also had a paper, the *Chronicle,* the result was a continual exchange of personalities, probably more vicious than at any period in history, at least in that of

[3] G. J. Clark, *Memoir of Jeremiah Mason,* 32.

New York State. Several duels resulted from this bitter warfare. Coleman challenged Cheetham, who displayed good sense by refusing to take the matter too seriously, and the differences were temporarily adjusted.

A harbor-master named Thompson, resenting the suggestion that Cheetham had weakened, declared that it was Coleman who had backed down. Coleman immediately sent him a challenge; the next day they met on the outskirts of the city, in a place called "Love Lane," now the foot of Twenty-first Street, and exchanged two shots without effect; because of the growing darkness the opponents moved closer, and at the next shot Thompson was mortally wounded. The editor of the *Evening Post* was at his office the next day as if nothing had occurred, at least nothing unusual in the life of an editorial publisher.[4]

It all seemed in the day's work, and no one recalled that an editor, not a hundred years before, had been threatened with imprisonment for printing; the community had progressed so far that now, not only was an editor printing his paper without let or hindrance, but he was supported by the government in so doing. What was more remarkable still, the editor now had the satisfaction of knowing that he might kill or be killed according to the Code.

Coleman's duel is a milestone in journalistic history, viewed in its relation to the Hamilton-Burr duel that resulted in the death of one of America's ablest statesmen. The Code itself was one evidence of the weaknesses of the Federalist cause, conveying the idea that the well-born had a code of their own that was superior to the laws that governed the common herd.

In 1804 came up the Croswell case, growing out of the

[4] Alexander, *Political History of New York State,* i, 128.

charges made by James Thompson Callender, whose attack on the Tories had led to William Cobbett's literary activities in Philadelphia. Callender had begun publishing, in 1795, an annual called *Political Progress* and later called the *American Annual Register.* It contained a reference to Hamilton's illicit relations with Mrs. Reynolds; a reference that led Hamilton, in self-defense, to put into print his whole statement of the Reynolds scandal, a most unfortunate confession. Callender was later employed by Bache on the *Aurora,* and when a strong Republican paper was needed in Virginia, he started the *Richmond Examiner.* For publishing a pamphlet called "The Prospect Before Us," in which he bitterly attacked Adams, the Federalists and the Alien and Sedition Acts, he was indicted; the infamous Chase, who commanded the marshal to see that none of the "rascally Democrats" were on the jury, presided at the trial. The trial was a mockery, and Callender was convicted before nightfall and sentenced to nine months' imprisonment. While in jail he defiantly continued his work and issued a still more savage attack on Jefferson's political opponents.

On Jefferson's election, Callender was granted a full pardon, his term of imprisonment having expired, but he was not content with this. He demanded the postmastership — ever the postmastership — of Richmond; when this was refused, he associated himself with the *Richmond Reporter,* filling its columns with slander and abuse of Jefferson.

By this sudden change in Callender's political faith the Federalists came into possession of what they considered the most damaging evidence against Jefferson, and it was used unsparingly, with Coleman demonstrating his ability as "Field-Marshal."

Jefferson, the believer in a free press, now tasted some

of its bitterness. Shortly after taking office he had begun to feel, apparently, that a free press had its disadvantages; he referred to the newspapers as "a bear-garden scene into which I have made it a point to enter on no provocation." [5]

On the other hand, shortly after his inauguration he set forth in a letter to Elbridge Gerry his attitude toward the press, as he consistently lived it out.

"The right of opinion," he said, "shall suffer no invasion from me. Those who have acted well have nothing to fear, however they may have differed from me in opinion; those who have done ill, however, have nothing to hope, nor shall I fail to do justice lest it should be ascribed to that difference of opinion. A coalition of sentiments is not for the interest of the printers. They, like the clergy, live by the zeal they can kindle, and the schisms they can create. It is contest of opinion in politics as well as religion that makes us take great interest in them, and bestow our money liberally on those who furnish aliment to our appetite. The mild and simple principles of the Christian philosophy would produce too much calm, too much regularity of good, to extract from its disciples a support from a numerous priesthood, were it not to sophisticate it, ramify it, split it into hairs, and twist its texts till they cover the divine morality of its author with mysteries and require a priesthood to explain them. The Quakers seem to have discovered this. They have no priests, therefore, no schisms. They judge of the text by the dictates of common sense and common morality. So the printers can never leave us in a state of perfect rest and union of opinion. They would be no longer useful, and would have to go to the plough. In the first moments of quietude which have succeeded the election they

[5] *Jefferson's Works,* x, 173.

seem to have aroused their lying faculties beyond their ordinary state, to re-agitate the public mind. What appointments to office they have detailed which had never been thought of, merely to found a text for their calumniating commentaries! However, the steady character of our countrymen is a rock to which we may safely moor; and notwithstanding the efforts of the papers to disseminate early discontents, I expect that a just, dispassionate and steady conduct will at length rally to a proper system the great body of our country." [6]

Under further newspaper attacks he showed that his mind was working somewhat sympathetically towards the point of view of the Federalists, and in a letter to Mrs. John Adams, dated September 11, 1804, he admitted that the state had the right to control the freedom of the press. "While we deny," he wrote, "that Congress have a right to control the freedom of the press, we have ever asserted the right of the States, and their exclusive right, to do so. They have accordingly, all of them, made provisions for punishing slander, which those who have time and inclination, resort to for the vindication of their characters. In general, the State laws appear to have made the presses responsible for slander as far as is consistent with its useful freedom. In those states where they do not admit even the truth of allegations to protect the printer, they have gone too far." [7]

While his mind was working in this way it was decided by some of his advisors that there should be a check put on the libels of the Federalists against the President, while at the same time the Federalists were given a taste of their own medicine.

The Hudson (New York) *Balance* was the paper se-

[6] *Jefferson's Works,* x, 254.
[7] *Jefferson's Works,* xi, 51.

lected, because of the vigorous editorship of Harry Croswell, who was an able assistant to Coleman of the New York *Evening Post* in disseminating Federalist doctrine through the Hudson Valley and up-state New York.

Following one of Coleman's vicious attacks on Jefferson, Croswell had printed a paragraph to the effect that Jefferson had paid James T. Callender to slander Washington and Adams. Croswell was pounced upon, and the Democratic party leaders felt that now they would exact payment in full for the oppression they had suffered under the Alien and Sedition Acts. The case went to court, the pack of Democratic editors in joyous pursuit, and Croswell was found guilty.

A touching letter exists which reveals old General Philip Schuyler appealing to his daughter to urge her husband to come to the aid of the Federal printer who is so sore beset by his political and editorial enemies. "I have had about a dozen Federalists ask me," he says, "entreating me to write to Your General if possible to attend on the 7th of next month at Claverack, as Council to the Federal printer there." [8]

It is a fine letter from a fine old gentleman, alive and sensitive to all the obligations of his leading position; not running off and letting the poor "Federal printer" languish in jail, as did the political associates of John Peter Zenger, who claimed poor Zenger's literary style and Latin quotations, but were entirely oblivious when the opportunity arose for furnishing his bail.

On the first trial Hamilton had been too busy to appear in Croswell's behalf, but when a motion was made for a new trial before the Supreme Court at Albany, he appeared and made one of the most notable arguments in

[8] Allan McLane Hamilton, *Intimate Life of Alexander Hamilton,* 180

his life; a speech that is, curiously enough, a continuation historically and legally of the great speech made by Andrew Hamilton in 1735 at the trial of John Peter Zenger. By Chancellor Kent it was declared to be Hamilton's "greatest forensic effort" and the ardor with which he threw himself into the cause is said to have made his pleading a memorable event. It was his last important speech and one cannot fail to mark that he, the genius who owed to journalism his education and his opportunity, ended his long record of service to humanity as he made his greatest legal effort for the freedom and protection of the press.

In declaring Croswell guilty the judge had ruled, as had Judge De Lancey in the Zenger case, that the truth of the libel could not be offered in evidence. It will be remembered that the venerable Andrew Hamilton had, in the face of all precedent, shattered this stand, at least so far as the jury was concerned.

Hamilton's Croswell speech itself has been lost,[9] but in his preparatory notes he emphasizes, as only he could emphasize, those principles the development of which in this country we have been tracing from the time of Benjamin Harris in 1690.

The outgrown dictum, "the greater the truth the greater the libel," was bad in morals and bad in law, he contended. "The liberty of the press," his notes read, "consists in the right to publish with impunity truth with good motives for justifiable ends, though reflecting on the Government, Magistracy or individuals."

The allowance of this right, he argued, was essential to the preservation of free government, the disallowance of it, fatal.[10]

[9] Lodge, *Hamilton*, 240.
[10] Allan McLane Hamilton, *Life of Alexander Hamilton*, 181.

The court divided after a long argument and the law was upheld, but so profound was the impression made on the lawmaking body by his speech, that the New York State legislature subsequently passed a statute authorizing the truth to be admitted in evidence and the jury to be the judges of the law as well as of the facts in libel cases.

It was during his attendance at court on this case that Hamilton made the remark, about Aaron Burr and his lack of principle, that later led the Vice-President to challenge Hamilton to a duel.

In the group sitting about the table in Lewis' tavern when Hamilton discussed Burr, was one who idly repeated the conversation. A letter quoting Hamilton found its way into the newspapers and this was called to Hamilton's attention by Burr. The offensive tone of Burr's communication shows that he was not to be contented without a duel; Hamilton's explanation was declared by Burr to be "a mere evasion," and a challenge was sent on June 27, 1804.

On the morning of July 11th they crossed the Hudson to Weehawken, and faced each other. Burr fired and Hamilton fell, dying thirty-one hours later. His pistol was undischarged and before he died he declared that he had never intended to fire at Burr.

Hamilton was one of America's greatest statesmen, and, despite his disbelief in the rule of the masses, he did more, not only to establish and to safeguard a free press, but to develop it, than any other man has done. The political ideas with which his name was associated in later life were doomed to pass with the Federalist party, which had been identified with disbelief in the stability of purely popular government, but his influence as a journalist continued for generations and still continues.

CHAPTER XV

EMIGRATION AND THE PAPERS OF THE WEST

Influence of Hamilton and Jefferson on Journalism — Trans-Appalachian emigration — John Scull and the *Pittsburgh Gazette* — He borrows "Cartridge Paper" — Paper-mills west of the Alleghanies — Old papers still surviving — List of Kentucky newspapers — Joseph H. Daveiss and Joseph Montford Street — Papers in northwest territory.

Never had a country greater need of human ingenuity and human resourcefulness than had this nation during the years immediately following the war for independence. In a new country, between the shore of the great ocean and the vast wilderness that lay on the other side of the Appalachian range, a new government was about to be formed, by men who were more conquerors of the soil than they were, by nature, statesmen.

If journalism established itself in this country in a way that amazed European critics; if it made progress and worked out developments that perplexed even our own astute thinkers, the explanation is to be found, not in one fact but in many facts. The most important was that in the great crisis in the history of the country and at an acute period in the development of the democratic idea in the world, it was through journalism that two of the country's most brilliant politicians, Hamilton and Jefferson, worked out a great political idea.

As we have said before, even at this distance of time, we are sensitive to the acrimony of that struggle between Hamilton and Jefferson. True, it degenerated into a personal contest of ambitions, but it was, nevertheless, a great epoch-making contest in the history of democracy, for it was to the reading public that they appealed; not to the House of Parliament, not to those alone who enjoyed the suffrage privilege,— a minority at that time — but to the reading public. Their battles in the public press influenced the character of development in the west, where the printing press almost anticipated the trader. So we find in the new settlements, those founded immediately after the Revolution, a vigorous belief in public affairs.

The thin line of colonies on the Atlantic coast had scarcely thrown off the British rule in 1783 when their power, influence and territorial aggrandizement began to develop in a way that was to make the next hundred years far more remarkable than the century just closed. With the end of the Revolutionary War, the country back of the Appalachian mountains began to swarm with new settlers, and in this wilderness the press was not only welcome but was considered a necessary symbol of the dignity of the settlement.

One of the reasons for the emigration after the Revolution was the fact that, for the poor working classes, life was but a miserable existence. They were daily in sharp contrast with those who had plenty. The stories of fertile fields, of easy and independent living, were attractive. Conditions in the wilderness could not be worse than they were in the so-called civilized places, and so these sons of hardy settlers packed their goods and chattels and trekked west.[1]

Two wagon roads penetrated the great wilderness that lay back of the thirteen colonies, one through Philadelphia to Pittsburgh and the other from the Potomac to the Monongahela. A third load led through Virginia

[1] McMaster, *History of the United States,* i, 70.

southwesterly to the Holston River and Knoxville in Tennessee.

Those who passed over these roads intending to farm had at least good prospects, but the printers who decided to cast their fortunes with the settlers beyond the mountains faced the probability of failure, for there was nothing to advertise. Even in the centers of western population, money was scarce and barter was still the principal mode of exchange.

The principal road had been completed in 1785, leading from Philadelphia, then the metropolis of the nation, to the forks of the Ohio,— a distance of three hundred miles. An express line of Conestoga wagons passed to and fro on this turnpike, and paper, type, ink and presses had to be transported over it, at the rate of six dollars a hundredweight.

Pittsburgh, at that time the frontier of civilization, was a shabby little river port with a population not exceeding three hundred souls, in less than forty log houses scattered along the levee where many flatboats and river craft waited to carry the immigrants and their goods into the western country.

To this uninviting settlement, with a noble purpose went John Scull, a Quaker boy of twenty-one and a true pioneer. He had seen the chaotic conditions in the country and had decided that it would be a fine thing to print and publish a journal that would arouse the western country to the necessity of standing by the union. He had come west with that idea in mind and on July 29, 1786, the *Pittsburgh Gazette* was printed. Following a historic precedent, Scull — who was known as " the handsome young man with the white hat," [2] — eked

[2] W. H. Venable, *Beginnings of Literary Culture in the Ohio Valley.*

out a livelihood by serving as postmaster of the port.

An ardent Federalist, he did the job he had set out to do. Even later he stood by the government so steadfastly during the Whiskey Insurrection that the local faction placed him under arrest. "It is difficult to estimate the services these men performed for the Community," says the historian of Pittsburgh, speaking of Scull and his son and successor. [3]

We get an inkling of the difficulties that beset the young printer — in addition to the disorganization that preceded the adoption of the Constitution — from a letter addressed by him to the commandant of the fort, asking for the loan of some paper with which to print his journal, none having arrived from the East. The commandant obligingly lent him "twenty-seven quires of cartridge paper."

While the *Gazette* was a Federal organ, it was liberally conducted, for Scull permitted H. H. Brackenridge to put forth the Jeffersonian ideas at some length. But the anti-Federalists felt that they were not properly supported in this section and in 1798 a paper called the *Herald of Liberty* was brought out at Washington, Pennsylvania, under the management of John D. Israel. This was followed two years later by one at Pittsburgh called the *Tree of Liberty*.

So pressing was the necessity for a paper-mill that one was established in 1793, at the Kentucky hamlet of Royal Spring. The second paper-mill west of the Alleghanies was established in 1796, but it was not until 1820 that a type foundry was established in the trans-Alleghany region. Although the pioneer journalists were apt to be adventurers and "frequently unsuccessful as business managers," they were, in the main, men who had to be

[3] Killikelly, *History of Pittsburgh*, 485.

reckoned with and men who, in addition to winning prominence in the political field, saw the business side of life, and the necessity for developing it.[4] The promptness with which they started paper-mills and type foundries was evidence that the printers were not content to be merely the mental feeders of the new country.

The *Pittsburgh Gazette* recently celebrated its one hundred and twenty-fifth anniversary. On that occasion it printed the names of the papers which antedated it and which, at that time, were still in existence,—a notable list:

The Courant, Hartford, Conn., 1764
The Connecticut Herald and Weekly Journal, New Haven, 1766
The Chronicle, Augusta, Ga., 1785
The Advertiser, Portland, Maine, 1785
The Maryland Gazette, Annapolis, 1745
The American, Baltimore, 1773
The Hampshire Gazette, Northampton, Mass., 1786
The Register and Mercury, Salem, Mass., 1768
The Journal, Elizabeth, N. J., 1779
The Gazette, Hudson, N. Y., 1785
The Eagle, Poughkeepsie, N. Y., 1785
The Philadelphia North American, 1728
The Saturday Evening Post, Philadelphia, 1728
The Mercury, Newport, R. I., 1758
The News and Courier, Charleston, S. C., 1732
The Journal, Windsor, Vt., 1783
The Gazette, Alexandria, Va., 1780
The New Hampshire Gazette, Portsmouth, 1756

The second paper west of the Alleghanies was established in Kentucky as a political necessity. Kentucky was then a part of Virginia, and there was an earnest movement on foot to separate it from the mother state. At a convention held in Danville in 1785, it was resolved that "to insure unanimity in the opinion of the people,

[4] Thwaites, *Proceedings of the Antiquarian Society,* xix, 350.

respecting the propriety of separating the district of Kentucky from Virginia, and forming a separate government, and to give publicity to the proceedings of the convention, it is deemed essential to have a printing press." [5] Here, in the wilderness, we see how strong was the idea that "publicity" was an essential of popular government.

Lexington, the most important town west of the mountains, offered inducements in the way of free land to the printers. John Bradford brought a printing press down the river on a flat-boat, had some type cut out of dogwood, [6] and on August 11, 1787, the *Kentucky Gazette* was issued, with the following editorial apology:

"My customers will excuse this, my first publication, as I am very much hurried to get an impression by the time appointed. A great part of the type fell into pi in the carriage of them from Limestone (Maysville) to this office, and my partner, which is the only assistant I have, through indisposition of the body, has been incapable of rendering the smallest assistance for ten days past."

Despite the wild condition of the country, the demand for newspapers increased to such an extent that, in 1793, as we have noted, the state was manufacturing its own paper. Newspapers were started in every part of the state where there were a few civilized beings. The rage for journalistic expression is shown in the way the papers sprang up in these towns and hamlets:

1798 *The Mirror,* Washington
1798 *The Palladium,* Frankfort
1798 *Guardian of Freedom,* Frankfort
1798 *Kentucky Telegraph*
1803 *Western American,* Bardstown
1803 *Independent Gazette,* Lexington

[5] *Pioneer Press* of Kentucky, 9.
[6] Roosevelt, *Winning of the West,* iii, 229.

1803 *Weekly Messenger,* Washington
1804 *Republican Register,* Shelbyville
1804 *The Mirror,* Danville
1805 *The Informant,* Danville
1806 *Republican Auxiliary,* Washington
1806 *Western World,* Frankfort
1806 *The Impartial Review,* Bardstown
1806 *The Mirror,* Russellville
1808 *The Lamp,* Lincoln County
1808 *Argus of Western America,* Frankfort
1808 *Louisville Gazette,* Louisville
1808 *The Reporter,* Lexington
1808 *Western Citizen,* Paris
1809 *Farmer's Friend,* Russellville
1809 *Political Theater,* Lancaster
1809 *The Dove,* Washington
1809 *The Globe,* Richmond
1810 *The Examiner,* Lancaster
1810 *American Republic,* Frankfort
1810 *The Luminary,* Richmond
1811 *American Statesman,* Lexington
1811 *Western Courier,* Louisville
1811 *Bardstown Repository,* Bardstown
1811 *The Telegraph,* Georgetown

The failure of the Federal government in 1797 to back up the ambitions of Kentucky led the powerful men of the state, through their organ, the *Gazette,* the only paper thus far published in the state, to attack the administration fiercely, and even General Washington himself. Writers then declared that, if the Federal government did not take Louisiana and put an end to the intolerable situation, they, themselves, would make the conquest of Louisiana. It was in this way that the Federalists, by their indifference to the demands of the west, lost control over a large section of the country. [7]

Joseph H. Daveiss, District Attorney, in his loyalty to the Union, attempted to arouse the community when he

[7] Roosevelt, *Winning of the West,* iv, 202.

found that Jefferson was indifferent to the machinations of Aaron Burr, who, after killing Hamilton, had wandered west. Daveiss twice presented Burr for treason to the grand jury, and twice the grand jury declared in Burr's favor. The leading Democrats of Kentucky were Burr's friends, while Henry Clay acted as his counsel, Daveiss, however, through the advent of two new settlers, was able to have a newspaper which exposed the treason of Burr and aroused the public.

It was in the summer of 1805 that there arrived in Frankfort, Kentucky, two pedestrians from far-off Virginia. John Wood had been a writer on the New York papers and had been connected with Aaron Burr; later he had gone to Virginia, where he had interested a young man named Joseph Montford Street and to him proposed starting a newspaper either in Kentucky or at New Orleans. Because of political enemies in New York, Wood's part, it was explained, must necessarily be a secret one. With the assistance of William Hunter, the editor of the *Palladium,* who allowed them to print their paper on his press, and with materials obtained from the editor of a paper published at Lexington, the first number of the *Western World* appeared on July 5, 1806. The paper was innocent-looking enough from a modern standpoint. The first article was entitled the "Spanish Conspiracy"; it aroused great excitement. Street was kept busy receiving challenges to duels, and finally notified the public that he would file all challenges in the order received and "from time to time give a list of them in the *Western World* for the information of the public at large." Not all of his opponents, however, gave him an opportunity to defend himself, for one legislator endeavored to assassinate him.

Street's next sensation was to further the prosecution

of Burr; when Burr was acquitted and a ball was given in honor of this event, Street was forcibly ejected from the ball-room. The success of the *Western World,* however, was such that, at the end of its fourth month, it had a circulation of 1,200, which was a most ample demonstration of its popularity. Meantime Street's partner, Wood, had sold out and tried to corrupt him. Failing in this, Wood left Frankfort for Washington and became attached to the cause of Burr, who had been denounced by President Jefferson, his arrest following shortly afterward. Street kept up the fight alone as best he could, but was finally impoverished by libel suits, and left the state to work among the Indians of Wisconsin, among whom he did notable service. [8]

More than ordinary importance attaches to the date of the first newspaper in the Northwest Territory, later to be known as the states of Ohio, Indiana, and Illinois. Here were to be the most effective forces in later American journalism; here the printer had no social disfavor to work down; here he was a desirable member of the community, even a necessary one, and the character of the men who had become conspicuous editors in this section was such as to give the community that they represented a country-wide reputation far beyond what it would have achieved in the old days when population was the sole method of determining a city's importance.

The historic relation between the post-office and the printing office, established by Campbell in 1704, persisted, as might be expected in a pioneer country where brawn was the first requisite and where those with the literary-political leaning would be few and in demand. The printer-editor, in addition to his educational qualifications for the postmastership of the place in which he settled,

[8] Register, *Kentucky State Historical Society,* iv, No. 12, 25.

had also the fact that by training he was something of a politician and knew how to obtain Federal recognition.

William Maxwell, the second postmaster of Cincinnati, established the first newspaper in that town and incidentally the first in the Northwest. This was the *Centinel of the Northwest Territory,* issued for the first time November 9, 1793. In 1796 Maxwell sold the *Centinel* to Edmond Freeman, who changed the name to *Freeman's Journal.* In 1800 it was moved to Chillicothe, the new capital of the Territory, and in October, 1801, Nathaniel Willis bought *Freeman's Journal,* merging it with his *Scioto Gazette,* which continues under that name at the present time. Joseph Carpenter brought out the *Western Spy and Hamilton Gazette,* May 28, 1799, at Cincinnati, changing the name in 1806 to the *Western Spy and Miami Gazette.* It was six years after the establishment of the first paper that the first General Assembly of the Northwest Territory met at Cincinnati, a small settlement of seven hundred and fifty people, surrounded by dense and impenetrable forests of the Miami country.

In 1810 there were sixteen newspapers in Ohio; already vigorous men were identified with the journalism of the state. The Rev. John W. Brown, a strong Jeffersonian, established in 1804 at Cincinnati a little sheet known as *Liberty Hall and Cincinnati Mercury,* which paper very shortly afterwards took into its office as apprentice Stephen l'Hommedieu, who was later to become its proprietor. L'Hommedieu, with Charles Hammond and William D. Gallagher, later gave vigorous support to the Free-soil cause in a community which might, because of material interests, have been led to side with the slave states.

Charles Hammond was one of the ablest journalists of

the country, also a distinguished lawyer. It was said of him that "he spoke at the bar as good English as Addison wrote in the *Spectator*." He started the *Ohio Federalist* in Belmont County, Ohio, in 1813, and moved to Cincinnati in 1826, where he became the first editor of the *Cincinnati Gazette*. Later he became a man of considerable influence in the city, displaying his independence in many ways, one of which was by wearing a long queue in contempt for social usages. He was a vigorous advocate of a free press and one of the few who realized that the slave-holding power, in endeavoring to throttle the press, was showing a greater arrogance than had ever before been shown on this continent. In the editorial columns of his paper he argued on great questions of constitutional law, and his ability, scholarship, and intellect affected the character of Ohio journalism.

He was a member of the first abolition society in Ohio, which was organized at Mt. Pleasant by Benjamin Lundy. It was Hammond, as we shall see, who demanded a fair hearing for James G. Birney, when the abolitionist went to Cincinnati to begin his fight against slavery. The editor of the *Gazette* saw that the slave-owners were striking at the freedom of the press in their demands that the abolition editors must be muzzled, and his pen was one of the most forceful in the country against any endeavor to stop public discussion. He provided Birney with much of the material that was used to show that the slave-owners were intimidating and assaulting writers who dared discuss the subject of slavery.

The settlement of the land beyond the Ohio was helped by untoward conditions in the east, where hard times, in 1814, had increased taxation. Liability to arrest for indebtedness caused many to sell everything they had and to move west, to the Great Lakes and to the eastern slope of the Mississippi valley. Mt. Pleasant, in Jefferson County, Ohio, which in 1810 was a hamlet of seven families, in 1815 contained ninety families, three taverns and seven stores, a meeting house, a school house, and a market house; within six miles were two grist-mills, twelve saw-mills, and a paper-mill. In a very short time there was a weekly newspaper, without which no community at that time was complete. This was but one of many similar instances of rapid growth, the emigration fever becoming so strong that it was said that in one day in 1818, there waited in Pittsburgh several thousand emigrants and goods worth $3,000,000 to be floated down the river.

In 1817 the distress throughout the country was so great that the public were asked to donate fruit and vegetables, as well as money, to take care of the starving Soup-houses sprang up in a number of cities and men labored, not for salary, but for their daily food. Sugar had risen from 12 cents to 25 cents per pound, and coffee from 18 cents to 37 cents a pound.

The immigration that followed caused the new settlers, when once in their new homes, to look back east with critical and questioning eyes, and with strong feelings against conditions that they believed should not have existed.

The feeling that the east was not so favorable to the development of the west had a great influence in developing an independent western journalism. It was first evidenced in the debate begun by Thomas E. Benton in the Senate, in January, 1830. The opposition of the east to the west was ascribed to the fact that emigration was so great that the east feared that there would be no men to work their factories. It was the continuation of this argument that led Senator Robert Young Hayne, of South Carolina, to make a speech along similar lines, attacking the owners of the woolen-mills and cotton-factories in the east on the ground that they wished to keep the people paupers so that they might make money. This speech of Hayne was the beginning of another nullification movement. It brought about Webster's famous reply in which, meeting Hayne's threat that the west and the south might unite to oppose the east, Webster spoke for the Union.

Despite the importance of the Webster-Hayne debate, not a word of it appeared in the Washington journals for two weeks, and a month went by before it was published in the newspapers of Philadelphia; it was this slowness in printing news when the public mind was becoming active and demanding action, that led to the introduction of real newspapers such as those of Bennett and Greeley.

Between 1810 and 1820 the population of the seaboard states suffered an actual decrease, due to migration; during the decade 1820-1830, however, there was an increase on account of immigration from Europe and a temporary cessation of westward migration. On account of this lessened immigration, the newspapers of Indiana and Illinois did not increase in number with the rapidity that had marked Ohio's development.

The first newspaper in Indiana appeared in 1804 at Vincennes, which was then the capital of the territory. Elihu Stout, a printer on the *Kentucky Gazette,* went to Vincennes to see what the prospects were for printing a paper, and was so encouraged by the citizens and officials that he immediately returned to Frankfort, purchased his outfit and, in July, 1804, issued the first number of the *Indiana Gazette.*

It became, in fact, a common occurrence for the town itself, where no individual showed a willingness to assume the financial obligations, to offer inducements to printers. The consequent demand for their services made it easy for journeyman printers to find employment wherever they went; this soon produced an itinerant class of printers, who gave to their trade a character and a reputation that outlasted, for many generations, the settling of the country in which they had so striking a part.[9]

The speed with which the towns developed was a source of amazement to travelers from eastern cities. The town of Vevay, Indiana, was laid out in 1813, in 1814 it was a mere collection of huts — two years later it was a prosperous county seat with a court-house, a school-house, and seventy-five dwellings, and was the boasted possessor of a weekly newspaper called the *Indiana Register*.[10]

The founder of the first paper in Indianapolis has left behind a picture of the manner in which the settlers of the west looked to the newspapers as an inevitable accompaniment to a real live town. In 1821 the site of Indianapolis was selected as the permanent seat of government for the new state. Two hundred persons immediately moved there, and within a year Nathaniel Bolton announced the publication of the *Indianapolis Gazette,* gotten out in a buckeye log cabin of but one room, "part of which was occupied for a family residence." The ink was put on with balls made of dressed deerskin, stuffed with wool. There was no post-office nearer than Connersville, a distance of sixty miles, and every four weeks a person was employed to bring the letters and other mail. President Monroe's message, delivered in December, arrived at Indianapolis in February, and

9 *See* Charles Edward Russell, *These Shifting Scenes.*

10 McMaster, *History,* iv, 385.

furnished, for three succeeding numbers of the *Gazette,* a thrilling serial. [11]

Nor was this an unusual condition, even in the east. An elderly relative of the writer remembers the time when her father, once every two months, walked sixty miles along the Susquehanna River from Laceyville to Wilkesbarre, Pennsylvania, to get the mail and the newspapers of the large cities.

In Illinois the development came later, and was marked by a lively interest in the Free Soil movement. The first General Assembly of Illinois convened at Kaskaskia on October 5, 1818, and John McLean of Shawneetown was the candidate for governor at the first election. In 1816 his rival, Daniel Pope Cook, who favored the Free Soil party, became part owner of the *Illinois Intelligencer,* the first newspaper in the territory." [12]

Other early newspapers printed in the state were in their order, the *Illinois Emigrant,* published by Henry Eddy and Singleton H. Kimmel at Shawneetown in 1818, its name being changed to the *Illinois Gazette* in 1824; the *Edwardsville Spectator,* by Hopper Warren in 1819; the *Star of the West,* at the same place in 1822, changed to the *Illinois Republican* in 1823; the *Republican Advocate* at Kaskaskia in 1823, by R. K. Fleming; the *Illinois Journal* at Galena, by James Jones in 1826; the *Sangamon Spectator* at Springfield, the same year, by Hopper Warren; the *Illinois Corrector* at Edwardsville in 1828; the *Galena Advertiser* by Newell, Philleo & Co., in 1829; the *Alton Spectator* in 1830, by Edward Breath; the *Telegraph* at the same place, by Parks and Treadway, afterwards controlled by John Bailhache, and still a leading paper in Madison County; the *Sangamon Journal,* now

[11] Bolton, *Early History of Indianapolis.*
[12] Moses, *Illinois,* i, 294.

the *State Journal,* in 1831, by Simeon Francis (and conducted by him until 1855) the publication of which has been uninterruptedly continued until the present time; and the *Chicago Democrat,* by John Calhoun, at Chicago in 1833. This last was later merged in the *Chicago Tribune,* the paper made famous by Joseph Medill, to whom we shall refer later.

In the northern section of the Northwest Territory, in what is now Michigan, the first newspaper appeared in 1809, in French and English. The first English paper in Detroit appeared in 1829 and was called the *Northwestern Journal;* it was later consolidated with the *Detroit Advertiser and Tribune,* now the *Detroit Tribune.* At the start, the *Journal* was a Whig paper, established by friends of John Quincy Adams to fight the Democratic party. To this, the opposition made answer two years later, in May, 1831, by the establishment of the *Detroit Free Press,* one of the country's famous and most successful newspapers.

As early as 1808 the first paper west of the Mississippi, the *Missouri Gazette,* was founded by Joseph Charless in St. Louis. The place was then a mere trading post, and it was announced that subscriptions were "payable in flour, corn, beef or pork." [13]

This paper afterwards became the *St. Louis Republic,* one of the leading papers of the west. When the question of Missouri's admission to the union came up, the territory's newspapers, the *Missouri Intelligencer,* the *St. Louis Gazette,* the *St. Louis Enquirer,* the *St. Charles Missourian* and the *Jackson Herald* united in vigorous editorial objections to congressional restriction, showing that the pro-slavery element was stronger in the state than were those opposed to the extension of slavery.

[13] Thwaites, in *Proceedings of the Antiquarian Society,* xix, 348.

The statistics of 1835 show how remarkably this western territory had taken to journalism. Even Missouri had seventeen papers with an annual circulation of 720,000 copies. Illinois, young state that it was, had eighteen, as many as Louisiana, where the first paper in French, *La Moniteur de la Louisiane,* had been printed in 1794, and the first one in English, the *Gazette,* in 1804. Indiana had twenty-three papers, while Ohio had one hundred and forty-five, and was only exceeded by New York and Pennsylvania, with two hundred sixty and two hundred, respectively. Even Massachusetts, the home of American newspapers, came after this progressive state, while Virginia, oldest of colonies, had only forty papers, less than a fourth of Ohio's count.

In noting the manner in which these new northern states outstripped the southern states in the growth of newspapers it is well to remember that slavery was forbidden in the former by the Ordinance of 1787. To this resolution Webster traced much of the character of the people of this section.

"We are accustomed," he said, "to praise the lawgivers of antiquity; we help to perpetuate the fame of Solon and Lycurgus; but I doubt whether one single law of any law-giver, ancient or modern, has produced effects of more distinct, marked, and lasting character than the Ordinance of 1787. . . . It fixed forever the character of the population in the vast regions northwest of the Ohio, by excluding from them involuntary servitude. It impressed on the soil itself, while yet a wilderness, an incapacity to sustain any other than freemen. It laid the interdict against personal servitude, in original compact, not only deeper than all local law, but deeper also than all local constitutions." [14]

[14] Rhodes, *History of the United States,* i, 16.

CHAPTER XVI

SUFFRAGE AND SLAVERY

Restrictions on suffrage — Gradual removal of limitations — President Monroe's tour of the country — Awakening of American spirit — Anti-Masonic papers — Beginning of crusade against slavery — Benjamin Lundy and William Lloyd Garrison — James G. Birney — Endeavor to muzzle anti-slavery press — Charles Hammond's influence assists Birney — Lovejoy murder — Negro publications.

Important as was the opening-up of the country geographically, still more remarkable were the political and social developments that came as a direct result of the belief in the democratic theory.

While the fathers of the Republic were firm believers in the political ideas which they had proclaimed, no attempt was made by them to put into practice, in the state governments, such theories as that of the equality of all men. It was to the state governments, however, that the Constitution later delegated the right to say what should be the qualifications for electors.

The consequence was that, when the Federal Constitution was adopted, the men who sat as delegates from the states were there more as representatives of the taxpayers than of the people at large. Thus, for example, the Massachusetts Senate consisted of forty men, apportionment among the counties being based on the amount of taxes each county paid. [1]

Only in Vermont did full manhood suffrage exist, while elsewhere the voter had to be a taxpayer. In the same

[1] McMaster, *History*, v, 376.

way, while liberty of conscience was guaranteed to all, in many states Catholics could not hold office, and, in most of them, the Jews were disfranchised.

The extension of manhood suffrage was an inevitable result of the assumption of political power by the press; indeed, it was the next logical step. With a suffrage based on the old ideas of property qualifications and special religious privileges, a free and untrammeled press was impossible, and it was equally true that a free press meant the breaking down of the privileged class. The paper with the large circulation was a power in the community, and it derived its power, not from the influential but from the non-voters.

Between 1790 and 1800 religious qualifications were abolished in many states; between 1800 and 1810 there was a broadening of the suffrage and, in the second decade of the century, when six states were admitted into the union, the property qualifications were done away with in a number, while throughout the entire country there was a steady movement to extend the rights of the people. In the three states — Mississippi, Connecticut and New York — legislation was passed admitting, in libel suits, a defense on the ground of the truth of the allegation.

The generation that had fought at Bunker Hill and Yorktown was passing away. The citizens of the states that were entering the union were the new type. They had none of the old prejudices in their consitutions; they were democratic and modern. Franchise was based on manhood. If there was a class distinction, it was between those who fought for their rights and those who were weaklings.

In 1816 there was a protest against the caucus method of nominating and the Republican party was split by the difference of opinion, but even those who upheld this method as advocates of Monroe's nomination, admitted that it was not truly representative of the people. This in itself was an indication of the growing democracy of the times.

To answer this growing democracy Monroe did what no other president since Washington had done, he started out to show himself to the people. From Philadelphia he went to New York, from New York to New Haven, Hartford and Providence; to Boston, to New Hampshire and Vermont; to Niagara Falls, to Buffalo, to Detroit and then back home. He was the first president to see his country as it was, the president of an era of good feeling for which he was so largely responsible.

There was much loose thinking, but still it was thinking. In the *Nashville Gazette,* in January, 1822, the idea was advanced that Andrew Jackson, the new type of man — the man representing, not the old "dynasty of the Secretaries" but the people who were developing the country — should be nominated for president.[2] It was in the election of 1824 that the people first began to show a deep interest in the choice of a president. Up to that time it may be truly said that the elections were handled for the people. Now, with the increased freedom and the broadening of the franchise, clubs were being formed, and small groups, composed of those who had formerly been considered ridiculous as political factors, now came into existence. In New York, in which property qualifications for voters were abolished by a new constitution adopted in 1821, organizations of the formerly disfranchised sprang into being within a year.

The spread of interest in human rights was evidence that the leaven of democracy was working. Moreover, the rise of the liberal movement in Europe, following

[2] McMaster, *History,* v, 57.

the formation of the Holy Alliance and the endeavor on the part of the Holy Allies to suppress liberal thought, had its reaction in America. The storm aroused throughout the South American republics, leading up to the enunciation of the Monroe Doctrine by President Monroe, awakened the thoughts of the people, who had never taken much cognizance of political matters except those immediately surrounding them. Americans began to be conscious of the fact that they had stimulated the world. They began to realize that they had established a democracy that was affecting the world and, as they saw the reaction, there came pride and conscious power and a greater determination to spread that power among the people. Foreign visitors declared that they had never seen such a proud, conceited people as these Americans.

Part of the same liberalizing movement was evidenced in a revival of religious feeling, which began in 1815 and was coincident with the formation of many philanthropic societies, among which were the Colonization, Tract, Bible, Foreign Mission, Home Mission, Sailors' Friend and Peace Societies. It was the time, too, when asylums, hospitals and libraries were founded and when there began to be great interest in the public school system.

One of the most interesting of these signs was the appearance of a labor party, following which came labor papers in numbers. Among the first of these was the *Workingman's Gazette,* appearing in October, 1824, advocating many things that were considered radical in those days, such as free education and the abolition of imprisonment for debt.

Many and strange were the phases of the reforming spirit which was spreading throughout the country, resulting in the establishment of a number of papers, some of which lasted but a short time, but which were, in their way, an influence in preparing the public for the higher issues. Some of these papers were: *The Telescope,* (New York City), *The Spirit of the Age,* (Rochester), *Southern Free Press,* (Charleston. S. C.), *The Spirit of the Age,* (Tuscaloosa), *Free Press,* (Wilmington, Del.), *The Friend of Equal Rights,* (New York), and the *Daily Sentinel,* (New York).

Given a cause and there was immediately a flood of publicity. It was the newspaper contract made in March, 1826, between William Morgan and David C. Miller, editor of the *Republican Advocate* — in which Morgan agreed to write an attack exposing the secrets of the Masonic craft — that led to the mysterious disappearance of Morgan. Almost immediately there was an anti-Masonic party, and a powerful party it became, too, with its organs and its fighting journalists, among them Thurlow Weed, whose *Albany Journal* was started as an anti-Masonic paper.

While the northwestern territory was yet in process of settlement, a movement began there,— a journalistic crusade, in fact — that was not to end until the great Civil War had rent the Union.

All history is more or less dramatic, but the American is justified in the feeling that the great elemental qualities, the qualities that abounded in the wilderness then so recently conquered, have appeared also in the doings of the conquerors in their relation with their fellow-men. Hardly, it would seem, had the original settlers finished building up communities to protect them from the savages and wild animals, before they were announcing, to a world old in civilization and laws, the new law for a free press. Before, by old world standards, they could be presumed to crawl, they were proclaiming themselves a defiant nation and they poured into the wilderness back of their shore line, new conquerors.

And now, though the paths through the forests had hardly been cleared, they were beginning a crusade which would have dumfounded and disheartened the Fathers of the Republic. It was in this wild west that obscure individuals were to begin the war on slavery. Under Quaker influence the Manumission Society of Tennessee was formed in Tennessee, as early as 1814, for the purpose of compulsory emancipation. This society published at Greenville a quarterly paper entitled the *Manumission Journal.*

The direct product of that organization was Benjamin Lundy. He was not a practical printer, not of those with whose history for a century we have been dealing; he was not of the type of the statesman using the press for his political ends, nor yet of the scholar drifting into a journalism that he despised. Lundy was a journalist by virtue of belief in the democracy that, even in the second decade of the nineteenth century, had become a more potent influence in the wilderness of Ohio than the Sage of Monticello ever dreamed possible. Forgotten though Lundy may be, it is well to remember that it was of this obscure saddler and editor that William Lloyd Garrison said, "I owe everything to Benjamin Lundy."

A native of New York, he had, while learning the saddler's trade at Wheeling, Virginia, seen the misery of slavery, and had become so deeply affected that in 1815 he formed an anti-slavery association, called the Union Humane Society, at St. Clairsville, Ohio. He was an unassuming Quaker, without eloquence or particular ability, but with great courage and great faith in his cause. He wrote appeals to the anti-slavery people throughout the country to form similar associations, and began to write articles on the subject for the *Philanthropist,* a paper published at Mt. Pleasant by a Quaker named Charles Osborn — the first publication in this country to advocate immediate emancipation.[3] Osborn having sold his paper, Lundy, with no further encouragement than that offered by its list of subscribers, decided to start another anti-slavery paper at Mt. Pleasant. He walked ten miles to Steubenville with the manuscript, and returned on foot, carrying on his back the entire edition of the first number of the *Genius of Universal Emancipation.*

It was while touring the country in search of new subscribers that he met, in Boston, William Lloyd Garrison, then a young man of twenty-three. Garrison, after learning to set type in the office of the *Newburyport Herald,* had gone to Boston to act as sub-editor of the *National Philanthropist,* the first temperance paper in the United States. Later he began editing a paper at Bennington called the *Journal of the Times,* an anti-slavery and temperance advocate. Lundy proposed that the two should join forces, which they did at Baltimore, where the anti-slavery sentiment was very strong, and in September, 1829, the publication of the *Genius* was resumed.

By this time many out-and-out anti-slavery publications had been started. Some of these were: *The Philanthropist,* first published in 1817; *The Emancipator,* (Tennessee, 1819); *The Genius of Universal Emancipation,* (1821); *The Abolition Intelligencer,* (Kentucky, 1822); *The Edwardsville Spectator* and the *Illinois Intelligencer,* 1822 and 1823 respectively; *The African Observer,* (Philadelphia, 1826); *Freedom's Journal,* (New York, 1827); *The National Philanthropist,* (Boston, 1826); *The Investigator,* (Providence, 1827); *The Free*

[3] McMaster, v, 209.

Press, (Bennington, 1828); and the *Liberalist,* (New Orleans, 1828). But the greatest came in 1831, when Garrison, only twenty-six years of age, founded the *Liberator* and began his historic fight on slavery.

The attitude of the Jackson administration in encouraging the slave-holding power to dominate the country, and the action of Jackson's Postmaster-General, Amos Kendall, in countenancing the non-delivery of northern newspapers in which there were abolition sentiments — as well as the burning of the newspapers in the public square of Charleston in 1835,— mean that, so far as the slaveholders were concerned, the reign of public opinion was at an end in the south. The post-office, which meant the government, here directly aligned itself with the small body of slaveholders and declared that sentiments which were objectionable to them should not pass through the mails. The situation would be equally anomalous if we could imagine the postmaster of the City of New York, in which Wall Street is located, taking the attitude, in the period of 1901-1908, that the western newspapers attacking the so-called "interests" were not to be allowed within the city because of their criticism of various financial concerns.

During the winter of 1835-1836 an effort was made in every free state legislature to pass bills making it a misdemeanor to publish or print writings that could be construed as inciting the slaves to rebellion. The vigilance committee in Louisiana offered $50,000 for the delivery of Arthur Tappan, who, with other abolitionists, had started the New York *Journal of Commerce* as an anti-slavery paper in 1827, putting at the head of it, as editor, a Virginia abolitionist, William Maxwell.

To cap the climax, President Jackson, in his annual message in December, 1835, recommended to Congress the passage of a law that would "prohibit, under severe penalties, the circulation in the southern states, through the mail, of incendiary publications intended to instigate the slaves to insurrection." That part of the message was referred to a committee which reported a bill prohibiting the circulation of any newspaper "touching the subject of slavery," and removing forthwith any postmaster who distributed such newspapers. This bill, however, was defeated on the final ballot, although, strange as it may seem, it was the vote of a New Yorker, Martin Van Buren, that reported it out of committee. The legislatures of the free states adjourned without a single one of them having passed any of the press-muzzling laws that had been submitted to them.

This attempt to stifle free discussion marked the beginning of the end of inert submission by the free state citizens to the autocratic domination of the slave-holding power; it now began to be evident to many of those who had sat quietly on the side lines hoping for peace, that when that power could dare to dictate what the North could print, and when its representatives could try to pass laws limiting the expression of public opinion in public print, it was time to stop hoping for a peaceful solution of this intricate matter, or at least time to show some courage in discussing it.

While thoughtful men throughout the country were beginning to look at the slave issue in this light, and while northern editors were turning over in their minds the question as to whether a policy of craven silence was, after all, the best one, there came a series of sensational events, all within the field of journalism and dealing with men identified with journalism, which aroused, if not the public, men who were destined in turn to arouse the public.

Few reformers, says Barrett Wendell, have lived to

such complete victory as did William Lloyd Garrison, who, when he died in 1879, had been for fifteen years a national hero. His fame might be said to have come to him as a result of his having lived to complete his work, whereas his co-laborer, James G. Birney, dying before the Civil War began, failed to obtain even posthumous reward, although he so richly deserved it.

James Gillespie Birney was a native of Kentucky, born about the time the first newspaper presses were being carried over the mountain roads. After graduating from Princeton, he had practiced law and, at the same time that Garrison was starting the *Liberator,* had become convinced, from his own accurate knowledge of slavery, that it was undermining the free institutions of the country and endangering the union of the states. He determined to liberate the few slaves that he owned and to move to Illinois, "the best site in the whole world for taking a stand against slavery." [4] His education, ability and firm Christian attitude had made him a national character, and when, in the spring of 1836, he began the publication of the *Philanthropist* in Cincinnati, interest was shown all over the country as to how far the threats of the pro-slavery element would be carried out.

Birney, in his paper, did more than a host of editors to show the North that the slave power in the South was not content with holding the black man in subjection. In issue after issue he set forth facts that showed that free speech and the free press were threatened by those in political control of the south. The speeches of the governors of Georgia, South Carolina and other states were printed with the speeches of Calhoun and other pro-slavery statesmen; these he backed up with editorials from the leading papers in the slave states, and the laws passed

[4] Birney, *James G. Birney and His Times,* 131.

in slave state legislatures, showing that freedom of speech and of the press was gradually being destroyed. Every time that a southern governor or southern legislature passed a bill demanding that the northern states muzzle the press or deliver some abolitionist editor to a southern governor for trial, Birney printed the demand in full.

It was due to the influence of Charles Hammond, editor of the *Gazette,* that Birney was permitted to remain in Cincinnati at all. The *Post,* the *Whig* and the *Republican,* the three papers which represented the Whig and Democratic parties, abused him unmercifully, and one of them even suggested lynching.

Amid the onslaught on Birney, Hammond administered to his fellow-editors and fellow-citizens a stern rebuke and emphatically re-asserted the right of freedom of speech and of the press, declaring forcibly that, if Mr. Birney wished to establish a paper in Cincinnati and to discuss slavery, it was his right to do so, and that men who should attempt to molest him would be striking at the fundamental principles of American institutions. For a while this had its effect, but the paper had not been established more than three weeks when a mob broke into the press-room and destroyed most of his material.

The murder of Elijah Lovejoy next stirred the country. Lovejoy was a graduate of an Eastern college, who had gone to St. Louis and had become the editor of a Henry Clay paper. In 1833 he established in St Louis a religious weekly called the *Observer,* in which he made frequent comments on slavery. It was not until 1835 that his paper became the subject of attack, at which time he, believing that it would be better to publish the paper on free soil, moved his press over to Alton, a small town across the river in Illinois.

When his press was delivered there, a mob smashed it

to pieces. A number of citizens promised to make good Lovejoy's losses, a new press was brought from Cincinnati, and for a year the *Observer* was published without molestation.

In July, 1837, an editorial calling for the formation of a state anti-slavery society infuriated the pro-slavery people and a mob entered the office and destroyed his press and type. Lovejoy issued an appeal for funds to buy a new press. The money was raised; the press arrived and, at the request of the Mayor of the town it was turned over to him for safe keeping. No sooner was this done than the Mayor allowed the mob to enter the warehouse where the press was stored. They smashed it into pieces and threw the important parts into the Mississippi.

A fourth press was ordered and delivered at St. Louis. Lovejoy and his friends gathered to protect it; while standing near the door of the warehouse, Lovejoy was shot five times and died almost immediately.

The northern papers almost unanimously denounced this crime. The southern papers took the attitude that Lovejoy had willfully courted destruction. The politicians turned their attention to other things, but it marked the beginning of the end.

Lundy, Birney, Lovejoy and Garrison are not usually acclaimed as great journalists, but it is due to the spirit of such men that journalism is great and democracy possible.

While it is not within the province of such a study as this to go into special developments of journalism, it is worth pointing out that it was not the white man alone who was developing a newspaper war against slavery. The negro began as early as 1827 to print his own paper, and from 1827 to 1837 were printed, in New York City, the *Freeman's Journal,* the *Rights of All,* the *Colored*

American, the *Elevator,* and the *Ram's Horn,* as well as the *National Watchman* at Troy, New York, the *Weekly Advocate* at Toronto, Canada, and the *North Star,* published by Frederick Douglas. [5]

[5] Penn, *The Afro-American Press,* 25.

CHAPTER XVII

NEWSPAPERS AND THE CAPITAL

Semi-official journals — Phases of Washington press — First publications — Samuel H. Smith — The *National Intelligencer* — Gales and Seaton — Jackson establishes the *Globe* — Amos Kendall — Patronage for newspapers — *Intelligencer* again in favor — Change in attitude toward "Official Organs" — Conspicuous Washington correspondents.

We go back to the seat of government to follow, practically to its end, the direction of public opinion by the heads of government, through semi-official newspapers. Hamilton's genius conceived the idea of such publications,— papers that should direct and inform the public, at the same time guiding them gently into such trains of thought as were desirable.

We know, however, that the publications set on foot by Hamilton soon led to the establishment of opposition papers by Jefferson. The chief protagonist of the democratic idea, when he came to the Presidency, did not hesitate to follow in Hamilton's footsteps. As we have seen, he gave to Duane and others such patronage and encouragement as served to keep them contented, and acceptably representative of his administration.

When the capital was moved to Washington, that city was not of sufficient size or importance to warrant the settling there of men of weight and standing in journalism. Consequently, it was in Philadelphia and New York that they found opportunities for producing papers that would affect the public.

In a capital that was not a historic city,— a capital, moreover, where the inhabitants were all citizens of other sections of the country — journalism was bound to assume a peculiar phase, radically different from any to be found in the European countries, where the journalism of the nation was dominated by that of the capital.

It is interesting to speculate as to the differences that might have been in the history of American journalism had Washington been the metropolis, and had the journals of that city swayed the thought of the country. The attempt to influence the country through Washington is part of the history of the slave power. The failure of the attempt and the rise of anti-slavery journalism which did so much to sweep the slave power out of Washington, is the story of northern journalism.

The geographical position of the capital brought the journals, as well as the social life, under the influence of the south. This was, as we shall see, to the distinct detriment of the newspapers, for, although there was no difference of mental or intellectual ability between northern and southern journalists, the social characteristics of the south were opposed to the democratic idea which was the life and breath of journalism. Moreover, American journalism, as it was to develop, could not live where the duello was so much in vogue as it was in the south. Here and there editors of extraordinary character might be found, men who could write and shoot with equal facility, but the usual intellectual development produced no such ambidexterity.

With the leading minds of the country gathered in Washington for the greater part of the year, it was natural that there should soon be the germ of great influence there. Because Washington was not the center of population, and because the papers there were under the immediate influence of the government, no national journals, such as those associated with the names of Hammond, Medill, Greeley, Bowles or Bennett, were ever developed at the capital.

Furthermore, Washington journals having little or no influence on the home constituents of the legislators, the editors were not men whom it became customary to take into the party councils. As in the case of Gales and Seaton, however, a few of the editors showed themselves to be such conspicuously able citizens that the leading statesmen of the country were glad and proud of their friendship.

As early as 1796, before the capital was located at Washington, a weekly paper had been printed there, under the auspices of Benjamin More. The year previous an unsuccessful attempt had been made by T. Wilson, who had founded the *Impartial Observer,* which lasted but a short time. [1]

Jefferson, for the benefit of the party, induced Samuel Harrison Smith, then the proprietor of the *Philadelphia Universal Gazette,* to move to Washington when that city became the capital. Smith had recently purchased the paper from Joseph Gales, one of the aliens at whom the Alien and Sedition laws had been aimed. Gales had been a conspicuous journalist in England and had fled because of threatened prosecution for political articles which had appeared in his paper, the *Sheffield Register.* It was said that he studied stenography during the long voyage to this country; one can readily believe that he might have mastered many sciences in the time such a voyage occupied in those days. He worked as a printer on the Philadelphia papers and was one of the first to report Congressional debates by stenography. In 1797 he

[1] Bryan, *History of the National Capital,* i, 264.

decided to move to Raleigh and sold his Philadelphia paper to Smith, who changed the name from *Independent Gazetter* to *Universal Gazette.* On the first of October, 1800, Smith inaugurated the *National Intelligencer and Washington Advertiser,* which was issued three times a week; he also transferred the *Universal Gazette* to Washington, making it the weekly edition of the *Intelligencer.*"[2] At about the same time Jefferson's opponents set up a paper called the *Washington Federalist;* it lasted but a very short time, while Smith's paper rapidly became prosperous and influential and was known as the "court journal."

In 1809 Smith admitted as partner Joseph Gales, Jr., son of the man from whom he had purchased the *Independent Gazetteer.* During the temporary retirement of Smith, Gales associated with him William W. Seaton, his brother-in-law, and the two became official stenographers to Congress, one reporting the Senate, the other the House of Representatives. They were the first official reporters of Congress; to them the country is indebted for the notes of the famous Missouri Compromise debates and other great oratorical clashes, including that of Webster and Hayne. Their seats were near those of the President of the Senate and the Speaker of the House, and, as one of the perquisites, they shared with those officials in the use of the official snuff-boxes.[3]

After the war of 1812, their position was even more important than it had been before, for the British, when they captured the city, were reported to have destroyed their office "in revenge."

Gales and Seaton became a famous partnership and both were important men in the City of Washington. Clay rushed to avail himself of the columns of the *In-*

[2] Bryan, i, 365. [3] Bryan, ii, 177.

telligencer when he was attacked by an unknown congressman in the *Columbia Observer,* and it was therein boldly denied that he had been guilty of making a coalition with John Quincy Adams by which he was to be made Secretary of State in return for his support of Adams for President. Webster is reported to have said that Gales and Seaton were the two wisest heads in the country, and that Gales knew more about the history of government than "all the political writers of the day put together."

It was Seaton who in 1824 entertained General Lafayette at his home, and the two partners, in turn, served as mayors of the City of Washington. Gales was elected Mayor in 1827 and again in 1828, while Seaton served for ten years. When Gales was not a candidate in 1830, it was intimated in his paper that national politics was playing a part in local affairs, which would indicate that Andrew Jackson was not allowing the editor of an opposition paper to advance politically with his permission. It was due to Gales and Seaton that the first attempt was made to publish under separate form the debates of Congress, and this was attempted at their own risk and expense.

In the last few months that Monroe held office, a number of personal organs appeared, papers intended to advance the political fortunes of various individual statesmen. During the administration of John Quincy Adams, the *National Journal* was the favored one. It was edited by Peter Force, another practical printer, who later achieved considerable influence in Washington life.

With Andrew Jackson's inauguration in 1829, both the *Intelligencer* of Gales and Seaton and Force's *National Journal* lost their semi-official positions, and Duff Green's *United States Telegraph* became the "official paper," although Green's warm friendship for John C. Calhoun led him to follow that leader rather than the President.

Amos Kendall, who was an assistant editor under Green, afterward became Jackson's confidential advisor. Green's friendship for Calhoun led the President to decide on having an organ of his own, edited by a man whom he could trust; he selected for this purpose Francis P. Blair, editor of the Frankfort *Argus,* a paper controlled by Kendall. Jackson brought Blair to Washington and established the *Globe,* and more directly than had Hamilton or Jefferson, he made the paper a vehicle for the expression of his personal views.

Green has left on record the statement that President Jackson's action in starting a new paper cost him $50,000 a year. Some one tried to patch up the differences between Jackson and Green and the latter says that, before the President's own cabinet, he, Green, refused to shake hands. How Harris and Zenger and Edes would have stared at that performance!

It was said that the President often turned his mail over to Blair, allowing him to edit it as he was disposed. Amos Kendall, becoming editorial writer on the *Globe,* had nightly private conferences with Jackson, at which the President would lie down and smoke and dictate his ideas "as well as he could express them," while Kendall would write and re-write until by alterations and corrections he had succeeded in getting his articles as the master mind wished them. "General Jackson needed such an amanuensis — intelligent, learned, industrious — as Mr. Kendall was," says Henry A. Wise of Virginia. "He could think but could not write; he knew what nerve to touch, but he was no surgeon skilled in the instrument of dissection. Kendall was." [4]

[4] Hudson, *History of Journalism,* 239.

Following the Whig victory of Harrison and Tyler in 1840, the *Globe* ceased to be the organ of the administration, but the *Intelligencer* was not restored entirely to its old position. A rival had developed in the *Madisonian,* which originally had been Van Buren's paper, but which, having seen a great light, had gone over to the Whigs.

The proprietor of the *Intelligencer* was made printer for the House of Representatives and the Senate selected the publisher of the *Madisonian* as its printer. When Harrison died most of the Whig journals deserted Tyler, but the *Madisonian* took up his cause, becoming a daily shortly afterward. The South Carolina or Calhoun section of the Democratic party blossomed forth about this time with a new paper, the *Spectator.* A change was also made in the method of doling out patronage to the papers. Since 1819 the practice had been to print the laws in newspapers in the different states and territories, whereas now it was directed that they should appear in at least two and not more than four of the principal papers in Washington, preference to be given to those with the largest circulation.

When the Democrats came back into power with James K. Polk in 1844, they returned to the old practice of scattering patronage throughout the Union, instead of giving it to the Washington organs. The wiser men in the party were beginning to see the uselessness of the administration organs, but there were still those who believed in them. " For want of an official organ to explain the principles of action," observed the *Boston Advertiser,* " the Polk administration has acquired no political character."

Consequently the *Globe* outfit was purchased,— the left-over organ was always supposed to have " claims " — and the *Washington Union* was issued in its place by

Thomas Ritchie, then seventy years of age, and one of the most influential political editors of the day. During this administration the dailies dropped to two, the *Intelligencer* and the *Union.*

On August 8, 1846, a law was enacted that, instead of each house selecting its own printer, the contract should go to the lowest bidder. In the meantime, Blair and Rives had more firmly established the *Congressional Globe,* in which the debates in Congress appear verbatim, so that the *Globe* became the recognized official reporter of Congress, a position it continued to hold until the work was taken over by the *Congressional Record.*

It was said of President Taylor that, although overruled in the selection of his official advisors, he was allowed to have his own way in the choice of a newspaper organ. As the *National Intelligencer,* under Gales and Seaton, had been very friendly to Daniel Webster and had denounced Taylor's nomination as "one not fit to be made," the President sought his editorial advisors in other quarters. Alexander Bullitt and John O. Sergeant, one from New Orleans and the other from New York, were brought to Washington to become editors of the *Republic,* the new official paper.

This organ had but little weight, and, when Fillmore succeeded to office and Webster became the head of his cabinet, the Massachusetts statesman saw to it that his favorites were immediately restored to favor. The *Intelligencer* was once more the official mouthpiece of the Whigs.[5]

But the selection was no longer a matter of national importance. It had degenerated into a mere designation of so much patronage.

It was Jackson's use of patronage that had lessened the

[5] R. R. Wilson, *Washington, the Capital City,* ii, 70.

influence of the administration organ as a molder of public opinion. Furthermore, the country had expanded, not only in population and wealth but in political independence and knowledge, to the point where the idea of administration papers was manifestly inadequate. A semi-official organ at the capital itself would necessarily be found ineffective, when so many of the papers had their own representatives writing and telegraphing news which, though it could carry a certain amount of color for a while, was obliged, in the long run, to be responsive to the demand for uncolored news or else to forfeit not only its standing but its existence. What was effective in a personal organ — friendly interpretation within judicious limits — might be obtained from some if not all of these Washington correspondents without the cost of supporting a paper. More important still, with a country growing as rapidly as was the United States, it was not the organ at the capital that was most effective; the newspapers in the large cities, or even in small ones,— those having able editors and writers — were the ones that were in a position to affect the public. Men who were leaders did not, as the country grew, look to the capital for guidance. Many of the men who swayed public opinion were not connected with Washington, and in many instances, when they did go to the capital in official positions, they went there with set opinions, carrying with them the endorsement of their own communities and expecting, not to be guided, but to guide.

Cheetham, the editor of the *Citizen* of New York, who had been Coleman's bitter antagonist, was one of the first to establish himself in Washington during the session of Congress, and, through his intimacy with Jefferson, he developed a correspondence for his paper that had some of the force of official utterances. Duane of the

Aurora, and Joseph T. Buckingham of the Boston *Galaxy* were also conspicuous figures in the early days.

It was during the exciting debates of 1824, however, that newspapers began sending their own representatives to report them, relying less on the papers printed in Washington. Any success of such semi-official journalism as Jackson planned was bound to be temporary at best, especially when the men outside the official circle were of such caliber as were James Gordon Bennett, who acted as correspondent to the New York *Courier* from 1827 to 1832; Richard Houghton, afterward editor of the Boston *Atlas,* the man responsible for undermining Daniel Webster's hold on the country and bringing about the nomination of William Henry Harrison; James Webb of the New York *Courier and Enquirer;* George D. Prentice of the *Louisville Journal;* Thurlow Weed of the *Albany Evening Journal;* Henry B. Anthony of the *Providence Journal;* Thomas Ritchie of the *Richmond Enquirer,* and later Horace Greeley, John W. Forney and Henry J. Raymond. Every one of these men would have scoffed at taking "dictation," even from a President.

CHAPTER XVIII

PENNY PAPERS AND THE *NEW YORK SUN*

Development of cheaper papers — De Tocqueville on personal journalism — Philadelphia first in field — Boston second — Appearance of *New York Sun* — Its many imitators — Immediate success — Amenities among editors — Locke and the moon hoax — The Philadelphia *Ledger* and the Baltimore *Sun* — Some rules for reporters — Penny papers debated in Congress.

Unnecessary emphasis has been placed on the price of the popular journals that came into existence in the early thirties. It has generally been asserted that their low price was the cause of their popularity; as a matter of fact, as we have seen, popular journalism was coming, and it was only a question of time when papers with a broader appeal than that of the old-fashioned six-cent sheet would be offered to the public.

Reduction in the cost of materials made possible the penny paper, which led many editors and journalists to appreciate more quickly the democratic movement that was going on around them. In offering a paper to a public that could afford but a penny, they were obliged to study the public and so came to appreciate the fact that what interested the penny public did not interest the six-cent public. In other words, details, such as could be obtained from the police courts, about the life of ordinary people, and the romance of the divorce courts were used to make the penny papers more appealing, thus bringing about a broader interest on the part of the journalists in the human side of the daily life of the city.

Of the many journals that were established to meet the demand thus created, only those survived by whom that demand was truly understood; those who satisfied it with newspapers of character, with an appreciation of the great curiosity on the part of the public for facts — or fiction — about their very interesting selves.

De Tocqueville, in his travels in this country, was struck with this very personal attitude on the part of American editors.

"The journalists of the United States," he wrote, "are usually placed in a very humble position with a scanty education and a vulgar turn of mind. . . . The characteristics of the American journalist consist of an open and coarse appeal to the passions of the populace, and he habitually abandons the principles of political science to assail the characters of individuals, to track them into private life and disclose all their weaknesses and errors. . . . The personal opinions of the editors have no kind of weight in the eyes of the public."

To this cultivated young man the journalistic expression of a raw young democracy, lacking all the traditions of the old European countries, was marked with crudities and vulgarities. The crudities were generally admitted and the vulgarities denied,— foolishly, for they are inevitable and unimportant when we consider the social and political changes of which they were simply surface manifestations.

Up to the early thirties, the price of newspapers in the large cities had remained practically prohibitive, so far as the average workingman was concerned. The papers were not sold on the streets and could only be obtained through subscription. Still more important, they were edited, not for the people on the street, but by and for the business institutions or the politicians.

The Whig party, which had replaced the Federalists as an opposition party to the Democrats, was the party of the business man, while the Democratic party, under Jackson, was becoming the party of the laboring class, especially at the north. As yet, however, no paper intended solely for this working class had appeared. The presses were still worked by hand, and the average circulation of the eleven six-cent dailies published in New York was said to be not more than 1,700 each.

Important indeed was the discovery that the papers were real business factors, and that the advertisements, rather than the circulation, were the means of making them profitable investments. The business world at large was now beginning to realize the value of the newspapers for making public announcements, and this tendency had increased so much that the matter of circulation was, in a great majority of instances, important only as it enabled the newspapers to command advertisements.

With such conditions before them it was inevitable that shrewd publishers, men possessed of initiative, would recognize the value of journals that would appeal to the great mass of the people who were then not readers of the papers; journals, also, which could be sold at a price that would be within the reach of the poorest.

It was in Philadelphia, where so many important journalistic innovations had begun, that the public was offered the first paper for one cent. It was called the *Cent,* and was issued in 1830 by Dr. Christopher Columbus Conwell, from a little office in Second Street, below Dock Street. Conwell had received his education at Mount St. Mary's and Georgetown Colleges and had graduated in medicine at the University of Pennsylvania.

He was said to be a young man of fine intellectual powers and was a prolific contributor to the current magazines of that time; he died of cholera in 1832 and his paper did not survive him.

Shortly after Conwell's time, an attempt was made in Boston to publish a one-cent paper called *The Bostonian,* but this, too, failed. Following this came the *Morning Post* in New York, January 1, 1833, notable principally for the fact that in this particular experiment Horace Greeley, the ambitious young printer, had an interest. The *Post,* however, was not really a penny paper, and its projectors, whose capital did not exceed two hundred dollars, ascribed their failure to the fact that the price — two cents — was too high. After a week's experiment, the price was reduced to one cent and, at the end of three weeks, the *Morning Post* died.

To this paper, however, was given the credit of inspiring the publication, in the following fall, of the New York *Sun,* the first permanent penny paper. On the other hand, it must be remembered that, since 1830, the illustrated penny magazine of London had been circulated in New York and other American cities and sold in large quantities. The experiments in Boston and Philadelphia had also attracted attention and discussion among printers. These printers and compositors were an intelligent body of men, seeking always to benefit their condition and studiously alive to the new ideas with which the country was then teeming.

With the founding of the New York *Sun,* we come to consider the history of great popular institutions. Older newspapers came to have something of the same influence as the *Sun,* notably the *Evening Post,* under Bryant and later under Godkin. But the *Sun* was the first popular paper; its story, as Mr. Edward P. Mitchell has said, is that of a living thing, altogether aside from the men who made it.[1]

Its founder, Benjamin H. Day, had learned the printing trade in the office of Samuel Bowles the elder, owner of the Springfield *Republican*. After working at his trade in New York, in the offices of the *Evening Post* and the *Commercial Advertiser*, he decided to print a penny paper. He hired a room, gathered or clipped all the news or advertisements, and by sitting up all night, brought out, on the third of September, 1833, the first issue of the New York *Sun*. In its treatment of news the paper differed little from the six-cent papers. It contained a few police items, which showed an endeavor to follow out its ambition as announced at the top of the first column of the front page:

"The object of this paper is to lay before the public, at a price within the means of every one, all the news of the day, and at the same time offer an advantageous medium for advertisements."

After two months Day announced that its success was assured, and that it had demonstrated that "the penny press, by diffusing useful knowledge among the operative classes of society, is effecting the march of independence to a greater degree than any other mode of instruction."[2]

The *Sun* at once took an active part in the life of the community, as can be seen in its announcement that the manager of the Park Theater, with whom Day had had a quarrel, was to appear, the announcement being phrased in this delicate fashion:

"DAMN THE YANKEES — We are informed by a correspondent (though we have not seen the announce-

[1] Frank M. O'Brien, preface to *The Story of the Sun*.

[2] November 9, 1833.

ment ourselves) that Farren, the chap who damned the Yankees so lustily the other day, and who is now under bonds for a gross outrage on a respectable butcher near the Bowery Theater, is intending to make his appearance on the Bowery stage THIS EVENING!"

The success of the paper of this period must be considered not only from the point of view of its financial returns, but from the part that it played in stimulating its rivals. It is this personal, competitive and aggressively combatant side of American journalism that makes its history so interesting, and so true an index of the democratic life of the people.

In commenting on the fact that other penny papers had all passed away, Day noted that since these papers had been printed they had begun "the most unlimited and reckless abuse of ourselves, the impeachment of our character, public and private."

The *Sun* was able to claim the credit of inspiring, not only the founding of the New York *Herald,* but numerous other sheets, among them *The Jeffersonian* — *The Man* — *The Transcript* — *The True Sun* — (established by some discharged employees) — *The Morning Star* — *The New Era* (established by Richard Locke, whose Moon Hoax story attracted wide attention) — *The Daily Whig* — *The Bee* — *The Serpent* — *The Light* — *The Express* — *The Union* — *The Rough Hewer* — *The News Times* — *The Examiner* — *The Morning Chronicle* — *The Evening Chronicle* — *The Daily Conservative* — *The Censor* and the *Daily News,* all of which were started within a period of fifteen years after the *Sun,* and all passed away with the exception of the *Express* and the *Daily News.*

Three years after it had been founded the *Sun* boasted that it had a circulation of 27,000 copies daily or 5,600 more than the combined sale of the eleven six-cent papers. [3]

Moreover, changes in the attitude of the public mind toward newspapers were set forth, statements important even as claims:

"Since the *Sun* began to shine upon the citizens of New York there has been a very great and decided change in the condition of the laboring classes and the mechanics, Now every individual, from the rich aristocrat who lolls in his carriage to the humble laborer who wields a broom in the streets, reads the *Sun;* nor can even a boy be found in New York City or the neighboring country who will not know in the course of the day what is promulgated in the *Sun* in the morning.

"Already we perceive a change in the mass of the people. They think, talk, and act in concert. They understand their own interest, and feel that they have numbers and strength to pursue it with success.

"The *Sun* newspaper has probably done more to benefit the community by enlightening the minds of the common people than all the other papers together." [4]

The "social" success of the paper, as shown in its relations with fellow editors, is evident from the fact that James Watson Webb was warned that the "three editors" of the *Sun* had pistols and would use them if Webb attempted a threatened assault.

When Webb assaulted Bennett in January, 1836, Day, in the *Sun,* illustrating the pleasant attitude of editors toward one another, thus sums up his own ideas as to the character of his confreres:

"Low as he has fallen, both in the public estimation and in his own, we are astonished to learn last evening

[3] *The Sun,* August 4, 1836.

[4] *The Sun,* June 28, 1838.

that Colonel Webb had stooped so far beneath anything of which we had ever conceived it possible for him to be guilty, as publicly, and before the eyes of hundreds who knew him, to descend to a personal chastisement of that villainous libel of humanity of all kinds, the notorious vagabond Bennett. But it is so."

In answer to Greeley's declaration that his paper, the *Tribune,* was to be the journal "of the virtuous and refined," the *Sun* a week later notified him that he must "go to school and learn a little decency."

Edgar Allen Poe, who occasionally found in cheap journalism an opportunity to make a needed penny, gave to the celebrated Moon Hoax story of Richard Adams Locke the credit for the success of penny journalism — a trifle too enthusiastically, as one might expect from a man of Poe's temperament:

"From the epoch of the hoax," he wrote, "the *Sun* shone with unmitigated splendor. Its success firmly established 'the penny system' through the country, and (through the *Sun*) consequently we are indebted to the genius of Mr. Locke for one of the most important steps ever yet taken in the pathway of human progress."

Although the story scarcely justifies Poe's encomiums nevertheless it gave the *Sun* international fame at a time when Day could not reasonably have expected to attract attention beyond the confines of New York City. Locke, a man of education and great ability — he had Poe's unstinted admiration — was a reporter on the *Sun* at twelve dollars a week. Needing more money, he outlined his moon story to Day, to whom the project was acceptable, and, after a preliminary announcement to the effect that great astronomical discoveries had been made by Sir John Herschel, the *Sun* published on August 25, 1835, three columns of what purported to be a reprint of Herschel's report, credited to the Supplement to the *Edinburgh Journal of Science.*

It purported to give an account of the astronomical observations of Herschel at the Cape of Good Hope, made through an enormous telescope. For the next four days the articles grew in interest until finally they were describing the appearances of man-bats and the most minute vegetation on the moon. They were so well written that even the scientists were deceived and most of the *Sun's* contemporaries, even the six-cent sheets which pretended to despise it, took for granted the truth of the reports.

In the office of the *Sun,* after the close of the Mexican War, a meeting was held to provide means for lessening the expense of gathering news. General Hallock, editor of the *Journal of Commerce,* presided, and the *Sun, Herald, Tribune, Express* and the *Courier and Enquirer* were represented. The Harbor Association was formed, by which one fleet of news-boats would do the work which half a dozen had been doing, and the New York Associated Press was formed to gather news in the large cities. [5]

To the success of the *Sun* may be traced the founding of two of the most important papers in the country, at least among those of later times. When Benjamin Day first conceived the plan of a popular penny paper, it was with two fellow printers, Arunah S. Abell and William M. Swain, that he first discussed it. They ridiculed Day's hopefulness, and Swain is said to have prophesied that the idea would be the ruin of Day. Swain later became foreman of the *Sun,* and three years after it was founded, with Abell and another printer named Azariah H. Simmons, decided to try the popular penny paper idea in other cities.

The three went to Philadelphia and there brought out,

[5] O'Brien, *The Story of the Sun,* 167.

on March 25, 1836, the first number of the *Public Ledger.* A month earlier a Philadelphia printer, William L. Drane, had issued the *Daily Transcript* as a penny paper, but before the year was over the *Transcript* was merged with the *Public Ledger.*

The firm of Swain, Abell and Simmons had had the benefit of watching the progress of penny journalism in New York, but they were unfortunate in their time, for their venture was but started when the whole country was threatened with bankruptcy.

The opening number of the *Public Ledger* contained a broader appeal than had been made in the *Sun,* for its projectors declared: "While its cheapness places it within the reach of the poorest artisan or laborer, we shall endeavor to furnish to the merchant and manufacturer the earliest and most useful information relating to their respective interests." It declared that it would devote itself with special energy "to a moral and intellectual improvement of the laboring classes, the great sinew of all civilized communities."

The public, which might not, it was presumed, be familiar with the journalistic revolution that had taken place in New York, where there were now three penny papers — two of them successful, the *Sun* and the *Herald* — was informed in the first announcement that "in the Cities of New York and Brooklyn, containing a population of 300,000, the daily circulation of the penny papers is not less than 70,000. This is nearly sufficient to place a newspaper in the hands of every man in the two cities and even of every boy old enough to read. These papers are to be found in every street, lane and alley; in every hotel, tavern, counting-house, shop, etc.; almost every porter, drayman, etc., while not engaged in his occupation, may be seen with a penny paper in his hands."

Philadelphia at first was cold to the proposition; so much so that both Swain and Simmons were inclined to give up the undertaking. Abell, however, had greater faith and business expectations for the paper. It occurred to him that it might be worth while to visit Baltimore to see what the prospects were for establishing a penny paper in that city. He found there none but six-cent papers and, despite the fact that the year was one of unprecedented gloom and business depression, he persuaded his partners that the field was a fertile one, with the consequences that, on May 17, 1837, the first number of the *Baltimore Sun* was issued, with Abell himself in charge.

Swain remained the editor in charge at Philadelphia, and these two enterprising men, one in Baltimore and the other in Philadelphia, were thus able to strengthen their property by their individual enterprise in separate cities.

The abolition riots in Philadelphia, in 1838, gave the *Ledger* an opportunity to show its courage and public spirit, when it denounced the mob and pleaded for the right of free speech and a free press. The courageous course of the paper attracted to it the support of the law-abiding people, and it strengthened its position by being one of the first papers to advocate independent voting. Twice the office was mobbed, but the courage of the editor never wavered.

Both Swain and Abell were enthusiastic supporters of the Morse magnetic telegraph and Swain was afterward president of the company for several years. For twenty years Swain was the master mind on the *Ledger,* and he is said to have accumulated a fortune of three million dollars, but at the beginning of the Civil War it was found that they were losing money because of the increased price of paper. Swain was unwilling to raise the price of his journal, and the partnership of Swain and Abell — Simmons having died — came to an end, when in 1864 the *Publc Ledger* was sold to George W. Childs.

The *Sun* at Baltimore, under Abell, rapidly became a more popular paper than the *Ledger,* for in three months it had a larger circulation than the Philadelphia paper had at the end of nine months. In a very short time it had a circulation twice as large as the oldest established six-cent paper in Baltimore.

George W. Childs, who took over the *Public Ledger* from Swain, was one of America's most distinguished philanthropists. He was one of the large school of Benjamin Franklin's disciples, men who at this time were becoming conspicuous as millionaires or business successes, having started in life without a penny, but with "industry, perseverance and a stout heart." Childs had been a member of a successful publishing house and had published a literary magazine, when he purchased the *Public Ledger.* His managing editor for years was William V. McKean, and to McKean should be given credit for the system of editorial ethics put forth as guiding principles of the *Public Ledger.* We read the constitutions of governments, but it is not often that we have the opportunity of reading the constitutional principles of a great newspaper:

"Always deal fairly and frankly with the public.

"A newspaper to be trusted and respected must give trustworthy information and counsel. It is a serious thing to mislead the people.

"Understate your case rather than overstate it.

"Have a sure voucher for every statement, especially for censure.

"There is a wide gap between accusation of crime and actual guilt.

"Deal gently with weak and helpless offenders.

"Before making up judgment take care to understand both sides, and remember there are at least two sides. If you attempt to decide, you are bound to know both.

"Do not say you know when you have only heard.

"Never proceed on mere hearsay. Rumor is only an index to be followed by inquiry.

"Take care to be right. Better be right than quickest with 'the news' which is often false. It is bad to be late, but worse to be wrong.

"Go to first hands and original sources for information; if you cannot, then get as near as you can.

"It is the reporter's office to chronicle events, to collect facts; comments on the facts are reserved for the editor.

"Let the facts and reasoning tell the story rather than rhetorical flourish.

"Don't be too positive. Remember always it is possible you may err.

"All persons have equal rights in the court of conscience, as well as in courts of law.

"Never add fuel to the fire of popular excitement.

"There is nothing more demoralizing in public affairs than habitual disregard of law.

"Uphold the authorities in maintaining public order, rectify wrongs through the law. If the law is defective, better mend it than break it.

"Nearly always there is law enough. It is the failure to enforce it that makes most mischief.

"There is no need, and therefore no excuse, for mob law in American communities.

"Numerous as bad men may be, remember they are but few compared with the millions of the people.

"The public welfare has higher claims than any party cry.

"Grace and purity of style are always desirable, but never allow rhetoric to displace clear, direct, forcible expression.

"Plain words are essential for unlearned people, and these are just as plain to the most accomplished." [6]

These three papers, the *Sun* in New York, the *Ledger* in Philadelphia, and the *Sun* in Baltimore, were products of a developing democracy. In turn they stood very stiffly for the democracy that had incubated them.

In the first years of penny journalism a reference during a congressional debate to the penny papers and their circulation brought forth an interesting defense of the new institution. A Congressman named Botts had declared, in an attack on the practice of giving government advertisements to the penny press, that they had "little or no circulation beyond the limits of the city from which they were published." To this the *Sun* made answer that its circulation was 30,000 in New York, Brooklyn, and Jersey City and 5,000 more without the city. The combined circulation of the *Boston Times,* the *New York Sun,* the *Philadelphia Ledger,* and the *Baltimore Sun* was put down as 96,000 copies; and the only places where the papers had not circulated, it was admitted, was in far-off farms and villages. In addition to this, it was claimed in their behalf that they had, in six years, accomplished more reforms than the party press had in twenty. They had rid Philadelphia of mobs, attacked the monopolies of the banks and profiteers in flour and beef, and had started a discussion tending to reform the debased currency system.

Politically, the penny press taught the higher priced

[6] See Appendix, Note C.

papers that party connection should be properly subordinated to the other and higher function of the public journals — the function of gathering and presenting the news as it is.

The *New York Sun* asserted that, by this mere presentation of the news, it had materially benefited the city. New York was a city undoubtedly in need of improvement in many ways. Although at this time it was the metropolis of the country and had a population of about 300,000, the principal streets were still badly paved and poorly lighted; although on lower Broadway at the fashionable hour, (from two to three o'clock,) there was a continuous procession of omnibuses, cabs, coaches, and carriages, as well as a throng of gorgeously dressed men and women, sightseers, shoppers and loiterers, yet barefoot girls swept the crossings and ragged urchins sold matches, and later, the penny papers.[7] Not until 1845 were there policemen in the daylight hours.

Thousands of penny newspapers were distributed each week in the country cities. They were sold in Boston, New York, Philadelphia, and Baltimore, at two-thirds of a cent a copy to the newsboys and carriers, who sold them on the street at a cent, or delivered them over their routes and collected six cents from each customer on Saturday. What seemed to amaze people most was the fact that in New York you would not see a laborer waiting or resting on a job, without also seeing a penny paper in his hands. Even the old six-cent journals admitted editorially that the new type of journalism had both spirit and intelligence and that all that was wanting to make it a real force in the community was a little common decency and honesty.

[7] McMaster, *History,* vii, 77.

CHAPTER XIX

JAMES GORDON BENNETT AND THE *HERALD*

Jackson's administration — Bennett's innovations — Impressions which influenced his course — First political conventions — Experience in politics — New York *Herald* — Characteristics of its founder — Assault by James Watson Webb — Announcement of his marriage — O. G. Villard's criticism.

In a democracy, all popular institutions should tend to identify the interest of the government with that of the people, and the newspaper has been the greatest means to that end. Throughout the fast-developing country, however, large numbers of people had, until the introduction of cheap newspapers, only that share in government that came from representatives of other people's selection.

The period of Andrew Jackson's presidency, during which the modern newspaper was first sold at a price within the reach of the laboring man's purse, was one of the most remarkable in the history of the world, and "nowhere more remarkable than in the United States," says John Fiske.

It was an industrial Periclean age, during which the railroads were introduced and developed, and agricultural machines invented; it was signalized by the introduction of anthracite coal and friction matches, and of the modern type of daily newspaper; by the beginning of such cities as Chicago, by the steady immigration from Europe, the rise of the Abolitionists and other reformers, the rapid expansion of the country and the consequent extensive changes in ideas and modes of living.

The *New York Herald* was the first successful attempt to provide a paper that dealt with the doings of the people aside from their activities as political communities; it was also the first newspaper to introduce what have since been described as "counting-room" methods. It was the first to sell news as news and not for the effect it would have on its readers. The founder's experiences in politics had been bitter enough to make him sympathize with the great mass of people who had very little more to do with government than to vote. Out of his own personal disappointments there had come the realization that there was a vast majority of the public for whom what usually passed for news could have but little interest, except as it stirred their imagination. For the average men on the street, news as printed in the current journals had the same interest that the cheap love story of a later generation had for the maid-of-all-work, who found therein an opportunity to throb over the misfortunes and adventures of titled persons, a belief in whose existence constituted one of the joys and opiates of her existence.

Bennett had in mind a paper for those who were unimportant, an entirely novel idea at that time — that it should be politically independent was not absolutely necessary, but this was a quicker way of achieving his goal. He was the first to aspire to build an institution that would be responsive to him and that would propagate the principles he believed in. Twenty years earlier this would not have been possible, for, twenty years earlier, the people to whom he was to appeal had not the vote, nor was there the interest in general education that made possible, among the great unknown mass, a large circulation.

The *New York Herald* was in the direct line of the development of American journalism, and its founder is, for the student of modern journalism, a most interesting figure, for he paved the way for things that were revolutionary in their day, though commonplace now. Furthermore, it came at a time when, on account of inventions and the great opening up of material opportunities, the introduction of the railroads, etc., there was every opportunity for his fertile genius.

It is easy enough now to see this and to appreciate how much he was indebted to the journalists and journalism that had come before him, and to understand that, if he had not done what he did, some one else would have worked out about the same time, and along nearly the same lines, the growing problems of journalism. But in his own time he was considered a daring innovator — and in some ways he was; though from much of what has been written about him one might assume that there was no journalism before him. It is true that his personal eccentricities gave his enterprise an individual flavor that caused the conservative element of society to view him with horror, though the same conservative element came later to regard the *New York Herald* as its special organ, and to look to it for the proper reports of its "social" doings.

It was the perusal of an edition of Franklin's autobiography, published in Scotland in 1817, that led young Bennett to come to America. In May, 1819, being then about twenty years of age, he landed in Halifax without a friend in the western continent and with less than twenty-five dollars in his purse.[1]

Between the day of that landing and the starting of the *New York Herald* sixteen years elapsed, during which time he worked in many parts of the country and obtained at first hand an accurate understanding of American politics. He made his way to Boston and there saw, for the

1 Parton, *Famous Americans,* 270.

first time, the curious tendency of the American reader to court what he most dreads. Joseph T. Buckingham's *New England Galaxy,* which violated all the traditions and decorous rules of the day, was the most abused paper in Boston, and the one that was most read. What most impressed Bennett on his first insight into American journalism was that, despite all the abuse, Buckingham possessed power, and that he achieved his distinction by his extravagant and severe style.

Going to New York, Bennett saw what he considered a justification for Buckingham. With the exception of Mordecai M. Noah of the New York *Advocate,* William L. Stone of the *Commercial Advertiser* and William Coleman of the *Evening Post,* the papers were unimportant and the editors too much given to personal and futile abuse.

After a short experience in Charleston as ship news reporter, Bennett returned to New York, and was soon made the Washington correspondent of the *Enquirer.* During the presidential election of 1828, he was in the thick of the fight and ardently supported Andrew Jackson, showing considerable aptitude as a politician for a man who had been only a few years in the country.

The following year he became an associate editor of the *Courier and Enquirer,* under James Watson Webb, and that journal was soon distinguished for its advocacy of many of the popular reforms. It was a strong Jackson organ, with Bennett enthusiastically leading the fight for the extension of democracy. The period was rough, with little regard for the refinement of editorial debate, but the young Scotchman seemed to enjoy it. Editors openly accused one another of the most disgusting acts,[2] and the pistol was an editorial accessory not infrequently

[2] Pray, *Memoirs of James Gordon Bennett,* 114.

used. So violent was the party spirit that one editor — in Columbia, South Carolina — sold his paper and announced that he retired from journalism with disgust.

The time, 1831–1832, was one in which political conventions first came to the fore, and became not only popular, but almost a fashion. It was at a convention of the National Republicans, held in Baltimore in December, 1831, that the first platform, in the form of an address, was adopted. One of the planks in this platform related to the corruption of the press by the Jackson administration. It was asserted that Jackson had cried out against the misuse of the press by the previous administration, but that under him "partisan editors were now the most favored class of pretenders to office."[3]

It was as the defender of the President, and incidentally of northern office-seeking editors, that Bennett first tested his ability to develop a discussion of national importance. Jackson had sent to the Senate the names of four editors for public office. Calhoun's differences with the President led him to oppose those whom he considered unfriendly, with the result that two southern editors were confirmed by the Senate, two northern editors being rejected. This led Bennett to attack the Senate. The papers throughout the country took this attack up and much debate ensued over the question — "Are editors eligible for office?" The question was an interesting one for that time, and most of the lawyers — who saw good offices going, from their point of view, astray — answered vigorously in the negative. All this was inspiring material for Bennett; the discussion was given another lively twist, with the press vigorously depicted by him as the "living jury of the nation."

From that time on Bennett became a political force, as-

[3] McMaster, vi, 130.

sisting in the nomination of Marcy as Governor and of Van Buren as Vice-president. This was a little too much for Webb, the proprietor of the *Courier and Enquirer,* and he and Bennett parted, Webb preferring to be the shining light of his own paper. The ill-feeling between the two began when Webb heard that Bennett was to start his own paper. This he did in 1832, establishing the *New York Globe* as a two-cent paper, but it received neither popular support nor that financial assistance that he believed would be forthcoming from his political associates.

When the first number was printed, November 29, 1832, he declared that for eight years he had labored in the cause of democracy,— he omitted no year that could possibly be counted, not even his year as a ship news reporter — that he had assisted in the election of Jackson and the advancement of Van Buren and that now he was through with politics. His next venture was in Philadelphia, where he invested, in a paper called the *Pennsylvanian,* the small sum of money which he had saved.

If his experience with politics and politicians had been disappointing in New York, it was bitter in Philadelphia. After he had sunk his own money, he needed a further sum of two thousand five hundred dollars, and applied to Van Buren and another political associate for it. After some correspondence, it was refused. From that time on, James Gordon Bennett was through with politics.

We have seen that the penny press, as it was called, originated in Philadelphia. Bennett, while there, gained some knowledge of Dr. Conwell's experiment with *The Cent.* When he came back to New York the *Sun* was the talk of the town, or at least, of the profession. The following year a paper called the *New York Transcript* was published as a rival of the *Sun*. Both papers had the same printers; to these printers Bennett went in 1834 and had them get him out a small sheet which appeared May 6, 1835, and which was called the *New York Herald*. A fire put him out of business for a short time, but he was not to be downed. He arose early and sat up late, did all his own reporting, collected all his own news, wrote the entire paper himself, posted his own books and made out his own bills. Thus began the *New York Herald,* famous on two continents.

It has been said of Bennett that he was one of the greatest news men this country has produced. What is more interesting to us is not what he did after he was successful but the manner of man he was in adversity. We can understand why the public would turn to him, despite all the abuse, when we see what he did in Wall Street. He knew, as others knew, that some of the editors of the six-cent "respectable" dailies were heavy speculators, and that articles were printed intended to affect the price of stocks. Bennett began boldly by asserting that these editors were "truly unfit by nature and want of capacity to come to a right conclusion upon any subject. They are still more unfit to give correct opinions on French affairs in consequences of their speculating mania, and deep interest in stock jobbing. They pervert every public event from its proper hue and coloring, to raise one stock and depress another. There is no truth in them."

This he followed up by printing an article that reflected on his former associate, the editor of the *Courier and Enquirer*. Webb waited for him in Wall Street and knocked him down with a stick. Bennett's next move had the advantage of distinct novelty. He printed an account of the assault.

"I have to apologize to my kind readers," he wrote,

" for the want of my usual life to-day." Referring to his assailant, he stated that Webb had, " by going up behind me, cut a slash in my head about one and one-half inches in length and through the integuments of the skull. The fellow, no doubt, wanted to let out the never-failing supply of good humor and wit, which has created such a reputation for the *Herald,* and appropriate the contents to supply the emptiness of his own thick skull. He did not succeed, however, in rifling me of my ideas, . . . He has not injured the skull. My ideas, in a few days, will flow as freely as ever, and he will find it so, to his cost."

Street fights between editors were not rare in these days; Philip Hone recorded in his diary that while shaving " this morning at eight o'clock I witnessed from the front window an encounter in the street nearly opposite, between William Cullen Bryant and William L. Stone; the former one of the editors of the *Evening Post* and the latter the editor of the *Commercial Advertiser.*"[4] Bryant, the poet, began this particular fight by hitting Stone, the historian, over the head with a cane, but judging from Hone's calm statement, the distinguished and urbane mayor of the city was so little disturbed that the argument did not even interfere with his shaving.

Bennett's method of treating his assault was an innovation, and a success — the circulation of the Herald containing this recital went up to 9,000 copies.

He was now a public character; something equally novel was expected from him with sufficient frequency to keep people buying his paper. He kept his promise as to Webb, with the result that a few months later he was able to report another assault by Webb.

" As I was leisurely pursuing my business yesterday in Wall Street, collecting the information which is daily

[4] Hone, *Diary,* i, 30.

disseminated in the *Herald,* James Watson Webb came up to me on the northern side of the street, said something which I could not hear distinctly, then pushed me down the stone steps leading to one of the brokers' offices, and commenced fighting with a species of brutal and demoniacal desperation characteristic of a fury. . . . My damage is a scratch about three quarters of an inch in length, on the third finger of the left hand, which I received from the iron railing I was forced against, and three buttons torn from my vest, which any tailor will reinstate for a sixpence. His loss is a rent from top to bottom of a very beautiful black coat, which cost the ruffian $40, and a blow in the face, which may have knocked down his throat some of his infernal teeth, for anything I know. Balance in my favor, $39.94. . . . As to intimidating me or changing my course, the thing cannot be done. Neither Webb nor any other man shall or can intimidate me. I tell the honest truth in my paper, and I leave the consequences to God. Could I leave them in better hands? I may be attacked — I may be assailed —I may be killed —I may be murdered — but I will never succumb — I will never abandon the cause of truth, morals and virtue." [5]

Webb's example was infectious, for in the same year Bennett was again assaulted, this time by a theatrical manager, Thomas H. Hamblin. "To me," was the editorial comment, "all these attacks, falsehoods, lies, fabrications are but as the idle winds. They do not ruffle my temper in the least. Conscious of virtue, integrity, and the purest principles, I can easily smile at the assassins, and defy their daggers.

"My life has been one invariable series of efforts, useful to the world and honorable to myself — efforts to

[5] *Herald,* May 10, 1836.

create an honorable reputation during life, and to leave something after my death for which posterity will honor my memory. I am building up a newspaper establishment that will take the lead of all others that ever appeared in the world, in virtue, in morals, in science, in knowledge, in industry, in taste, in power, in influence. No public reputation can be lasting unless it is built on private character and virtue. My whole private life has been one of virtue, integrity and honorable effort, in every relation of society. Dissipation, extravagance, and fashionable follies never had any charms for me. . . . This has been the cause of the success attending the *Herald*." [6]

The sophisticated reader will feel that there is a great deal of the ridiculous in this, but — viewing Bennett as an instrument, as one affecting thousands,— it must be remembered that it was better than shooting those who resented his attacks. It must not be supposed for a moment that he was the exponent of non-resistance — on the contrary, he made those who injured him suffer — but he was just Scotch enough to select his own weapons, and fortunately they are the weapons of which civilization has approved.

Of the personal tributes to himself, perhaps the most individual was that contained in his announcement of his forthcoming marriage. With proper headlines, it appeared as follows: [7]

[6] Pray, *Memoirs*, 214, 215.
[7] *Herald*, June 1, 1840.

"TO THE READERS OF THE *HERALD* — DECLARATION OF LOVE — CAUGHT AT LAST — GOING TO BE MARRIED — NEW MOVEMENT IN CIVILIZATION.

"I am going to be married in a few days. The weather is so beautiful; times are getting so good; the prospects of political and moral reforms so auspicious, that I cannot resist the divine instinct of honest nature any longer; so I am going to be married to one of the most splendid women in intellect, in heart, in soul, in property, in person, in manner, that I have yet seen in the course of my interesting pilgrimage through human life.

". . . I cannot stop in my career. I must fulfill that awful destiny which the Almighty Father has written against my name, in the broad letters of life, against the wall of heaven. I must give the world a pattern of happy wedded life, with all the charities that spring from a nuptial love. In a few days I shall be married according to the holy rites of the most holy Christian church, to one of the most remarkable, accomplished, and beautiful young women of the age. She possesses a fortune. I sought and found a fortune — a large fortune. She has no Stonington shares or Manhattan stock, but in purity and uprightness she is worth half a million of pure coin. Can any swindling bank show as much? In good sense and elegance another half a million; in soul, mind, and beauty, millions on millions, equal to the whole specie of all the rotten banks in the world. Happily the patronage of the public to the *Herald* is nearly twenty-five thousand dollars per annum, almost equal to a President's salary. But property in the world's goods was never my object. Fame, public good, usefulness in my day and generation; the religious associations of female excellence; the progress of true industry,— these have been my dreams by night and my desires by day.

"In the new and holy condition into which I am about to enter, and to enter with the same reverential feelings as I would enter heaven itself, I anticipate some signal changes in my feelings, in my views, in my purposes, in my pursuits. What they may be I know not — time alone can tell. My ardent desire has been through life, to reach the highest order of human intelligence, by the shortest possible cut. Associated, night and day, in sickness and in health, in war and in peace, with a woman of this highest order of excellence, must produce some curious results in my heart and feelings, and these results the future will develop in due time in the columns of the *Herald*.

"Meantime, I return my heartfelt thanks for the enthusiastic patronage of the public, both of Europe and of America. The holy estate of wedlock will only increase my desire to be still more useful. God Almighty bless you all."

"JAMES GORDON BENNETT."

A distinguished journalist, Oswald Garrison Villard, in his criticism of the Bennetts,[8] speaking from the vantage ground of social superiority and of impeccable morality, sees in the elder Bennett only a lack of moral fiber. He admits that the Bennetts, father and son, were the most remarkable news men this country has ever produced. "The father revolutionized the whole science of news-getting, and the son outdid him by creating exclusive news." Even this adverse critic finds that in the

[8] *Nation,* May 25, 1918, cvi, 615.

Herald for 1858–1859, "printed on splendid rag paper which is white and strong to this hour," the news is treated in a manner very mild compared to the conservative dailies of to-day, and what is more, the accounts are accurate. Yet Bennett, to his contemporaries, was a blackguard and all that was horrible, and Mr. Villard, who fails to see Bennett as an instrument and whose attention is concentrated on him as an individual and a sensationalist, can only see by the reflected light of the past.

This seeing the past in the light of present-day developments — developments which our ancestors could not foretell — must be studiously avoided in making historical judgments. Mr. Villard's horror over the elder Bennett is no greater than the disgust with which the good people of Boston viewed his own distinguished grandfather, William Lloyd Garrison, and it must be remembered that, a century ago, the editors of even the conservative papers were men who did things that the editors of the radical papers of to-day would consider barbarous and vulgar.

The elder Bennett was pro-slavery and pro-Tammany, and it was said that not until a mob had gathered in front of his office did he become a loyal supporter of the Union. And yet Count Gurowski wrote in his diary, in August, 1861, that it was "generally believed that Lincoln read only the *Herald*."

In the study of the history of journalism the personal characteristics of the editor are not of vital importance, unless those personal characteristics are obtruded in such a way as to corrupt the public mind. There is great danger that, in writing history and in making historical judgments, we may use the phraseology and assume the moral tone of those who would arrogate to themselves the exclusive control of moral standards.

It was said that the elder Bennett "horrified" and "shocked" New York by his disregard of the conventions. This is a loose way of speaking and a looser way of thinking. Instead of New York, with its 300,000 inhabitants, being "shocked" or "horrified," it is probable that not more than five hundred people — which would include the socially elect and the conservative editors — were at all seriously disturbed by his peculiar and, as we view it now, rather amusing style of journalism. It is hard to imagine the draymen and laborers being "shocked" or "horrified" at Bennett's writings, but we can readily understand how his dynamic outbursts attracted them, where the old conservative sheets would have sent them to sleep, had they had either the money or the inclination to purchase them.

CHAPTER XX

GREELEY AND THE *TRIBUNE*

Reasons for the *Tribune* — Greeley's early life — Through Pennsylvania — *Morning Post* — Thurlow Weed — Seward, Weed & Greeley partnership — Description of Weed — *Log Cabin* and Harrison campaign — *Tribune* open for liberal ideas — Hard times in New York — Free soil party encouraged.

Nominally, the *New York Tribune* was brought out as a protest against the sensational journalism that Bennett was offering in the *Herald*. There were also political reasons, the principal one being that the Whigs desired a paper that would appeal to the laboring classes, who were unable to get a Whig paper for a penny.

" I had been incited to this enterprise," Greeley relates, " by several Whig friends, who deemed a cheap daily, addressed more especially to the laboring class, eminently needed in our city, where the only two cheap journals then and still existing — the *Sun* and the *Herald* — were in decided, though unavowed, and therefore more effective, sympathy and affiliation with the Democratic party.

" My leading idea was the establishment of a journal removed alike from servile partisanship on the one hand and from gagged, mincing neutrality on the other. Party spirit is so fierce and intolerant in this country that the editor of a non-partisan sheet is restrained from saying what he thinks and feels on the most vital, imminent topics; while, on the other hand, a Democrat, Whig, or Republican journal is generally expected to praise or blame, like or dislike, eulogize or condemn, in precise accordance with the views and interest of the party. I believed there was a happy medium between these extremes,— a position from which a journalist might openly and heartily advocate the principles and commend the measures of that party to which his convictions allied him, yet frankly dissent from its course on a particular question, and even denounce its candidates if they were shown to be deficient in capacity or (far worse) in integrity. I felt that a journal thus loyal to its guiding convictions, yet ready to expose and condemn unworthy conduct or incidental error on the part of men attached to its party, must be far more effective, even party-wise, than though it might always be counted on to applaud or reprobate, bless or curse, as the party's prejudices or immediate interest might seem to prescribe. Especially by the Whigs — who were rather the loosely aggregated, mainly undisciplined opponents of a great party, than, in the stricter sense, a party themselves — did I feel that such a journal was consciously needed, and would be fairly sustained." [1]

The story of Horace Greeley and the *New York Tribune* is of the best American tradition. It is a more important part of American history than the stories of some presidential administrations. It has been accepted as an important event in the history of the press, but has not been given its proper place in that of American politics.

The history of American journalism that begins with Benjamin Harris and *Publick Occurances* might properly end with Greeley and the *Tribune*. The world that pilloried and imprisoned Harris atoned amply to Greeley. The battle for the right to criticize government and to make it more human, the battle that began with Harris,

[1] Greeley, *Autobiography*, 136, 137.

was brought to a victorious and dramatic close by Greeley. From the time when Harris presumed to tell the government what it should not do in the matter of waging barbarous warfare, till the time when Greeley did tell the government what to do, when he became the most influential single figure in the selection of the country's presidents, there is a steady, never-failing progression. One might almost expect to find a blood descent from one to the other; indeed, the rise of journalistic power, from Harris to Greeley, moves with a precision such as marked the development of an ancient dynasty.

But Greeley, for all the good that he did and all the power that he had — and he never used power but for good — was not a happy man, and he founded no dynasty. The great paper that he founded passed to another on his death, and Whitelaw Reid, the man who succeeded him — with none of his struggles or handicaps — was a much happier man, and achieved far greater honors.

Greeley himself tells us [2] that from childhood he so loved and devoured newspapers that he early resolved to be a printer. Born on a rocky farm in New Hampshire in 1811, he was only eleven years of age when, hearing that an apprentice was wanted in a newspaper office at Whitehall, he went with his father to obtain the job, but he was rejected because of his youth.

In the spring of 1826 another opportunity came, when the *Northern Spectator* at East Poultney, Vermont, advertised for an apprentice. The spirit of the times is revealed in the fact that the citizens of the town of East Poultney had decided to finance the journal, private capital having come to the conclusion that there was no profit in the undertaking.

Greeley's father was moving for the west, one of the

[2] *Recollections of a Busy Life*, 61.

great number who had grown tired of the struggle for existence in the east, and in consequence was very glad to allow young Horace to make arrangements with the publishers at East Poultney. This was done, and the boy went to work for his board, with the understanding that after he became twenty years of age, he was to receive $40 a year — less than a dollar a week. This helps us to understand why men were willing to seek opportunity in the western wilderness.

His apprenticeship over, Greeley started out to seek his "future," a cardinal belief of young America of that time being that the golden opportunity awaited him who persistently sought it. Romantic though this seems now, it was the spirit that made possible the emigration of great numbers. He traveled from East Poultney to Lake Erie and thence to his father's house in Pennsylvania, catching steamboats when possible, or a canal boat now and then, but, for the greater part of the journey, afoot. Such a trip, which now takes but ten or twelve hours, at that time could not be made in less than two weeks.

After exhausting the possibilities of the printing shops in Chautauqua County, Greeley visited Erie, Pennsylvania (about 1830), and worked on the *Gazette*, which had been started twenty years before by Joseph M. Sterrett; this was, he says, the first newspaper on which he had ever worked that made any money for its owner.

On his way back he applied, unsuccessfully, for a position on the *Wyoming Herald* in Wilkesbarre, Pennsylvania. He now began to realize that there was a surfeit of printers traveling about the country, and he turned toward the great city.

Between 1818 and 1830, he tells us, thousands and tens of thousands of men were unwillingly idle. The country that had once boasted its political unanimity was now torn in dissension. As men contemplated their condition, they turned bitterly to the government for some kind of relief. The country suffered from a dearth of money and, as the pressing need for money increased and merchants and banks struggled to avert bankruptcy, the political furies enveloped the East, especially the city of New York, which was rapidly becoming the financial center of the nation.

When Greeley arrived in New York in August, 1831 — a tall, thin country boy of twenty — he had not a friend within two hundred miles and only ten dollars in his pocket.

On the first day he visited two-thirds of the printing offices on Manhattan Island, before securing employment. For the next eighteen months he worked at odd jobs, but managed to save money; he was then induced by Dr. D. H. Shepherd to start a small printing shop, with the idea of putting out a cheap paper. The forty dollars' worth of type needed for this enterprise was bought on credit.

Shepherd was the originator of the idea of a cheap paper, his belief being that a paper sold on the streets by newsboys would be a great success. The *Morning Post,* as the new venture was called, came out January 1, 1833, but, a terrible storm having driven the people off the streets, no one bought the paper. The enterprise lasted but three weeks.

This experience had given Greeley a taste for editorship, and with only enough money to pay the printer, he shortly afterward brought out the *New Yorker,* a small paper of literary and general intelligence. This was established in 1834 and attracted immediate attention among those interested in politics. "Those who read it became Whigs." His mind acted upon other minds of a certain constitution with wonderful magnetism, attracting thousands of readers by his marvelous gift of expression and the broad sympathies and clear discernments that characterized his writings.[3]

Although Bennett never referred to it, Greeley's friendly biographer is authority for the statement that, while he was conducting his job office, under the name of Greeley and Company, James Gordon Bennett, "a person then well known as a smart writer for the press," visited him one day and, exhibiting fifty dollars and some other notes of smaller denomination as his cash capital, invited him to join in setting up a new daily paper.[4]

With his modest venture, the *New Yorker,* Horace Greeley began his rise to power and influence, for among those attracted by his writings was one of the strongest and most interesting characters in American history,—Thurlow Weed, the "man behind the scenes." Weed was the first real political boss of New York State. He was a journalist of ability, but his sole interest in life was politics. To a great extent he modeled his life on that of the man whom he later displaced, Edwin Croswell. Croswell was state printer, the editor of the *Albany Argus,* a politician of consummate ability and the journalistic advisor of the "Albany Regency," the powerful ring that governed Democratic politics. What he did in a small way, Weed did on a large scale, achieving such wealth, power and influence as no politician before him had even dreamed of.

Weed's early life was not unlike that of Greeley, though not marked by the same poverty. He began his active journalistic career by enlisting Whig support for a paper with which to fight the influential *Albany Argus,*

[3] Alexander, ii, 27.

[4] Parton, *Life of Greeley,* 117.

and, on March 22, 1830, he established the Albany *Evening Journal.*

At the time when Greeley came to Weed's attention the Whigs were about to enter the campaign of 1838, with William H. Seward, then the bright particular star of the party, as their candidate for governor. Weed was Seward's friend and advisor — a very Warwick. He was preëminently "practical"; being political boss of the state, he knew how to raise large campaign contributions. A weekly Whig paper was needed for this campaign, and Weed decided that the editor of the *New Yorker,* whose name he did not even know at the time, was the man to edit the paper. He went to New York and called at Greeley's office on Ann Street, inquiring for the editor. "A young man with light hair, blond complexion, with coat off and sleeves rolled up, was standing at a case with 'stick' in hand, and he replied that he was the editor, and that his name was Horace Greeley." [5]

Greeley accepted Weed's offer, agreeing to edit the paper as desired, and also to spend at least two days each week in Albany. The paper was called the *Jeffersonian* and gave much satisfaction to the political dictator. Greeley's work even then was marked by such maturity of thought and felicity of expression as was given to few men in his day. While he was editing the *Jeffersonian* in Albany, he was Weed's personal guest, and the two became intimate, not only politically but socially. That was the beginning of the famous Seward-Weed-Greeley political partnership, the dissolution of which resulted in the nomination of Abraham Lincoln, instead of William H. Seward, for the Presidency in 1860.

There was idealism and patriotism in this partnership, but there was also a sordid side, as we shall see later. In

[5] *Weed's Autobiography,* 466.

a personal way there was not missing, however, an appealing note, such as was revealed in the correspondence of Seward, when he wrote to his wife that Weed had gone to New York "on an errand of love and tenderness to Greeley," who was worried under the weight of domestic grievances, and whose health had been impaired "from exposure in his nightly walks from his office." "He brought Greeley's child home," Seward wrote, "to keep until Greeley himself had recovered his health."

When Seward was elected governor in 1838, Weed was the acknowledged boss. He was consulted on all appointments, and there were, according to Seward, fourteen hundred of them. The State Senate, however, was under Democratic control, but Weed overcame that difficulty by going to New York, using his new-found power to collect $8,000, and putting the money into Democratic districts, thus gaining control of the entire Legislature.

Later in life, after their bitter quarrel, Greeley wrote concerning Weed and Seward:

"Mr. Thurlow Weed was of coarser mold and fiber — tall, robust, dark-featured, shrewd, resolute, and not over-scrupulous —keen-sighted, though not far-seeing. Writing slowly and with difficulty, he was for twenty years the most sententious and pungent writer of editorial paragraphs on the American press.

"In pecuniary matters, he was generous to a fault while poor; he is said to be less so since he became rich; but I am no longer in a position to know. I cannot doubt, however, that if he had never seen Wall Street or Washington, had never heard of the Stock Board, or had lived in some yet undiscovered country, where legislation is never bought nor sold, his life would have been more blameless, useful and happy." [6]

[6] *Busy Life,* 313.

When the Harrison and Tyler campaign came on in 1840, Greeley, having come to be considered a valuable member of the party, was made the editor of another political journal, the *Log Cabin.* This title was the result of an article that, at the time of Harrison's nomination, the *Baltimore American* had written:

"Give him a barrel of hard cider and settle a pension of two thousand a year upon him, and, our word for it, he will sit for the remainder of his days contented in a log cabin." This sneer was the basis of a historic battle-cry, which was first used at Harrisburg, Pennsylvania, January 20, 1840, with the result that "the log cabin and hard cider" became the slogan of the Whig party.

In his biography of Henry Clay, Carl Schurz declared that "there has never been a presidential canvass in which there has been less thought." The parades, the songs and the log cabin cries were all part of an extraordinary excitement, but that excitement meant that the people were tired of the party in power and their ebullience was simply the outward evidence of their intention to throw off their bonds.

Greeley claimed much credit for the Whig victory that followed. He asserted that the *Log Cabin* had helped arouse most of the enthusiasm, citing the fact that it achieved the phenomenal circulation of 80,000.[7] He therefore determined to try a greater field and, with a capital of $1,000, lent him by a Whig friend, he brought out the *Tribune* on April 10, 1841.

When the *Tribune* appeared, the *Courier and Enquirer,* the *New York American,* the *Express,* and the *Commercial Advertiser* were Whig papers, all in the six-cent class. The *Evening Post* and the *Journal of Commerce* leaned to the Democratic party, while the *Sun* and the *Herald,*

[7] *Busy Life,* 134.

though affecting to be neutral, were really inclined to be Democratic.

From the very beginning Greeley established the fact that he was ready to fight for his place in the newspaper world; he had as his assistant Henry J. Raymond, of whom we shall speak later, and he very quickly attracted to himself and his paper all those who had reform causes at heart; all, indeed, who were in sympathy with the oppressed. Margaret Fuller was not only a contributor to the *Tribune,* but lived with Mr. and Mrs. Greeley at their country home on Forty-ninth Street. In this way he became, with her, a devoted champion of the emancipation of women and a believer in the fullest recognition of social and political equality with "the rougher sex."

The same spirit led him to open his columns to the socialists of that day. Fourier was then the rage among the intellectuals, due in great measure to the efforts of Alfred Brisbane, who presented Fourier's ideas to the public in a series of articles, which ran for two or three years in the *Tribune.*

Greeley attributed his own conversion to Fourierism to the fearful conditions that he saw in the winter of 1837-38, when destitution and suffering pervaded the city.

"I lived that winter," he says, "in the Sixth Ward,—then, as now, eminent for filth, squalor, rags, dissipation, want, and misery. A public meeting of its citizens was duly held early in December and an organization formed thereat, by which committees were appointed to canvass the ward from house to house, collect funds from those who could and would spare anything, ascertain the nature and extent of the existing destitution, and devise ways and means for its systematic relief. Very poor myself, I could give no money, or but a mite; so I gave time instead, and served, through several days, on one of the visiting committees. I thus saw extreme destitution more closely than I had ever before observed it and was enabled to scan its repulsive features intelligently. I saw two families, including six or eight children, burrowing in one cellar under a stable,—a prey to famine on the one hand, and to vermin and cutaneous maladies on the other, with sickness adding its horrors to those of a polluted atmosphere and a wintry temperature. I saw men who each, somehow, supported his family on an income of $5 a week or less, yet who cheerfully gave something to mitigate the suffering of those who were *really* poor. I saw three widows, with as many children, living in an attic on the profits of an apple stand which yielded less than $3 a week, and the landlord came in for a full third of that. But worst to bear of all was the pitiful plea of stout, resolute, single young men and women: "We do not want alms; we are not beggars; we hate to sit here day by day, idle and useless; help us to work,— we want no other help; why is it that we have nothing to do?"[8]

Greeley's socialistic beliefs led to a warm debate with his erstwhile protégé, Henry J. Raymond, when the latter, leaving Greeley and the *Tribune,* went to work for James Watson Webb on the *Courier and Enquirer.* This was an additional reason for the coolness, which developed into actual enmity, between the two.

It was, however, by his vigorous championship of the Free Soil party and by the whole-souled manner in which he later threw himself into the Republican party, that Greeley achieved his greatest fame before the war. The Democratic party was dominated by the South; the Whigs were a weak opposition, led mainly by men who did not have the courage of their convictions and who did not sense the struggle that was coming. The Free Soil party

[8] Greeley, *Busy Life,* 145.

grew up in the attempt to check the endeavors of the slaveholders to extend slave territory; it eventually supplanted the Whig party, which was never more than a party of opposition. Although it included all those who, for various reasons, were opposed to the Democrats, the Whig party never had strong and uniting principles of its own.

Despite the fact that there were Free Soil Democrats, the Democratic party had become the party of the South and of slavery, even at this time, 1840–1850. True it was that in the Whig party was to be found the only effective opposition to the extension of slavery, but many of its leaders were so anxious to conciliate sentiment among pro-slavery Northerners that a new party with firmer principles was inevitable. In the movement for such a party, Greeley and the *Tribune* rapidly became leaders.

So excellent a political authority as James G. Blaine gives credit to Greeley for having a national influence as early as 1848. He says that Seward's influence, backed by the organizing skill of Thurlow Weed and the editorial power of Horace Greeley, was responsible for the election of General Taylor, and adds, "Perhaps in no other national election did three men so completely control the result." [9]

"There were many other journals in both the North and the South," says another writer, "but there was only one *Tribune* in the entire country." [10]

The weekly *Tribune* had become the great anti-slavery journal of the period, and "went into almost every parsonage, college, and farmer's home in the Northern states." It was "the spokesman of the most numerous

[9] *Twenty Years in Congress,* i, 82.
[10] Wilson, *Life of Dana,* 99.

and determined body of men ever associated for public purposes in the United States."[11] "The *New York Tribune*," says Charles Francis Adams, "during those years was the greatest educational factor, economically and morally, this country has ever known."[12]

[11] Pike, *First Blows of the Civil War*, xiv.
[12] *An Undeveloped Function*, 64.

CHAPTER XXI

THE *TIMES* AND GREELEY'S TRIUMPH

Greeley's Characterization of Raymond — Need for the *Times* — Greeley a great moral factor — Faults in New York papers — *Times* issued — Birth of Republican party — Weakness of Seward — Greeley's longing for leadership — Interview with Weed — Raymond nominated for lieutenant-governor — Letter to Seward — Weed and Seward lacking in perception — Lincoln-Douglas debates — Chicago convention of 1860.

As Bennett and the *Herald* had inspired Greeley to make in the *Tribune,* a better paper, so it was Greeley and his *Tribune* that inspired Raymond to be the sponsor of a paper that would be less radical, less addicted to all the "isms," than the *Tribune.*

Raymond, as we learn from his correspondence with R. W. Griswold, had gone to Greeley when a youth, brimming over with idealism and literary ambition. "I never found another person, barely of age and just from his studies, who evinced so much and so versatile ability in journalism as he did," Greeley wrote later of Raymond. "Abler and stronger men I may have met; a cleverer, readier, more generally efficient journalist I never saw. He is the only assistant with whom I ever felt required to remonstrate for doing more work than any human brain and frame could be expected to endure. His services were more valuable in proportion to their cost than those of any one who ever worked on the *Tribune.*" [1]

As Raymond came to know the city and the men influential in politics, he saw that there was room for another

[1] Alexander, ii, 160.

paper, a journal that would appeal to those who thought Greeley extreme and Bennett impossible. His political associates, Weed and Seward, also saw that a conservative paper, at a popular price, would tend to bring into the Whig party a conservative element that had not hitherto been attracted. Weed, the practical man, saw that there were business men who could be brought into the party, if some of the radicalism could be curbed.

The *Times* entered the field at a time when the anti-slave forces in the east needed such an organ. The success of Seward was the success of the new party, and Weed and Seward needed just such a paper. The years between 1850 and 1860 were filled with cross currents; the wisest men declared that they were unable to foretell the future, although it was only those who were called "hotheads" who realized the truth that lay in Seward's words,— that a conflict was inevitable. No one could foresee that Greeley, Seward, Weed, and Raymond, the four men who had made the Republican party possible, would quarrel among themselves, over a mere matter of patronage, to the discomfiture of all of them, but to the benefit of the nation.

Nor would the boldest prophet have suggested that the introduction of penny journalism, producing such pro-slavery journals as the *New York Sun* and the *New York Herald,* would ever be considered as one of the important steps that led to the spread of journalism among the masses, and eventually made the question of slavery the one that held the North as a political unit. Had the question of secession come before the country disassociated from slavery, it is difficult to conceive that Lincoln would have received the support that he did. Strong abolitionist as he was, Greeley was one of those in favor of allowing the South to take her slaves and go.

As we have contended all through this book, the moral issue lay with the people; it was hammered out by agents as blind and as grimy, politically, as the men who work before an actual furnace. The contentions and political maneuverings of these men were but the means to an end.

When Thurlow Weed, in 1848, wished to retire from the *Albany Evening Journal,* a banker of Albany, George Jones, (who afterwards became Raymond's partner,) offered the *Journal* to Raymond, but the negotiations fell through. Later Raymond began planning for a newspaper in New York. As interesting as was Bennett's visit to Greeley, to interest him in the *Herald,* is the fact that Raymond enlisted in his initial negotiations, Charles Anderson Dana, then of the *Tribune.*

Seward's son, at that time a writer on the *Albany Journal,* tells of a call made by Dana of the *Tribune* and Raymond of the *Courier and Enquirer* on Thurlow Weed, to seek his advice regarding plans for a new morning journal in New York. Raymond felt that somewhere between the *Herald* and the *Tribune* there was room in the city for a paper that would be conservative in politics, carefully accurate in its news, and without "reforms or sensations." Dana believed that Weed's short, crisp editorial articles, critical and humorous, were the kind that would be most popular.

Raymond spent the two years following Weed's offer in Albany, first as a member of the legislature, and then as Speaker of the Assembly. During those winters he had many conversations with George Jones; what finally led to the decision to undertake the paper was information received by Jones, to the effect that the *Tribune* had made a profit of $60,000 in one year.

The time selected for the introduction of a new paper was, as Raymond's associate and biographer has set forth, exceedingly propitious. The *Journal of Commerce* was dull; the *Express*, a morning paper, "behind the times"; the *Sun*, too much patronized by "domestics in quest of employment and by cartmen dozing at street corners waiting for a job." The *Evening Post*, which published one edition at half-past two in the afternoon, was noted chiefly for "its vigorous espousal of the doctrines of free trade." The *Commercial Advertiser* was merely a rival of the *Post*. The *Herald* contained much "printed filth"; the *Tribune* "had got into bad ways" — mainly through its editor's enthusiastic advocacy of the theories of Charles Fourier.[2]

After many difficulties the first number of the *Times* was brought out on September 18, 1851. Raymond's salutation was as cautious as could be,— there was not even a declaration of principles. He had declared in a preliminary statement that the *Times* would not "countenance any improper interference on the part of the people of one locality with the institutions, or even the prejudices, of any other." His opening editorial showed the same cautious regard for the sensitive Southerner, in the statement, "there are few things in the world which it is worth while to get angry about; and they are just the things that anger will not improve." [3]

What all three — Raymond, Weed and Seward — failed to realize was the fact that all the temperate discussion in the world was not going to bridge the chasm between the slave-holding South and those men and women of the North who believed that slavery was a crime. As politicians, they hoped that, by a careful policy of drift, immediate difficulties might be avoided and, now and then, a political victory achieved.

[2] Maverick, *Henry J. Raymond*, 52.
[3] *New York Times*, September 18, 1851.

The political situation might have continued unchanged for several years had not Stephen A. Douglas introduced in December, 1853, in the Senate, the famous "Nebraska Bill," which affirmed that the Clay compromise of 1850 had repealed the Missouri Compromise of 1820. Almost immediately the country was in a ferment, and the anti-slavery Whigs found themselves able to enroll under the same banner with the Free Soil Democrats. The parties in the country now came to be distinguished as "Nebraska" or "anti-Nebraska." In Jackson, Michigan, on July 6, 1854, the Republican party was born, the result of this last move of the slave power.

Here Seward distinguished himself. In the struggle for the repeal of the Missouri Compromise, he made a greater fight in 1854 than Rufus King had made in 1820 over the original enactment. It was Seward who answered arguments and marshaled the opposition; whose final great appeal concluded in words that few people at that time realized as fundamental truth: "The slavery agitation you deprecate so much is an eternal struggle between conservatism and progress; between truth and error, between right and wrong. . . . You may legislate and abrogate and abnegate as you will, but there is a superior power that overrules all; that overrules not only all your actions and all your refusals to act, but all human events, to the distant, but inevitable result of the equal and universal liberty of all men." [4]

An anti-Nebraska State convention was held at Saratoga on August 16, 1854; Horace Greeley offered the resolutions and Raymond was a conspicuous figure. It was here that Greeley was doing his greatest work, in urging the formation of a new party made up of Whigs, Free Soilers and the anti-Nebraska Democrats; it was

[4] F. W. Seward, *Life of W. H. Seward,* ii, 221.

here that Seward, Raymond and Weed, showed their lack of vision. The New York Senator — whose position in view of his opposition to the Kansas-Nebraska bill, was a commanding one — felt that the Whigs were still numerically strong enough to be the leaders in the movement and that a new party was not needed. "Seward hangs fire," wrote Dr. Bailey; "he agrees with Thurlow Weed."[5]

Strong in debate, Seward was weak in council, due to his great susceptibility to Weed and to Weed's advice. That Weed, in this crisis, was actuated by any other than the highest motives, is incredible, to any one who reads and studies his life; what is evident is that Weed, like any man whose bent has been thoroughly political, was naturally opposed to anything so revolutionary as the formation of a new party, and was most unsympathetic, as are all practical politicians, toward the initiator or the moral enthusiast. Raymond, in the *Times,* naturally reflected the views of Seward and Weed, but furnished a plausible defense for their position. The result was that at the Saratoga convention in August, nothing was done except to agree to re-assemble in September. When the regular Whig convention met in September, the differences among the Democrats made it appear that the Whig candidate for governor would be elected. This prospect, as much as anything else, was what had held Weed back from a sympathetic reception of the idea of a new party.

Greeley, who had vision, yearned for leadership. The issues that had gone to make the Whig party strong were issues that he had made. Whatever feeling he may have had about Raymond personally, there is no question but that he resented the growing importance of his former associate, and the fact that it was toward him (Raymond)

[5] *First Blows of the Civil War,* 237

that Weed and Seward were more and more inclined to lean. He harbored the idea that this was the time for him to present himself as a candidate for governor.

In addition to the Nebraska question, the one absorbing topic before the people of the State of New York at that time was prohibition. An anti-liquor wave had swept over the country and the Prohibitionists were popular. Greeley had been ardent in the cause and had, to a large extent, fought its battles; this was to him an additional reason for believing that the time had come for him to run for office. To Weed, therefore, as the acknowledged boss of the Whig party in New York State, went Greeley, and there is very little doubt that there was also in his mind a determination to find out exactly what his own position was in the "firm," that had been known as the Weed-Seward-Greeley partnership.

Nowhere in the history of American politics is there a more lamentable exhibition of the weakness of the system that had grown up, the system of which Weed was the chief exponent, than the following account of the interview, taken from Weed's reminiscences:

"Mr. Greeley called upon me at the Astor House and asked if I did not think that the time and circumstances were favorable to his nomination for Governor. I replied that I did think the time and circumstances favorable to his election, if nominated, but that my friends had lost control of the state convention. This answer perplexed him, but a few words of explanation made it clear. Admitting that he had brought the people up to the point of accepting a temperance candidate for Governor, I remarked that another aspirant had 'stolen his thunder.' In other words, while he had shaken the temperance bush, Myron H. Clark would catch the bird. . . . I informed Mr. Greeley that Know-Nothing or 'Choctaw' lodges had been secretly organized throughout the state, by means of which many delegates for Mr. Clark had been secured. Mr. Greeley saw that the 'slate' had been broken, and cheerfully relinquished the idea of being nominated. But a few days afterward Mr. Greeley came to Albany, and said in an abrupt, but not unfriendly way, 'Is there any objection to my running for Lieutenant-Governor?' . . . After a little more conversation, Mr. Greeley became entirely satisfied that a nomination for Lieutenant-Governor was not desirable and left me in good spirits." [6]

Weed was either very stupid or very canny when he assumed that Greeley left him in good spirits; he had insulted the man as far as was possible,— short of actually throwing him out of the room,— for he had practically informed him that there was no place for him anywhere on the state ticket as long as Weed controlled the machine. In addition to this, his excuses were of the most superficial and insulting kind.

Myron H. Clark, the man selected in place of Greeley, was a fanatic of very slender attainments, originally a cabinet-maker. He had introduced an anti-liquor bill, passed it through the legislature, and was made a state hero by Governor Horatio Seymour's veto. While he was well liked, his popularity was not so great that Weed could not have beaten him had he so wished. To make matters worse, the convention nominated Raymond for lieutenant-governor,— "No other name could have been put on the ticket so bitterly humbling to me," Greeley admitted afterward in a letter to Seward. It was an unnecessary humiliation, although Weed insisted that the convention had acted on its own responsibility and that he had never thought of Raymond until his name had been suggested by others. It was also a fatal error, for then

[6] *Life of Thurlow Weed,* ii, 225.

began Greeley's quarrel with the other members of the triumvirate and, in a letter to Seward, he withdrew from the partnership. It was this quarrel that culminated in the defeat of Seward in the Chicago Republican Convention in 1860.

Greeley's letter to Seward, which did not come to light until years later, shows a rather pathetic willingness to have taken a minor place in the triumvirate. It reveals that his more practical and hard-headed associates had grown very tired of this crank reformer, with his fanatical ideas. It is pathetic in the fact that it shows how Greeley,— the man who was then probably the greatest journalist in the country,— was destined to break himself on the rock of political ambition.

This letter was written immediately after the election, in which he loyally supported the unimportant Clark, who was successful. Greeley recited with great pains how he had assisted both Seward and Weed; how they had both advanced politically and how, when he had suggested that he be nominated for lieutenant-governor (he denied that he had asked for the governorship), he had been humiliated by Weed's refusal.[7]

The nomination of Raymond, he frankly said, was more than he could bear, and he thus concluded this remarkable letter:

"Governor Seward, I know that some of your most cherished friends think me a great obstacle to your advancement — that John Schoolcraft, for one, insists that you and Weed shall not be identified with me. I trust, after a time, you will not be. I trust I shall never be found in opposition to you; I have no further wish but to glide out of the newspaper world as quietly and as speedily as possible, join my family in Europe, and, if

[7] See Appendix, Note D.

possible, stay there quite a time,— long enough to cool my fevered brain and renovate my overtasked energies. All I ask is that we shall be counted even on the morning after the first Tuesday in February, as aforesaid, and that I may thereafter take such course as seems best without reference to the past." [8]

Seward's inability to see the political mistake that had been made is shown by the off-hand manner with which, in a note to Weed, he refers to this extraordinary letter, suggests that something be done for poor Greeley and asks if there is a place on the Board of Regents that could be made for him, as if history could be patched up with a place on the Board of Regents!

In the new Republican party that was formed Greeley had, over Seward and Weed, the advantage that he had been an ardent believer in the movement, and had been in frequent consultation with, and had greatly encouraged those who were for the new party, and was said to have been the one who suggested the name, "Republican." [9] On the other hand, Seward and Weed had never given the Republican movement, in the West and in New England, a word of encouragement in 1854,— a mistake that cost them dearly before many years had passed.

When Seward made his great speech favoring the immediate admission of Kansas, and defending the settlers in maintaining their struggle for admission as a free state, Greeley enthusiastically endorsed it as "unsurpassed in its political philosophy." The day that it was printed in the weekly *Tribune,* the circulation rose to 162,000 copies.

It was this friendliness on Greeley's part when he and they were at one on a matter of principle, that led Seward

[8] *Busy Life,* 320.
[9] Alexander, ii, 216.

and Weed to underestimate the extent of the hurt they had done Greeley. They might have realized that the ex-partner was not inactive in the convention of 1856, which nominated Fremont and — although he was most anxious to be nominated, even against the advice of his friend Weed — passed Seward completely over. Weed believed that it was impossible to elect the Republican candidate in 1856, and for that reason did not support Seward, wishing to save him for 1860; by that time, he believed, the Republican party would be strong enough to elect its candidate. Greeley "sided" with Weed in this sage view of the situation. It was Borgian unanimity.

Two years later the debates in Illinois between Stephen A. Douglas,— whose theory of popular sovereignty had appealed not only to northern Democrats but to many northern Republicans,— and Abraham Lincoln, an unknown Republican "politician," brought to the front the man who was to solve the questions of this grave period. It was during these debates that Lincoln had declared that "a house divided against itself cannot stand." Several months later Seward, in his Rochester speech, summed up the impending clash as "an irrepressible conflict between opposing and enduring forces, and it means that the United States must and will, sooner or later, become either entirely a slave-holding nation, or entirely a free labor nation." Both of these statements arrived at the same point at practically the same time and Seward, with his greater reputation, was given the credit of having antedated Lincoln.

Bennett, who had remained Democratic and around whom an agitation had developed without any apparent disturbance of his own self-satisfaction, denounced Seward as a more dangerous person than Beecher or Garrison, declaring that no conflict existed, except the one

Seward was fermenting. Even Samuel Bowles, in the *Springfield Republican,* thought that Seward had made a mistake, but Greeley saw and declared that the position was "calm, sagacious, profound and impregnable, showing a masterly comprehension of the present aspect and future prospects of the great question which now engrosses our politics."[10] Seward's speech was a bid for the Presidency. James Watson Webb, in the *Courier and Enquirer,* declared that it settled the question of Seward's nomination.

Lincoln, however, was moving up on him. He came to New York in 1860, and was introduced to his audience at a meeting over which William Cullen Bryant presided. Although Bryant and Weed had both met Lincoln years before, neither of them could recall him. Greeley's enthusiasm for Lincoln's address in Cooper Union was unbounded. "He is one of nature's orators," the *Tribune* declared.[11] To add to the increasingly favorable impression that Lincoln was making, Seward, in a speech before the Senate, showed a weakening in his position, leading Wendell Phillips to declare, in the *Liberator,* that he was phrasing his speech to suit Wall Street.

When the Republican Convention met in Chicago in 1860, Seward was the leading candidate and the Eastern politicians assumed that he would be nominated. Surrounded by the strongest men of New York, Weed attended, confident and arrogant, to direct the victory. He had not included Greeley in his list of delegates, but Greeley,—holding a proxy from far-off Oregon,—was just as busy, if not so confident or so arrogant, as Weed.

What was more important, the West knew him, knew him favorably and believed that his analysis of Seward's

[10] *New York Tribune,* October 27, 1858.
[11] *Ibid,* March 1, 1860.

character revealed the true weakness of Weed's candidate. In this way he did more to defeat Seward's candidacy than did any other man in the country.

Both Seward and Weed insisted that Greeley had given them to understand that he was supporting the former. The failure of both men to appreciate Greeley's position, however, is as evident as their failure to appreciate the fact that the Western Republicans, admire Seward though they did, were unable to countenance his political methods and his close association with Thurlow Weed. William Cullen Bryant declared that what injured Seward as much as anything else was the "project of Thurlow Weed to give charters for a set of city railways, for which those who received them are to furnish a fund of from four to six hundred thousand dollars to be expended for the Republican cause in the next presidential election."[12]

Another witness tells us that Weed took an Indiana politician aside, and "pleaded with him to turn the Indiana delegation over to Seward, saying that they would send enough money from New York to insure his election for Governor, and carry the state later for the New York candidate."[13]

It was a moneyed convention, if we are to believe Greeley's statements, and there is every indication that they are true; but the West was firm and, when it was over, Lincoln had been nominated. A Western politician was able to write, "Greeley slaughtered Seward, and saved the party. He deserves the praises of all men and gets them now. Wherever he goes he is greeted with cheers."[14]

[12] Godwin, *Life of Bryant,* ii, 127.
[13] A. K. McClure, *Lincoln and Men of War Times,* 25.
[14] Hollister, *Life of Schuyler Colfax,* 148.

CHAPTER XXII

THE AUTOCRACY OF THE SLAVEHOLDERS

Backwardness of Southern press — First abolition movement at South — Effect of arrogance of slave-holders — Government without newspapers — Reasons for attitude of "poor whites" — South commercially outstripped — Northern papers steadily improved — Contrast between sections shown by press — "Honor" — Exemplified by Jennings Wise — Robert Barnwell Rhett — *Charleston Mercury* — Suggested resumption of slave importation — George D. Prentice.

We have followed thus far the development of journalism and its influence on democracy in the United States, but it has been to a large extent a story of the North and West. What was the progress at the South, where, with the literary inclinations of a wealthy leisure class, there was certain to be interest in a political press? How far did the ideas of the slaveholders affect the journalism of that section, and what were the processes that led to so sharp a division? These questions are important, especially when we consider that from the leading southern state, Virginia, came the democratic ideas that were to rule the country. The ideas of Thomas Jefferson, as we have seen, eventually dominated the Republic, and it was as a result of these democratic ideas that there sprang up a great democratic cheap press. The anomaly is that the section of the country in which it might be assumed that Jefferson had the greatest influence was the one that lagged farthest behind, in the development of both journalism and democracy.

The cause of this backwardness was the development

of slavery as an economic factor in the South, following the invention of the cotton-gin. The South believed that, through the growth of the cotton industry, it was to be the wealthy section of the country; the cotton-gin made the use of slave labor imperative.

Up to the time that Whitney invented the cotton-gin, there was not, even in the South, a strong pro-slavery sentiment; in fact, in the early part of the century there was a great abolition sentiment in the South. Washington had, on his death, freed his slaves, and some of the most distinguished statesmen of that region, although they held slaves, believed that at some time or another slavery would be abolished.

Jefferson had, in his original draft of the Declaration of Independence, a clause condemning slavery. It was omitted, however, because it was thought that such a clause might give offense to those in the North who had been engaged in the slave-traffic. Years afterward, this reproach came back to plague the abolitionists of the North, for the truth was that there were, at the North, as many who were willing to make profit out of the slaves as there originally were in the South. Even after the agitation against slavery had been fully launched, merchants of the North who had profitable business relations with the cotton states were opposed to all contention that might interfere with their profits.

As we have seen, it was in the slave states that the abolition feeling first developed, but we have also seen that that feeling was very quickly put down. This suppression, together with the fact that the South had come under the domination of an autocracy that brooked no public discussion, except within lines of its own setting, was the reason for the minor place in journalism occupied by the southern papers.

The first abolition newspapers were started in the South and the bitterest speeches against slavery were made there. But the movement was driven out and driven North by the slave-holding class, who, although in the minority, represented the material wealth of the country and were, under the social, political and economic conditions which they had fostered, the sole representatives of public opinion. In those early days when abolition papers were being started in the South, it was a battle of principle against interest, of ideas against force.

But there can be no idealists, no great editors or journals, where brute force and material wealth so completely control, and the result was that the southern men of idealism were ignored in their own communities, or that they went North.

Making due allowances for population, it is interesting to compare the newspaper growth in the free soil states,— Ohio, Indiana or Illinois, for example,— with that of Louisiana, in which there had been, since before the beginning of the nineteenth century, a prosperous city. Even while Louisiana was a French colony, New Orleans had supported a paper; its first English paper, however, was not published until 1804. But in 1828 there were only nine papers in Louisiana, while Ohio had sixty-six, Indiana seventeen and even Illinois could boast of four.

In 1810 Ohio showed fourteen papers, as compared with Louisiana's ten, but in the period from 1810 to 1828, Ohio gained no less than fifty-two, while Louisiana actually shows a loss of one paper. In 1840 the figures were: Ohio, one hundred twenty-three, Indiana, seventy-three, Illinois, forty-three, Louisiana, thirty-four.

There may have been many reasons for this; the chief one undoubtedly was that, where men are not free to discuss questions without endangering their lives, and where a small oligarchy, such as the slaveholders constituted, is in the ascendant and is the political power, a strong journalistic spirit cannot be developed. Had there been men in the South of the temper of old Ben Harris, or Zenger, or Sam Adams, there would have been a different story to tell. The slave-holders of the South were never so numerically strong that they could not have been crushed by the South itself. [1]

By appealing to the other white inhabitants on the ground of fear and race prejudice, however, they succeeded in crushing out whatever minority there might have been. What was more important, they drove to the North the very men that they needed, men of independent judgment, of the type of Edward Coles, second Governor of Illinois,— a slave-holder in Virginia who left that state in order that he might liberate his slaves.

More important still, they discouraged those restless spirits who sought better conditions in life, and who, as emigrants, took into undeveloped territory a vigor and a freshness that made for liberty of discussion and democracy, the very life of Americanism.

This side of the Southern question still remains to be explained — preferably, one would think, by a student of Southern sympathies, broad enough to understand that the sentiment in the North was an inevitable political-sociological development. That the sentiment in the South was also inevitable, one is forced to believe when one finds such exponents of it as Governor Henry A. Wise, who declared that he was thankful there were few papers in Virginia,— almost a paraphrase of the statement of Governor Berkeley of Virginia in 1671, when he thanked God that "we have no free schools nor printing,— God keep us from both."

[1] *See* Appendix, Note E.

The astounding thing is that this was supposed to be the sentiment of the state that gave to the world Jefferson, whose belief was that he would rather live in a land where there were newspapers and no government than in one where there was a government, but no newspapers.

What happened in the South was exactly what Jefferson considered the undesirable alternative, a government without newspapers,— that is, newspapers as the North knew them and in the proportion and relation to the people that the North had them. The number of white illiterates in the South was one of the results of a lack of democracy; it was also one of the causes. Journalism would have helped to cure this condition, paradox though that may seem. In recent times the success of a clever journalist,— Arthur Brisbane, editor of the *New York Evening Journal,*— has been due, in great measure, to the fact that he printed a certain section of his paper in type large enough to be read by many who could almost be classed as illiterates.

The people who eventually aroused the North were not the so-called aristocrats, not people of the type of Philip Hone, who suffered a nervous shock when he saw a *Herald* reporter enter Mrs. Brevoort's exclusive ballroom. It was the class of people who corresponded to the illiterates of the South who became a vital, moving power under the stimulation of free discussion; whose susceptibility to ideas and sensitiveness to moral conditions acted on northern journalism even when its beginnings were of the basest and most sordid description. These people, the "plain people," evolved their own leaders and champions,— Lincoln, Greeley, Samuel Bowles of the *Springfield Republican,* William Lloyd Garrison,— whereas the same class at the South remained an inert mass, responsive only to the virtual command of the so-called better-class whites.

How thoroughly the "poor whites" were in the hands of their superiors is shown by the statement of a modern student of the South as to the reason why this particular class fought so valiantly for the Confederacy:

"An acute observer, a Confederate veteran, once said to me, 'When I was serving in the Army of Northern Virginia, I took great interest in finding out why mountaineers and poor whites, men who had never owned a slave, men who had no interest in slavery, were as keen for the war as any of us. I concluded that it was a war of caste. Rightly or wrongly, they had the notion that, if the North won, they would be reduced to the level of the negro. They were animated by an intense racial feeling. They fought for the racial idea.'"[2]

In this connection it is well to recall that slavery was never formally established by statute in any of the southern states. It was a "tolerated anomaly." Had an effort been made to pass such statutes, there is no telling what the effect might have been on these lethargic "poor whites"; it might have stirred them to realization that their own condition, in a community where they had so little political power, was not too secure.

We must not be led into the error of thinking that there was, in the beginning, any difference in ability between the journalists at the North and those of the South.

A southern critic of the South, Hinton Rowan Helper, insisted that there were able journalists there, and that it was the lack of enterprise and the lack of freedom which made them seem inferior to their brethren at the North. At this day, looking calmly back over this turbulent period, we can realize how true this statement was.

[2] N. W. Stephenson, *Atlantic Monthly*, June, 1919.

What is more, for the men who were fighting the battles of the slave power, slavery had little real influence, and that influence was unquestionably deadened by the fact that the very breath of the institution of journalism was freedom. Their bitter denunciations of those northern politicians and fanatical abolitionists,— who wished, they declared, to rob them of their property,— concealed in many a case the heavy sense of impending doom.

Although the South claimed to be wealthier than the North, its people were fast being confronted on all sides with evidences that, commercially, the North was leaving them far behind. Little as the local southern editors wished to call attention to this fact, they were frequently obliged to do so, in order to stir their constituents. In the early fifties the *Whig*, of Vicksburg, Mississippi, complained that the Mississippi Legislature had been obliged, not only to send its session laws to Boston to be printed, but to appropriate $3,000 to pay one of its members to go there and read proofs. "What a commentary on the Yankee-hater!"— A little later, the Greensboro' *Patriot* criticized the legislature of North Carolina for doing the same thing, adding, "It is a little humiliating that no work except the commonest labor can be done in North Carolina; that everything which requires a little skill, capital, or ingenuity, must be sent North." [3]

For twenty years preceding the war, the fact was evident that the northern papers were steadily becoming more comprehensive in their scope and more complete in every department, and that they were enlisting more talent than were those at the South. It was the complaint of the southerner, Helper, that "the very highest literary ability in finances, in political economy, in science,

[3] Helper, *The Impending Crisis*, 391.

in statism, in law, in theology, in medicine, in the *belles-lettres,* is laid under contribution by the journals of the non-slave-holding states." Certainly, the same could not be said of the southern journals.[4]

It was stated in 1850, undoubtedly with truth, that the press of the South, taken as a whole, was about twenty years behind that of the North, and that, while it was exceptional at the North to find a newspaper or magazine that had not improved during the decade from 1840 to 1850, in the South the reverse held true.[5]

This book, Helper's *Impending Crisis,* was indeed an anomaly, for its thesis was that slavery depressed the poor whites and enabled the slave-owners to profit at their expense; but it was unsuccessful as an attempt to arouse the non-slave-holding whites.[6]

For twenty years or more the wide difference between the two sections of the country showed itself more openly in the newspapers and journals than in any other way. The assumption on the part of southerners that their people were descendants of the Cavaliers, while those of the north represented the socially inferior Roundheads, resulted, once the cleavage began, in a sharpness of treatment of each by the other. The lack of ambition, lack of mobility, and the very sensitive "honor," so characteristic of the Southerner, made it more and more impossible for the man at the North to understand his Southern brother, especially when, to avenge his honor, the Southerner was obliged to employ personal violence, as in the case of Brooks and Sumner.

This class "honor" was at the very base of the difference between the two sections; it made the Southern

[4] *Impending Crisis,* 387.

[5] *See* Appendix, Note F.

[6] T. C. Smith, *Parties and Slavery,* 288.

editor and thinker, who was a victim to it, unable to appreciate the truth of either Turgot's conception of progress or the immorality of slavery.

In fifty years there had been no change in the attitude of mind of the people south of the Mason and Dixon line, with the result that society was encrusted with a leadership, social and political, through which it was impossible for either an individual or an idea to break. The election to the Governorship of his state and to the United States Senate of such a man as Andrew Johnson, a really illiterate tailor, was a great exception; we have seen in the cases of Coles of Illinois, Birney and others how, the moment men began to think contrary to the views of the slave-holding leadership, it became necessary for them to move north. It has been pointed out that, with all the literary inclination on the part of the educated southerners, only one book, that of Helper, was written to stimulate thought as to the possible social effect of slave-holding on the poor whites.

An example of the absurd lengths to which this self-established superiority led some of its votaries is related of young Jennings Wise,— editor of the *Richmond Enquirer,* and son of the Wise who was thankful that there were few papers in Virginia. The young man had had unusual opportunity for broadening of character, having served in the American Embassies at Paris and Berlin, but he returned to Virginia apparently more than ever imbued with the aristocratic ideas of that section. He was said to be so amiable that "he never had a personal quarrel," but in two years of his career as the editor of the *Enquirer,* he fought eight duels in defense of his father, for he thought it was his duty to challenge anyone who criticized the Governor in the slightest way. This young man was not only a model of all the virtues, but genuinely religious, according to his brother. Were such characters the exception, they would baffle psychology. They were not rare, however, and the fact that they appeared in number shows why it was easy for this class idea to finally become a political one, until there had developed a local patriotism that burned far more fiercely than did the love of the entire country, at the North.

The chief exponent of that brand of patriotism was Robert Barnwell Rhett, editor of the Charleston *Mercury,* who, ten years before the war, was an ardent advocate of secession, and who saw in South Carolina's struggle a repetition of the story of the Greek republics. "Smaller states," he said, "have before us struggled successfully for their freedom against greater odds." Rhett's paper was the intellectual voice of the South. When Calhoun died in 1852, it was Rhett who took his place in the United States Senate; it was he who wrote South Carolina's appeal to the other states to secede; [7] when Jefferson Davis was inaugurated President of the Confederacy, it was on the arm of Rhett that he leaned when he entered the hall. The testimony of Rhodes is paid to Rhett, without mention of his name:

"Before the war," he states, "Charleston was one of the most interesting cities of the country. It was a small aristocratic community, with an air of refinement and distinction. The story of Athens proclaims that a large population is not necessary to exercise a powerful influence on the world; and, after the election of Lincoln in 1860, the 40,000 people of Charleston, or rather the few patricians who controlled its fate and that of South Carolina, attracted the attention of the whole country. The story of the secession movement of November and

[7] Wilson, *Rise and Fall of the Slave Power,* iii, 110.

December, 1860, cannot be told with correctness and life, without frequent references to the Charleston *Mercury* and the Charleston *Courier.* The *Mercury* especially was an index of opinion, and so vivid is its daily chronicle of events that the historian is able to put himself in the place of those ardent South Carolinians and understand their point of view." [8]

Given a man of Rhett's temperament, (his real name was Smith, which he changed to Rhett on entering Congress in 1837), one can understand the development of a local feeling of nationality; one cannot grasp as easily the reasons for the failure to see where the slave issue was leading. We have shown that there were those, here and there, who admitted that the South was falling far behind the North in the things that made for progress, but it remained for Rhett's paper,— though the article was signed by another — to suggest, a few years before the war began, a return to the barbarous practice of slave importation, a relic of the preceding century.

" There are many minds among us," said this writer, " firmly convinced that the Slave Trade is almost the only possible measure, the last resource to arrest the decline of the South in the Union. They see that it would develop resources which have slept for the great want of labor; that it would increase the area of cultivation in the South six times what it is now; that it would create a demand for land and raise its price, so as to compensate the planter for the depreciation of the slaves; that it would admit the poor white man to the advantages of our social system; that it would give him clearer interests in the country he loves now only from simple patriotism that it would strengthen our representation in Congress,

[8] *Historical Essays,* 91, 92.

and that it would revive and engender public spirit in the South." [9]

But there was one southern editor and one southern journal that maintained independence, and that was George D. Prentice and his *Louisville Journal.* It was said of Prentice that "he built the city of Louisville," [10] and to him is also given the credit of "preventing the secession of Kentucky."

Henry Watterson, his distinguished successor, says that "from 1830 to 1861 the influence of Prentice was perhaps greater than the influence of any political writer who ever lived." Prentice was a Connecticut Yankee, who could shoot as well as write, and when he established himself in Louisville, he identified himself at once as a man ready and willing to fight. His course after that was smoother.

When Fort Sumter was fired upon, Prentice wavered, and his "indecision was fatal to his national influence. He opposed the Rebellion but not for radical reasons and not with zeal." [11] Behind the arras, even here, there was tragedy. Prentice fought to keep Kentucky in the Union, he was loyal — but both his sons, his only children, were in the Confederate army.

[9] *Charleston Mercury,* February 17, 1857.

[10] Venable, 391.

[11] *Ibid,* 399.

CHAPTER XXIII

CIVIL WAR

The fourth estate in war time — Lincoln and newspapers — Trouble with editors — Sympathy for South — Attack on Fort Sumter arouses Northern papers — Greeley ignored — "Forward to Richmond" — Bull Run — Factional differences at North — Malignant papers excluded from mails — "Prayer of Twenty Millions" — Joseph Medill's antagonism to Seward — Downfall of Weed — *Tribune* office mobbed — Baltimore convention — Two papers suspended — High office promised to Greeley.

That journalism may make war was the opinion of no less an expert on the latter than Bismarck, who declared, in 1877, that the press was "the cause of the last three wars."[1] The Crimean war was credited to the *London Times,* while the Spanish-American war has been ascribed to the activities of William Randolph Hearst. On the other hand, war, although it does make news, cannot be said to make for journalism in its larger sense. In the two great American wars with which journalism had much to do, the Fourth Estate did not increase in power during the war; it suffered rather a diminution of influence. Sam Adams, who had so much to do with the struggle leading to the Revolutionary war, was a spent figure after it was over; so, after the Civil war, the men who had cleared the ground for the struggle gave way to those who had distinguished themselves during the conflict, particularly on the field of battle.

The soldier's belief that, in war, editors are less im-

[1] Rhodes, *Essays,* 89.

portant than fighters, is appreciated by no class of men so little as by the editors. In a democracy the latter are still entitled to full freedom of expression, up to the point where they begin to interfere with the waging of the war — the very war which, as a rule, they have been largely instrumental in bringing about. A position subservient to the exigencies of the situation is not easy for them to take, and we see, in the story of the Civil War, how the very leaders of the Fourth Estate who brought about the conditions that made the war inevitable were, because of the political power they still possessed and the frequency with which elections came, a source of embarrassment and perplexity to the government.

There is no rule,— there can be no rule,— as to the degree of freedom to be extended to the press in time of war, or as to how much it shall be abridged. In the great European war just ended, we have seen Great Britain,— a country less democratic than America,— through the efforts of Lord Northcliffe, turn out its Prime Minister and change its attitude toward the struggle in which it was engaged. The British form of government made that possible; there is very little doubt that there were several times, in the course of the Civil War, when Lincoln would have been turned out, had this country, in the sixties, been under such a Parliamentary government as England's.

Giving due consideration to the fact that Lincoln's task was that of putting down a rebellion, with a North far from unanimous, while the war of Great Britain was with another race, one outside its borders, the wisdom of our system seems to have amply justified itself. War must be waged by autocratic power, with only such checks as will keep those having that power from using it for any other purpose than waging war. It is generally admitted now that the change which Northcliffe brought about in England was a wise one, but it is not impossible to conceive of an unwise change. The advantage of our system was that, having once committed to Lincoln the conduct of the government, with the power to wage war in its defense, it was not possible to remove him except for actual malfeasance in office,— rage as the Fourth Estate might, and did. The value of the checks that a constitutional government puts on all power, including that of the press, was never more clearly demonstrated or more fully justified.

A study of Lincoln's relations with the newspapers leaves one filled with wonder, as does a study of every aspect of his career, at the gifts with which nature had endowed this great son of American democracy. Whence came his vision? His uncanny overview of the men and problems about him is one of the mysteries of the story of civilized man. There is nothing like it in history; indeed, there is nothing in history like his calm use of all that was usable in the new power that had developed since the war of the Revolution. What was not usable, what was malignant and raging in the Fourth Estate, was calmly allowed to beat itself against the rocks.

The pity was that mere political manipulation kept Lincoln from close and sympathetic touch with the great journalist of his time — Horace Greeley. They should have been understanding friends; probably, but for Weed, they would have been. They had much in common, and the humble origin of both proves that great men are not born and left in the midst of the wilderness; rather are they born in the wilderness and transported by seeming miracles to the exact point where they are needed.

Lincoln's troubles with the editors began immediately

after his nomination. Raymond and Weed,— whose futures, not only politically but as journalists, were wrapped up so closely with that of Seward,— suffered greatly in prestige, while the *Tribune* was given credit for great political sagacity and power. The result was that Raymond, goaded by Greeley's self-satisfaction, made his famous attack, [2] in which he charged Greeley with having secretly betrayed Seward while pretending to be his friend. Neither Weed nor Raymond would admit that it was the domination of the former that had ruined Seward.

In his answer to Raymond, Greeley avowed that his writings in the *Tribune* were sufficient evidence of his belief that Seward could not be nominated. With reference to his having betrayed the candidate, he called on Seward to produce his letter of six years before, stating that Seward had been showing this letter to other people. He asserted that, as he had not kept a copy of the letter, he had a right to have it back, in order that he might publish it. Seward took his time about complying with Greeley's request, but finally the letter was turned over to Thurlow Weed.

The outcome of this bitter controversy was that Lincoln had, in New York, a divided house. While all parties to the controversy were loyal in the highest degree, there was such division in the councils as gave the leader of his party many anxious and disturbing moments. The secession of South Carolina found Lincoln's advisors hopelessly at sea, and Greeley went so far that he declared: "If the Cotton States shall become satisfied that they can do better out of the Union than in it, we insist on letting them go in peace. The right to secede may be a revolutionary one, but it exists

[2] *New York Times,* May 25, 1860.

nevertheless. When any considerable section of our Union shall deliberately resolve to go out we shall resist all coercive measures designed to keep it in. We hope never to live in a Republic where one section is pinned to the other by bayonets."

"If the Cotton States, unitedly and earnestly, wish to withdraw peacefully from the Union," he said again, "we think they should and would be allowed to go. Any attempt to compel them by force to remain would be contrary to the principles enunciated in the immortal Declaration of Independence, contrary to the fundamental ideas on which human liberty is based." [3]

Giving strength to this wrong counsel, the Mayor of New York City, Fernando Wood, proposed to make New York a free city. An important meeting, at which were present John A. Dix, William B. Astor, Charles O'Connor and others, was held for the purpose of seeing that the South was "treated fairly" — further evidence of what slender support the new president was receiving from the city which had had so much to do with his nomination and election, and with the issues that elected him.

The newspapers of New York then had,— what they now have not,— an influence throughout the country; an influence which they lost gradually, as the great western cities began to develop after the war. None of them was very helpful to Lincoln between his election and his inauguration; in fact, one day after the fall of Fort Sumter, the *Sun* prodded the *Herald* on its friendliness for the South, and declared that if its publisher had not hung out an American flag there would not have been another issue of the paper. The *Herald* was also charged with having had in its office a full set of Confederate colors,

[3] *New York Tribune,* November 9th and 26th, 1860.

"ready to fling to the breeze of treason which it and the mayor hoped to raise in this city."

The firing on Fort Sumter brought a much-needed realization of the seriousness of the situation, and put an end to the sympathy for the Southern cause. The Southern papers viewed with bitter anger and disgust this boldness of front on the part of journals and politicians formerly considered neutral, if not friendly. The *Charleston Mercury* called the roll of the statesmen whom the South had counted friends. "Where," it asked, "are Fillmore, Van Buren, Cochrane, McKeon, Weed, Dix, Dickinson and Barnard, of New York, in the bloody crusade proposed by President Lincoln against the South? Unheard of in their dignified retirement, or hounding on the fanatic warfare, or themselves joining 'the noble army of martyrs for liberty' marching on the South."

"The proposition to subjugate," said the *Richmond Examiner,* "comes from the metropolis of the North's boasted conservatism, even from the largest beneficiary of Southern wealth — New York City."

Meanwhile Lincoln had taken Seward into his Cabinet, and James Watson Webb, another bitter enemy of Greeley, had been offered the post of Minister to Constantinople. Rejecting that, he had been made Ambassador to Brazil. Greeley was left without political recognition, and his temper was such that he could not but be unhappy, especially considering that, only a few months before, he had been proclaimed as the man who had brought about Lincoln's nomination.

He was indeed "a power without the government," left to fight the struggle in his own way. While his editorials in November and December, 1860, doubtless had much to do with alienating Lincoln from him, the fact that his bitterest enemy stood between him and the President was the real hindrance to a better understanding.

From the very first, Greeley felt that things were not moving properly at the capital, and he was not the only one. "Something seems not right with Scott," wrote Count Gurowski. "Is he too old or too much of a Virginian, or a hero on a small scale? . . . Scott is against entering Virginia, against taking Baltimore, against punishing traitors. Strange, strange!" [4]

Greeley's fear that the war might not be properly conducted by men whom he disliked led to a series of articles calling for action. These appeals culminated in the *Tribune's* voicing what was described as the Nation's war-cry: "Forward to Richmond!" This appeared on June 27, 1861, a four-line, triple-leaded leader, printed in small capitals, entitled "The Nation's War-Cry." It was as mandatory as it was conspicuous: "Forward to Richmond! Forward to Richmond! The Rebel Congress must not be allowed to meet there on the 20th of July!"

It seemed strange that Greeley, who only a short time before, had shown so conciliatory a spirit about secession, should now be so suspicious of others. "Do you pretend to know more about military affairs than General Scott? ask a few knaves, whom a great many simpletons know no better than to echo. No, Sirs! we know very little of the art of war, and General Scott a great deal. The real question — which the above is asked only to shuffle out of sight — is this: Does General Scott contemplate the same ends, and is he animated by like impulses and purposes, with the great body of the loyal, liberty-loving people of this country? Does he want the Rebels routed, or would he prefer to have them conciliated?" [5]

Lincoln finally gave way, and ordered General Mc-

[4] *Gurowski's Diary,* i, 35.

[5] *Tribune,* July 1, 1861.

Dowell,— who had, in the vicinity of Bull Run, 30,000 men, of whom only 1,600 were regulars, however,— to move forward, with the result that the North suffered the shock of losing the first battle of the Civil War. This calamity, however, was not without its advantages, for it aroused the free states to the fact that a stern conflict confronted them.

Greeley paid, in many ways, for the *Tribune's* part in bringing about the battle of Bull Run. James Gordon Bennett suggested that he be tried for murder, and a bitter newspaper war ensued. The four important papers, edited by four of the most influential editors in the country — Greeley, Bennett, Raymond, and Bryant — were more bitterly opposed to one another than to the South. Despite their differences, they were all loyal, which was not true of some few minor papers.

The Federal grand jury for the southern district of New York suggested that some of these other New York papers should be indicted. "Their conduct is, of course, condemned and abhorred by all loyal men, but the grand jury will be glad to learn from the Court that they are also subject to indictment and condign punishment." [6]

The bitterness between the Northern factions — Greeley on one side, and Weed, Seward and Raymond on the other — was intensified by the fact that Weed and Seward believed that, by putting the slave issue to the rear, a compromise might be effected with the South, or at least with the border states.

Senator Sumner in Congress, and Secretary Chase in the Cabinet, backed the policy of Greeley, who now became the outspoken oracle of what was known as the radical element at the North. While this faction was critical of Lincoln in the beginning, it was critical mainly

[6] *Appleton's Encyclopedia*, iv, 1861, 329.

because it was suspicious of the influence of Weed and Seward, and because it was keenly sensitive to the fact that the former was susceptible to material considerations. Additional strength was given to these critics by the fact that Weed had made himself unpopular in the West, after Lincoln's nomination, by his insulting refusal to entertain the suggestion that Seward might take second place on the ticket.

The loyalty of these radicals, however, could never be questioned, nor could they be confounded with another group of critics, virulent and malignant, such as were referred to in the charge of the grand jury, quoted above. Some of these papers the postmaster had excluded from the mails, the action calling forth bitter denunciation from editors who had, but a few years before, chortled with glee when Jackson's Postmaster-General, Amos Kendall, had excluded anti-slavery papers from the mail. On the whole, the number of papers affected by the restrictions imposed by Lincoln and his cabinet, in time of war, never equaled the number that had suffered interference, in a time of peace, under Jackson and his pro-slavery postmaster, Kendall.

The intense feeling on the part of both radicals and conservatives as to the emancipation of the slaves was reflected in Congress, with the radicals in the ascendant. It was then that Greeley, urged on by his friends,— who believed that a blow must be struck — wrote and printed his famous "Prayer of Twenty Millions," an editorial signed by himself and addressed to Abraham Lincoln.

The "prayer" — a signed, three-column editorial, heavily leaded,— began by stating that those who had assisted in making Lincoln President expected from him enforcement of the laws, and that the President had been remiss in the discharge of his "official and imperative duty with regard to the emancipation provisions of the new Confiscation Act. These provisions were designed to fight Slavery with Liberty. They prescribe that men loyal to the Union and willing to shed their blood in her behalf shall no longer be held, with the Nation's consent, in bondage to persistent malignant traitors, who for twenty years have been plotting and for sixteen months have been fighting to divide and destroy our country."

He complained that the President had given too much consideration to the advice of "fossil politicians." "The Union cause has suffered and is now suffering immensely, from mistaken deference to Rebel Slavery."[7]

"I close, as I began, with the statement that what an immense majority of the Loyal Millions of your countrymen require of you is a frank, declared, unqualified, ungrudging execution of the laws of the land, more especially of the Confiscation Act. That act gives freedom to the slaves of Rebels coming within our lines, or whom these lines may at any time inclose,— we ask you to render it due obedience by publicly requiring all your subordinates to recognize and obey it. The Rebels are everywhere using the late anti-negro riots in the North, as they have long used your officers' treatment of negroes in the South, to convince the slaves that they have nothing to hope for from a Union success,— that we mean in that case to sell them into bitterer bondage to defray the cost of the war. Let them impress this as a truth on the great mass of their ignorant and credulous bondmen, and the Union will never be restored — never. We cannot conquer Ten Millions of people united in solid phalanx against us, powerfully aided by Northern sympathizers and European allies. We must have scouts, guides, spies, cooks, teamsters, diggers and choppers from the Blacks

[7] *New York Tribune,* August 20, 1862.

of the South, whether we allow them to fight for us or not, or we shall be baffled and repelled. As one of the millions who would gladly have avoided this struggle at any sacrifice but that of Principle and Honor, but who now feel that the triumph of the Union is indispensable not only to the existence of our country but to the well-being of mankind, I entreat you to render a hearty and unequivocal obedience to the law of the land."

The appeal attracted so much attention that Lincoln replied to it himself in the *National Intelligencer:*

"I would save the Union. If there be those who would not save the Union unless they could at the same time save slavery, I do not agree with them. If there be those who would not save the Union unless they could at the same time destroy slavery, I do not agree with them. My paramount object in this struggle is to save the Union, and it is not either to save or destroy slavery. If I could save the Union without freeing any slave, I would do it; and if I could save it by freeing all the slaves, I would do it; and if I could save it by freeing some and leaving others alone, I would do that. What I do about slavery and the colored race, I do because I believe it helps to save the Union; and what I forbear, I forbear because I do not believe it would help to save the Union. I shall do less whenever I believe what I am doing hurts the cause, and I shall do more when I shall believe doing more will help the cause." [8]

At the meeting of the Cabinet on July 22, 1862, Seward opposed the Emancipation Proclamation; Weed, who had just returned from London, backed up the opinion of Seward; Raymond, who had made the *Times* the organ of the President, was always for the suppression of the slavery question. The *Herald*, the only other journal of

[8] *Lincoln's Works,* ii, 227.

weight in New York, was against anything that Greeley was for. It was, in fact, a Democratic organ when it possibly could be without being absolutely disloyal.

Greeley was not the only one dissatisfied with conditions. "The Union is in awful peril," wrote Joseph Medill, of the Chicago *Tribune*,— whose power and influence were increasing,— to Schuyler Colfax. "We have fought for 'Union and Slavery' for sixteen months. The crisis has come at last. One or the other must be given up, both cannot endure. We as a nation have rowed against Niagara's stream, but have drifted steadily toward the chasm, and the roar of the cataract can be heard by all but the wilfully deaf. The Governors have petitioned the President, and he has consented to receive three hundred thousand more volunteers. But they will not come. Tell the President he must call louder. He must either touch the popular heart by calling on men to fight for 'Union and Liberty,' or he must resort to conscription, and draft his recruits. Tell him not to be deceived. He needs these recruits now. If he adopts the former policy, a million men will obey the summons. But he must give us freedom-loving generals to lead them." [9]

A later criticism, also written by Medill to Colfax and intended to be transmitted to Lincoln, shows great bitterness toward Seward: "McClellan in the field and Seward in the Cabinet have been the evil spirits that have brought our grand cause to the very brink of death. Seward must be got out of the Cabinet. He is Lincoln's evil genius. He has been President de facto, and has kept a sponge saturated with chloroform to Uncle Abe's nose all the while, except one or two brief spells, during which rational intervals Lincoln removed Buell, issued the Eman-

[9] Hollister, *Life of Schuyler Colfax*, 186.

cipation Proclamation, and discharged McClellan. Smith is a cipher on the right hand of the Seward integer — by himself, nothing but a doughface. Bates is a fossil of the Silurian era — red sandstone, at least — and should never have been quarried out of the rocks in which he was imbedded. Blair was thrown into a retrograde position by the unfortunate quarrel of his brother Frank with Fremont. There must be a reorganization of the Cabinet; Seward, Smith and Bates must go out." [10]

Greeley was right, and his success as the moral voice of the North was soon to be demonstrated in a way that he could scarcely have anticipated,—by the downfall of Thurlow Weed, his former partner, but now his bitter enemy.

In 1863 Greeley and Weed, in a stiff battle in the New York Legislature, backed opposing candidates for the U. S. Senate. Weed succeeded in electing Edwin D. Morgan, with the assistance of Morgan's money, but announced, practically at the same time, his withdrawal from the *Albany Evening Journal.* He was rich and independent, but, although at the time of his retirement he had spent thirty years in building up a powerful political machine, he was so unpopular throughout the state that he was obliged to give up his long-cherished idea of removing to a farm near Rochester, there to spend his last days. So hostile was the feeling toward him in that section that he abandoned this idea and settled in New York City.

Commenting on this change in Weed's political fortunes, Greeley took the opportunity to compare the statements previously made by Weed and Raymond about his own ambitions:

"Let it pass whether or not the editor of the *Tribune* has been intensely ambitious for office. It would have

[10] Hollister, *Life of Schuyler Colfax,* 186.

been a blessed thing for the country if the editor of the *Journal* (Weed) had been impelled by the same passion. For avarice is more ignoble than ambition, and the craving for jobs has a more corrupting influence, alike on the individual and the public, than aspiration to office." [11]

He was a good hater, was Horace Greeley.

With so bitter a journalistic rival as Bennett on one side, such sharp and unrelenting party rivals as Weed and Raymond on another, and the anti-Union journals constituting a third point of attack, it was not surprising that, when the draft riots came, Greeley and his office were war centers. On July 13, 1863, the office of the *Tribune* was attacked; the rioters forced an entrance, threw books and papers out of the window and set fire to the place. The police charged, dispersing the mob with a number of cracked skulls, and managed to put out the fire.

One of Greeley's many enemies started the rumor that during the excitement he had sought refuge under a table in a restaurant. His reply to the slur was characteristic. He stated that, against the advice of many friends, who had warned him of the danger of attack and the peril of life in which he stood, he had gone as usual to his office. At the usual time for his evening meal he left his office by the main entrance, "went over to Windust's eating house for his dinner, passing through a howling mob for nearly the entire distance and was recognized by several of them." The next day he returned to the office, "now being armed," and was at his desk every day that week. And whoever "asserted that he at any time 'was hiding under Windust's table' is a branded liar and villain."

Near the completion of Lincoln's first term, when the time arrived for the nomination of his successor, it was

[11] *New York Tribune,* December 12, 1862.

observable that he had not, among all his so-called journalistic supporters, a real friend. Although Seward was loyal, Weed sulked in his camp over some petty appointment. In order to bring him back into the field, the President was obliged to write him a humble and somewhat apologetic letter.

"I have been brought to fear recently," the President wrote, with characteristic tenderness, "that somehow, by commission or omission, I have caused you some degree of pain. I have never entertained an unkind feeling or a disparaging thought towards you; and if I have said or done anything which has been construed into such unkindness or disparagement, it has been misconstrued." [12]

From Greeley, who had become to a large extent a party leader, Lincoln could expect little. Weed, as well as Greeley, praised General U. S. Grant, insinuating that he might possibly be a candidate to succeed Lincoln, but when the convention assembled at Baltimore, on June 7, 1864, the opposition had weakened. The platform, agreeable to both conservatives and radicals, was written by Henry J. Raymond, who reached, at this convention, the zenith of his power and influence. [13]

The development of a presidential boom for Horatio Seymour resulted in Bennett's veering once more toward the Democratic party, though he had been a merciless critic of Seymour as Governor. One reads the speeches and letters of the Democratic governor with amazement at the man's stupidity and bad manners. The only political platform that men like Seymour had was the very honest criticism of Lincoln by men of the type of Greeley. Unfortunately for himself, Seymour never realized that men like Greeley and Raymond, or even Weed, while

[12] Barnes, *Life of Thurlow Weed,* ii, 440.

[13] Alexander, iii, 95.

they might be led into disagreeing with Lincoln, would be utterly unable to associate with the "copperheadism" of Seymour.

On May 18, 1864, the *World* and the *Journal of Commerce* printed the bogus proclamation of Joseph Howard, Jr. Both papers were immediately suspended, and not allowed to resume until Monday, May 23rd, when Manton Marble, the editor of the *World,* in a three-column editorial, upbraided the President. Howard had been city editor of the *Times,* and, when arrested, was at his desk as city editor of the *Brooklyn Eagle.* Seymour at once endeavored to make political capital out of the suspension of the two papers, by ordering the District Attorney to arrest all those who had entered the offices of either paper.

McClellan was nominated, and Bennett was inclined to support him. Lincoln wrote privately to Bennett and asked him to accept the mission to France. The editor declined the offer, but his vanity was tickled; the *Herald* slowly veered about and, before the campaign was over, was advocating Lincoln's election. [14] It was at this time that Greeley made his Quixotic trip to Niagara Falls, to negotiate with the ambassadors of Jefferson Davis. Although the futility of this was evident,— to no one so much as to Lincoln — the trip was good for Greeley, as the offer of the mission to France was good for Bennett.

A month before the election, Greeley and Weed were of the opinion that Lincoln could not avoid defeat, and Raymond wrote to the President that his stand on the slavery question was affecting his chances of success. [15] The importance of this statement,— the crime of it, from a political point of view — is that it was made by the Chairman of the Republican National Executive Committee.

[14] McClure, 80.

[15] Nicolay-Hay, ix, 218.

But Lincoln stood firm, despite his editorial advisors and detractors; he wrote Grant to "hang on like a bull-dog and keep choking and chewing" and, in September, the tide turned. The nation was thrilled by Sheridan's defeat of Early, and Grant was able to proclaim that "The rebels have now in their ranks their last man."[16] The spirit of the North responded to the eloquence of George William Curtis, the young editor of *Harper's Weekly,* who, referring to the farewell speech of Alexander Stephens on his retirement from public life in 1859, said:

"Listen to Mr. Stephens in the summer sunshine six years ago. 'There is not now a spot of the public territory of the United States over which the national flag floats where slavery is excluded by the law of Congress, and the highest tribunal of the land has decided that Congress has no power to make such a law. At this time there is not a ripple upon the surface. The country was never in a profounder quiet.' Do you comprehend the terrible significance of those words? He stops; he sits down. The summer sun sets over the fields of Georgia. Good-night, Mr. Stephens — a long good-night. Look out from your window — how calm it is! Upon the Missionary Ridge, upon Lookout Mountain, upon the heights of Dalton, upon the spires of Atlanta, silence and solitude; the peace of the Southern policy of slavery and death. But look! Hark! Through the great five years before you a light is shining — a sound is ringing. It is the gleam of Sherman's bayonets, it is the roar of Grant's guns, it is the red daybreak and wild morning music of peace indeed, the peace of national life and liberty."[17]

Lincoln was swept into office with 179 electoral votes

[16] Alexander, iii, 120.

[17] Cary, *G. W. Curtis,* 186.

to 21 for McClellan, but the record of New York was not one of which its citizens should feel proud. In a total of 730,821 votes, Lincoln had only 6,749 more than McClellan. At the same election Raymond went to Congress,— to his own surprise, it was said,— carrying by 386 a Tammany Hall district that in 1862 had given a Democratic majority of 2,000. "It was the greatest victory of the year," says Alexander, "and in the end led to the saddest event of his life."

The election was to have brought to Greeley, also, the reward that he craved. Lincoln had sent word to him, during the campaign, that in the event of his re-election, Seward would probably go to England as Ambassador; in that event, "Greeley would make an admirable successor to Benjamin Franklin, the first Posmaster General."

Shortly after the inauguration, Greeley sent a messenger to the President, to remind him of his suggestion of the previous fall. The messenger arrived in Washington the morning after John Wilkes Booth had fired the fatal shot.[18]

[18] Alexander, iii, 126.

CHAPTER XXIV

AFTER THE WAR

Attempt of press to control politics — Failure of Raymond — Widespread indifference to corruption — Samuel Bowles — Platform of new reform movement — Carl Schurz — Liberty party — Greeley's candidacy — His defeat — Blaine on Greeley — Joseph Medill — Correspondence with Greeley, Webb and Seward — Chicago *Tribune*.

The story of journalism now enters directly into the field of political reform. The question is no longer one of the newspaper in its proper field, representing the people, but of its controlling the machinery of politics. Greeley, Raymond and Weed came to grief, as we have seen, in their attempts to control.

Raymond, acting as spokesman for President Lincoln, had been largely instrumental in bringing about the nomination of Andrew Johnson for Vice-President. Shortly after Johnson took office, Weed breakfasted with him, and from now on Raymond and Weed were his advisors and spokesmen; on the floor of Congress Raymond championed his cause, to his own humiliation and defeat. As he aligned himself with the President in his reckless disregard of the wishes of Congress, Raymond was watched with amazement by his own party. With the assistance of Raymond, Seward and Weed, Johnson attempted to organize a National party, at the convention held in Philadelphia in August, 1866. Raymond, in his loyalty to the President, went so far as to declare that the southern states, no matter how great their disloyalty, could not be deprived of their rights. Within two weeks he was removed from the chairmanship of the Republican National Committee, and later removed from the Committee. His career was ended, and he died three years later.

Brilliant, diplomatic, forceful, Raymond's failure as a legislator was ascribed to the fact that he had not begun his congressional career until he was too old to learn what was practically a new vocation. On the other hand, he was only forty-five years of age, and, of the men who distinguished themselves in Congress, many had made their maiden efforts at a much later time in life. James G. Blaine suggested that if, when he was elected Lieutenant-Governor, he had instead been elected to Congress, the story might have been different.

The student of journalism will see a far different reason for Raymond's failure. A journalist can never succeed unless he is fathering popular or moral causes. Weed, who made a fortune out of politics, who was for years the political boss of his state — even aspiring, under Johnson, to be the political boss of the nation,— was also a failure, despite his great wealth. He failed to appreciate the drift of public sentiment, and so lost control of the politics of New York State to so Quixotic and temperamental a figure as Greeley.

At the time when Raymond started the *New York Times,* there was a broad field of usefulness for the conservative journal that he had planned, but, just as Greeley ran to an extreme in his fanaticism, his individualism, and his pursuit of everything that seemed human or idealistic, so Raymond in the field of conservatism, guided by the very materialistic Weed and influenced by the disappointed Seward, ran to a narrow conception of politics and government; he was obsessed by the idea that political power could do little wrong. His mistake was that of the man in office — the blindness of those in power, competing with men who had no such weakness and who still had the eagerness of unfulfilled ambition. It illustrates the truth of the statement that great journalism is journalism in attack; great journalism is never journalism in office.

The month after Raymond's removal, the New York State Republican Convention was held, and both Weed and Raymond were conspicuously absent. They had risen to the zenith of political power, but had fallen; their fall was due less to a political catastrophe than to an awakening of the moral sense of the people.

Immediately after the Civil War,— as there is likely to be after every war, after every great moral ebullition — there had sprung up, in the wake of material progress, an indifference to the finer questions of morality. For twenty-one years the struggle on slavery had so engrossed the nation that many other important problems had been neglected — practically pushed aside.

The attention of the nation had been concentrated on the larger issues, and unscrupulous men had availed themselves of the opportunities afforded by that concentration to encompass their own ends, often to the detriment of the public welfare.

"Great projects of money-making throve and multiplied," says the biographer of Samuel Bowles, "corporations enriched by the government used their wealth to corrupt legislation; the tendency to speculate was stimulated by a currency of fluctuating value; business expansion and private extravagance went on till checked by the disaster of 1873. Bestowal of public office as a reward for partisan service, an evil of long standing, had been confirmed when Lincoln virtually transferred the patronage from his overworked Administration to the Republican Congressmen. Its mischief was widened by the multiplication of executive officers; its wrong was only slowly appreciated by the people at large. The Democratic party at the north had been debauched and demoralized by its attitude during the war, and the Republican party had become so sacred in the eyes of most of its adherents that under its shelter abuses found easy tolerance. The progressive political work of the years from 1868 on was largely of a very disagreeable kind. It consisted very much in the rooting out of abuses both old and new. A great deal of it resembled more the work of a policeman than a prophet." [1]

We have seen in the Republican convention of 1860, particularly on the part of those from the West, a distrust of the type of politician represented by Seward and Weed. The references at that time to the use of money indicated that, though the question had not yet become a primary one, corruption in politics was sooner or later to be a matter of absorbing public interest. The time had now come for warfare on this corruption, and in the reconstruction period, the Springfield (Mass.) *Republican,* under Samuel Bowles, became a journal of national influence, through its vigorous and continued denunciation of corrupt leaders and their connection with politics.

Bowles had very sharply delineated the character of James Fisk, Jr., a notorious stock gambler and corruptionist. When Bowles later visited New York, Fisk had him arrested and locked up in Ludlow Street jail. The affair attracted nation-wide attention, and many prominent citizens of Boston, wishing to do Bowles honor, tendered him a dinner. The editor declined, but in so doing he wrote the platform of the new reform movement.

" The corruption in politics and the corruption in busi-

[1] Merriam, *Life of Samuel Bowles,* ii, 88.

ness affairs," he said, " have become offensive and startling within the past few years, and the moral sense of the community seems at times to have become blunted by the successful display and repetition of practices that violate every principle of fair dealing and integrity and put the control of government and the value of many kinds of property at the mercy of political adventurers and ruthless stock-gamblers. The press really seems to be the best, if not the only instrument, with which honest men can fight these enemies of order and integrity in government and security in property . . . American journalism is now but in its feeble infancy; — but we have more to fear at present from its good nature, from its subserviency, from its indifference, from its fear to encounter prosecution and loss of patronage by the exposure of the wrong and the exposition of the right. A courageous independence and integrity of purpose, coupled with a fearless expression of truth as to all public individuals, corporations and parties, are the features in its character to be most encouraged.

" My own observation is that the Press rarely does injustice to a thoroughly honest man or cause. It may be deceived with regard to a private individual, and misrepresent him for a time; but with reference to public men and measures, its knowledge is more intimate and competent than that of any other agency possibly can be; and I know that it withholds unjustly to the public one hundred times, where it speaks wrongly once of the individual. Certainly, nine out of ten of all libel-suits against the Press are brought by adventurers, and speculators, and scoundrels, whose contrivances to rob the public have been exposed. . . ."

Almost the same sentiments were being expressed by equally courageous men, in different sections of the country, and a coalition of these forces was bound to occur. In Missouri, the leader of the protest was a very remarkable character, Carl Schurz, the editor of the St. Louis *Westliche Post*. Schurz had been a general in the Union army; he was one of the German patriots who had been driven out of their native land because of their battle for liberty.

Nominally, the Liberal movement had its origin in the state of Missouri in 1870. The state had not seceded, but thousands of its citizens had joined the rebel ranks. To prevent these men fighting against the Union as civilians, an amendment to the Constitution had deprived them of the rights of citizenship, and the Republicans, who held control of the legislature, were not inclined to restore these rights at once. Then and there, headed by Carl Schurz and Benjamin Gratz Brown, began the formation of the new movement. These Liberals combined with the Democrats and Missouri was turned over to Democratic control.

In many northern states, different conditions were bringing about a feeling, among a vigorous minority, that the Republican party had failed to avail itself of its possibilities, despite its conduct of the war. It must be remembered that the Republican party was very young, and that to it there was not the attachment that was to be expected of the Democratic party, which had existed ever since the first president. On the Democratic party, however, was the stain of disloyalty, and many men, although they found themselves out of sympathy with the Republicans, were still unable to forget the record of the opposition during the war. They turned with enthusiasm to the third party, made up principally of bolters from the Republican ranks.

Originating with Carl Schurz, the new party was almost "newspaper made," for the leading figures included many of the famous editors of the North. In every northern state there was opposition within the Republican party to the administration of Grant, and Schouler in the *Cincinnati Commercial,* Medill in the *Chicago Tribune* and Greeley in the *New York Tribune,* all helped to fan the flames.

The national convention of the Liberal Republicans, called by the Liberals of Missouri, was held at Cincinnati in May, 1872. Among the leaders of the convention were Colonel A. K. McClure, editor of the Philadelphia Times, Carl Schurz and Joseph Pulitzer of Missouri, and Horace White, one of the owners of the *Chicago Tribune.*

The politicians who had gone to the convention with the intention of controlling the nominations, viewed the result of the balloting with disappointment and surprise — Horace Greeley was nominated. The Free Trade Liberals in New York, at a meeting presided over by William Cullen Bryant, at once disowned the new Liberal party and its candidate.

Friends had told Greeley that it would be impossible for the Democrats to support him for the Presidency. His reply to this shows the same weakness that he had exhibited in similar circumstances in an interview with Thurlow Weed for the governorship of New York. He immediately suggested that if he were not an available candidate for President, he hoped he would be considered acceptable for the second place on the ticket.[2]

His nomination put no heart into the men who had to make the fight for him. Even the state of New Hampshire, in which he had spent his boyhood, rebelled against his nomination and, in the October elections, the Republicans won in a landslide. He made a sturdy,

[2] McClure, 301.

statesmanlike fight, but it was soon apparent that the battle was hopeless. While he was still bearing up under the gloom that followed the October elections, he was called home to nurse his dying wife; he passed a month of sleepless nights, and was at her bedside when she died, a week before his defeat in November. A few weeks later, November 29, 1872, his own death came.

"I was an abolitionist for years," he said a few days before he died, "when to be one was as much as one's life was worth even here in New York,—and the negroes have all voted against me. Whatever of talents or energy I have possessed, I have freely contributed all my life to protection, to the cause of our manufacturers; and the manufacturers have expended millions to defeat me. I even made myself ridiculous in the opinion of many whose good wishes I desired, by showing fair play and giving a fair field in the *Tribune* to Women's Rights; and the women have all gone against me."

So passed Horace Greeley, one of the greatest of American journalists, human in his faults, human in his greatness. He represented better than any other man in history what is noble and lasting in journalism. Of all that was written of him, none wrote with more understanding than did James G. Blaine.

"The strain through which he had passed, following years of incessant care and labor, had broken his vigorous constitution," wrote Blaine after Greeley's death. "His physical strength was completely undermined, his superb intellectual powers gave way. Before the expiration of the month which witnessed his crushing defeat he had gone to his rest. The controversies which had so recently divided the country were hushed in the presence of death; and all the people, remembering only his noble impulses, his great work for humanity, his broad impress upon the age, united in honoring and mourning one of the most remarkable men in American history.

"His mind was original, creative, incessantly active. His industry was as unwearying as his fertility was inexhaustible. Great as was his intellectual power, his chief strength came from the depth and earnestness of his moral convictions. In the long and arduous battle against the aggression of Slavery, he had been sleepless and untiring in rousing and quickening the public conscience. He was keenly alive to the distinctions of right and wrong, and his philanthropy responded to every call of humanity. His sympathies were equally touched by the suffering of the famine-stricken Irish and by the wrongs of the plundered Indians. Next to Henry Clay, whose ardent disciple he was, he had done more than any other man to educate his countrymen in the American system of protection to home industry. He had on all occasions zealously defended the rights of labor; he had made himself an oracle with the American farmers; and his influence was even more potent in the remote prairie homes than within the shadow of Printing-House Square. With his dogmatic earnestness, his extraordinary mental qualities, his moral power, and his quick sympathy with the instincts and impulses of the masses, he was in a peculiar sense the Tribune of the people. In any reckoning of the personal forces of the century, Horace Greeley must be counted among the foremost — intellectually and morally." [3]

What Greeley and the *New York Tribune* were to the East, Joseph Medill and the *Chicago Tribune* were to the West. Without Greeley's temperamental difficulties and without Greeley's great ambition, Medill succeeded in developing a great newspaper. That was to him ample

[3] *Twenty Years in Congress*, ii, 532-536

satisfaction,— although it brought with it political honors, they never gave him such disturbing moments as those with which the great eastern editor had to contend.

Such education as Medill received he obtained while working on his father's farm in Stark County, Ohio. He studied law and was admitted to the bar in 1864; his association with the editor of the local paper attracted him to journalism, however, and he learned to set type and work a hand press. The result was that he gave up the idea of practicing law, and in 1843 he bought out the *Coshocton Whig,* changing the name to *Coshocton Republican.* Like so many young men in the middle west at that time, he burned with indignation over the aggressiveness and the arrogance of the South, and in his little paper the editorials were so bitter that on one occasion sundry Democrats waylaid him and answered his editorial attacks with cuts and bruises. Two years later he moved to Cleveland, and established the first Free Soil morning paper in that city. This paper, the name of which was changed to the *Cleveland Leader,* is to-day one of the important papers of the country.

Medill's great work was to unite the Free Soil and the Whig parties. The Whigs were controlled by the slave element, and it was Medill's task to draw such of the Whigs as were not under the domination of the pro-slavery element, into a new party, which he proposed to call the "Republican." He wrote to Horace Greeley to ask his advice about his proposed third party; we see from this how easy it was for Greeley to influence the country, when men like Joseph Medill looked to him as a leader.

"Go ahead, my friend, with your proposed Republican party, and God bless you," Greeley replied. "I hope you will have the best of luck. The time has indeed come to bury our beloved party; it is dead. But we have many fool friends who insist it is only in a comatose state and will recover, but I tell them it is dead — still, I dare not yet in New York announce the demise of the party and call for the organization of a new one. But do you go ahead on the Western reserve and commence the work. I like the name for it (Republican). I was opposed to J. Watson Webb when he changed the name Democrat-Republican to Whig, but at that time he had the public ear. If you can get the name Republican started in the West it will grow in the East. I fully agree to the new name and the new christening."

James Watson Webb and Thurlow Weed, to whom he also wrote, scolded him for such a suggestion, but William H. Seward suggested that the idea was worth trying out. Finally, one night in March, 1854, a meeting was called in the office of the *Cleveland Leader,* and there was born the National Republican party, the platform of which was "No more slave states; no more slave territory; resistance to pro-slavery aggression; slavery is sectional; liberty is national."

The following year an opportunity came and Medill went to Chicago to take an interest in the *Chicago Tribune.* From 1855 until the time of his death in 1888 he was, in the public mind, the editor and controller of the *Tribune,* though during several periods, notably the time that he served as mayor of Chicago, he was not in editorial control.

CHAPTER XXV

EDITORS OF THE NEW SCHOOL

Charles Anderson Dana — His broadness of view — Brook Farm colony — Fourteen years with *Tribune* — Assistant secretary of war — Editor of *Sun* — Opposition to Grant — Attitude toward Tweed — Bennett the younger and the *Herald* — The *Times* — Whitelaw Reid — Henry Watterson — His views on journalism.

Art comes into journalism late, as it comes into so many of the artifices of men. It is impossible to do justice to the life and work of Charles Anderson Dana unless one views him as a journalist in whom the artistic side of his profession was dominant. A common point of view has been that of the literary critic who declared that "in its exercise of its recording functions it (journalism) is a useful trade, and in its commenting office it takes rank as a profession, but it is never an art." [1]

We have here an old-fashioned criticism, a point of view not so common now as it was before Charles Anderson Dana made of journalism an art. He saw his great profession as no one had seen it before him, as a whole, as a very human whole, and he left an impression on his time that can only be compared to that made by Addison and Steele on the essayists of the early eighteenth century. Despite his cynicism and the errors of taste and judgment into which his personal disappointments led him, his entire period of editorial control was suffused with such an optimism as regards the intelli-

[1] Boynton, *Journalism and Literature,* 5.

gence of the American people that one is led to feel that there was much virtue in the "vice" that so aroused his doleful critics.

Dana was born in New Hampshire in 1819 and, when twelve years of age, went to Buffalo to become a clerk in his uncle's store. Here Indians were sometimes customers and he learned the Seneca language, adding to it Latin and Greek, and later on prepared himself to enter Harvard, which he did in 1839. When he was obliged to leave college he joined the Brook Farm Colony and, to pay his way, taught Greek and German in addition to waiting on the table. He was thus early associated with all that was cultured and scholarly in America and it was through his Brook Farm experiences that he came to know Horace Greeley and to be employed by him in February, 1847, as the city editor of the *Tribune*, at $10 a week. On the *Tribune* he soon became an important factor, so much so that credit was given to him for many of the editorials that were commonly ascribed to Greeley. His was the broader culture, and Greeley deferred to it, as is shown by the frequent letters that he wrote to him from Washington when Dana was acting as managing editor and Greeley was writing on the politics of the nation.

On one occasion Dana, who was much interested in the new Opera House, left Greeley's Washington article out of the paper to make way for his favorite subject. Greeley good-naturedly protested:

"What would it cost to burn the Opera House? If the price is reasonable, have it done and send me the bill."

The campaign in the *Tribune* for an early movement of the northern troops in 1861 was Dana's, though it was Greeley who had to stand for the pleasant suggestion of Bennett that hanging was too good for the man who started the cry "On to Richmond." The parting between Greeley and Dana came, however, as a shock to the younger man. Greeley notified the stockholders that if he, Dana, did not leave, Greeley would. This was a blow to Dana, whose relations with Greeley had recently been most friendly and he thought that some misunderstanding must be at the bottom of it. He sent a friend to Greeley to test him out and found that it was true. Accordingly he resigned on March 28, 1862, and found himself at the age of forty-three, after fourteen years on the *Tribune,* one of the best equipped newspaper men in America, but with no place open for him.[2]

His ability, however, was known in Washington and the most important work of his life came through the accident of his non-employment. In 1863 he was asked to come to Washington, and President Lincoln and Secretary of War Stanton employed him, not to spy on General Grant, but to tell them frankly whether it was true, as his enemies declared, that Grant was drinking himself into idiocy. His reports on Grant resulted in the General's receiving from Washington the heartiest coöperation.

The war over, he resigned as Assistant Secretary of War and went to Chicago to become the editor of the *Republican.* The paper, however, was not sufficiently financed, and again he was the journalist without the journal.

At a time when most men are settled in life, Dana was yet to begin a career. On January 25, 1868, a number of prominent Republicans paid Moses S. Beach $175,000 for the *New York Sun* and made Dana editor-in-chief. From that time on he was a national figure, not always of the greatest influence, but never in obscurity.

[2] O'Brien, *Story of the Sun,* 215.

During Grant's first administration Dana became, to the surprise of many, a bitter critic of the President. This was generally ascribed to the fact that Grant had not appointed him Collector of the Port of New York, a position for which he had been urged by his friends. His attack on the President began with the bestowal of public offices in reward for campaign contributions. But he went further and practically accused the President of being responsible for the corruption of the public services. He declared that Grant had " done more to destroy in the public mind all distinction between right and wrong, to make it appear that the great object of life and the chief purpose of official authority is to acquire riches, and that it makes no difference by what means this object is attained. Had Grant been a pure man of high moral sense, a delicate feeling of honesty, and a just conscience, his example, his influence, and his power would long since have sufficed to turn back the rising tide of corruption and to rescue the government from the dangerous evils with which it was struggling."

He accused the President of having twenty-four relatives holding office, and as an evidence of the corruption in Washington he obtained and printed a letter, a phrase of which rapidly became the shibboleth of corruption; it was as follows:—

Treasury Department of Pennsylvania,
Harrisburg, March, 1867.

MY DEAR TITIAN,—Allow me to introduce to you my particular friend Mr. George O. Evans. He has a claim of some magnitude that he wishes you to help him in. Put him through as you would me. He understands Ad*dition,* Di*vision,* and Si*lence.*

"TO TITIAN J. COFFEY, ESQ.,
Washington, D. C."

Yours,
"W. H. KEMBLE."[3]

[3] Wilson, *Life of Charles A. Dana,* 427.

The attitude of Charles A. Dana toward the corrupt political boss of New York City, William M. Tweed, has been defended by the historian of his paper on the ground that Dana's support of Tweed was satirical.[4] The paper on December 7, 1870, printed a short announcement of the fact that ten cents had been sent in to start a monument for Tweed and a semi-sarcastic editorial endorsement of the proposal. Tweed himself was obliged to order the money that had been collected to be returned, but the fact that a considerable sum had been contributed would indicate that a great many people had failed to appreciate the joke of Dana, and were taking it seriously. Two such serious students as Gustavus Myers and Dr. Henry Van Dyke construed the Dana support of the Tweed statue proposal as serious. There was not in Dana's ridicule of Tweed any of the relentless attitude that he showed in his attack on President Grant; and it was for this reason that he lost friends.

What Dana said about journalism was always acute and always sound. When shortly after Greeley's death he was being criticized throughout the country for the manner in which he had supported Greeley's nomination for the presidency, Dana spoke of the profession which none knew better than he and incidentally spoke of himself.

" A great deal of twaddle is uttered by some country newspapers just now over what they call personal journalism. They say that now that Mr. Bennett, Mr. Raymond, and Mr. Greeley are dead, the day for personal journalism is gone by and that impersonal journalism will take its place. That appears to mean a sort of journalism in which nobody will ask who is the editor of a paper or the writer of any class of article, and nobody will care.

[4] O'Brien, *Story of the Sun.*

"Whenever, in the newspaper profession, a man rises up who is original, strong, and bold enough to make his opinions a matter of consequence to the public, there will be personal journalism; and whenever newspapers are conducted only by commonplace individuals whose views are of no consequence to anybody, there will be nothing but impersonal journalism." [5]

There was nothing erratic about Dana personally. The men who knew him not only admired but loved him. He had none of Greeley's passion for reform and although he was perhaps a more profound student than Godkin he had rather a disdain for the seriousness with which Godkin and his associates viewed life. He was accused of not having a high moral outlook; he retaliated by expressing his abhorrence of sham.

It is a strange thing that this man who had such a genius for journalism should have arrived so late in life, but the answer probably is that he loved his books and loved culture more than he really loved success.

Dana's judgment of personal journalism was more than justified by the career of the men who succeeded the three great personal journalists, Greeley, Raymond and Bennett.

The younger Bennett, as he was called, has but recently died. It is interesting that he made his paper the organ — as far as there could be an organ — of the very people who had so publicly expressed their contempt for his father and the *New York Herald*. If the paper had a fatal defect as a journal it was this very catering to the vanity of snobocracy. It was the younger Bennett's own weakness. He cluttered the office of the Paris *Herald* with useless and impoverished nobility and in the desire to make a "gentleman's" paper he treated the news from

[5] *New York Sun,* December 6, 1872.

an angle that frequently produced disproportions. His own vanity led him to the most Quixotic measures such as ordering the omission of the Russian Emperor's name from the paper because of some personal affront. The "personal column," on account of which he narrowly escaped being sent to prison, showed how far his sojourn in Paris had led him away from healthy American opinion.[6]

The immediate successor of Raymond was his partner, George Jones, under whom the *Times* became a power, particularly in municipal affairs, when it was the instrument by which the corruption of W. M. Tweed was exposed. For a period it lost its influence, but later it came under the ownership of Adolph S. Ochs, by whom it has been developed as a conservative but enterprising journal, one of the most widely read in the country.

The success of Whitelaw Reid more than justified the statement of the editor of the *Sun*. Reid had hardly assumed control of the *Tribune* when he was offered in 1878 the appointment of Minister to Germany, an honor far greater than any that ever came within the grasp of Greeley, and an honor that he was wise enough to decline. It was repeated within a few years and again he declined. He afterward became a candidate for Vice-President of the United States, without one-tenth of the effort that Greeley made to obtain a nomination as Lieutenant-Governor of the State of New York. He was made Ambassador to France, he died Ambassador to Great Britain, and his body was brought home under escort of the battleships of two nations.

What Reid, Jones, Bennett, Jr., and Dana realized more than others of their day, and what the later comers, Pulitzer and Hearst, also recognized, was the fact that not

[6] See appendix, Note G.

so much the views of the editors as the news that the papers contained would sell papers, and all of them made their papers successful by fitting their publications to the spirit of the times. It is this understanding that has made Ochs, the present owner of the *Times,* the proprietor of possibly the most successful paper, financially, in the country, exclusive of the Chicago *Tribune.*

Credit has been given to Godkin of the *Post* and Dana of the *Sun* for their influence on the journalism of the country; it would be an injustice to Whitelaw Reid to fail to point out the credit due to him for the liberalizing influence which the *Tribune* had on the American press, both during the war, when he was managing editor under Greeley, and after he had become the chief owner. As did Bowles and the *Springfield Republican,* Reid set a standard for the politically independent paper and showed that it could not only live, but that it could lead. The *Chicago Tribune, Cincinnati Commercial* and the *Louisville Courier Journal* were papers that breathed the same spirit. Later, it is true, Reid made the *Tribune* the organ of the Republican party, but it was a chastened and refreshed Republican party and the independence he had shown in the time referred to had its effect on the growth of American independent journalism.

Of the personal journalism that Dana said was bound to arrive whenever the newspaper had back of it a strong figure, no greater exemplar could have been conceived than another journalist who rose contemporaneously with Reid, Henry Watterson of the Louisville *Courier-Journal,* the successor of George D. Prentice.

No journalist, no individual, in the country has done so much since the Civil War to bring about a better understanding between the North and the South.[7] No one

[7] Had he lived, Henry W. Grady, of the *Atlanta Constitution,*

was better fitted for the task and he has for years been the "Well-Beloved" of the profession, endeared to many who opposed him politically. He was one of those ardent journalists who led the liberal movement in 1872 and he has since been a leader, and nearly always a liberal. His recently published reminiscences have shed new light on that interesting time. Watterson, Samuel Bowles of the *Springfield Republican,* Horace White of the *Chicago Tribune* and Murat Halstead of the *Cincinnati Commercial* were the men who ran the national convention in that year. With Carl Schurz they formed a combination to control the nominations. Whitelaw Reid was present as a representative of Horace Greeley and the *Tribune,* and when he heard of the "combine" he insisted that the *Tribune* should be admitted.

Watterson urged Reid's admission, on the ground that Greeley never would be considered as a candidate, and the seemingly ingenuous and very polite young man from New York was taken into camp. As a matter of fact, as he wrote in later years, Reid knew full well what he was doing; it later proved to be themselves and not Reid that had been taken in, for Greeley *was* nominated.

The combination took to itself much credit for the formation of the convention, although outside of the circle were many men of influence and power, men of the type of Alexander K. McClure of the Philadelphia *Times,* an ardent supporter and friend of Lincoln during the war, and one of the most insistent of the reformers who brought about the liberal movement.

Watterson is now eighty years of age. He is one of the few men living who knew the great men of the country before the Civil War; he is the only great editor who

would undoubtedly have been not only one of the great editors of the country but one of its leading statesmen.

was friendly with the giants of that time. He has loved his profession, he has dignified it, it is as much indebted to him as he is to it. He speaks therefore of the mission of journalism with authority.

"Assuming journalism equally with medicine and law to be a profession," he writes, "it is the only one of the three in which versatility is not a disadvantage. Specialism at the bar or by the bedside leads to perfection and attains results. The great doctor is the great surgeon or the great prescriptionist — he cannot be great in both — and the great lawyer is rarely great, if ever, as counselor and advocate.

"The great editor is by no means the great writer, but he ought to be able to write and must be a judge of writing. The newspaper office is a little kingdom. The able editor needs to know and does know every range of it between the editorial room, the composing room and the pressroom. He must hold well in hand everybody and every function, having risen, as it were, step by step from the ground floor to the roof. He should be level-headed yet impressionable; sympathetic yet self-possessed; able quickly to sift, detect and discriminate; of varied knowledge, experience and interest; the cackle of the adjacent barnyard the noise of the world to his eager mind and pliant ear. Nothing too small for him to tackle, nothing too great, he should keep to the middle of the road and well in rear of the moving columns; loving his art — for such it is — for art's sake; getting his sufficiency, along with its independence, in the public approval and patronage, seeking never anything further for himself. Disinterestedness being the soul of successful journalism, unselfish devotion to the noble purpose in public and private life, he should say to preferment as to bribery, 'Get behind me, Satan.'

" Whitelaw Reid, to take a ready and conspicuous example, was a great journalist; but rather early in life he abandoned journalism for office and became a figure in politics and diplomacy so that, as in the case of Franklin, whose example and footsteps in the main he followed, he will be remembered rather as the ambassador than as the editor.

" More and more must these requirements be fulfilled by the aspiring journalist. As the world passes from the rule of force — force of prowess, force of habit, force of convention — to the rule of numbers, the daily journal is destined, if it survives as a power, to become the teacher — the very Bible of the people. The people are already beginning to distinguish between the wholesome and the meretricious in their newspapers. Newspaper owners likewise are beginning to realize the value of character. Instances might be cited where the public, discerning some sinister but unseen power behind its press, has slowly yet surely withdrawn its confidence and support. However impersonal it pretends to be, with whatever of mystery it affects to envelop itself, this public insists upon some visible presence. In many states the law requires it. Thus personal journalism cannot be escaped and whether the one-man power emanates from the counting room or the editorial room, as they are called, it must be clear and answerable, responsive to the common weal, and, above all, trustworthy."

CHAPTER XXVI

AFTER-WAR PROBLEMS AND REFORM

Direct part of newspapers in government — E. L. Godkin — Editor of *Nation* — Real power — Fitness of *Post* as an influence for good — Criticism of Godkin — His pessimism — Contrast with early writings — Bryce's opinion — William Rockhill Nelson — Kansas City *Star* — Their extensive influence — "In His Spirit."

The war left many newspapers in a stronger position than before the struggle; the power wielded by the important journalists had established their right to be heard and had set a standard of conduct for those who were to come after. Newspapers were hereafter to play a direct part in government through their influence on those extra-constitutional forces, the political parties. There had been, it is true, a Greeley, a Weed, a Medill and a Forney; now there was not a state — perhaps but few counties — where the political policy was not inspired by some active editor or owner. The political organization without its organ was an anomaly; what became necessary was the paper that would fight the political organ.

The paper with the largest circulation was necessarily the most influential, and the larger circulation generally meant affiliation with the dominant party. These facts, together with the increased cost of manufacturing a newspaper, would tend toward a purely commercial morality, were it not for the check that lies in the newspaper of small circulation but stiff idealism.

The part in politics played by such editors as Greeley,

Prentice, Rhett, Raymond, Medill or Weed, was not congenial to all men; aside from their ability or inclination to take such an active interest in politics, newspapers had become such large business undertakings that concentration on their own interests was imperative. Particularly was this the case with the men best fitted and inclined to edit conservative journals.

From the close of the Civil War to the end of the nineteenth century the leading conservative editor of the country was Edwin Lawrence Godkin, declared by Rhodes to be one of the greatest editors of this country, and by Bryce to be one of the greatest editors of the world.

"To my generation," declared William James, "Godkin was certainly the towering influence in all thought concerning public affairs, and indirectly his influence has certainly been more pervasive than that of any other writer of the generation, for he influenced other writers who never quoted him, and determined the whole current of discussion."

"When the work of this century is summed up," wrote Charles Elliot Norton to Godkin, "what you have done for the good old cause of civilization, the cause which is always defeated, but always after defeat taking more advanced position than before — what you have done for this cause will count for much." — "I am conscious," wrote President Eliot of Harvard to Godkin, "that the *Nation* has had a decided effect on my opinions and my action for nearly forty years; and I believe it has had a like effect on thousands of educated Americans."[1]

These were the opinions of men of deep feeling and fine intellect, and they encouraged Godkin in a work which, as he said himself, was difficult because he knew

[1] Rhodes, *Historical Essays*, 270 271.

he was making himself odious to a large mass of people. It was a new and strange road in journalism. It was an absolutely unheard-of road in a democracy; a road that had its dangers, as was shown in the case of one of Mr. Godkin's associates on the *Nation,* who so confused unpopularity with success, that every time the *Nation* lost a subscriber he chortled with glee.

Godkin was born in Ireland and was educated at Queen's College, Belfast, during a time when the philosophy of John Stuart Mill and Jeremy Bentham was in the ascendant, a fact that explains many of his own tendencies. After serving as correspondent to the *London Daily News* in the Crimean War, he came to America and, during the last three years of the Civil War, was the correspondent of the same paper.

For sixteen years, it was as the editor of the *Nation* that he was making his mark in the country, but it is as the editor of the *Evening Post,* with which the *Nation* was merged, that he will be best remembered.

The *Nation* was started in 1865 and merged with the *Post* in 1881, Godkin becoming associate editor of that paper with Carl Schurz as editor-in-chief. Two years later Schurz retired and Godkin became editor-in-chief, a position in which he remained until 1900, when he retired because of failing health. During that time the *Evening Post* was one of the world's famous newspapers; it was the leader in "reform" in the United States.

Godkin rose to real power at a time when looseness of political thinking marked journalism. At the root of much of the corruption of the times was unquestionably the spoils system, its sponsors grown arrogant through the fact that, as the Democratic party was discredited, the nation was under, not a two-party, but a one-party government.

There had been, too, a slipping away from the common standards of honesty. The growth of the large corporation and the rise of public utilities had given political power a financial value hitherto unknown. The tendency was to apply material rather than moral standards; to ask, "What has he?" rather than "What is he?" A nation-wide influence for good was sadly needed.

The *Evening Post* was a paper fitted to be such a national influence. It had been founded as a conservative organ; the men who had edited or controlled it from its inception had been men who, if not followers of Hamilton politically, agreed with him in viewing with distaste the "excesses" of journalism. Some of these conservatives, in the old days, were robust men — Coleman for instance or Bryant, who carried constructive criticism to the point of belaboring W. L. Stone, the editor of the *Commercial Advertiser,* over the head with a cane. But no paper in America was better fitted for the work in hand.

It is unquestionably true, as William James says, that Godkin influenced the men who wrote editorials more than any other individual in the country. On the other hand it was also said by intellectual men that he was not always fair in his criticism of those men and measures that he did not favor, and that "he was apt to convey the idea that if any one differed from him on a vital question, like the tariff, or finance, or civil service reform, he was necessarily a bad man." [2]

It was this tendency that led many to believe that his influence on the intelligent youths of the country was not for the best, and he was blamed for painting the condition of the country and of politics as so bad that the one was not worth while entering and the other was not worth while saving. The result was that many educated

[2] *Historical Essays,* 276.

young men avoided politics, considering themselves superior to those who took an interest in their country's welfare.

His influence was as potent in the West as in the East. Many were the strong and able men who owed to him their interest and activity in favor of civil service reforms, their ideas on " sound " money, their belief in free trade, and their interest in a clean city government. These were his main teachings, and he taught them with a vigor and distinction of expression that led James Bryce to say that the *Nation* was not only the best publication of its kind in America, but the best in the world. On the other hand it was said that he never " made a retraction or rectification of personal charges shown to be incorrect."[3] When General Francis A. Walker died in 1897, Godkin refused even to notice his funeral in the *Nation,* although Walker was one of the distinguished economists of the country, because the two had taken opposite sides on the gold question in 1896.

In the latter part of his life the inevitable, or rather what might be expected of a disciple of Bentham, happened. He became a thorough pessimist and regarded the democratic experiment in America as a hopeless failure. He returned to England, despairing entirely of America, and, writing to Charles Eliot Norton, said:

" But the situation to me seems this: An immense democracy, mostly ignorant, and completely secluded from foreign influences, and without any knowledge of other states of society, with great contempt for history and experience, finds itself in possession of enormous power and is eager to use it in brutal fashion against any one who comes along, *without knowing how to do it,* and is therefore constantly on the brink of some frightful catastrophe

[3] Rhodes, 282.

like that which overtook France in 1870. The spectacle of our financial condition and legislation during the last twenty years, the general silliness and credulity begotten by the newspapers, the ferocious optimism exacted of all teachers and preachers, and the general belief that we are a peculiar or chosen people to whom the experiences of other people is of no use, make a pretty dismal picture, and, I confess, rather reconcile me to the fact that my career is drawing to a close. I know how many things may be pointed out as signs of genuine progress, but they are not in the field of government. Our two leading powers, the legislature and the press, have to my knowledge been running down for thirty years. The present crisis is really a fight between the rational business men and the politicians and the newspapers, and the rational business men are not getting the best of it.

"The press is the worst feature of the situation, and yet the press would not be what it is without a public demand for it as it is. I have been having cuttings about the present situation sent in to me from all quarters, and anything more silly, ignorant, and irrational you could not imagine. I am just now the object of abuse, and the abuse is just what you would hear in a barroom row. You are lucky in being a professor, and not obliged to say anything about public affairs except when you please. I have had a delightful and characteristic letter from William James urging me not 'to curse God and die,' but to keep on with 'the campaign of education.'"[4]

With the Spanish War he lost all hope of the American people ever retrieving themselves. It is unfair, however, in judging the great work that Godkin did, to be influenced by this later pessimism. It was his belief in American institutions, as he expressed it in a letter to

[4] Ogden, *Life of E. L. Godkin*, ii, 202, 203.

the *London Daily News* in 1868, that made possible all his achievements as well as the great influence that he acquired. Later in life he met with disappointments,— intellectual disappointments in his case; for he was too sincere in his nature to seek political office,— and those intellectual disappointments acted on him as disappointments of other varieties acted on other great journalists — they soured him and made him appear a man without faith and without belief.

The good that he did was not accomplished when he was bereft of the enthusiasm that moves men, but rather when he felt as he did in 1868, shortly after the Civil War; incidentally the country was then facing far more serious conditions than it faced when Godkin was so doleful.

"There is no careful and intelligent observer," he wrote, "whether he be a friend to democracy or not, who can help admiring the unbroken power with which the popular common sense — that shrewdness, or intelligence, or instinct of self-preservation, I care not what you call it, which so often makes the American farmer a better politician than nine-tenths of the best read European philosophers — works under all this tumult and confusion of tongues. The newspapers and politicians fret and fume and shout and denounce; but the great mass, the nineteen or twenty millions, work away in the fields and workshops, saying little, thinking much, hardy, earnest, self-reliant, very tolerant, very indulgent, very shrewd, but ready whenever the government needs it, with musket, or purse or vote, as the case may be, laughing and cheering occasionally at public meetings, but when you meet them individually on the highroad or in their own houses, very cool, then, sensible men, filled with no delusions, carried away by no frenzies, believing firmly in the future greatness and glory of the republic, but holding to no other article of faith as essential to political salvation." [5]

Coming when he did, Godkin was a tonic as well as an irritant. One of the causes of irritation among those who had to contend with him in editorial debate was the fact that he was a foreigner, but this, as Bryce says, gave him detachment and perspective. It is for the great ability that he had and for his great influence on the younger minds, his influence against corruption and for honesty and culture, that the country must be grateful.

"His finished criticism," says Bryce, "his exact method, his incisive handling of economic problems, his complete detachment from party, helped to form a new school of journalists, as the example he set of a serious and lofty conception of an editor's duties helped to add dignity to the position. He had not that disposition to enthrone the press which made a great English newspaper once claim for itself that it discharged in the modern world the functions of the mediæval Church. But he brought to his work as an anonymous writer a sense of responsibility and a zeal for the welfare of his country which no minister of State could have surpassed.

"His friends may sometimes have wished that he had more fully recognized the worth of sentiment as a motive power in politics, that he had more frequently tried to persuade as well as to convince, that he had given more credit for partial installments of honest service and for a virtue less than perfect, that he had dealt more leniently with the faults of the good and the follies of the wise. Defects in these respects were the almost inevitable defects of his admirable qualities, of his passion for truth, his hatred of wrong and injustice, his clear vision, his indomitable spirit.

[5] Rhodes, 287.

"Mr. Godkin was not only inaccessible to the lures of wealth — the same may happily be said of many of his craft-brethren — he was just as little accessible to the fear of public displeasure. Nothing more incensed him than to see a statesman or an editor with 'his ear to the ground' (to use an American phrase), seeking to catch the sound of the coming crowd. To him, the less popular a view was, so much the more did it need to be well weighed, and if approved, to be strenuously and incessantly preached. Democracies will always have demagogues ready to feed their vanity and stir their passions and exaggerate the feeling of the moment. What they need is men who will swim against the stream, will tell them their faults, will urge an argument all the more forcibly because it is unwelcome. Such a one was Edwin Godkin. Since the death of Abraham Lincoln, America has been generally more influenced by her writers, preachers, and thinkers than by her statesmen. In the list of those who have during the past forty years influenced her for good and helped by their pens to make history, a list illustrated by such names as those of R. W. Emerson and Phillips Brooks and James Russell Lowell, his name will find its place and receive its well-earned meed of honor."[6]

By no possible conception could his life be called a failure. The pessimism of his later years was not due to any fault of his adopted country, but to his failure to remain youthful in spirit; a failure due, in turn, to the fact that he had, as De Quincey says of Kant, "no faith, no self-distrust, no humility, no child-like docility." Men to be right, had to agree with him.

That spirit was against the very idea of government by public opinion; it was bound to breed the belief that,

[6] *Contemporary Biography*, 380, 381.

not alone the country, but the world, had gone wrong. We, who have traced the story of journalism, know that there was no greater cause for despair at the time that he lived and was active, than there was at any other time in the history of the nation. He was undoubtedly one of the great editors of the country, but he had less trying times to face than either of his notable predecessors, Bryant or Coleman, who paved the way for him and his achievements. Had he lived to see the *Evening Post* of to-day, with its black headlines, he would have despaired utterly of salvation in this world or the next, yet we know that these things are comparatively unimportant. His dogmatism, which was his strength, prevented him from seeing things in true relation, and from realizing that the men who see humanity laid open and at its worst, — they of the medical profession,— are the most hopeful and the men most marked by " faith, self-distrust, humility and child-like docility."

We find a healthier view of reform journalism in the West. Never was the spirit of the liberal and reform movement better exemplified than in the case of the Kansas City *Star,* founded by William Rockhill Nelson at about the same time that Godkin took over the *Evening Post.* The story of the *Star* was really that of hundreds of newspapers which, under the inspiring example of leaders in the profession, refused to be merely the organs of party, and became,— where the community was not large enough to make itself heard in national politics — of local and state-wide power for political and civic reform and for the betterment of the community.

Nelson was educated for the law, and became a successful business man; he was attracted to politics by the spirit of the day, partly through his acquaintance with Samuel J. Tilden. The fight against the Tweed ring stirred him, and the failure of the Democratic party to renominate Tilden in 1880 made him an independent. He was the owner of the *Fort Wayne Sentinel* when he decided to embark in a larger field and selected Kansas City. The *Star* appeared for the first time in September, 1880, when Kansas City was the muddiest town in the United States; it had no pavements and but a few plank sidewalks. It was a town apparently hopelessly corrupt. Sunday was a day for unlimited drunkenness. In the very first election that took place after the paper was started, Nelson served notice that the *Star* was out for better conditions:

"The *Star* has no ax to grind, no candidate to elect, no party to serve. Its only interest is in the growth and prosperity of Kansas City and the proper administration of the city government. It is for the best men, entirely regardless of party. It is, however, forced to admit that most of the men who are seeking nominations from both parties are utterly unfit for the positions to which they aspire. Briefless barristers, to whom no sane man would entrust a lawsuit involving five dollars, want to be city attorney. Irresponsible and incapable men, whom no one would think of selecting for cashier or bookkeeper, ask for the city treasurership. Ignorant peddlers of whiskey aspire to the city council. Such of these men who seek nominations may expect that the *Star* will tell the truth about them. The voters of the city have a right to know all the facts as to the character and capacity of those who ask their suffrage. These they cannot find in their party organs." [7]

The fight that followed was long and bitter, but Nelson won. A new Kansas City took the place of the one with the mud streets and the plank walks, and it was said of the

[7] *The Star,* March 10, 1881.

Star that not a situation arose in the affairs of the city, "the location of a park, the undertaking of public works or what not," but its voice was always potent and usually decisive. In fact, the *Star* became the most influential paper between the Mississippi and the Pacific. Few indeed were the papers or the editors that attained to such power and influence, such distinction and wealth, as did the *Star* and Nelson; throughout the country, nevertheless, many men were inspired to follow in the same path, even though they did not achieve the same success. On Nelson's death his wife and his daughter, Mrs. Kirkwood, dedicated the paper to the people of Kansas City "In his spirit." The editorial signed by them summarized well the attitude of the great majority of editors, those in whom machine politics or indifference had not entirely deadened the sense of responsibility:

"The *Star* was dedicated by Mr. Nelson to great purposes and high ideals in the service of humanity — to honest elections, to democratic government, to the abolition of special privilege, to fair dealings on the part of public service corporations, to larger opportunities for boys and girls, to progress toward social and industrial justice, to all things that make for the richer, fuller life that he coveted passionately for every man, woman and child.

"Particularly was it dedicated to the advancement of Kansas City. Whatever helped the city the *Star* was for. Whatever hurt the city the *Star* was against. For thirty-five years this newspaper had warred against election thievery, against the boss rule, against grasping corporations that came to the town only to make money out of it, against the whole brood of enemies of Kansas City. There has been no citizen, no matter what his station, but has known that if he came forward with a practical, efficient plan for the city's benefit, he could count on the heartiest help and coöperation of the *Star*.

"Those to whom this trusteeship has fallen recognize the heavy responsibility and obligation now theirs. In meeting this responsibility and this obligation they are depending on his associates on the staff who are in complete sympathy with his ideals, and who will have the active management of the paper. It is the one aim of the trustees and associates alike that his spirit shall direct the *Star's* policy, and that it shall continue to fight, as he would have it fight, for righteousness and justice and the common good, and for the greater, nobler city of his dreams." [8]

[8] *Biography of William Rockhill Nelson,* 182, 183.

CHAPTER XXVII

THE MELODRAMA IN THE NEWS

Genius of Pulitzer unappreciated — His earlier career — Association with Carl Schurz — Buys St. Louis *Post-Dispatch* — Takes over New York *World* — Case of Judge Maynard — Bond issue of 1896 — School of journalism suggested — Criticism as necessary as reform.

What was said of Pulitzer has been said of many other editors by their political opponents. Political adversaries are not inclined to admit that rivals may be moved by equally high motives, as in politics an admission of merit in an opponent is frequently considered a strategical mistake. That Pulitzer was out to sell as many papers as he could, no matter by what means, was all that his critics could see; it was not until his death that some of his conservative critics appreciated that he was able to turn his initiative and genius into the fields of culture that they had held particularly their own.

Had the idea of an academic training for journalists come from a college man or from one of the conservative journalists, it would doubtless have been just as successful, but it would have been less characteristic of the history of journalism; a history which abounds in curious human developments, in revelations of beauty of character, like those the wilderness traveler finds in unbeaten paths and deep woodland pools.

Having traced the developments of American journalism from its very beginning, it is not a difficult task that confronts us when we come to analyze what was called the "modern journalism" of Joseph Pulitzer.

Pulitzer did only what was inevitable. In his desire to achieve the greatest influence for the paper that he controlled, he reached for closer contact, between the papers and the people, than had existed up to his time; it was his genius that discovered the way in which that might be done. It was not surprising, viewed in the past history of journalism, that in so doing he aroused the adverse criticism of the conservatives.

Great as was the impression that he left on his time, he was no more an innovator than was Greeley with his passion for reform or Bennett with his sense of news; no more so than were Freneau and Duane, with their recklessness of attack on the very head of the government, and other men — some forgotten — who, in their turn, advanced journalism one step more, and thus made possible, if not a reputation for themselves, at least power and influence for those who were to come after.

The career of Pulitzer, a poor half-educated idealist, was much like that of Greeley. Born in Hungary, he was absolutely friendless when he arrived in New York, and had to sleep in City Hall Park, though later a fireman allowed him to sleep in a furnished room at French's Hotel in Park Row. Twenty years later he bought this same hotel for $680,000 and tore it down to put up the present World Building. In 1864 he enlisted as a private dragoon in the First New York Cavalry, served with the Army of the Shenandoah until peace was declared, and was then honorably discharged. He worked at menial occupations in order to escape starvation, but never lost faith or courage and never wasted an opportunity to read and study. He drifted West, obtained a position on the *St. Louis Post*,— then edited by Carl Schurz — showed ability as a speaker and, in 1869, was elected a member of the legislature of Missouri. In Jefferson City, while serving in the Legislature, he was attacked by a political grafter, and shot the man. He put his savings into the *Post,* and in 1871 he became managing editor of the paper. He was one of the organizers of the Liberal Republican movement in Missouri, and it was through his strategy that Carl Schurz was made Chairman of the Cincinnati Convention, which met May 1, 1872, and nominated Horace Greeley for president.

Schurz refused to support Greeley, but Pulitzer stumped the West for him and made many speeches in his behalf. The political differences between himself and Schurz caused him, in 1875, to sell his interest in the *Post;* following this he acted as Washington correspondent for the *New York Sun,* returning to St. Louis in 1878 and buying the *Evening Dispatch* and *Evening Post,* which he issued as one paper.

His success with the *St. Louis Post-Dispatch* was such that his income reached $200,000 a year. He was but thirty-six years of age, yet had a national reputation as a public speaker and editor. He was about to go abroad when the possibility of purchasing the *New York World* was presented to him.

In the days of his association with Carl Schurz he had been a radical and a socialist. Later he had grown more conservative, but he was still in a frame of mind to be stirred by the newspaper condition in New York, a condition epitomized by John Bigelow, one of the editors of the *New York Evening Post,* when he declared that there were too many newspapers for the educated class. [1]

Pulitzer had this in mind when, in 1883, he bought the *New York World,* and instituted what his contemporaries and his biographer have called " a totally new system of newspaper conduct." As we have seen however, there

[1] George Cary Eggleston, *Recollections,* 289.

was nothing extraordinary in the system that Pulitzer inaugurated. The papers which, in the early thirties, had been founded for the purpose of catering to the laboring classes had grown staid and conservative. A new generation of laboring people had come up, several of them in fact, and the papers that were supposed to appeal to them, appealed rather to the preceding generation. The Pulitzer journalism was, therefore, not so much the inauguration of a new system as the re-birth of an old one.

The appeal to the laboring or semi-educated classes was, as it had been in the thirties, immediately successful; as had been the case with the first penny papers, it was demonstrated that, while the *World* gained in circulation by hundreds of thousands, no other morning paper lost. The conservative morning papers that looked with so much horror on Pulitzer's innovations gradually found, as their predecessors had found in the case of the penny papers and the news system inaugurated by Bennett, that by adopting some of his methods they were able to increase their constituency.

It was the discovery that in New York,— or, for that matter, in every city in the country — there was a large uneducated or semi-educated population who were not reading newspapers, that led William M. Laffan, then a subordinate on the *Sun* and later the proprietor and editor of that paper, to bring out, on March 17, 1887, the *Evening Sun,* an afternoon paper that was to address itself, not to the educated class but to those less fortunately conditioned. Its success led to the *Evening World,* and to an entire change in the character of the evening papers of the country; so much so that the *New York Evening Post,* with its great traditions, is even to-day making, through large type and black headlines, the same appeal for the patronage of the uneducated that the *Sun* and the *Evening World* made thirty years ago.

We gather some of the strength of the Pulitzer journalism, and we begin to understand why it was successful, when we read some of his instructions to his editorial writers. A famous case in the history of the New York judiciary was that of Judge Maynard, who, after questionable conduct in a certain election proceeding, came up for re-election on the Democratic ticket. Mr. Pulitzer, it is to be remembered, was a Democrat. Calling in his chief editorial writer, George Cary Eggleston, he said to him:

"I want you to go into the Maynard case with an absolutely unprejudiced mind. We hold no briefs for or against him, as you know. I want you to get together all the documents in the case. I want you to take them home and study them as minutely as if you were preparing yourself for an examination. I want you to regard yourself as a judicial officer, oath-bound to justice, and when you shall have mastered the facts and the law in the case, I want you to set them forth in a four column editorial that every reader of the *World* can easily understand."

There were model instructions. They are the praecepta of journalism as the defender and upholder of democracy.

Another illustration of his large, democratic and unusual view of the mission of journalism, was his handling of the 1896 bond issue. The government was about to sell two hundred million dollars of bonds to a Wall Street syndicate at 104¾, when it was demonstrated that the bonds were bringing in the market as high as 122. Pulitzer sent for the heads of his departments and the head of the editorial page and gave them rapid-fire instructions, in which, in a few hundred words, the entire national campaign was outlined.

"We have made our case in this matter of the bond issue. We have presented the facts clearly, convincingly, conclusively, but the Administration refuses to heed them. We are now going to compel it to heed them on pain of facing a scandal that no administration could survive.

"What we demand is that these bonds shall be sold to the public at something like their actual value and not to a Wall Street syndicate for many millions less. You understand all that. You are to write a double-leaded article to occupy the whole editorial space to-morrow morning. You are not to print a line of editorial on any other subject. You are to set forth, in compact form and in the most effective way possible, the facts of the case and the considerations that demand a popular or at least a public loan instead of this deal with a syndicate, suggestive as it is of the patent falsehood that the United States Treasury's credit needs 'financing.' You are to declare, with all possible emphasis, that the banks, bankers, and people of the United States stand ready and eager to lend their government all the money it wants at three per cent. interest, and to buy its four per cent. bonds at a premium that will amount to that. . . .

"Then as a guarantee of the sincerity of our conviction you are to say that the *World* offers in advance to take one million dollars of the new bonds at the highest market price, if they are offered to the public in open market.

"In the meanwhile, Chamberlin has a staff of men sending out dispatches to every bank and banker in the land, setting forth our demand for a public loan instead of a syndicate dicker, and asking each for what amount of the new bonds it or he will subscribe on a three per cent. basis. To-morrow morning's papers will carry with your editorial its complete confirmation in their replies, and the proposed loan will be over-subscribed on a three per cent. basis. Even Mr. Cleveland's phenomenal self-confidence and Mr. Carlisle's purblind belief in Wall Street methods will not be able to withstand such a demonstration as that. It will compel a public loan. If it is true that the contract with the syndicate has already been made, they must cancel it. The voice of the country will be heard in the subscription list we shall print to-morrow morning, and the voice of the country has compelling power, even under this excessively self-confident administration." [2]

With his idealism and his own knowledge of the suffering and poverty of the submerged world about him, Joseph Pulitzer could never have been content with the mere exploitation of the news, even if that exploitation had been, financially, twice as successful as it proved to be. What esentially appealed to him in journalism was its opportunity to touch the heart; because he was a sentimentalist he was successful in arousing public interest and establishing his papers as great, powerful, popular organs.

He could not see things calmly and philosophically as could Godkin, but he could express in his own way his feelings about the same crimes. So, while he stood for honest government, the reforms that he advocated most successfully were those that dealt with liberty and freedom; with the abolition of cruelty in the prisons, with the stopping of oppression by petty officers of the law, and with the ending of graft, the graft that hit mainly those who were trying to earn a mere living.

The critics who were unable to understand the Pulitzers, or Bennetts, or Greeleys, were generally those who failed

[2] Eggleston, *Recollections,* 329, 330.

to appreciate the value of sentiment — direct sentiment as it were. Otto H. Kahn tells of a famous financier who was unable to endure listening to a violinist play Chopin's "Funeral March," because it always moved him to tears; there are many who are sensitive to beauty in the same way, yet the knowledge that the violinist was starving would move them little. Yet it is such men, keen for subtle beauties, who, in democratic leaders, see mere exponents of demagogy.

Pulitzer was distinguished from most of his predecessors in journalism, not so much for his financial success, or for his sentimental treatment of the news, but by the fact that he saw that the Fourth Estate was so great a power in the country that the men who were to be its votaries should be trained, as well and as thoroughly as those who entered any of the other professions. It was this knowledge of the responsibility that is placed on every man in the profession that led him to suggest the school of journalism at Columbia University. Like most of the great editors of the country he had been obliged to work for his own education — and a great education it had proved to be — but he desired that there should be some better system; so that those who were to take up a career fraught, when that career was a downward one, with so much of peril to the public, should be trained under auspices that would tend to develop character.

Pulitzer has been called an adventurer in journalism, but such characterization takes little account of the depth and genius of the man. When we find that the journalism with which his name is associated had the qualities of romance and sentiment of drama, we must remember that such was the man. He had lived a most melodramatic life. Was it possible that the journalism that bore the stamp of his personality could be otherwise than melodramatic?

When we find that criticism against journalism that is at all democratic has always, from the very beginning up to to-day, proceeded from the educated or superior class, it is most logical to assume that there is, and that there will continue to be, natural opposition. The journals of the educated class will never be able to see those of the uneducated class in anything but the most critical light. To a certain extent this is wise, because healthy, sound, vigorous criticism is as necessary for radicalism as reform is necessary for conservatism.

The idea of the School of Journalism came, curiously enough, from a man of the people,— from one of their champions. We have seen how, for almost two hundred years, the attitude of many of the educated and cultured was that this new vocation was not a profession. We have seen them even deny its power, the power that was deciding the questions of the day,— self-evident as that power was.

Pulitzer was the first to recognize the new profession was drawing to it young men of brains and ability who had been trained for some other profession. Aside from the idealism which led to his suggestion and to his bequests founding the new school, there was the desire to eliminate the great waste of time that came through training men to be journalists, who had started out to be something else.

"What is everybody's business," he said once, "is nobody's business — except the journalist's. It is his by adoption. But for his care almost every reform would be stillborn. He holds officials to their duty. He exposes secret schemes of plunder. He promotes every hopeful plan of progress. Without him public opinion would be shapeless and dumb. Our republic and its press will rise or fall together. An able, disinterested, public-spirited press, with trained intelligence to know the right and courage to do it, can preserve that public virtue without which popular government is a sham and a mockery."[4]

[4] *Review of Reviews,* February, 1912, p. 187.

CHAPTER XXVIII

CONCLUSION

William Randolph Hearst — Position in newspaper world not unique — Loyalty to California — Eastern Opinion vs. Spirit of the West — Early days on Pacific coast — Brannan and Colton — Discovery of gold — James King of William — His murder — Conclusion — Gregory Humes — The genius of journalism.

Psychologically, as well as chronologically, the journalism of William Randolph Hearst succeeded that of Joseph Pulitzer. It is an interesting fact that, though both editors were of the same political faith and though both, as inventors of the "yellow press," had to suffer the opprobrium of the conservative and Republican journals, their antagonism toward each other was more bitter than that between them and their political opponents. It was in the case of the papers of these two editors that the large amount of capital invested in the modern press began to show influence;— where circulation or business success is concerned there is no common cause in journalism.

At least a dozen serious people have asked in the course of the preparation of this work, "What are you going to do with Hearst?" In treating of contemporary characters, the difficulties are obvious, and the easiest way is always avoidance. The purpose of this study would be belied, however, if we were to endeavor even a lesser makeshift. What little we may have imbibed of the spirit of the men who have inspired these pages would have miscarried, if we ourselves hesitated to apply the rules of fair measurement that we, by implication, are urging on others.

The best way to arrive at a correct historic judgment is to try to conceive of the man under dissection as being thoroughly dead and completely forgotten. He is resurrected for the purpose of finding out what he did, and what effect he had on his contemporaries. The abuse showered on him by his rivals then frequently becomes an evidence that he wielded some power. The question is, Did he wield that power for good or for evil? Was he selfish? Was he (and this is important in a democracy) corrupt?

In the matter of arousing bitter hatred, Hearst's position in American journalism has not been unique. The feeling against the elder Bennett, when the papers of the city united against him in the famous *Herald* war,— going to the extent of abusing the manager of the Astor House for permitting him and his wife to live there,— was far greater than it ever was against Hearst. Yet we know now that Bennett violated no law, other than the canons of good taste. The office of Greeley was almost sacked, and his life was threatened; Bennett urged for him a public hanging; he was a thorn in Lincoln's side,— but we know now that Greeley was one of the great moral forces in this nation. The "rascally Pulitzer," as his contemporaries called him, was the subject of a most scurrilous pamphlet, he was derided for his humble beginnings; yet his contribution to journalistic advancement, through his school of journalism, is greater than that of any other individual, unless it be Jefferson.

What the final judgment on Hearst will be depends very largely on his own actions, for the popularity or unpopularity of the cause espoused has much to do with the final judgment passed by the people on the journalist. He has certain deep ingrained prejudices, which, if he were a statesman, might be grave defects; to the journalist, however, they are often, if his vision is correct, a source of strength. Journalism is the only profession where prejudice, like versatility, may be an asset.

In analyzing Hearst and his two principal papers, the New York *American* and the New York *Evening Journal,* one fact has been ignored. Though a New Yorker by adoption, he has always remained a loyal Californian. He has a thoroughly western contempt for the things that the East reveres; his success has been made over their heads; being financially able, he has bitterly attacked the banking influence that predominates in the East, and in turn has had visited on him all the social disfavor that his opponents could command. As nearly as possible, the war between Hearst and his opponents has been a class war, for the dispassionate historian must admit, despite all the criticism of Hearst, that he has been a vigorous American and has never advocated reforms outside the line of law or against the constitution, but has always been in full sympathy with his patron saint, Jefferson.

Hearst represents a West that has always been more or less, in Eastern opinion, an appendage to the political sentiment of the country. This interesting view was represented in the declaration of a distinguished statesman who said to the writer, within the last decade, that a political battle then imminent would have to be won by the forces he represented, in order "that the political control of the country might remain in the East." The tone in which he spoke indicated his strong belief that the passing of the control from the East would be not only a political catastrophe but a menace to the country.

As a matter of fact, it has been the West and not the East that, since the Civil War, has generated the power back of those reforms and those progressive measures that have developed and strengthened the democracy of the country. A racy people will always be nearer to the springs of government, and, being near the source, will carry out the ideas more vehemently and spontaneously, than a people steeped in tradition and custom. Attrition wears away impulse sometimes with curious results. In the last decade or two we find growing up in the East the feeling that the Federalist party was not, after all, the party of error that for over a hundred years we have assumed it to be. Such a sentiment could never, during the last fifty years, have found any encouragement west of the Mississippi.

The spirit of that country, developed with the printing press as well as with the pick and the spade, would be a separate study in itself; we have been able only to hint at this spirit, in the story of the settlement of the western reserve. When we come to the bloody settlement of Kansas, we find that the printing press anticipated even the pick and the spade.

There were, among the Mormons, many printers, at least enough to be conspicuous as a class, and these men, as the new sect pushed itself westward, identified frontier life with the printing press. A group of New York and New England Mormons, led by a printer named Samuel Brannan, who had already printed a Mormon paper in New York, established a colony on the bay of San Francisco in September, 1846. Brannan had brought out with him printing press, type, paper, etc., and within four months after the founding of this colony he printed the first issue of the *California Star*. A few weeks before, on August 15, 1846, the first newspaper in the Territory of California had been printed at Monterey by the American alcalde, Walter Colton, a former editor of the Philadelphia *North American.* On taking over the alcalde's office from his retreating predecessor, Colton had discovered an old press and some Spanish type. By using cigarette paper, the sheets of which were a little larger than ordinary foolscap, he was able to bring out the *Californian* within a few weeks after the raising of the American flag.[1] The paper was printed in both English and Spanish and, as the Spanish font contained no "W," that letter in the English section of the paper was represented by two " V's."

The following spring the *Californian* moved to San Francisco, and a year later both the *California Star* and the *Californian* were obliged to suspend publication because all the employees, including the printer's devil, had hurriedly quit when they heard of the discovery of gold. The whole country, from San Francisco to Los Angeles, responded to one cry — gold! [2]

In the strange and feverish times that followed, the name of James King of William stands out. Between 1849 and 1856 a thousand murders had been committed in San Francisco, but only one legal execution had taken place. The government was admittedly rotten, business was uncertain and failures common; corruption, gambling and crime were so rampant that the better class of citizens absolutely despaired.

James King of William — the very name he adopted showed him to be a man of strong opinions — was a native of Georgetown, in the District of Columbia, and had worked in the banking house of Corcoran and Riggs at Washington. Before the knowledge of the discovery

[1] Walter Colton, *Three Years in California,* 33.
[2] Hittell, *History of California,* ii, 689.

of gold had reached the East, he had sailed for California, hoping to find, through the change of climate, a renewal of health. He succeeded in establishing himself in the banking business and became widely known as a man of intelligence and courage, as well as of integrity. His open refusal to fight a duel attracted to him that element of the community that was struggling, almost hopelessly, against the lawless element. In the various explanations and statements that he had been called on to make as a business man, he had developed a crisp, direct style that led his friends to suggest the feasibility of his starting a newspaper. On October 5, 1855, the first number of the *Daily Evening Bulletin* was issued; from the first number it began an attack on the corruption and fraud of the politicians and bankers. From the beginning he refused to accept low medical advertisements, and, though his paper was unrestricted in abuse and vehement denunciation of public and private criminals, King asserted that he would print nothing that was not fit to be read at his own fireside.

The paper was a sensation and greatly heartened those who, until it made its appearance, had believed that the conditions in San Francisco were irremediable.

A month after the publication of the *Bulletin,* a United States marshal was shot down by a disreputable gambler. King, in the *Bulletin,* while urging the citizens to be cautious, called on the community to watch the sheriff and to hang him if the murderer escaped. So boldly had King attacked the vicious element in San Francisco that it was decided to kill him. A ruffian named Casey picked a quarrel, and King, as he left his office to walk to his home, was shot before he could defend himself. The San Francisco *Herald,* a rival paper, referred to the shooting as " an affray between Mr. J. P. Casey and Mr. James

King," which reference aroused such indignation that the paper was obliged to suspend. The result of this murder was the formation of the Vigilance Committee of 1856.

To the Eastern mind, such a beginning will seem to have no reflection in the orderly and well-edited papers that now abound in the far West, nor will it seem to offer the slightest excuse for a wealthy young Californian's having stirred, angered and irritated the East — and having been successful. Unfortunately, the Eastern mind that takes an interest in the subject is, at best, little given to understanding the West,— even its simpler aspects. Frank students of our policy admit this, while others irritably protest, "Nonsense; we're all alike — like us." It isn't so, but although the West knows that it is not so, the East does not. Whatever is to be the final analysis of Hearst it will be one in which the call of men for strange and lonely venture, the nervous dislike of check and convention, will largely enter. Meanwhile, the student of journalism finds food for thought in the fact that the greatest exponent of personal journalism, in the city that produced the Titans of the profession, was a Californian; one who, whatever his faults, has never been harnessed and certainly never afraid.

We have followed the line of a development strange in the history of civilization. We have seen the rise of journalism from the time, less than two centuries ago, when it had little relation with government and public opinion,— so little that the suppression of the first paper by the government aroused no protest; the records, in fact, indicate that the suppression was regarded with a complacency tantamount to approval. So far as we know there was — save the individual concerned financially — no one to protest, or to resist the complete subjugation of what we call public opinion, which in this instance we may call public soul. Harris stands out as almost the single point of protest against conditions as they were in 1690, as opposed to conditions as they should be. He represented, as did no other man in that community at that time, the idea of rule by public opinion, as it has since developed. He represented the theory of public rights in a community that, while it was founded on the idea of liberty and public rights, still failed to realize that within itself it had created an autocracy just as hateful as the one from which it had fled.

The community had not — in fact, the world had not — grown to realize that liberty or freedom of conscience cannot be had without freedom of discussion. Harris' impotence, as well as his strength, was the fact that he represented an idea, and used an invention, that was as yet hardly developed — the printing press and the new idea of journalism.

In 1690 Harris was the sole point of contact between the great mass of people in America — a vast majority of whom did not even know that he lived — and what we call public opinion. To-day there is no section or group of the people in this country not represented in the court of public opinion; none which has not, in some form or some way, a journalistic representative in the field, battling for its proper share of attention in a democracy where the will of the people, as exercised under a constitution, is the law of the land.

What our study of this development has shown us is that a system has slowly evolved, whereby the people are given the fullest measure of control and are made, in the final analysis, the direct sponsors of the government that they control. A more complete circle of delegation of power and return has never existed, and it is not easy to conceive of making it more responsive without producing a chaos that would negative all human effort. As our problems have arisen, the elasticity of the self-devised checks has been proved; imperfections, so-called, have really been the results that are inevitable in a country growing and developing in unprecedented ways. Dangers and failures have been found and will be found, as must be expected under any government into which the human element enters to so great an extent. But it is in this particular regard that the American democracy has achieved its greatest triumph — there has never been in high office a man, with the exception of Aaron Burr, who has shown a vicious intent toward the people, nor have there been, among the thousands of unfettered editors, any conspicuous examples of men who have not had their country's interest first at heart, wrong though some of them have been in their methods.

There is no profession, unless it is medicine, that calls for a higher regard for the simple truth than does journalism. "A good reporter is one who is never deceived by a lie." There have been men, there are men, into whose consciousness this fact never penetrates, but for the vast majority of the men who have achieved distinction in journalism it has been an actuating and primal principle.

From the very humble beginning of journalism in America to this day, there has been a devotion to duty that shows how fundamental is this ethical principle, in those who are drawn into this profession, where success is not measured by fame or by money. Those who, like Bucher, see but the commercial side, or, like Boynton, recognize only a shadowing and imitation of literature, miss something — something fine that lies in the soul of men whose deep interest in their fellowmen satisfies them with positions in life far below what their talents could command.

Walter Pater speaks somewhere,— in *Marius,* I think,— of the æsthetic charm that lies in mere clear thought. There is indeed an æsthetic charm in the simple and truthful recital of events in the world we live in — it may not be evident to those who soar high, those whose minds are attuned to the rhythm of greater beauties, but it is there; men know it, and carry that knowledge through life whether they have learned it in the grimy, unattractive office of some "patent-inside" weekly or, with greater force, as part of the large, keen organization that prints, in the small hours of the morning, a great metropolitan daily.

No newspaper man reaches forty without having met and talked with thousands of fellow-workers; they leave, in their entirety, an ineffaceable impression of optimism, of high purpose, of indomitable energy and courage. Considered as individuals, no two are alike; twin brothers have curiously opposing facets, overshadowing mere physiognomical resemblances. A regiment of reporters will hear the same speech or witness the same convention, yet what they write will have such rare diversity that one will wonder by what miracle there were gathered together so many intellects so strangely dissimilar.

If their own opinion were sought, the vast majority of these newspaper men, dissimilar as they are in character and point of view, would explain their attraction to their calling,— one long considered unworthy the name of a profession,— by the "love of the game."

The "game" — a child's word; there the explanation greatly lies. For men, like children, must love what they do more than they love themselves, if they are to wield the force that makes youth and romance so omnipotent. The flavor of adventure is never lacking in successful journalism because, underlying it all, is the consciousness, a consciousness curiously aggressive, that evil is being overthrown; that that incomprehensible thing, the public, is being served through the medium of the particular journal for which the work is undertaken.

The "game," however, has behind it a purpose, a deep and serious purpose, as this book, I believe, has shown. Expressed or unexpressed, there is always a strong belief that this country is different from others, and that the making of a happier and better nation is in the hands of each individual, working his own way. There is ever present, under cynical cover at times, the missionary spirit — the sense of personal responsibility for the right conduct of our government and our people, a spirit that leads even to the greatest sacrifice.

Of that spirit two examples come to mind — there must be hundreds that are known to others. At an engagement near Santiago, Cuba, just previous to the battle of El Caney, in the Spanish-American War, there was a correspondent, named Edward Marshall, of the New York *Journal*. He was where, if he had had due regard for his own life, he would not have been — in the front with the soldiers. A bullet struck his thigh, making him a cripple for life; as he lay bleeding and wounded — how seriously, it was not possible to tell — he dictated to a comrade his story for his paper. It was foolhardy, some one afterward suggested,— but was it not also magnificent?

In the editorial office of the New York *World* is a bronze tablet bearing the inscription:

IN MEMORY OF
GREGORY T. HUMES
Reporter on the *World*
Mortally injured in the Stamford Railroad Wreck.
He thought first of his paper and with indomitable courage sent the news of the disaster.
Born April 22, 1878
Died June 13, 1913

Humes was a passenger on the train when the wreck occurred. When he was lifted out, dying, his first request was that his paper be notified that there was "a big story" at Stamford, and that he was sorry that he could not write it as he was "all smashed up." Not until his duty was done would he ask that his mother be telephoned to come to him.

"For those who see the newspapers from the outside," commented a paper at that time, "and with more suspicion and criticism than understanding, this reporter's example should at least suggest the thought that no trade, business, profession, which can enlist such men and retain such loyalty can quite deserve that fine scorn visited upon it so frequently by those thoughtless cynics who do not see behind its necessary impersonality the keen and vital individuality of hundreds of men like Gregory Humes, whose occupation he has dignified by his complete fidelity to its highest standards and its unwritten code." [3]

I have said that there must be others. There is scarcely an editor whose experience will not bear witness of the youths, many from homes of comfort and luxury, who have, at no matter what discomfort, shown equal spirit. That spirit is not to be explained away by any sordid analysis; it is the finest of American spirit enlisted in the finest of causes — the public weal.

"But," says the critic, "it is not benefiting the public

[3] *New York Sun,* June, 1913.

to report a railway wreck." "It wasn't necessary to report it at once; the facts would have come out at the investigation before the grand jury," I hear some distinguished graybeard of a jurist say. The man who feels that way, who thinks that way, does not know the American public. Whether it is in the crowded, congested section of the city, amid the clatter of push-carts and the din of the itinerant peddlers, or far away in the hills where the cowbell at evening echoes for miles, there is caught up, more than all the fulminations of the statesman, the spirit of the "game" — the spirit of sacrifice of the reporter Humes; the spirit that made America free and that has made her people trusting and confident.

APPENDIX — NOTE A

THE BEGINNING OF "NEWES"

No papers of so early a date as the reign of Elizabeth are preserved in the British Museum, but we have been kindly favored by Dr. Rimbault with the following list, which has fallen under his observation, all of which, with the exception of the last, are of that reign:

"Newe newes, containing a short rehersal of Stukely's and Morice's Rebellion," 4to, 1579.

"Newes from the North, or a Conference between Simon Certain and Pierce Plowman," 4to, 1579.

"Newes from Scotland, declaring the damnable life of Doctor Fian, a notable sorcerer, who was burned at Edenborough in January last," 4to, Gothic, 1591.

"Newes from Spaine and Holland," 1593.

"Newes from Brest, or a Diurnal of Sir John Norris," 4to, 1594 (printed by Richard Yardley).

"Newes from Flanders," 1599.

"Newes out of Cheshire of the new found well," 1600.

"News from Gravesend," 4to, 1604.

We may add to Dr. Rimbault's list the following:

"Wonderful and strange newes out of Suffolke and Essex, where it rayned wheat the space of six or seven miles," 12mo., 1583.

The titles of most of these pamphlets direct us to a very fair estimate of their contents; it must be confessed they were somewhat of the stamp of the "Full, True, and Particular Accounts" of Seven Dials. The public asked for news — and got it in its first crude form, yet still in disjointed fragments: —

"Lamentable newes out of Monmouthshire in Wales, containinge the wonderful and fearfull accounts of the great overflowing of the waters in the said countye," etc., 1607.

"Woful newes from the west partes of England, of the burning of Tiverton," 4to, 1612, with a frontispiece.

"Strange newes from Lancaster, containing an account of a prodigious monster born in the township of Addlington in Lancashire, with two bodies joyned to one back," April 13th, 1613.

The appetite for news is whetted and increased efforts are made to appease it. The pamphlets begin to assume a more definite form:

"Newes from Spaine," published in 1611.

"Newes out of Germany," 1612.

"Good newes from Florence," 1614.

"Newes from Mamora," 1614.

"Newes from Gulick and Cleve," 1615.

"Newes from Italy," 1618.

"Newes out of Holland," published May 16th, 1619. (Dr. Burney's collection.)

"Vox Populi, or Newes from Spaine," 1620.

"Newes from Hull," "Truths from York," "Warranted tidings from Ireland," "Newes from Poland," "Special passages from several places," etc., etc.

Such are samples of the titles of news books preserved in the British Museum and other collections, most of them purporting to be translations from the Low Dutch.

Andrews, *History of British Journalism,* vol. i, pp. 25–27.

APPENDIX — NOTE B

THE CHARACTER OF WILLIAM BRADFORD

It is not perhaps the least praise of a man so long and so closely connected as Bradford was with the great engine of parties, that while he was a steady supporter of the administration of Governor Cosby and Lieutenant-Governor Clark against the fierce opposition made by the *Weekly Journal* of Zenger and the party of Van Dam who controlled it, he seems to have gone to extreme lengths with no one; but to have pursued a long career of creditable industry, unmarked by "those incidents which arrest the attention by agitating the passions of mankind." It was the natural result of such a course that he accumulated a large estate which he lived long to enjoy.

It is an evidence of Bradford's strong capacity that, although "the darkness of old age" had now begun to invade him, and his concerns were both various and extensive, he should have carried himself and them successfully against the rivalry and interests of Benjamin Franklin. Through the whole term of Franklin's connection with the press in Philadelphia, the elder Bradford and his son or grandson conducted their journals with an ability which perfectly sustained them; and against the efforts, not very scrupulous ones either, of this celebrated man — to whom through four generations of their own families, they were constantly opposed, alike on concerns of business which touched very sharply the pecuniary interests of the great "economist and calculator"; on the exciting feuds of provincial politics, and finally, on the great questions of the Stamp Act,— to which the Bradfords were actively opposed — and the course of the Colonies in the early stages of the Revolution, wherein these persons were bold and confident — managed the concerns of their offices generally with steady success and honorable liberality. Franklin, with all his address and all his power, and an animosity difficult to understand in a temper so apparently placid as his, but equal to either, was never able to break them down. And in this country of quick changing names and scenes, it deserves a record, that long after the great philosopher and his successful rival in the business of printing, Andrew Bradford (son of that William whom we now commemorate) were moldering in the dust beside each other in the quiet graveyard of Christ Church, in that same place where more than a century before, the king of printers had been received and entertained a friendless boy by a son of the aged colonist [1]— there yet stood, in a fifth generation — one hundred and forty years, at least, from the time it had been planted on that soil — pursuing still its labor, and bearing still its ancient and proprietary name, "THE PRINTING PRESS OF WILLIAM BRADFORD." [2]

[1] Franklin mentions in his Autobiography that when he first went to Philadelphia, in his seventeenth year, he dressed himself as neat as he could and went to Andrew Bradford, the Printer. "He received me civilly, gave me a breakfast; told me 'I should be welcome to lodge at his house and he would give me a little work to do now and then till fuller business should offer.'"

[2] It appears, from the imprint of many books yet to be seen, that

APPENDIX — NOTE C

BRYANT INDEX EXPURGATORIUS[1]

Above and over (for "more than")
Artiste (for "Artist")
Aspirant
Authoress
Beat (for "defeat")
Bagging (for "capturing")
Balance (for "remainder")
Banquet (for "dinner" or "supper")
Bogus
Casket (for "coffin")
Claimed (for "asserted")
Collided
Commence (for "begin")
Compete
Cortege (for "procession")
Cotemporary (for "contemporary")
Couple (for "two")
Darky (for "negro")
Day before yesterday (for "the day before yesterday")
Début
Decease (as a verb)
Democracy (applied to a political party)
Develop (for "expose")
Devouring element (for "fire")
Donate
Employe
Enacted (for "acted")
Endorse (for "approve")
Enroute
"Esq."
Gents (for "gentlemen")
Graduate (for "is graduated")
"Hon."
House (for "House of Representatives")
Humbug
Inaugurate (for "begin")
In our midst
Is being done (and all passives of this form)
Item (for "particle, extract or paragraph")
Jeopardize
Jubilant (for "rejoicing")

this press was in operation at Philadelphia in the year 1825, being then still under the management of William Bradford, of New York, a great-great-grandson of the original founder of it in 1685. This gentleman was the last of this ancient family of printers; and it is calculated to inspire a sentiment of pathetic feeling that, with him, the office is finally closed. He left "no son of his succeeding."—"Commemorative Address on William Bradford," John William Wallace, p. 93. This citation covers the entire Note B.

[1] Compiled by William Cullen Bryant when editor of the *Evening Post*.

Juvenile (for "boy")
Lady (for "wife")
Last (for "latest")
Lengthy (for "long")
Leniency (for "lenity")
Loafer
Loan or loaned (for "lend" or "lent")
Located
Majority (relating to places or circumstances for "most")
Mrs. President, Mrs. Governor, Mrs. General, and all similar titles
Mutual (for "common")
Official (for "officer")
On yesterday
Ovation
Over his signature
Pants (for "pantaloons")
Partially (for "partly")
Parties (for "persons")
Past two weeks (for "last two weeks" and all similar expressions relating to a definite time)
Poetess
Portion (for "part")
Posted (for "informed")
Progress (for "advance")
Quite (prefixed to "good," "large," etc.)
Raid (for "attack")
Realized (for "obtained")
Reliable (for "trustworthy")
Rendition (for "performance")
Repudiate (for "reject" or "disown")
Retire (as an active verb)
Rev. (for "the Rev.")
Rôle (for "part")
Roughs
Rowdies
Secesh
Sensation (for "noteworthy event")
Standpoint (for "point of view")
Start, in the sense of "setting out"
State (for "say")
Taboo
Talent (for "talents" or "ability")
Talented
Tapis
The deceased
War (for "dispute" or "disagreement")

APPENDIX — NOTE D

HORACE GREELEY'S FAMOUS LETTER TO WILLIAM H. SEWARD

"New York, Saturday evening,
November 11, 1854.

"Governor Seward,— The election is over, and its results sufficiently ascertained. It seems to me a fitting time to announce to you the dissolution of the political firm of Seward, Weed, and Greeley, by the withdrawal of the junior partner — said withdrawal to take effect on the morning after the first Tuesday in February next. And as it may seem a great presumption in me to assume that any such firm exists, especially since the public was advised, rather more than a year ago, by an editorial rescript in the *Evening Journal,* formally reading me out of the Whig Party, that I was esteemed no longer either useful or ornamental in the concern, you will, I am sure, indulge me in some reminiscences which seem to befit the occasion.

"I was a poor young printer and editor of a literary journal — a very active and bitter Whig in a small way, but not seeking to be known out of my own Ward Committee — when, after the great political revulsion of 1837, I was one day called to the City Hotel, where two strangers introduced themselves as Thurlow Weed and Lewis Benedict, of Albany. They told me that a cheap campaign paper of a peculiar stamp at Albany had been resolved on, and that I had been selected to edit it. The announcement might well be deemed flattering by one who had never even sought the notice of the great, and who was not known as a partisan writer, and I eagerly embraced their proposals. They asked me to fix my salary for the year; I named $1000, which they agreed to; and I did the work required to the best of my ability. It was work that made no figure and created no sensation; but I loved it, and did it well. When it was done, you were governor, dispensing offices worth $3000 to $20,000 per year to your friends and compatriots, and I returned to my garret and my crust, and my desperate battle with pecuniary obligations heaped upon me by bad partners in business and the disastrous events of 1837. I believe that it did not then occur to me that some one of these abundant places might have been offered to me without injustice; I now think it should have occurred to you. If it did occur to me, I was not the man to ask you for it; I think that should not have been necessary. I only remember that no friend at Albany inquired as to my pecuniary circumstances; that your friend (but not mine), Robert C. Wetmore, was one of the chief dispensers of your patronage here; and that such devoted compatriots as A. H. Wells and

John Hooks were lifted by you out of pauperism into independence, as I am glad I was not; and yet an inquiry from you as to my needs and means at that time would have been timely, and held ever in grateful remembrance.

"In the Harrison campaign of 1840, I was again designated to edit a campaign paper. I published it as well, and ought to have made something by it, in spite of its extreme low price; my extreme poverty was the main reason why I did not. It compelled me to hire press-work, mailing, etc., done by the job, and high charges for extra work nearly ate me up. At the close, I was still without property and in debt, but this paper had rather improved my position.

"Now came the great scramble of the swell mob of coon minstrels and cider-suckers at Washington — I not being counted in. Several regiments of them went on from this city; but no one of the whole crowd — though I say it, who should not? — had done so much toward General Harrison's nomination and election as yours respectfully. I asked nothing, expected nothing; but you, Governor Seward, ought to have asked that I be postmaster of New York. Your asking would have been in vain, but it would have been an act of grace neither wasted nor undeserved.

"I soon after started the *Tribune,* because I was urged to do so by certain of your friends, and because such a paper was needed here. I was promised certain pecuniary aid in so doing; it might have been given me without cost or risk to any one. All I ever had was a loan by piecemeal of $1000 from James Coggeshall, God bless his honored memory! I did not ask for this, and I think it is the one sole case in which I ever received a pecuniary favor from a political associate. I am very thankful that he did not die till it was fully repaid.

"And let me here honor one grateful recollection. When the Whig Party under your rule had offices to give, my name was never thought of; but when, in 1842–3, we were hopelessly out of power, I was honored by the party nomination for state printer. When we came again to have a state printer to *elect* as well as nominate, the place went to Weed, as it ought. Yet it was worth something to know that there was once a time when it was not deemed too great a sacrifice to recognize me as belonging to your household. If a new office had not since been created on purpose to give its valuable patronage to H. J. Raymond, and enable St. John to show forth his *Times* as the organ of the Whig state administration, I should have been still more grateful.

"In 1848 your star again rose, and my warmest hopes were realized in your election to the Senate. I was no longer needy, and had no more claim than desire to be recognized by General Taylor. I think I had some claim to forbearance from you. What I received thereupon was a most humiliating lecture in the shape of a decision in the libel case of Redfield and Pringle, and an obligation to publish it in my own and the other journal of our supposed firm. I thought, and still think, this lecture needlessly cruel and mortifying. The plaintiffs, after using my columns to the extent of their needs or desires, stopped writing, and called on me for the name of their assailant. I proffered it to them — a thoroughly responsible name. They refused to accept it unless it should prove to be one of the four or five first men in Batavia — when they had known from the first who it was, and that it was neither of them. They would not accept that which they had demanded; they sued me, instead, for money, and money you were at liberty to give them to your heart's content — I do not think you *were* at liberty to humiliate me in the eyes of my own and your public as you did. I think you exalted your own judicial sternness and fearlessness unduly at my expense. I think you had a better occasion for the display of these qualities when Webb threw himself untimely upon you for a pardon which he had done all a man could do to demerit. (His paper is paying you for it now.)

"I have publicly set forth my view of yours and our duty with respect to fusion, Nebraska, and party designations. I will not repeat any of that. I have referred also to Weed's reading me out of the Whig Party — my crime being, in this as in some other things, that of doing to-day what more politic persons will not be ready to do till to-morrow.

"Let me speak of the late canvass. I was once sent to Congress for ninety days merely to enable Jim Brooks to secure a seat therein for four years. I think I never hinted to any human being that I would have liked to be put forward for any place; but James W. White (you hardly know how good and true a man he is) started my name for Congress, and Brooks's packed delegation thought I could help him through, so I was put on behind him. But this last spring, after the Nebraska Question had created a new state of things at the North, one or two personal friends, of no political consideration, suggested my name as a candidate for governor, and I did not discourage them. Soon the persons who were afterward mainly instrumental in nominating Clark came about me and asked if I could secure the Know-Nothing vote. I told them I neither could nor would touch it; on the contrary, I loathed and repelled it. Thereupon they turned upon Clark.

"I said nothing, did nothing. A hundred people asked me who should be run for governor. I sometimes indicated Patterson; I never hinted at my own name. But by-and-by Weed came down, and called me to him to tell me why he could not support me for governor. (I had never asked nor counted on his support.)

"I am sure Weed did not mean to humiliate me, but he did it. The upshot of his discourse (very cautiously stated) was this: If I were a candidate for governor, I should beat, not myself alone, but you. Perhaps that was true; but, as I had in no manner solicited his or your support, I thought this might have been said to my friends rather than to me. I suspect it is true that I could not have been elected governor as a Whig; but, had he and you been favorable, there *would* have been a party in the state ere this which could and would have elected me to any post without injuring itself or endangering your reëlection.

"It was in vain that I urged that I had in no manner asked a nomination. At length I was nettled by his language — well intended, but *very* cutting as addressed by him to me — to say, in substance, 'Well, then, make Patterson governor, and try my name for lieutenant. To lose this place is a matter of no importance, and we can see whether I am really so odious.'

"I should have hated to serve as lieutenant-governor, but I should have gloried in running for the post. I want to have my enemies all upon me at once; I am tired of fighting them piecemeal; and, though I should have been beaten in the canvass, I know that my running would have helped the ticket and helped my paper.

"It was thought best to let the matter take another course. No other name could have been put on the ticket so bitterly humbling to me as that which was selected. The nomination was given to Raymond, the fight left to me. And, Governor Seward, *I have made it,* though it be conceited in me to say so. What little fight there has been I have stirred up. Even Weed has not been (I speak of his paper) hearty in this contest, while the journal of the Whig lieutenant-governor has taken care of its own interests and let the canvass take care of itself, as it early declared it would do. That journal has (because of its milk-and-water course) some twenty thousand subscribers in this city and its suburbs, and of these twenty thousand I venture to say more voted for Ullmann and Scroggs than for Clark and Raymond; the *Tribune* (also because of its character) has but eight thousand subscribers within the same radius, and I venture to say that of its habitual readers nine-tenths voted for Clark and Raymond—very few for Ullmann and Scroggs. I had to bear the brunt of the contest, and take a terrible responsibility in order to prevent the Whigs uniting upon James W. Barker in order to defeat Fernando Wood. Had Barker been elected here, neither you nor I could walk these streets without being hooted, and Know-nothingism would have swept like a prairie fire. I stopped Barker's election at the cost of incurring the deadliest enmity of the defeated gang, and I have been rebuked for it by the lieutenant-governor's paper. At the critical moment he came out against John Wheeler in favor of Charles H. Marshall (who would have been your deadliest enemy in the House); and even your colonel-general's paper, which was even with me in insisting that Wheeler should be returned, wheeled about at the last moment and went in for Marshall, the *Tribune* alone clinging to Wheeler to the last. I rejoice that they who turned so suddenly were not able to turn all their readers.

"Governor Seward, I know that some of your most cherished friends think me a great obstacle to your advancement—that John Schoolcraft, for one, insists that you and Weed shall not be identified with me. I trust, after a time, you will not be. I trust I shall never be found in opposition to you; I have no further wish but to glide out of the newspaper world as quietly and as speedily as possible, join my family in Europe, and, if possible, stay there quite a time — long enough to cool my fevered brain and renovate my overtasked energies. All I ask is that we shall be counted even on the morning after the first Tuesday in February, as aforesaid, and that I may thereafter take such course as seems best without reference to the past.

"You have done me acts of valued kindness in the line of your profession; let me close with the assurance that these will ever be gratefully remembered by, "Yours,

"HORACE GREELEY."

APPENDIX — NOTE E

GROWTH OF NEWSPAPERS FROM 1776 TO 1840

STATES	1776	1810	1828	1840
Maine	....	....	29	36
Massachusetts	7	32	78	91
New Hampshire	1	12	17	27
Vermont	....	14	21	30
Rhode Island	2	7	24	16
Connecticut	4	11	33	33
New York	4	66	161	245
New Jersey	....	8	22	33
Pennsylvania	9	72	185	187
Delaware		2	4	6
Maryland	2	21	37	45
District of Columbia	....	6	9	14
Virginia	2	23	34	51
North Carolina	2	10	20	27
South Carolina	3	10	16	17
Georgia	1	13	18	34
Florida	....	1	2	10
Alabama	....	....	10	28
Mississippi	....	4	6	30
Louisiana	....	10	9	34
Tennessee	....	6	8	46
Kentucky	....	17	23	38
Ohio	....	14	66	123
Indiana	....	....	17	73
Michigan	....	....	2	32
Illinois	....	....	4	43
Missouri	....	....	5	35
Arkansas	....	....	1	9
Wisconsin	....	....	....	6
Iowa	....	....	....	4
TOTAL	37	359	861	1,403

NORTH, *Census of 1880*, viii, 47.

APPENDIX — NOTE F

STATISTICS OF THE DAILY AND WEEKLY NEWSPAPERS IN THE UNITED STATES IN 1840

FREE STATES	Daily	Weekly	SLAVE STATES	Daily	Weekly
California	..	...	Alabama	3	25
Connecticut	2	31	Arkansas	..	9
Indiana	..	73	Delaware	..	6
Illinois	3	40	Florida	..	10
Iowa	..	4	Georgia	5	29
Maine	3	33	Kentucky	5	33
Massachusetts	10	81	Louisiana	11	23
Michigan	6	26	Maryland	7	35
New Hampshire	..	27	Mississippi	2	29
New Jersey	4	32	Missouri	6	29
New York	34	211	North Carolina	..	27
Ohio	9	114	South Carolina	3	14
Pennsylvania	12	175	Tennessee	2	44
Rhode Island	2	14	Texas	..	...
Vermont	2	28	Virginia	4	47
Wisconsin	..	6			
TOTAL	87	895		48	360

The following table shows that in 1850 the north was rapidly outstripping the south in newspapers, periodicals and circulation:

FREE STATES	Number	Copies printed annually
California	7	761,200
Connecticut	46	4,267,932
Illinois	107	5,102,276
Indiana	107	4,316,828
Iowa	29	1,512,800
Maine	49	4,203,064
Massachusetts	202	64,820,564
Michigan	58	3,247,736
New Hampshire	38	3,067,552
New Jersey	51	4,098,678
New York	428	115,385,473
Ohio	261	30,473,407
Pennsylvania	309	84,898,672
Rhode Island	19	2,756,950
Vermont	35	2,567,662
Wisconsin	46	2,665,487
TOTAL	1,792	334,146,281

SLAVE STATES	Number	Copies printed annually
Alabama	60	2,662,741
Arkansas	9	377,000
Delaware	10	421,200
Florida	10	319,800
Kentucky	62	6,582,838
Louisiana	55	12,416,224
Maryland	68	19,612,724
Mississippi	50	1,752,504
Missouri	61	6,195,560
North Carolina	51	2,020,564
South Carolina	46	7,145,930
Tennessee	50	6,940,750
Texas	34	1,296,924
Virginia	87	9,223,068
Georgia	51	4,070,868
TOTAL	704	81,038,695

HELPER, *The Impending Crisis,* 290.

ILLITERATE WHITE ADULTS IN THE FREE AND IN THE SLAVE STATES — 1850

FREE STATES	Native	Foreign
California	2,201	2,917
Connecticut	826	4,013
Illinois	34,107	5,947
Indiana	67,275	3,265
Iowa	7,043	1,077
Maine	1,999	4,148
Massachusetts	1,055	26,484
Michigan	4,903	3,009
New Hampshire	893	2,064
New Jersey	8,370	5,878
New York	23,241	68,052
Ohio	51,968	9,062
Pennsylvania	41,944	24,989
Rhode Island	981	2,359
Vermont	565	5,624
Wisconsin	1,459	4,902
TOTAL	248,830	173,790

SLAVE STATES	Native	Foreign
Alabama	33,618	139
Arkansas	16,792	27
Delaware	4,132	404
Florida	3,564	295
Georgia	40,794	406
Kentucky	64,340	2,347
Louisiana	14,950	6,271
Maryland	17,364	3,451
Mississippi	13,324	81
Missouri	34,420	1,861
North Carolina	73,226	340
South Carolina	15,580	104
Tennessee	77,017	505
Texas	8,037	2,488
Virginia	75,868	1,137
TOTAL	493,026	19,856

HELPER, *Impending Crisis,* 291.

APPENDIX — NOTE G

For the year ending June 30, 1882

Newspapers	Postage paid on Daily and Weekly editions
New York Tribune	$27,290.56

NEWSPAPERS	Postage paid on Daily and Weekly editions
The New York Herald	$21,930.78
The Inter-Ocean	16,609.36
The St. Louis Globe-Democrat	16,386.60
The New York Sun	14,769.66
The New York Times	14,598.56
The Cincinnati Enquirer	13,154.42
The St. Louis Republican	11,799.96
The Toledo Blade	9,817.42
The St. Paul Pioneer Press	9,209.52
The Chicago News	7,789.14
The Louisville Courier-Journal	7,305.06
The Chicago Times	6,581.10
The Cincinnati Gazette	6,561.44
The Chicago Tribune	5,644.02
The Boston Journal	5,555.42

The Detroit Free Press	5,308.98
The Kansas City Times	5,230.23
The Philadelphia Record	5,087.44
The Cleveland Leader	4,474.48
The Cincinnati Commercial	4,154.48
The Philadelphia Times	3,883.78
The Detroit Post and Tribune	3,490.22
The Boston Herald	3,351.74
The Philadelphia Press	2,858.68
The Cleveland Herald	2,595.10
The Cincinnati Times-Star	2,575.78
The Boston Advertiser	1,955.12

Pamphlet, *N. Y. Tribune,* 22.

APPENDIX — NOTE H

ZENGER'S TRIAL

"Viewed in the light of that day, before the colonies had learned the use and power of newspapers, before John Wilkes had defied parliament and crown in behalf of the right to deal in type with public questions, the case and its results marked a complete change in theory and practice. It was the development of a new motor in affairs. It was the creation of an implement for the people, which rulers and courts must forever regard. The Christian era doubtless would have come without John the Baptist and his preaching. So American independence would have been wrought out, without this triumph for the liberty of printing the truth. But as events have occurred, the trial of Zenger and his acquittal stand forth as the one incident which molded opinions, which strengthened courage, which crystallized purpose on this continent in the grand movement whose termination perhaps no man foresaw, whose direction few suggested above a whisper, and yet whose logic was as direct as the laws of the universe.

"Why should the press be wholly free, if this continent was to bow before a king seated beyond the ocean, and to receive its statutes from a parliament in which it could have no representatives? A generation was required for the question to stir men's minds, and to bring them face to face with the answer. If Zenger had been convicted, no estimate can determine the time which would have been demanded to strike

[1] Roberts, *New York,* i., 277, 278.

the fetters from discussion, and therefore from deliberation and action for the rights of the people.

"This verdict in New York was an achievement for the freedom of the press, and so for the liberty of man, of which the colonies soon began to reap the benefit, and for which the thought and speech of mankind all over the globe are braver and more affluent of noble life."

APPENDIX I

THE SUN-HERALD MERGER

The merging of the New York *Herald* in the *Sun* has brought to a dramatic close the story of the *Herald* and that chapter of American journalism which deals with the two Bennetts. Frank A. Munsey, whose ownership of both properties led to their combination, has, unlike most of the great editors of the country, been associated with no one great newspaper. Indeed he has reversed the process by which most editors have obtained influence. In combining the *Sun* and the *Herald* in one sheet, both Dana and Bennett become the pedestal for his fame. At a time when patriotic utterance is much needed in this country, the *Sun* has assumed a conspicuous leadership. It can hardly be expected that the addition of the *Herald* will do aught but strengthen its position.

BIBLIOGRAPHY

ANONYMOUS:

The Life and Writings of James Gordon Bennett. New York, 1844.

William Bradford, His Connection with Early Printing. New York, 1893.

The Freedom of Speech and Writing. London, 1776.

Reminiscences of the "Evening Post." New York, 1851.

Chicago's First Half Century, Inter-Ocean Publishing Company, 1883.

Notable Men of Chicago and Their City, Daily Journal, Chicago, 1910.

Early Chicago — Reception to the Settlers by the Calumet Club, Chicago, 1879.

Fifth Annual Review of the Commerce of Chicago.

Public Papers of George Clinton, First Governor of the State of New York, 9 vol. Third Annual Report of State Historian, N. Y. and Albany, 1899–1911.

ADAMS, BROOKS: *The Emancipation of Massachusetts.* Cambridge, 1887.

ADAMS, CHARLES FRANCIS (Editor): *The Works of John Adams,* vols. i to x. Little, Brown & Co., Boston, 1850–56.

ADAMS, CHARLES FRANCIS: *An Undeveloped Function.* Washington, Government Printing Office, 1902.

ADAMS, CHARLES FRANCIS: *Massachusetts — Its Historians and Its History.* Boston, 1898.

ADAMS, CHARLES FRANCIS: *Three Episodes of Massachusetts History,* 2 vols. Houghton Mifflin & Co., Boston, 1892.

ADAMS, HENRY: *History of the United States of America, 1801–1817,* 9 vols. New York, 1889.

ADAMS, JOHN: *Familiar Letters of Adams and His Wife, Abigail Adams,* New York, 1876.

ADAMS, JOHN: *Letters of John Adams addressed to his wife,* vols. i and ii. Little, Brown & Co., Boston, 1841.

ADAMS, JOHN QUINCY: *Memoirs,* 12 vols. Philadelphia, 1874–77.

ALDEN, H. M.: "Why the Ancients had no Printing Press," in *Harper's Monthly,* vol. xxxvii, p. 394.

ALEXANDER, DEALVA STANWOOD: *A Political History of the State of New York,* 3 vols. New York, 1906.

ALLEN, WILLIAM B.: *A History of Kentucky.* Louisville, 1872.

ALLIBONE, SAMUEL AUSTIN: *A Critical Dictionary of English Literature,* 3 vols. Philadelphia, 1863–71.

AMERICAN ANTIQUARIAN SOCIETY: Proceedings, N. S. 23, 24, 25, 26, 27, years 1913–1914–1915–1916–1917. Bibliography of American Newspapers, 1690–1820, by Clarence S. Brigham.

AMERICAN ARCHIVES: Fifth Series, vol. i. Washington, 1848.

AMERICAN HISTORICAL RECORD: vol. i. Phila., 1872.

ANDREAS, A. T.: *History of Chicago from the earliest period to the present time,* 3 vols. Chicago, 1884–86.

ANDREWS, ALEXANDER: *The History of British Journalism,* 2 vols. London, 1859.

ARMSTRONG, EDWARD: *Address before the Historical Society of Pennsylvania, Nov. 8, 1851.*

ARMSTRONG, F. LEROY: The Daily papers of Chicago. *Chautauquan, 1898,* vol. xxvii, pp. 538–545.

ARNOLD, ISAAC NEWTON: *William B. Ogden; and early days in Chicago.*

ARNOLD, SAMUEL GREEN: *History of the State of Rhode Island,* 2 vols. New York, 1859.

ARTHUR, T. S., and CARPENTER, W. H.: *The History of Georgia.* Philadelphia, 1852.

AUSTIN, GEO. LOWELL: *The History of Massachusetts.* Boston, 1876.

AYER, MARY FARWELL: *Boston Common in Colonial and Provincial Days.* Boston, 1903.

BACHE, BENJAMIN FRANKLIN: *Truth Will Out!* Philadelphia, 1798.

BALL, TIMOTHY HORTON: *Northwestern Indiana from 1800 to 1900.* Chicago, 1900.

BANCROFT, GEORGE: *History of the United States of America,* 6 vols. New York, 1882.

BANKS, ELIZABETH L.: "American Yellow Journalism," *Nineteenth Century,* vol. xliv, p. 328. London, 1898.

BARBER, JOHN WARNER: *Historical Collections, Connecticut.* New Haven, 1849.

BARBER, JOHN WARNER: *Historical Collections, Massachusetts.* Worcester, 1839.

BARBER, JOHN WARNER and HOWE, HENRY: *Historical Collections of the State of New York.* New York, 1841.

BARRY, JOHN STETSON: *History of Massachusetts,* vol. i (1st) Colonial Period, vol. ii (2nd) Provincial Period, vol. iii (3rd) Commonwealth Period. Boston, 1855–57.

BARSTOW, GEORGE: *History of New Hampshire.* Boston, 1853.

BASSETT, JOHN SPENCER: *The Federalist System,* forming *The American Nation: a History,* vol. xi of. Harper, New York, 1906.

BELKNAP, JEREMY: *The History of New Hampshire,* 2 vols. Dover, N. H., 1812.

BENTON, JOSIAH HENRY: *The Story of the Old Boston Town House.* Boston, 1908.

BERNARD, SIR FRANCIS: *The Barrington-Bernard Correspondence and Illustrative Matter.* Cambridge, 1912.

BIGELOW, JOHN: *William Cullen Bryant.* Houghton Mifflin & Co., Boston, 1897.

BIGELOW, JOHN: *The Complete Works of Benjamin Franklin,* 9 vols. New York, 1887.

BINNEY, HORACE: "Leaders of the Old Bar of Philadelphia," in *Pennsylvania Magazine of History and Biography,* vol. xiv, No. 1, p. 1. 1890.

BIRNEY, WILLIAM: *James G. Birney and His Times.* Appleton, New York, 1890.

BIRRELL, AUGUSTINE: *Thomas Paine,* in his *In the Name of the Bodleian,* pp. 195–206. New York, 1905.

BISHOP, CORTLANDT F.: *History of Elections in the American Colonies.* New York, 1893.

BLAINE, JAMES GILLESPIE: *Twenty Years of Congress,* 2 vols. Norwich, Conn., 1884–86.

BLANCHARD, RUFUS: *The Discovery and Conquests of the Northwest,* 2 vols. Chicago, 1880.

BLANCHARD, RUFUS: *The Rise and Fall of Political Parties in the United States.* Chicago, 1884.

BOBIN, ISAAC: *Letters of Isaac Bobin,* New York Colonial Tracts. No. iv. Albany, 1872.

BOLTON, NATHANIEL: Lecture delivered before the Indiana Historical Society. Indianapolis, 1853.

BOOTH, MARY L.: *History of the City of New York.* New York, 1867.

BORGEAUD, CHARLES: *The Rise of Modern Democracy in Old and New England.* London, 1894.

BOURNE, H. R. FOX: *English Newspapers,* vol. i. London, 1887.

BOURNE, R. R. FOX: *The Life of John Locke,* 2 vols. New York, 1876.

BOYNTON, HENRY WALCOTT: *Journalism and Literature.* Houghton Mifflin & Co., Boston, 1904.

BRADFORD, ALDEN: *History of Massachusetts, 1620 to 1820.* Boston, 1835.

BRADFORD, ALDEN: *Memoir of the Life and Writings of Rev. Jonathan Mayhew, D.D.* Boston, 1838.

BRIGHAM, CLARENCE SAUNDERS: Burke, Major, fourth paper presented by, with other papers edited and published by Roger Williams, in London, 1652. Providence, R. I., 1903.

Brooks, Noah: Henry Knox, a Soldier of the Revolution (*American Men of Energy*). New York, 1900.

Bross, William: *History of Chicago*. Chicago, 1876.

Brown, George Washington: *The Truth at Last. Reminiscences of Old John Brown*. Rockford, Illinois, 1880.

Brown, Henry: *The Present and Future Prospects of Chicago*. Chicago, 1876.

Brown, John Mason: *The Political Beginnings of Kentucky*. Louisville, 1889.

Browne, William Hand: *Maryland*. Boston, 1904.

Bryan, Wilhelmus Bogart: *History of the National Capital*. 2 vols. Macmillan, New York, 1914.

Bryce, James: *Studies in Contemporary Biography*. Macmillan, New York, 1903.

Buckingham, Joseph T.: *Personal Memoirs*, 2 vols. Boston, 1852.

Buckingham, Joseph T.: *Specimens of Newspaper Literature*, 2 vols. Boston, 1850.

Buecher, Carl: *Industrial Evolution*. H. Holt & Co., New York, 1912.

Burnet, Gilbert (Bishop): *Bishop Burnet's History of His Own Time, etc.*, 2 vols. Oxford, 1823.

Butler, Mann: *A History of the Commonwealth of Kentucky*. Louisville, 1834.

Campbell, Douglas: *The Puritan in Holland, England and America*, 2 vols. New York, 1892.

Capen, Nahum: *The History of Democracy*. Hartford, 1874.

Carlile, Mary Anne: *Suppressed Defence*. London, 1821.

Carlyle, Edward Irving: *William Cobbett*. London, 1904.

Carpenter, Francis Bicknell: *Anecdotes and Reminiscences of Abraham Lincoln*. New York, 1865; *Six Months at the White House with Abraham Lincoln*.

Houghton Mifflin & Co., New York, 1866.

CARPENTER, STEPHEN CULLEN: *Memoirs of Thomas Jefferson,* 2 vols. New York, 1809.

CARPENTER, WILLIAM H.: *History of Massachusetts.* Philadelphia, 1853.

CARPENTER, WILLIAM H.: *The History of Ohio.* Philadelphia, 1884.

CARY, EDWARD: *George William Curtis.* Houghton Mifflin & Co., Boston, 1895.

CHALMERS, GEORGE: *An Introduction to the History of the Revolt of the American Colonies,* 2 vols. Boston, 1845.

CHALMERS, GEORGE: *Life of Thomas Ruddiman.* London, 1794.

CHAMBERLAIN, REV. N. H.: *Samuel Sewall and the World He Lived in.* Boston, 1897.

CHANNING, EDWARD, and HART, A. B.: *Guide to the Study of American History.* Ginn and Co., Boston, 1896.

CHAUNCEY, CHARLES: *A Discourse Occasioned by the Death of the Rev. Jonathan Mayhew, D.D.* Boston, 1766.

CHEETHAM, JAMES: *The Life of Thomas Paine.* New York, 1809. *Letters of James Cheetham,* Massachusetts Historical Society Proceedings, vol. i, p. 41, 1908.

CHEVES, LANGDON: *Letter to the Editors of the Charleston Mercury.* Charleston, S. C., 1844.

CHILDS, GEORGE WILLIAM: *Recollections.* Lippincott, Philadelphia, 1890.

CLAFLIN, ALTA BLANCHE: *Political Parties in the United States.* New York, 1915.

CLARK, GILBERT JOHN: *Memoir, autobiography and correspondence of Jeremiah Mason.* 1917.

CLEAVER, CHARLES: *Early Chicago Reminiscences.* Chicago, 1882.

CLEWS, HENRY: *Twenty-eight Years in Wall Street.* New York, 1888; *Fifty Years in Wall Street.* New York, 1908.

CLINTON, GEORGE: *Public Papers of George Clinton, First Governor of the State of New York,* 9 vols. Appendix N to third annual report of State Historian. N. Y. and Albany, 1899–1911.

COBB, SANFORD H.: *The Story of the Palatines.* New York, 1897.

COBBETT, WILLIAM: *The Life of W. Cobbett.* Philadelphia, 1835.

COBBETT, WILLIAM: *The Life of Thomas Paine.* London, 1796.

COBBETT, WILLIAM, EDITOR: *Parliamentary History of England,* 24 vols. London, 1803.

COLEMAN, WILLIAM: *An Appeal to the People.* New York, 1810.

COLLET, C. D.: *History of the Taxes on Knowledge,* 2 vols. London, 1896.

COLLINS, LEWIS: *Historical Sketches of Kentucky.* Maysville, 1850.

COLTON, REV. WALTER: *Three Years in California.* A. S. Barnes and Co., New York, 1850.

COMAN, KATHARINE: *Economic Beginnings of the Far West,* 2 vols. New York, 1912.

CONANT, CHARLES ARTHUR: *Alexander Hamilton.* Houghton Mifflin & Co., Boston, 1901.

CONARD, HOWARD LOUIS: *Encyclopedia of the History of Missouri,* 6 vols. St. Louis, 1901.

CONGDON, CHARLES TABOR: *Reminiscences of a Journalist,* Boston, 1880.

CONNELLEY, WILLIAM ELSEY: *An Appeal to the Record.* Topeka, 1903.

CONRAD, HENRY CLAY: *History of the State of Delaware,* 3 vols. Wilmington, 1908.

CONWAY, MONCURE DANIEL: *The Life of Thomas Paine,* 2 vols. Putnam, New York, 1892; *Omitted Chapters of History disclosed in the life and papers of Edmund Randolph.* Putnam, New York, 1889.

CONWAY, MONCURE DANIEL (Ed.): *The Writings of Paine,* 4 vols. Putnam, New York, 1894–1896.

COOK, ELIZABETH CHRISTINE: *Literary Influences in Colonial Newspapers.* Columbia University Press, New York, 1912.

COOKE, GEORGE WINGROVE: *The History of Party,* 3 vols. London, 1840.

COOPER, THOS. VALENTINE, and FENTON, HECTOR TYNDALE: *American Politics from the Beginning to Date (1884).* Chicago, 1884.

COXE, DANIEL: *A Description of the English Province of Carolana, by the Spaniards called Florida and by the French, La Louisiane.* Philadelphia, 1850.

CRAIG, NEVILLE BURGOYNE: *The History of Pittsburgh.* Pittsburgh, 1917.

CRAWFORD, MARY CAROLINE: *Old Boston in Colonial Days.* Boston, 1908.

CURREY, JOSIAH SEYMOUR: *Chicago; Its History and Its Builders,* 3 vols. Chicago, 1912.

DANA, CHARLES ANDERSON: *Lincoln and His Cabinet.* Marion Press, New York, 1899.

DANVERS, JOHN THIERRY: *A Picture of a Republican Magistrate of the New School.* New York, 1808.

DARLING, CHARLES W.: *New Amsterdam, New Orange, New York, with chronological data.* Utica, N. Y., 1889.

DAVENANT, CHARLES: *Political and Commercial Works,* 5 vols. London, 1771.

DAVIS, A.: *History of New Amsterdam,* New York, 1854.

DAWSON, HENRY BARTON: *Introduction to the Federalist.* New York, 1864.

DAWSON, HENRY BARTON: *The Fœderalist, a Collection of Essays,* 2 vols. Scribner, New York, 1863.

DEAN, JOHN W.: *Sketch of the Life of William B. Towne.*

DE TOCQUEVILLE, ALEXIS: *Democracy in America,* 2 vols. Cambridge, 1862.

De Witt, Cornelius: *Jefferson and the American Democracy,* trans. by R. S. H. Church. London, 1862.

Dillon, John Brown: *History of Indiana.* Indianapolis, 1859.

Disraeli, Rt. Hon. Benj.: *The Literary Character.* 1881.

Disraeli, Isaac: *Amenities of Literature.* New York, 1881.

Disraeli, Isaac: *Calamities and Quarrels of Authors.* London and New York, 1881.

Disraeli, Isaac: *Curiosities of Literature,* 4 vols. New York, 1881.

Disraeli, Isaac: *Literary Character of Men of Genius.* New York, 1881.

Dix, Morgan: *Memoirs of John Adams Dix,* 2 vols. Harper, New York, 1883.

Doyle, John Andrew: *The English in America,* 5 vols. London, 1882.

Drake, Samuel G.: *The History and Antiquities of the City of Boston.* Boston, 1854.

Drake, Samuel G.: *News from New England.* Albany, 1865.

Duane, William: *Politics for American Farmers.* Washington, 1807.

Duane, William: *Reports of a debate in the Senate of the United States.* Philadelphia, 1804.

Duane, William (supposed author): *Sampson against the Philistines.* Philadelphia, 1805.

Du Bose, John Witherspoon: *The Life and Times of William Lowndes Yancey.* Birmingham, 1892.

Duniway, Clyde Augustus: *The Development of Freedom of the Press in Massachusetts.* New York, 1906.

Dunning, Wm. Archibald: *Reconstruction, political and economic,* vol. xxii, *The American Nation: a History.* Harper, New York, 1907.

Dunton, John: *Letters written from New England,* A. D. *1686.* Boston, 1867.

DUNTON, JOHN: *Life and Errors of . . . D., Citizen of London.* London, 1818.

Edinburgh Review: English edition, vol. xxxvi. October, 1821.

Edinburgh Review: January, 1878, to April, 1878, vol. cxlvii. Edinburgh, 1878.

EDWARDS, GEORGE WILLIAM: *New York as an Eighteenth-Century Municipality.* Longmans, Green and Co., New York, 1917.

EGGLESTON, GEORGE CARY: *Recollections of a Varied Life.* Holt, New York, 1910.

FARIS, JOHN T.: *The Romance of Old Philadelphia.* Philadelphia, 1918.

FELT, JOSEPH B.: *Annals of Salem,* 2 vols. Salem, 1845.

FENTON, HECTOR TYNDALE: (*See* Cooper, Thomas V.)

FESS, SIMEON D.: *History of Political Theory and Party Organization in the United States.* Ginn and Co., Boston, 1910.

FISHER, E. T. (trans.): *Report of a French Protestant Refugee in Boston, 1687.* Brooklyn, 1868.

FISHER, GEORGE PARK: *The Colonial Era.* New York, 1892.

FISKE, JOHN: *American Political Ideas.* Houghton Mifflin & Co., Boston, 1911.

FISKE, JOHN: *The American Revolution,* 2 vols. Houghton Mifflin & Co., 1891, 1892; *The Critical Period of American History, 1783–1789.* Houghton Mifflin & Co., Boston, 1916; *The Dutch and Quaker Colonies in America.* Boston, 1899.

FOOTE, WILLIAM HENRY: *Sketches of Virginia,* 2 vols. Philadelphia, 1855.

FORCE, PETER: *Tracts and other Papers relating principally to the origin, settlement and progress of the Colonies of North America,* vol. iv. Washington, 1846.

FORD, EMILY E. F.: *Notes on the Life of Noah Webster.* New York, 1912.

FORD, HENRY JONES: *The Rise and Growth of American Politics.* Macmillan Co., New York, 1898.

FORD, PAUL LEICESTER: *Bibliotheca Hamiltoniana.* Knickerbocker Press, New York, 1886.

FORD, PAUL LEICESTER, and BOURNE, EDWARD GAYLORD: *The Authorship of the "Federalist."* New York, 1897.

FORD, PAUL LEICESTER: *A list of editions of the "Federalist."* Brooklyn, 1886; *Franklin Bibliography.* Brooklyn, 1889; *The Many-Sided Franklin.* New York, 1899; *The Journals of Hugh Gaine, printer,* 2 vols. Dodd, Mead and Co.. New York, 1902; *The New England Primer.* New York, 1896; *John Tucker and His Writings.* Chicago, 1894.

FORD, WORTHINGTON C.: *Massachusetts Hist. Society Proceedings,* Series 2, vol. xx, pp. 257–394. Boston, 1907.

FORMAN, SAMUEL E.: *The Political Activities of Philip Freneau* (included in *Johns Hopkins University Historical and Political Studies,* vol. xx, 1902). Baltimore, 1902.

FOSTER, WILLIAM EATON: *Stephen Hopkins, a Rhode Island Statesman,* 2 vols. S. S. Rider, Providence, 1884.

FOWLE, DANIEL: *A Total Eclipse of Liberty.* Boston, 1755.

FOX, CHARLES JAMES: *A History of the Early Part of the Reign of James II.* London, 1856.

FRANKLIN, BENJAMIN: (*See* Sparks, Jared); *Collected Works,* edited by John Bigelow (10 vols.).

FRENEAU, PHILIP: *The Miscellaneous Works of Philip Freneau.* Philadelphia, 1788.

FROTHINGHAM, RICHARD: *The Rise of the Republic of the United States.* Boston, 1905.

GALE, EDWIN O.: *Reminiscences of Early Chicago and Vicinity.* Revell, Chicago, 1902.

GENET, GEORGE CLINTON: *Washington, Jefferson and "Citizen" Genet, 1793.* New York, 1899.

GIBBS, GEORGE. *Memoirs of the Administrations of Washington and John Adams,* 2 vols. New York, 1846.

GIHON, JOHN H.: *Geary and Kansas.* Philadelphia, 1857.

GODDARD, DELANO A.: *The Mathers weighed in the balance and found not wanting.* Boston, 1870.

GODKIN, EDWIN LAWRENCE: *Life and Letters,* 2 vols. Macmillan, New York, 1907; *Reflections and Comments.* Scribner, New York, 1907.

GODKIN, EDWIN LAWRENCE: *Unforeseen Tendencies of Democracy.*

GODWIN, PARKE: *A Biography of William Cullen Bryant,* 2 vols. Appleton, New York, 1883.

GORDON, ELEANOR LYTLE K.: *John Kinzie, the "Father of Chicago."* Savannah, 1910.

GORDON, WILLIAM: *The History of the Independence of the United States of America.* New York, 1801.

GORDY, JOHN PANCOAST: *A History of Political Parties in the United States,* 4 vols. Holt, New York, 1900.

GRAYBILL, JAMES EDWARD: *Alexander Hamilton, Nevis-Weehawken.* New York, 1898.

GREELEY, HORACE: *The Autobiography of Horace Greeley.* New York, 1872.

GREELEY, HORACE: *The American Conflict,* 2 vols. Hartford, 1864–6.

GREEN, JOHN RICHARD: *Short History of the English People.* New York, 1884.

GREEN, SAMUEL: *Diary by Increase Mather, March, 1675, to December, 1676.* Cambridge, 1900.

GREENE, GEORGE WASHINGTON: *A Short History of Rhode Island.* Providence, 1877.

GRIFFIN, APPLETON P. C.: *List of works relating to Political parties in the United States.* Washington, 1907.

GRIFFIN, JOSEPH (Editor): *History of the Press of Maine*—Brunswick. 1872.

GUROWSKI, ADAM: *Diary.* 2 vols. Boston, 1862; New York, 1864.

GUYER, I. D.: *History of Chicago.* Chicago. 1862.

HALSTEAD, MURAT: *Caucuses of 1860 — A History of the National Political Conventions.* Columbus, 1860.

HAMBLETON, JAMES PINCKNEY: *A Biographical Sketch of Henry A. Wise.* Richmond, 1856.

HAMILTON, ALEXANDER: *See* H. C. Lodge.

HAMILTON, ALLAN McLANE: *The Intimate Life of Alexander Hamilton.* Scribners, New York, 1910.

HAMILTON, J. C.: *The Life of Alexander Hamilton.* New York, 1834.

HAMILTON, JOHN CHURCH: *History of the Republic of the United States, as traced, etc.*, 7 vols. Philadelphia, 1864.

HAMMOND, JABEZ D.: *The History of Political Parties in the State of New York,* 3 vols., Cooperstown, New York, 1844.

HARLEIAN MISCELLANY: Collection of pamphlets and tracts from the Earl of Oxford's library in 12 volumes. London, 1808.

HARRISON, C. C.: (*See* under Lamb, Martha J.)

HART, ALBERT BUSHNELL: *Handbook of the History, Diplomacy and Government of the United States.* Cambridge, 1903.

HART, A. B.: (*See* Channing, Edward.)

HATCH, LOUIS CLINTON: *The Administration of the American Revolutionary Army,* Harvard Historical Studies, vol. x. Longmans, Green & Co., New York, 1904.

HAWKINS, RUSH C.: *Some late statements about early printing* — Bibliographer, vol. i. New York, 1902.

HAY, JOHN: *See* Nicolay, J. G.

HAYNE, I. W.: *The Mercury's Course.* Charleston, 1857.

HAZEN, REV. HENRY A.: *New Hampshire and Vermont.* Concord, N. H., 1894.

HELPER, HINTON ROWAN: *Compendium of the Impending Crisis of the South.* A. B. Burdick, New York, 1860;

HELPER, HINTON ROWAN: *The Impending Crisis of the South.* New York, 1860.

HENRY, J.: *Notes concerning William Winston Seaton,* Smithsonian Institute, vol. xviii, 1880.

HENRY, WILLIAM ELMER: *Some Elements of Indiana's Population.* Indianapolis, 1908.

HERNDON, WILLIAM HENRY, AND WEIK, JESSE W.: *Abraham Lincoln,* 2 vols. Appleton, New York, 1909.

HILDEBURN, CHARLES R.: *A Century of Printing — The Issues of the Press in Pennsylvania, 1685–1784,* 2 vols. Philadelphia, 1885.

HILDRETH, RICHARD: *The History of the United States of America,* 6 vols. Harper, New York, 1880.

HILLARD, GEORGE STILLMAN: *Memoir and Correspondence of Jeremiah Mason.* Cambridge, 1873.

Historical Magazine: Of notes and queries concerning the Antiquities, History and Biography of America. New York, 1867.

HITTELL, THEODORE H.: *History of California,* 4 vols. San Francisco, 1897.

HOAR, GEORGE FRISBIE: *Autobiography of Seventy Years,* 2 vols. Scribners, New York, 1903.

HOCKETT, HOMER C.: "The Influence of the West on the Rise and Fall of Political Parties," *Mississippi Valley Historical Review,* vol. iv, p. 459. Cedar Rapids, 1918.

HOLLEY, O. L.: *Life of Benjamin Franklin.* Boston, 1856.

HOLLISTER, GIDEON HIRAM: *History of Connecticut,* 2 vols. Hartford, 1857.

HOLLISTER, OVANDO J.: *The Life of Schuyler Colfax.* Funk and Wagnalls, New York, 1886.

HONE, PHILIP: *The Diary of Philip Hone, 1828–1851,* 2 vols. Dodd, Mead and Co., New York, 1889.

HOSMER, JAMES KENDALL: *Samuel Adams.* Houghton Mifflin & Co., Boston, 1885.

HOUGHTON, HENRY OSCAR: *Address on Early Printing in America.* Montpelier, 1894.

HOUGHTON, WALTER RALEIGH: *Conspectus of the History of Political Parties and the Federal Government.* Indianapolis, 1880.

HOWE, HENRY: *Historical Collections of Ohio.* 1891; *Historical Collections of Virginia.* 1856.

HOWE, HENRY, AND BARBER, JOHN W.: (*See* under Barber, John W.)

HOWELL, T. B.: *A complete collection of State Trials,* vol. vii. London, 1816.

HOWELLS, W. C.: *Recollections of Life in Ohio from 1813–1840.* R. Clark Co., Cincinnati, 1895.

HUDSON, FREDERIC: *Journalism in the United States.* New York, 1873.

HUIDEKOPER, FREDERIC LOUIS: *The Military Unpreparedness of the United States.* Macmillan, New York, 1915.

HUNT, F. KNIGHT: *The Fourth Estate,* 2 vols. London, 1850.

HUNT, GAILLARD (Editor): *The Writings of James Madison,* 8 vols. Putnam, New York, 1902.

IRELAND, ALLEYNE: *Joseph Pulitzer.* New York, 1914.

JEFFERSON, THOMAS (Edited by Andrew A. Lipscomb): *Writings,* Monticello Edition, 20 vols. Washington, 1904.

JONES, HORATIO GATES: *Andrew Bradford, Founder of the Newspaper Press in the Middle States of America.* Phila., 1869; *Reports of the Committee of the Historical Society of Pennsylvania of their visit to New York, May 20th, 1863, at the celebration of the two hundredth birthday of William Bradford, who introduced the art of printing into the middle Colonies of British America.* Phila., 1863; *Selections from Duane Papers,* Historical Magazine, Second series, vol. iv. Morrisania, 1868.

JONES, THOMAS: *History of New York during the Revolutionary War,* 2 vols. New York, 1879.

KENDALL, AMOS: *Autobiography.* Boston, 1872; *Secession Letters.* Washington, 1861.

Kentucky State Historical Society: *Register, January, 1918,* vol. xvi, No. 46. Frankfort, 1918.

KILLIKELLY, SARAH H.: *The History of Pittsburgh.* Pittsburgh, 1906.

KING, CHARLES R.: *The Life and Correspondence of Rufus King,* 6 vols. Putnam, New York, 1894.

KING, JOHN: *Animadversions on a Pamphlet entitled "Letter of Advice by a Divine of the Church of England."* London, 1701.

KING, WILLIAM L.: *The Newspaper Press of Charleston, S. C.* Charleston, 1882.

KINKEAD, ELIZABETH SHELBY: *A History of Kentucky.* New York, 1896.

KITCHIN, GEORGE: *Sir Roger L'Estrange.* London, 1913.

KNOX, THOMAS WALLACE: *The Republican Party and Its Leaders.* P. F. Collier, New York, 1892.

LAMB, MARTHA J. R., AND HARRISON, C. C.: *History of the City of New York.* A. S. Barnes Co., New York, 1877–96.

LEAKE, ISAAC Q.: *Memoir of the Life and Times of General John Lamb.* Albany, 1850.

LECKY, W. E. H.: *Democracy and Liberty.* New York, 1899.

LECKY, W. E. H.: *The American Revolution, 1763–1783.* Appleton, New York, 1898.

LECKY, W. E. H.: *A History of England in the 18th Century,* 8 vols. New York, 1882–90.

LEE, JAMES MELVIN: *History of American Journalism.* Boston, 1917.

LEWIS, WILLIAM DRAPER: *Great American Lawyers,* 8 vols. Philadelphia, 1907.

LILLY, LAMBERT: *The History of the Middle States.* Boston, 1846.

LINN, WILLIAM: *The Life of Thomas Jefferson.* Ithaca, 1834.

LIPSCOMB, ANDREW A. (Editor): (*See* under Thomas Jefferson.)

LOCKWOOD, MARY SMITH: *Yesterdays in Washington.* Roslyn, Virginia, 1915.

LODGE, HENRY CABOT: *Boston.* New York, 1891; *Alexander Hamilton.* Boston, 1882; *Studies in History.* Boston and New York, 1884.

LODGE, HENRY CABOT (Editor): *The Works of Alexander Hamilton,* 9 vols. Putnam, New York, 1885.

LOSSING, BENSON J. (Editor): *The American Historical Record.* Phila., 1872; *History of New York City.* New York, 1884; *The Pictorial Field Book of the Revolution,* 2 vols. Harpers, New York.

Lowell, Mass.: Old Residents' Historical Association, vol. i, August, 1875. Lowell, 1875.

LUNDY, BENJAMIN: *Life, Travels and Opinions of Benjamin Lundy.* Philadelphia, 1847.

LUTTRELL, NARCISSUS: *A Brief Historical Relation of State Affairs from September, 1678, to April, 1714,* vols. i, ii, iii, v, vi. Oxford, 1857.

LYMAN, T. P. H.: *The Life of Thomas Jefferson.* Philadelphia, 1826.

MCCALL, CAPT. HUGH: *History of Georgia.* Atlanta, 1909.

MCCLINTOCK, JOHN N.: *History of New Hampshire.* Boston, 1889.

MCCLURE, ALEXANDER KELLY: *Abraham Lincoln and Men of War Times.* Philadelphia, 1892.

MCKINLEY, ALBERT EDWARD: *The Suffrage Franchise in the Thirteen Colonies in America.* No. 2, publications of the University of Pennsylvania.

MCMASTER, JOHN BACH: *Benjamin Franklin as a Man of Letters.* Houghton Mifflin Co., 1900; *A History of the People of the United States,* vols. i, ii, iii. Macmillan, New York, 1900.

MACATAMNEY, HUGH: *Cradle Days of New York.* New York, 1909.

MACY, JESSE: *Political Parties in the United States.* Macmillan, New York, 1900.

MAGAZINE OF AMERICAN HISTORY: Nos. for January, February and August, 1887. New York, 1887.

MARSHALL, HUMPHREY: *History of Kentucky.* Frankfort, 1824.

MARTIN, CHARLOTTE M., AND MARTIN, BENJAMIN ELLIS: *The New York Press and Its Makers in the 18th Century, in Historic New York,* vol. ii. New York, 1899.

Maryland Historical Magazine: Vols. i to viii.

MASON, EDWARD GAY: *Early Chicago and Illinois.* Chicago, 1890.

MASON, JEREMIAH: *Memoir, Autobiography and Correspondence of Jeremiah Mason.* Kansas City, Mo., 1917.

Massachusetts Colonial Society Publications, vol. ix. Boston, 1907.

Massachusetts Historical Society: *Commemoration of Tercentenary, John Milton.* Cambridge, 1909.

Massachusetts Historical Society: *Collections,* 1st Series, vols. iv, v, vi. Boston, 1806–09.

Massachusetts Historical Society: *Collections,* 5th Series, vols. i, v, vi, vii, ix, x. Boston, 1878.

Massachusetts Historical Society: *Proceedings,* Second Series, 20 vols.

MATHER, REV. COTTON: *History of King Philip's War.*

MATHER, INCREASE: *Early History of New England.* Boston, 1864; *Remarkable Providences.* London, 1856.

MATHER, RICHARD: *Journal of Richard Mather, 1635—His Life and Death, 1670.* Boston, 1850.

MAVERICK, AUGUSTUS: *Henry J. Raymond and the New York press.* Hartford, 1870.

MAY, SIR THOMAS ERSKINE: *The Constitutional History of England,* 2 vols. New York, 1882; *Democracy in Europe,* vols. i and ii. London, 1877.

MEAD, EDWIN D.: *The Old Home Week in New Hamp-*

shire, Reprinted from the New England Magazine, May, 1899.

MELONEY, WILLIAM BROWN: "Joseph Pulitzer, the Blind Editor of the *World*," *American Magazine*, November, 1909.

MERRIAM, GEORGE SPRING: *The Life and Times of Samuel Bowles*, vols. i, ii. New York, 1885.

MINOT, GEORGE RICHARDS: *History of Massachusetts*, 2 vols. Boston, 1798.

MIX, JAMES B.: *The Biter Bit* (re "Blackmailing operations" of N. Y. *Sun*). Washington, 1876.

MONROE, JAMES (STANISLAUS M. HAMILTON, Editor): *The Writings of*, 3 vols. New York, 1900.

MOORE, HUGH: *Memoir of Col. Ethan Allan.* Plattsburgh, 1834.

MORDECAI, SAMUEL: *Richmond in By-gone Days.* Richmond, 1856.

MORRIS, ANNE CARY: *The Diary and Letters of Gouverneur Morris.* New York, 1888.

MORRIS, GOUVERNEUR: *Notes on the United States of America.* Phila., 1806; *An Oration on George Clinton.* New York, 1812.

MORSE, ANSON ELY: (*See* Richardson, E. C.)

MOSES, JOHN: *Illinois Historical and Statistical*, 2 vols. Chicago, 1889.

MOTLEY, JOHN LOTHROP: *History of the United Netherlands*, 4 vols. Harper, New York, 1861–80.

MUNSELL, J.: *Outline of the History of Printing.* Albany, 1839.

NASON, ELIAS: *Sir Charles Henry Frankland.* Albany, 1865.

NELSON, WILLIAM: *Check-List of the Issues of the Press in New Jersey, 1723, 1728, 1754–1800.* Paterson, 1899; *Notes toward a History of the American Newspaper.* New York, 1918.

New York Colonial General Assembly: *Journal of the*

votes and proceedings of the General Assembly of the Colony of New York, vol. ii. (Hugh Gaine), New York, 1766.

New York Documents Relative to the Colonial History of the State of New York, vols. v, vi, vii. (*See* under O'Callaghan.) Albany, 1855.

NICOLAY, JOHN GEORGE, AND HAY, JOHN: *Complete Works of Abraham Lincoln,* 2 vols., Century, New York, 1894. *Abraham Lincoln, a History,* 10 vols. Century Co., New York, 1890.

NILES, H.: *Things as They Are.* Baltimore, 1809.

NOBLE, JOHN: *The Libel Suit of Knowles and Douglass.* Cambridge, 1897.

NORCROSS, GRANVILLE H.: *Southern Newspapers Printed on Wall Paper,* Massachusetts Historical Society Proceedings, vol. xlvi, pp. 241–43. Boston, 1913.

NORRIS, J. W.: *General directory, etc., of Chicago with historical sketch.* Chicago, 1844; re-printed 1902.

NORTH, S. N. D.: *The Newspaper and Periodical Press.* In vol. viii, Tenth Census of the United States. Washington, 1884.

NOWLAND, JOHN H. B.: *Early Reminiscences of Indianapolis.* Indianapolis, 1870.

OBERHOLTZER, ELLIS PAXSON: *The Literary History of Philadelphia.* Phila., 1906; *Philadelphia, a History of the City and Its People,* 4 vols. Phila., 1912.

O'BRIEN, FRANK MICHAEL: *The Story of The Sun.* Doran, New York, 1918.

O'CALLAGHAN, EDMOND BAILEY: *The Documentary History of the State of New York,* 4 vols. Albany, 1850–51; *Documents Relative to the Colonial History of the State of New York,* 8 vols. Albany, 1858.

ODGERS, W. BLAKE: *An Outline of the Law of Libel.* New York, 1897.

OGDEN, ROLLO (Editor): *Life and Letters of Edwin Lawrence Godkin.* Macmillan, New York, 1907.

OHIO: Celebration of the 47th anniversary of the First Settlement of the State of Ohio, by native citizens. Cincinnati, 1835.

OHIO ANTI-SLAVERY SOCIETY: *Narrative of proceedings against the liberty of the Press in Cincinnati.* Cincinnati, 1836; *Historical and Philosophical Society of Ohio, Quarterly Publication,* vols. x, xii. 1915–17, Cincinnati.

Ohio Hundred Year Book: A handbook of the Public Men and Public Institutions of Ohio, 1879–1901. Columbus, 1901.

ORTH, SAMUEL PETER: *The Boss and the Machine.* New Haven, 1919.

OSTROGORSKI, M.: *"De l'organisation des partis politiques aux Etats Unis."* Paris, Fr., 1889.

PAINE, ALBERT BIGELOW: *Thomas Nast — his period and his pictures.* Macmillan, New York, 1904.

PAINE, THOMAS: *The Genuine Trial of Thomas Paine, etc.* London, 1793; (*See* Conway, Moncure Daniel; Birrell, Augustine; Cobbett, William; Cheetham, James; Carlile, Mary Anne.)

PALFREY, JOHN GORHAM: *History of New England,* 5 vols. Boston, 1858–1890.

PARTON, JAMES: *Famous Americans of Recent Times.* Houghton Mifflin & Co., Boston, 1884; *Life of Thomas Jefferson.* Boston, 1874.

PARTON, JAMES: *Life of Horace Greeley,* 1893 Edition. Houghton Mifflin & Co., Boston, 1893; *Life of Andrew Jackson,* 3 vols. New York, 1860.

PATTON, JACOB HARRIS: *Political Parties in the United States.* (New Amsterdam Book Co.), New York, 1902.

PELLEW, GEORGE: *John Jay.* Boston, 1892.

PENDLETON, JOHN: *Newspaper Reporting in Olden Time and To-day.* London, 1890.

PENN, IRVINE GARLAND: *The Afro-American Press and Its Editors.* Springfield, Massachusetts, 1891.

Pennsylvania Colonial Records, vol. viii. Harrisburg, 1852.

Pennsylvania Historical Society: *Memoirs of,* edition of 1826, reprinted in 1864, vol. i. Phila., 1864.

The Pennsylvania Magazine, vols. xiv, xvi. Phila., 1892.

PERRIN, WILLIAM HENRY: *The Pioneer Press of Kentucky.* Filson Club Publications No. 3. Louisville, 1888.

PETERSON, EDWARD: *History of Rhode Island.* New York, 1853.

Philadelphia North American: In *Editorial Review* (May). Phila., 1911.

PIKE, JAMES SHEPHERD: *First Blows of the Civil War.* New York, 1879.

POWELL, LYMAN PIERSON: *Historic Towns of the Western States.* Putnam, New York, 1901.

PRAY, ISAAC C.: *Memoirs of James Gordon Bennett and His Times.* New York, 1855.

PRIME, SAMUEL I.: "On the Public Ledger," *N. Y. Observer,* Oct. 31, 1878. New York, 1878.

Providence Typographical Union, No. 33: *Printers and Printing in Providence, 1762–1907.* (Providence Publishing Co.), Providence, 1907.

PULITZER, JOSEPH: *The School of Journalism in Columbia University.* New York, 1904.

Quarterly Review, vol. cxli, January and April, 1878. London, 1878.

QUINCY, JOSIAH: *A Municipal History of the Town and City of Boston from September 17, 1630, to September 17, 1830.* Boston, 1852.

RANDALL, EMILIUS OVIATT, AND RYAN, DANIEL JOSEPH: *History of Ohio,* 5 vols. (The Century History Co.), New York, 1912.

RANDALL, HENRY STEPHENS: *The Life of Thomas Jefferson,* 3 vols. New York, 1858.

RAYNER, B. L.: *The Life of Thomas Jefferson.* Boston, 1834.

REID, WHITELAW: *American and English Studies,* 2 vols. Scribner, New York, 1913.

RHETT, ROBERT BARNWELL: *American Historical Review, 1854,* vol. xiii. Lancaster, Pa., 1908.

RHOADES, LILLIAN IONE: *The Story of Philadelphia.* New York, 1900.

RHODES, JAMES FORD: "Edwin Lawrence Godkin," *Atlantic Monthly,* Sept., 1908. Boston, 1908; *Historical Essays.* Macmillan, New York, 1909.

RICHARDSON, CHARLES FRANCIS: *American Literature, 1607–1885.* New York, 1887.

RICHARDSON, ERNEST C., AND MORSE, ANSON ELY: *Writings on American History.* Princeton, N. J., 1904.

RIDPATH, JOHN CLARK: *James Otis, the pre-revolutionist,* Milwaukee, 1903.

RITENOUR, JOHN S.: Early newspapers of Southwest Pennsylvania, *Inland Printer,* 1913, vol. li. Chicago, 1913.

ROBERTS, ELLIS H.: *New York,* 2 vols. New York, 1904.

ROBERTSON, GEORGE: *Scrap Book on Law and Politics, Men and Things.* Lexington, 1855.

ROBINS, EDWARD: *Benjamin Franklin.* New York, 1898.

ROBINSON, WILLIAM A.: *"Party Organization and Campaign Methods," Washington University Studies,* vol. iii, Part 2. St. Louis, 1916.

ROGERS, JAMES EDWIN THOROLD: *The Story of Holland.* Putnam, New York, 1892.

ROOSEVELT, THEODORE: *The Winning of the West,* vols. i–iv. Putnam, New York, 1889–1896.

RUSSELL, CHARLES EDWARD: *These Shifting Scenes.* Hodder and Co., New York, 1914.

RUTHERFORD, LIVINGSTON: *John Peter Zenger, His Press, His Trial.* New York, 1904.

RYAN, DANIEL JOSEPH: (*See* Randall, E. O.)

SABINE, LORENZO: *The American Loyalists.* Boston, 1847.

SAFFELL, WILLIAM T. R.: *Records of the Revolutionary War.* Pudney and Russell, New York, 1858.

SANBORN, EDWIN DAVID: *History of New Hampshire.* Manchester, 1875.

SCHARF, COL. J. THOMAS: *The Chronicles of Baltimore.* Baltimore, 1874; *History of Maryland.* Baltimore, 1879.

SCHARF, J. THOMAS, AND WESTCOTT, THOMPSON: *History of Philadelphia,* 3 vols. Phila., 1884.

SCHOULER, JAMES: *History of the United States Under the Constitution, 1783–1865,* 6 vols. Washington, 1886.

SCHOULER, WILLIAM: *History of Massachusetts in the Civil War,* 2 vols. Boston, 1868–71.

SCHURZ, CARL: *The Condition of the South.* 1865; "Correspondence; James Rood Doolittle," *Missouri Historical Review,* vol. xi. p. 20. Columbia, Mo., 1916.

SCUDDER, HORACE E.: *Noah Webster.* Boston, 1899.

SEARS, LORENZO: *American Literature in the Colonial and National Periods.* Boston, 1902.

SEATON, JOSEPHINE: *William Winston Seaton.* J. R. Osgood and Co., Boston, 1871.

SEDGWICK, THEODORE, JR.: *A Memoir of the Life of William Livingston.* J. and J. Harper, New York, 1833.

SEWALL, SAMUEL: *Diary of Samuel Sewall* (Massachusetts Historical Society Collections). Boston, 1872–82.

SEWARD, FREDERICK WM.: *Autobiography of William H. Seward, with a Memoir,* 3 vols. New York, 1877–1891; *Reminiscences of a War-time Statesman and Diplomat.* Putnam, New York, 1916.

SHEA, GEORGE: *The Life and Epoch of Alexander Hamilton.* Houghton Mifflin & Co., Boston, 1881.

SIMMS, WILLIAM GILMORE: *History of South Carolina.* Charleston, 1866.

SKELTON, EDWARD OLIVER: *The Story of New England.* Boston, 1910.

SMITH, EDWARD: *William Cobbett — a Biography,* 2 vols. London, 1878.

SMITH, HORACE WEMYSS: *Life and Correspondence of Rev. William Smith,* 2 vols. Phila., 1879–80.

SMITH, J. ALLEN: *The Spirit of American Government.* Macmillan, New York, 1907.

SMITH, SAMUEL GEORGE: *Democracy and the Church.* New York, 1912.

SMITH, THEODORE CLARKE: "*Parties and Slavery, 1850–1859,*" *The American Nation — A History,* vol. xviii. Harper, New York, 1907.

SMITH, WILLIAM: *History of the Province of New York,* 2 vols. New York, 1830.

SMITH, WILLIAM HENRY: *Charles Hammond and His Relations to Henry Clay and John Quincy Adams.* Chicago, 1855.

SMITH, ZACHARIAH FREDERICK: *The History of Kentucky.* Louisville, 1892.

SMYTH, ALBERT H.: *The Philadelphia Magazines and their contributors, 1741–1850.* Phila., 1892.

SPARKS, JARED: *Life of Ethan Allen.* Harper, New York, 1854; *The Life of Gouverneur Morris,* 3 vols. Boston, 1832.

SPARKS, JARED (Editor): *The Works of Benjamin Franklin, etc.,* 10 vols. London, 1882; *The Writings of George Washington,* 12 vols. Harper, New York, 1847.

STACKPOLE, EVERETT S.: *History of New Hampshire,* 3 vols. New York, 1916.

STEPHEN, SIR JAMES FITZ JAMES: *A History of the Criminal Law of England,* 2 vols. London, 1883.

STEVENS, BENJ. FRANKLIN: *Facsimiles of Mss. in European Archives Relating to America.* London, 1895.

STEVENS, DAVID H.: *Party Politics and English Journalism, 1702–1742.* Chicago, 1916.

STEVENS, WALTER BARLOW: *Missourians One Hundred Years Ago.* Columbia, Mo., 1917.

STILLE, CHARLES JANEWAY: *The Life and Times of John Dickinson.* J. B. Lippincott Co., Phila., 1891.

STREETER, SEBASTIAN F.: *Early History of Maryland.* Baltimore, 1876.

SULGROVE, B. R.: *History of Indianapolis and Marion County, Indiana.* Phila., 1884.

SUMNER, WILLIAM GRAHAM: *Alexander Hamilton.* Dodd, Mead and Co., New York, 1890.

SUMNER, WILLIAM GRAHAM: *Andrew Jackson.* Houghton Mifflin & Co., Boston, 1899.

THOMAS, ISAIAH: *The History of Printing in America,* 2 vols. Worcester, 1810.

THWAITES, REUBEN GOLD: "The Ohio Valley Press before the War of 1812," Published in the *Proceedings of the Antiquarian Society,* vol. xix. Worcester, Mass., 1909.

TODD, CHARLES BURR: *The Story of Washington — (Great Cities of the Republic).* Putnam, New York, 1889.

TOMPKINS, H. B.: *Bibliotheca Jeffersoniana.* Putnam, New York, 1887.

TRUMBULL, JOHN: *M'Fingal: an epic poem.* Boston, 1813.

TUCKER, GEORGE: *The History of the United States from colonization to 1841,* 4 vols. Phila., 1856; *Life of Thomas Jefferson,* 2 vols. Phila., 1837.

TUDOR, WILLIAM, JR.: *The Life of James Otis.* Boston, 1823.

TUFTS, JAMES H.: *The Real Business of Living.* New York, 1918.

TYLER, LYON GARDINER: *Williamsburg, the Old Colonial Capital.* Richmond, Va., 1907.

TYLER, MOSES COIT: *Literary History of the American Revolution,* 2 vols. Putnam, New York.

United States: *10th Census — 1880,* vol. viii; *Special Reports on Newspapers and Periodicals.* Washington, 1884; *Reports of Committees — 25th Congress, 2d Session, 1837–8,* vol. iv.

VALLANDIGHAM, CLEMENT LAIRD: *The Record of . . . V. on Abolition.* Cincinnati, 1863.

VAN BUREN, MARTIN: *Inquiry into the Origin and Course of Political Parties.* New York, 1867.

VAN FOSSAN, W. H.: *Clement L. Vallandigham,* in Ohio Archaeological Quarterly, vol. xxiii, p. 256. Columbus, 1914.

VENABLE, W. F.: *Beginnings of Literary Culture in the Ohio Valley.* R. Clarke and Co., Cincinnati, 1891.

VILLARD, OSWALD GARRISON: *The James Gorden Bennetts and Their Newspaper. Nation,* New York, vol. cvi. New York, 1918.

VIOLETTE, EUGENE MORROW: *History of Missouri.* D. Heath and Co., New York, 1918.

VOLTAIRE: *Age of Louis XIV.*

WALKER, FRANCIS A.: *The Making of the Nation, 1783–1817.* London, 1896.

WALLACE, JOHN WILLIAM: An Address Delivered at the Celebration by the New York Historical Society on the 200th Birthday of Mr. William Bradford, etc. Albany, 1863.

WASHBURNE, E. B.: *Sketch of Edward Coles, Second Governor of Illinois.* Chicago, 1882.

WATSON, JOHN FANNING: *Annals of Philadelphia and Pennsylvania, in the olden time, etc.,* 2 vols. Phila., 1856–57.

WEBB, JAMES WATSON: *General J. Watson Webb vs. Hamilton Fish and E. R. Hoar.* 1875.

WEBBER, CHARLES WILKINS: *Historical and Revolutionary Incidents.* Philadelphia, 1861.

WEED, HARRIET A., AND BARNES, THURLOW WEED (Editors): *Thurlow Weed—Life, Including His Autobiography,* 2 vols. Houghton Mifflin & Co., Boston, 1883–4.

WEED, THURLOW: *What I Know About Horace Greeley's . . . Record.* J. McGee, New York, 1872.

WEEDEN, WILLIAM BABCOCK: *Economic and Social His-*

tory of New England, 2 vols. Houghton Mifflin & Co., Boston, 1890.

WEIK, JESSE W.: (*See* Herndon, William Henry.)

WELLS, WILLIAM VINCENT: *The Life and Public Services of Samuel Adams,* 3 vols. Little, Brown & Co., Boston, 1866.

WENDELL, BARRETT: *A Literary History of America.* Scribner, New York, 1911.

WESTCOTT, THOMPSON, and SCHARF, J. THOMAS: (*See* under Scharf, J. Thomas.

Western Journal: Vol. iv. 1850.

WHARTON, FRANCIS: *State Trials of the United States during the administrations of Washington and Adams.* Carey and Hart, Phila., 1849.

WHITE, ANDREW D.: *Autobiography,* 2 vols. Century Co., New York, 1905.

WHITE, PLINY HOLTON: *Life and Services of Matthew Lyon.* Burlington, 1858.

WHITON, JOHN MILTON: *Sketches of the History of New Hampshire.* Concord, 1834.

WILLIAMSON, WILLIAM DURKEE: *History of the State of Maine.* Hollowell, 1832.

WILSON, HENRY: *History of the Rise and Fall of the Slave Power in America,* 3 vols. J. R. Osgood and Co., Boston, 1874–77.

WILSON, JAMES HARRISON: *The Life of Charles A. Dana.* Harper, New York, 1907.

WILSON, RUFUS ROCKWELL: *Washington — The Capital City.* Lippincott, Phila., 1901.

WINSOR, JUSTIN (Editor): *The Memorial History of Boston, 1630–1880,* 4 vols. Boston, 1880.

WINSOR, JUSTIN (Editor): *Narrative and Critical History of America.*

WISCONSIN: State Historical Society of Wisconsin — Proceedings at 44th Annual Meeting. Madison, 1897.

WISE, BARTON HAXALL: *The Life of Henry A. Wise.* Macmillan, New York, 1899.

WISE, JOHN SERGEANT: *The End of an Era.* Houghton Mifflin & Co., Boston, 1902.

WOLFE, SAMUEL M.: *Helper's Impending Crisis Dissected.* New York, 1860.

WOODBURN, JAMES ALBERT: *Political Parties and Party Problems in the United States.* Putnam, New York, 1914.

WOODWARD, FRANK E.: *Reference List of Works Relating to Thomas Jefferson.* Malden, Mass., 1906.

WRIGHT, HENRY CLARKE: *No Rights, No Duties.* Boston, 1860.

WRIGHT, JOHN STEPHEN: *Chicago: Past, Present, Future.* Chicago, 1870.

YOUNG, JOHN P.: *Journalism in California.* Chronicle Pub. Co., San Francisco, 1915.[1]

[1] For the preparation and supervision of the Bibliography the author is indebted to Mr. James William Davis.

INDEX

A

H

S